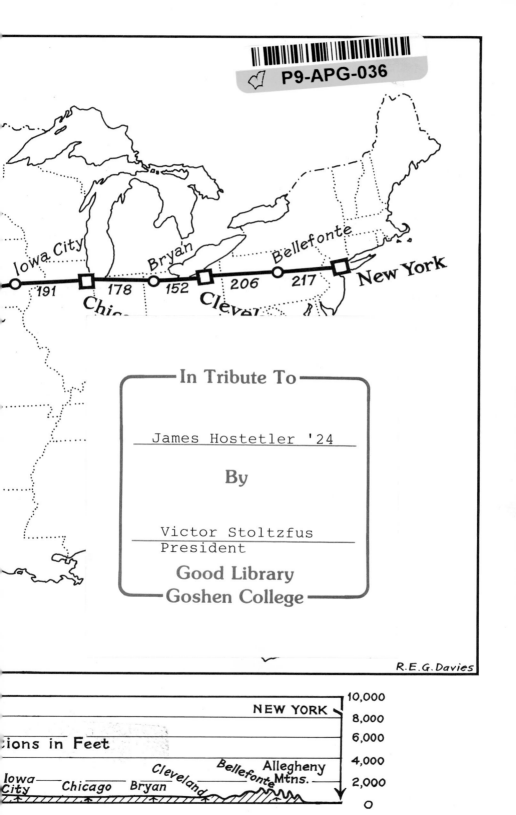

Iowa City Bryan Bellefonte New York

191 178 152 206 217

Chi... Cleve...

R.E.G. Davies

NEW YORK

10,000
8,000
6,000

...ions in Feet

4,000

Cleveland Bellefonte Allegheny
Iowa Chicago Bryan Mtns.
City

2,000

0

William M. Leary is a professor of history at the University of Georgia. He has written numerous books and articles on aviation history.

Aerial Pioneers

Pilots Henry G. Boonstra (*left*) and James F. Moore, September 1920.

Aerial Pioneers

The U.S. Air Mail Service, 1918-1927

William M. Leary

SMITHSONIAN INSTITUTION PRESS
Washington, D.C.

This book was edited by Ruth W. Spiegel,
and designed by Christopher Jones.
Type was set by G & S Typesetters, Inc., Austin, Texas,
and the printing was by The Maple Press Company, York, Pa.
∞ The paper used in this publication meets the minimum requirements of the
American National Standard for Permanence of Paper for Printed Library
Materials Z39.48−1984.

Library of Congress Cataloging-in-Publication Data
Leary, William M. (William Matthew), 1934−
    Aerial pioneers : the U.S. air mail service,
1918−1927.
    Bibliography: p.
    Includes index.
    1. Air mail service—United States—History.
I. Title.
HE6496.L43   1985   383′.144′0973   85-600033
ISBN 0-87474-610-8

ENDPAPER MAP: Transcontinental air route, 1923.
NOTE ON THE MAPS AND PHOTOGRAPHS: All maps in this book were drawn by
    R. E. G. Davies, curator, National Air and Space Museum. Photographs not
    listed below are from the collection of the **National Air and Space Museum**:
photo p. 21, courtesy **Praeger family**;
photos pp. 36 and 37, courtesy **National Archives**;
photos pp. 69, 124, 141, 228, courtesy **Marie Miller Ricker**;
photos pp. 130 and 157, courtesy **Mrs. James P. Murray**;
photos pp. 133, 189, 235, from the **author's collection**.
NOTE ON CITATIONS OF TIME: All such citations are in local time.

Contents

To My Wife,
Margaret MacGregor Leary

Preface

THE U.S. AIR MAIL SERVICE belongs to a long and honorable tradition of federal support for projects to improve transportation and communication. The federal government built the great National Road, extending from Maryland to Illinois, during the first half of the nineteenth century; it subsidized the construction of canals in the Midwest; and it spent money to improve navigation for steamboats on western rivers. In 1843–44 Congress funded and the Post Office operated the first magnetic telegraph line in the United States. Transcontinental railroads benefited from federal largess to the tune of 170,000,000 acres of public land, or 9.5 percent of the total land areas of the twenty-six states west of the Mississippi River. The national government promoted these advances in transportation and communication as a way to facilitate economic progress and to strengthen the bonds of union. For the most part, the American people enthusiastically supported the policy.

Washington played a similar role in nurturing the development of aviation. Anxious to exploit this new mode of transportation to advance the mails, the Post Office took the lead in fostering the use of airplanes for peaceful purposes. While European governments early decided to assist commercial aviation through direct subsidy to private companies, American officials reached a similar conclusion only after lengthy debate. In the interim, the U.S. Air Mail Service pioneered air routes, tested equipment, and developed operational techniques that would provide a solid and necessary foundation for the rapid expansion of commercial airlines after 1927.

When I first became interested in the origins of commercial aviation in the United States, I was surprised to learn that a reliable history of the government-sponsored Air Mail Service did not exist. I decided that there was a need for a narrative account of this important organization, one that would emphasize its pivotal operational contributions to later airline development.

I began work on the project during the summer of 1976, thanks to a

8

fellowship provided by the National Air and Space Administration. Monte D. Wright, director of NASA's history office, gave me working space and a free hand to go my own way; I am grateful for his understanding and support. The knowledgeable staff at the National Archives facilitated my use of the postal records which form the core of my study. Alex Roland, then at NASA and now on the faculty of Duke University, generously shared with me the fruits of his research into the National Advisory Committee for Aeronautics. Nick A. Komons of the Federal Aviation Agency and Richard P. Hallion of the National Air and Space Museum, both of whom were busy with important studies of their own, provided insights and inspiration. I also learned a great deal from Richard K. Smith, a talented historian with a refreshingly acerbic approach to the past.

Progress came slowly after 1976, as other projects commanded my attention. However, I continued to collect material, a process that was greatly facilitated by an Air Force Historical Foundation fellowship and by summer research grants from the University of Georgia. Lester D. Stephens, head of the history department at Georgia, offered unflagging support over the years, along with friendship, encouragement, and an abiding sense of excellence.

A number of people read and commented on various drafts of the manuscript. Captain Joseph F. Ross (Pan American Airways, retired) spent countless hours trying to improve my prose; my debt to him can never be repaid. My busy colleague William Stueck actually volunteered to critique an early draft of *Aerial Pioneers*, then forced me to address important questions that I had ignored. Alex Roland responded to a plea for help and provided the kind of constructive criticism that facilitates revision. Richard Smith made important comments on early chapters, while Wesley P. Newton of Auburn University reviewed the manuscript with patient understanding. None of the above bears any responsibility for the final version of *Aerial Pioneers*.

My son Peter deserved many of the hours that I spent in my study, trying to capture in words an elusive past; I hope that one day he will understand why I thought the effort was worth such a high price. My partner in life took time from her impossibly demanding role of wife-mother-teacher to read the manuscript and correct my erratic grammar. This book is dedicated to Margaret, a very special lady who keeps the center of my life together and prevents things from falling apart.

WILLIAM M. LEARY
Athens, Georgia
February 2, 1985

It is difficult to make history live— equally difficult to embody the reality of these seven league planes which overleaped great regions of the continental United States. It was hard work for those of us who participated; a sense of romance and adventure sustained us. It elated us to conquer time and space.

—*James Clark Edgerton*

1 Decision to Fly the Mail

THE WONDER OF FLIGHT has long passed. Although a few enthusiasts remain enamored of the airplane, most people accept the marvels of air transportation as a commonplace facet of daily life. But it was not always so. There was a time when tales of men's triumph over gravity filled the pages of newspapers across the country, an era when flying was a great adventure. During this heroic age of aviation, pioneer airmen made hundreds of remarkable voyages, most of them long forgotten. One that had lasting consequences took place on June 13, 1910, when Charles K. Hamilton captured the public's attention for a brief but glorious moment by flying *round trip* between New York and Philadelphia.

Charlie Hamilton seemed drawn to the airman's world by a compelling fascination. He began his love affair with flight as a youngster, startling his parents by plunging out of an upstairs window with an umbrella firmly clutched in hand. Several years after surviving this attempt to imitate a county fair parachute jumper, Hamilton ran away from home, assumed the name of H. A. Milton, and toured fairs and carnivals in the southwestern United States as a hot air balloonist. Hamilton took to the air in every conceivable fashion, piloting gliders and airships, riding in kites, and gaining a reputation as the most daring parachutist of his day. In 1909 he was touring Japan with the first airship ever seen in East Asia when he read about Louis Blériot's epochal cross-channel flight between France and England. He hurried home and managed to talk Glenn L. Curtiss into giving him flying lessons. Impressed by Hamilton's natural talent and daring, Curtiss hired the twenty-four-year-old airman as an exhibition pilot.[1]

Hamilton did not take a scientific approach to aeronautics. He was a performer, a daredevil who soon became known as the "Demon of the Skies." He perfected the "Hamilton Dive," a vertical drop from 1,000 feet, pulling out at the last minute in front of the grandstands, then zooming across the field at full power. Crashes were frequent, and Hamilton liked to boast that he had managed to break every bone in his body. Although this was an exaggeration, the reality was impressive enough. Despite two broken collar bones, two fractured ribs, a dislocated left arm, a broken ankle, and two broken legs, he continued to fly with abandon. "For daring and skill in the manipulation of an aeroplane," one contemporary proclaimed, "this rough rider of the sky has no superior."[2]

A small, wiry man, weighing about 110 pounds, with unruly red hair and large, prominent ears, Hamilton became a fixture at air meets across the country. His trademark was a cigarette, held constantly in his mouth. Never one for half-measures, he tied a piece of lighted punk to the seat of his open cockpit airplane so that he could light up in the air. Known as a hard drinker, he often hired a boy to meet him upon landing with a glass of beer.[3]

The high point of Hamilton's career came in 1910. The Philadelphia *Public Ledger* and the *New York Times* had offered a prize of $10,000—a small fortune at a time when gold sold for $20 an ounce —for the first round trip to be completed in one day between New York and Philadelphia. Determined to claim this lucrative award, Hamilton and Curtiss arrived at Governors Island, starting point for the flight, shortly before dawn on June 13. While Curtiss made last minute adjustments on the *Golden Flyer* (finest airplane of its day, used by Curtiss on May 29 to win $10,000 for the first flight between New York and Albany), Hamilton wrapped five inflated automobile tires around his body; they were designed to act as life preservers in the event of a water landing. Struggling into a leather jacket, Hamilton climbed into the pusher biplane and began his take-off run at 7:10 A.M. It ended abruptly when the propeller blade hit a stake that protruded some six inches above the ground. Curtiss quickly fitted a new propeller to the 50-hp, 8-cylinder, liquid-cooled engine, and Hamilton was on his way again at 7:37 A.M.[4]

Hamilton circled Governors Island, slowly gaining altitude, then leveled off at 300 feet and headed southwest until he located the special train that he was supposed to follow to his distant destination. Battling head winds, he took one hour and forty-eight minutes to cover the eighty-five miles to Philadelphia. Nevertheless, the average speed of nearly fifty miles per hour impressed contemporary observers.[5]

Thousands of spectators lined the stretch of vacant lots east of Front Street and Erie Avenue that served as Philadelphia's landing field. Unable to resist the opportunity to perform, Hamilton circled overhead three times before diving to a landing. Gov. Edwin S. Stuart, resplendent in top hat and morning coat, strode forward to greet the smiling aviator. Hamilton delivered a letter from New York's Gov. Charles Evans Hughes. Stuart immediately penned a reply for the return trip. After the governor inspected the airplane, the crowd called upon him to make a speech—or so one report has it. Happy to oblige, Stuart climbed the steps of a nearby hotel and said:

> *My friends, you have witnessed a great sight today. A peep into what the future might hold for your children has been offered to you. Some day it is likely that the air will be filled with machines such as that which you have just seen. A great era is at hand. I am proud to be here, and was proud to take the hand of the man who accomplished such a feat as flying from New York to Philadelphia.*[6]

Following a light lunch with officials and prominent citizens, Hamilton returned to the field and took off at 11:43 A.M. This time he had a tail wind, and he quickly outdistanced the guide train. Hamilton followed the Pennsylvania Railroad tracks, but at Metuchen, New Jersey, he mistook the Lehigh Valley tracks for the Pennsylvania and headed in the wrong direction. Engine trouble developed. Lost, and with a sputtering motor, Hamilton made a forced landing in a muddy meadow near South Amboy, breaking the propeller of his biplane.

For a time it seemed that Hamilton would be unable to complete his trip before dark (as stipulated in the contest rules). But he would not be denied. Eager volunteers were pressed into service, and they carried the machine through waist-deep slime to a nearby stretch of dry and level ground while Hamilton telephoned New York for help. Curtiss and a mechanic dashed to the site by automobile. Spark plugs cleaned, rudder repaired, and propeller replaced, Hamilton set off for Governors Island at 6 P.M. This time he found New York. The tired but jubilant flyer, cigarette in mouth, landed at 6:41 P.M. He had established a new world's record—170 miles—for the longest distance flown in one day.[7]

Hamilton's career was brief. He quarreled with Curtiss later in the year, and Curtiss successfully sued him for breach of contract. Early in 1911, Hamilton fell ill with tuberculosis. Following several months in a sanatorium, he had a reconciliation with Curtiss and returned to the exhibition circuit. But he was never the same. On January 22, 1914, Hamilton died in bed from an internal lung hemorrhage at the age of twenty-nine.[8]

Hamilton's moment of fame has special importance in the historical evolution of air mail service in the United States. His New York to Philadelphia flight received wide publicity and drew attention to the commercial possibilities of aviation. One aeronautical journal—not for the last time—quoted Alfred Lord Tennyson's "Locksley Hall" about "pilots of the purple twilight" and the "heavens filled with commerce." A French observer gushed: "After the Wrights, with their white wings, and Curtiss, with his wings of gold, now you have Hamilton flying from city to city. The day of real aerial voyages has come. It is a revolution that was begun in your country."[9]

Among the many people touched by the event was Congressman Morris Sheppard. Known to his colleagues in Congress as single-minded, ambitious, diligent, and an ardent prohibitionist and reformer, Sheppard was not a man given to visionary enthusiasms. The thirty-five-year-old Texas Democrat nevertheless grew so excited as he read the morning newspaper accounts of Hamilton's feat that he decided to take immediate action. On the afternoon of June 14, Sheppard introduced a bill in the House that directed the postmaster general to make a study of the practicality of operating an experimental air mail service between Washington and some other suitable point.[10]

As Sheppard likely realized, movement of mail by air was not new. Pennsylvanian John Wise had made the world's first official flight with regular mail (there had been earlier unofficial flights) when his gas-filled balloon *Jupiter* rose from the ground at Lafayette, Indiana, on August 17, 1859. Bound for New York, Wise encountered contrary winds and was forced down near Crawfordsville, Indiana, thirty miles away, after four and a half hours aloft. The French had operated the first air mail service during the Franco-Prussian War. Between September 1870 and January 1871, balloons carried over German lines more than 2,000,000 letters from besieged Parisians. The most recent movement of mail by lighter-than-air craft had come early in the twentieth century, following the perfection of dirigibles by Count Ferdinand von Zeppelin. In fact, on June 22, 1910, nine days after Hamilton's intercity flight, the German company DELAG (Deutsche Luftschiffahrt Aktien Gesellschaft) would open the world's first passenger and mail commercial airline between Friedrichshafen and Dusseldorf with powered, steerable Zeppelins.[11]

Although Sheppard's bill—the first to envision the use of heavier-than-air machines to carry mail—was fated to die in committee, Postmaster General Frank H. Hitchcock needed little prodding. A supporter of aviation ever since he had observed the trial flights by the Wright brothers at Fort Myer in 1909, he appreciated the advantages of airplanes to advance the mail—provided that this could be done without expense to the government. In early November, Hitchcock authorized the first official mail flight, an attempt by John A. D. ("Douglas") McCurdy to fly off a platform on the deck of the Hamburg-American line steamship *Kaiserin Auguste Victoria* while the vessel was fifty miles from New York. Bad weather, however, forced McCurdy to cancel the daring flight.[12]

The following week, on November 10, 1910, Hitchcock attended an aviation meet near Baltimore. In the afternoon, the avid birdwatcher and lifelong bachelor became the first postmaster general to go aloft when he made a circuit of the field with Count de Lesseps in a Blériot monoplane. Hitchcock announced that he was "greatly pleased" with the experience, spoke about his "keen interest" in aviation, and predicted that airplanes ultimately would be "extensively used for carrying mail."[13]

Despite Hitchcock's "keen interest," the Post Office took no further action for nearly a year. In late September 1911, organizers of an international aviation meet, to be held at the Garden City Estates on Long Island, sought permission from postal authorities to feature a special airplane mail service as part of the program. Hitchcock, surely aware that the first British aerial mail service had been flown on September 9, readily assented.[14]

Aviation meets were gala social events in 1911. On September 23, despite clouds and cold temperatures, a steady stream of people made their way out Nassau Boulevard by automobile and special train to the Garden City Estates. Ladies carried fashionable Japanese parasols; many wore green and blue goggles. Gen. Frederick Dent Grant and his guest, Rear Adm. Ching Pai Kwong of the Imperial Chinese Navy, sat in a special box festooned with the Stars and Stripes and the dragon-adorned yellow flag of China. A band in red coats and caps played lively airs as 10,000 spectators filled the freshly painted bright green grandstand. Mlle Gaby Deslys created a stir when she strolled in front of the temporary hangars in a gown that was split up one side to reveal a section of black stocking. Paris might have been ready for such attire, but New York was not. The young lady attracted such a crowd of gawkers that she was forced to take refuge in a nearby automobile.

With Mlle Deslys safely in seclusion, attention focused on the aviators and their machines. Thirty-six noted flyers were on hand to compete for $40,000 in prizes. Americans Eugene B. Ely and Harry N. Atwood ("Undisputed Eagle of the Air") vied against Englishmen Claude Grahame-White and Thomas O. M. Sopwith. Capt. Paul W. Beck and Lts. Thomas de Witt Milling and Henry H. Arnold represented the American military services. Women flyers included Mlle Helen Dutrieu (brought over from France for the meet at a rumored cost of $2,500), Harriet Quimby, and Matilde Moisant. Farman, Nieuport, Curtiss, and Wright airplanes dotted the field, along with more exotic models.

The meet got underway at 3:15 P.M. with a series of racing and scouting contests. The first authorized mail service in the United States came shortly after 5 P.M. Hitchcock had established a special post

Postmaster General Frank H. Hitchcock hands mail to Earle Ovington on September 25, 1911, two days after Ovington had made the first official air mail flight.

office ("Aeroplane Station No. 1") in the middle of the field, together with twenty collection boxes in the grandstand and surrounding areas. Earle H. Ovington was duly sworn in as the first U.S. air mail pilot, then A. H. Bartsch of the Bosch Magneto Company handed him a bag that contained 640 letters and 1,280 postcards. The tiny cockpit of Ovington's Blériot monoplane could hardly accommodate the load. With difficulty, he stuffed the sack between his legs. Although this restricted movement of the control stick, Ovington decided to go ahead.

The graceful monoplane, aptly named *Dragonfly* and bearing the number 13 on its tail, made a pretty sight as it took off at 5:26 P.M. and headed toward Mineola, five and a half miles away. Covering the distance in six minutes, Ovington circled overhead while he worked the mail bag up until it rested on the upper longeron of the fuselage. All the while, Postmaster William McCarthy of Mineola waited below, frantically waving a handkerchief. Ovington flew close to the ground, took aim as best he could, and tossed the bag over the side. The mail sack landed on target, but it burst on impact. "I can see to this day,"

Ovington later recalled, "said postmaster gathering mail from the field as I circled to return to my home field." [15]

Hitchcock had wanted to be present for the first mail flight, but official duties detained him in Washington. Although postal authorities in New York had tried to reschedule the event, meet organizer Timothy L. Woodruff declined, claiming that widespread advance publicity precluded any delay. [16] The postmaster general did attend on September 25 and 26. Once described as "tall, broad-shouldered, red-haired, aloof in bearing, and inclined to foppishness in dress," Hitchcock seemed to enjoy himself immensely. He handed the mail to Ovington, posed for pictures, and spoke at length to reporters, indicating that the Post Office surely would designate "aerial routes" at some point in the near future. He even flew to Mineola in a Curtiss biplane with Captain Beck, carrying a mail sack on his lap. [17]

Encouraged by events on Long Island, Hitchcock decided that the time was right for the federal government to take a more direct role in fostering commercial aviation. "The progress being made in the science of aviation," he wrote two months later in the Post Office's *Annual Report* for 1911, "encourages the hope that ultimately the regular conveyance of mail by this means may be practical." In remote geographical areas where other means of carrying the mail have proved difficult, air transportation might be a viable alternative. In order to test this method under "practical conditions," Hitchcock asked Congress to appropriate $50,000 for experimental contract operations. [18]

On January 17, 1912, Second Assistant Postmaster General Joseph Stewart appeared before the House committee that was examining appropriations for the Post Office. Asked about the $50,000, he said that the money would be used to try air mail in places where such service would be superior to existing means of transportation. Most likely, this would mean the western part of the country, especially Arizona and New Mexico, where airplanes could reduce from days to hours the transit time for mail across mountains, canyons, and rivers. The committee questioned Stewart on this point for only a few minutes. Finally, the chairman asked the postal official if he were satisfied that airplanes, at their present stage of development, could be relied upon to provide dependable service. Stewart replied, "I think so." [19]

Apparently unimpressed, the committee failed to include the $50,000 in the Post Office appropriations bill. But other members of the House were not prepared to let the matter drop. Led by Congressman William G. Sharp, Ohio Democrat and avid astronomer, they tried to amend the bill on the floor of the House. Although in favor of efforts to curb federal expenditures, Sharp argued that $50,000 for an aerial experiment did not seem excessive at a time when the government was paying the railroads $47,000,000 to carry mail. Sounding a theme that often would be heard in the years to come, he pointed out that Congress should support the development of aeronautics because the field held such enormous potential in terms of national defense, commercial advantage, and scientific research. The Wright brothers had invented the airplane, but Europeans had assumed leadership in this vital area. "Our nation," Sharp concluded, "should not lag behind other powers in the progress of human achievement."

Sharp's amendment provoked opposition from both sides of the aisle, mainly on the grounds of economy and impracticality. John A. Moon (Democrat, Tennessee) termed the proposal "a useless expenditure of money." Joseph G. Cannon (Republican, Illinois), the powerful former speaker of the House, argued that aeronautical experiments should be confined to the Army. "I do not wish to be put down as opposed to any progressive measure," Congressman Thomas L. Reilly (Democrat, Connecticut) explained, "but it occurs to me that the postal service and the Post Office have been up in the air high enough for a long time and now let us get down to terra firma for once." A majority of the House agreed, and the amendment went down to defeat, 43 to 25.[20]

Hitchcock continued to promote the air mail by authorizing local postmasters to send mail by air—"without expense to the Department"—during aviation meets or when special intercity flights were made. Between October 1911 and December 1912 he approved forty-seven such requests for "official" sanction (not all were flown). However, Hitchcock's plans for an experimental air mail service ended with the failure of Sharp's amendment.[21]

IN NOVEMBER 1912 Woodrow Wilson triumphed over William Howard Taft and brought to an end sixteen years of Republican domination of the presidency. As the outgoing postmaster general had failed to request funds for air mail in his *Annual Report* for 1912, submitted shortly after the election, the new administration would have to deal with the issue.

The Aero Club of America, major spokesman for aeronautical interests in the country, welcomed the change of government and stood ready to offer advice. In March 1913 a lead editorial in *Flying*, the organization's official publication, took the outgoing administration to task for failing to perceive the profound changes that had taken place in the science of aeronautics, especially in the military sphere. It voiced the hope that Wilson would bring a more enlightened attitude to the subject and sponsor the development of both military and commercial aviation.[22]

The following month, Henry Woodhouse, associate editor of *Flying*, put forth a series of specific proposals. In order to bring the United States abreast of aeronautical progress elsewhere in the world, the Wilson administration should support four programs. The Army needed $1,000,000 to expand its aviation component, while the Navy required $150,000 for prizes to be awarded in an aircraft design competition. Wilson should accept the recommendation of a Taft-appointed commission and establish a National Aerodynamic Laboratory. Finally, the new administration should seek $50,000 from Congress for air mail experiments in Alaska, Arizona, and Colorado. The airplane, Woodhouse argued, "can, birdlike, cross chasms, fields, ravines, mountains, and rivers, traveling in a straight line where other vehicles would have to make detours, thus saving time which, in the matter of mail carrying, means saving money also." [23]

The administration's attitude toward aeronautics, at least with respect to its postal applications, would depend on the new postmaster general. Albert Sidney Burleson, Wilson's choice for the position, was an impressive figure. Tall, erect, usually dressed in black, and carrying an umbrella in all weather (to conceal gout), the Texas congressman was known as an able legislator and shrewd politician. An early supporter of Wilson's (he had directed the Speaker's Bureau during the campaign of 1912), Burleson had wanted a cabinet post as a reward. At first, Wilson had not favored the appointment; only reluctantly had he given in to pressure from conservative House Democrats. Wilson never had cause to regret the decision: Burleson proved a loyal and capable subordinate.[24]

The new postmaster general had deep Texas roots. His grandfather, Edward Burleson, had served as vice-president of the Texas Republic in the 1840s. Graduating from Baylor-Waco University in 1881, Burleson matriculated to the University of Texas where in 1884 he became valedictorian of the school's first law class. He joined the firm of Sneed & Poindexter after graduation, learning the law and making influential friends. In 1898 Burleson won election to Congress from the Tenth District; he would be returned to his seat every two years until selected postmaster general. Cultivating a rustic manner that masked a penetrating intelligence, Burleson soon became a powerful figure on the Hill. An unflinching party loyalist (he even would support Al Smith in 1928 despite intense opposition from most Texas Democrats), he zealously guarded the interest of the cotton growers of his district.[25]

"The post office system is essentially a business institution," Burleson announced in his first *Annual Report*. In tune with the spirit of the times, he placed great emphasis on efficiency. Burleson set out to eliminate waste, to battle special interests that were more concerned about profit than service, and "to promote efficiency." With regard to air mail, Burleson made clear his views in a letter to Henry Woodhouse. "I fully realize the necessity of keeping abreast of the needs of the postal service for the rapid transportation of mail," he wrote on November 21, 1913, "and of using every possible facility to this end." The Post Office had kept a careful eye on progress in aeronautics, he assured Woodhouse, and the time was rapidly approaching "when the Department will be called upon to give serious consideration to the feasibility of aerial mail transportation." However, the postmaster general concluded, such means of transportation will be adopted only "after it is demonstrated that they can be furnished and maintained within the proper limits of economy." [26]

In early December a subcommittee of the House Post Office Committee took up consideration of a bill—again offered by Congressman Sharp—to authorize the postmaster general to contract for air mail. Hoping to drum up support for the measure, subcommittee chairman David E. Finley (Democrat, South Carolina) sent a copy to Burleson and asked for his opinion. "I recommend the favorable consideration of the bill," the postmaster general replied. If a suitable appropriation were made, he continued, the department would be able "to ascertain to what extent aeroplanes may be employed at the present time in the mail transportation services." [27]

Burleson, clearly, was willing to experiment with air mail. But the cautious tone of his letter, as well as his lack of other action, indicated that this was not a project of particularly high priority. Representative Finley, on the other hand, bubbled with enthusiasm. Reporting the bill favorably, he stressed recent progress in aeronautics in Europe. He quoted French aviator Roland Garros, who recently had flown across the Mediterranean at its widest point, as an expert witness: "'The aeronautical motors are on the threshold of perfection; their reliability is increasing daily; they can be relied upon to fly hours without trouble, and to give their rated horsepower continually; this state of perfection makes possible almost anything.'" Finley pointed out that hundreds of flights were being made every day without accident. In fact, the French government was carrying air mail across the Sahara Desert. "We believe," the South Carolinian concluded, "the carrying of mail and light packages by aeroplane has passed beyond the experimental stage." [28]

Minority leader James R. Mann (Republican, Illinois) led the opposition when the measure came before the House on December 15, 1913. Despite Finley's claim, Mann pointed out (with accuracy) that "there is no place in the world to-day where mail is regularly carried by aeroplanes—in the Sahara Desert or anywhere else." While not opposed to appropriations for the development of aviation, Mann considered Finley's proposal to be premature. "There is no need or demand for this experiment," he argued.

William E. Cox (Democrat, Indiana) and John J. Fitzgerald (Democrat, New York) agreed with Mann. Aviation was not yet practical; the only agitation for this scheme had come from three or four airplane manufacturers, intent on profit. Congressman William H. Murray (Democrat, Oklahoma) mocked the idea of progress: "Along with the spineless cactus, the motherless chicken, the seedless raisin, the wireless telegraphy, you want a trackless travel?"

Finley made an impassioned speech in support of the measure, emphasizing that the United States was falling far behind other nations in the development of aeronautics. Other congressmen voiced their support, including Halver Steenerson (Republican, Minnesota), Frank B. Willis (Republican, Ohio), H. Robert Fowler (Democrat, Illinois), and that indefatigable champion of the air mail, William G. Sharp. But the air mail proposal was not a partisan issue. Without party discipline, and lacking pressure from powerful economic groups or vocal constituents, members of the House were free to decide the question on an individual basis. A majority apparently agreed that the air mail was impractical and uneconomical; the bill was defeated, 54 to 28.[29]

THE YEARS 1914 AND 1915 saw remarkable progress in aeronautics, brought about by the demands of war in Europe. Despite the new prominence of aviation, prospects for air mail in the United States continued to languish. Burleson asked Congress for $50,000 in his *Annual Report* for 1913 and for 1914, Second Assistant Postmaster General Stewart spoke in favor of the request when he appeared before House committees that examined postal appropriations, and aeronautical periodicals published supportive editorials—but nothing happened. Aeronautical development simply was not a priority for the Wilson administration, and Congress was not prepared to act without strong presidential leadership.

Yet this quiescent period was not without significance. Two events loom large in retrospect. In March 1915 Congress authorized the formation of the National Advisory Committee for Aeronautics (NACA). A prestigious body, with representatives from the military services, Smithsonian Institution, Weather Bureau, National Bureau of Standards, and civilian scientific community, NACA had a mandate "to supervise and direct scientific study of the problems of flight, with a view to their practical solution. . . ." It would soon play a key role in the establishment of an air mail service. The other important event—one that would have a profound effect on the course of commercial aviation in the United States—took place on September 1, 1915, when Burleson appointed Otto Praeger as second assistant postmaster general.[30]

Although a number of men have claimed the title of "Father of the Air Mail," none deserves it more than Otto Praeger. Praeger himself wanted to give the credit to Burleson. The postmaster general, Praeger wrote in his unpublished autobiography, conceived the plan for introducing aircraft as a permanent fixture in the postal service. All others directly or indirectly involved in the scheme were "only the favored instrumentality for translating Postmaster General Burleson's vision into the far-flung operation known as the United States Air Mail."[31]

Perhaps so, but knowledgeable and respected contemporary figures such as Charles G. Grey, editor of the British weekly *The Aeroplane* and the annual *Jane's All the World's Aircraft,* and Gill Robb Wilson, noted aviation columnist and author, held different views. Grey, who did not

Otto Praeger.

dispense praise lightly, once told Praeger: "I have always regarded you as the world's pioneer of air mails." Wilson wrote after Praeger's death in 1948: "His vision during the formative days of national air policy was one of the truly opportune assets of United States air history." Praeger may have lacked a detailed technical knowledge of the subject, but he grasped the broader political implications of aeronautics. "He saw," Wilson concluded, "that if the nation could be compacted and unified in domestic economy, it could move more positively and swiftly on the international stage. He knew that a sprawling democracy had handicaps in this respect, and he seized with enthusiasm upon the airplane as an agent to tie together the nation's areas of diversified local interests."[32]

Praeger, like Burleson, took pride in his Texas heritage. Herman Praeger, Otto's father, emigrated with his father from Dresden in 1851. Grandfather Praeger opened a hardware store in Victoria, Texas. There, in 1845, Herman married Louisa Shultz, a native of Berlin who wrote poetry and liked to play the guitar. Otto, the third of four children, was born in Victoria on February 27, 1871.[33]

Herman Praeger moved to San Antonio in 1879 and opened a hardware store on East Commerce Street. Otto grew up in the midst of a large German-American community that had taken root on the southwestern frontier. Praeger later recalled the San Antonio of his youth as a developing city of 50,000 people, featuring open-air Mexican restaurants and gambling houses and saloons that did a thriving business twenty-four hours a day, seven days a week. Stagecoaches still passed through town, and gun fights often broke out in the saloons. Praeger met "Judge" Roy Bean ("the law west of the Pecos") and other frontier notables. One day on the way home from school he encountered John L. Sullivan, heavyweight boxing champion of the world—and suffered the first of many disillusionments. The Great John L. was not wearing tights or a diamond-studded belt, as pictured in the *Police Gazette*; instead, "he looked just like any other old drunk making a fool of himself, parading the streets with a seedy looking rabble at his heels."[34]

Praeger attended a German-American school where all subjects (except English) were taught in German. From there, he went on to San Pedro High School. His boyhood ambition was to become editor of a great newspaper. M. Koenigsberg, a classmate who went on to gain fame as a newspaperman, recalled that Praeger's intensity could be intimidating; fellow students "talked about him in whispers." Praeger owned a small printing press on which he regularly printed a four-page newspaper that contained news of the high school. "Young

Praeger had the passion of an evangelist," Koenigsberg remembered. "Through journalism, we agreed, ran the path of modern knighthood."[35]

Praeger left high school before graduation ("something went amiss with my mathematics") for a job as cub reporter on the San Antonio *Express*. Experiencing the usual joys and sorrows of a newspaper apprenticeship, he followed political candidates, reported on trials, interviewed such public figures as Buffalo Bill Cody and Kit Carson, and watched editors reduce to a few simple sentences his carefully crafted prose ("those fine pieces into which I poured my very soul, and which were garlanded with the choicest metaphors, similes and adjectives"). His best remembered assignment was a self-promoted bicycle tour of Mexico in 1892. Praeger spent three months on the road, pedaling through the Sierra Mojada desert and over the Sierra Madre mountains. He traveled 1,772 miles, from San Antonio to Mazatlan on the Pacific coast, then to Mexico City, where he interviewed President Porfirio Diaz. The young reporter enjoyed his work. Later, he reflected "that a live, small town newspaper is a better journalist kindergarten than anything a metropolitan city has to offer. . . ."[36]

After six years with the *Express*, Praeger felt the need for further formal schooling as a foundation for "solid journalistic work." He left his job and enrolled in the University of Texas as a nondegree student. Praeger spent three years in Austin, taking courses in political economy, psychology, history, and literature, and acquiring a grounding in the sciences. Along the way, he learned the most valuable lessons that a university can impart to a student: "To observe, to analyze and to weigh are the priceless gifts that I carried back into my profession from my alma mater. . . ."

Praeger returned to the *Express* in 1897 and undertook more important assignments, as befitted a growing maturity. Three years later, he had his first taste of public office. During an interview with a newly elected reform mayor, Praeger was offered the position of city clerk. He accepted. Praeger held the office for two years, supervising the widening and repaving of streets (asphalt replaced bricks and wooden blocks), construction of a new civic center, and creation of an extensive park system. When the reformers were voted out in 1902, Praeger rejoined the *Express* as city editor. Although rising to news editor, Praeger realized that his prospects had come to an end: the editor owned the newspaper and showed no inclination of relinquishing the top position. Praeger resigned in 1904 and went to Washington, D.C., as correspondent for three Texas newspapers, including the influential *Dallas News*.

Praeger spent ten happy years as a member of the Washington press corps. He loved the excitement of the capital, the feeling of being at the center of national events. He quickly discovered that congressmen could be relegated to three categories: effective ("wizards"), pompous ("stuffed shirts"), and failures ("duds"). "The large number of colorless, mediocre men in Congress who passed for statesmen among their constituents," he recalled, "was to me a great surprise." Praeger most admired Progressive reform leaders. Watching closely from the press gallery, he observed "each move in the stirring events that marked the rise, sweep and eclipse of the Progressive movement in our national politics."

Early in 1914 Praeger had a conversation with one of President Wilson's associates about the administration's patronage problems. Wilson and Burleson, he learned, faced a dilemma. Secretary of State William Jennings Bryan, whose passion for patronage was without equal, was pushing the selection of a clearly unqualified individual for postmaster of Washington, D.C. The only way out, said Praeger's informant, was for Burleson to name someone else on personal grounds. Bryan would understand *that*. Praeger, as an old fishing and hunting buddy of Burleson's, volunteered for the position. The postmaster general, after teasing him about an "itch for office," appointed Praeger postmaster of Washington, D.C., on April 1, 1914.

Praeger later recalled his first day at his new post. At the end of business, an assistant postmaster brought in a large pile of correspondence for signature. "How do I know what I am signing?" Praeger inquired. The experienced bureaucrat assured him that the material had been properly initialed and that all was in order. Furthermore, it would not do any good to read the letters because they were based on extensive memoranda and reports. "Alright," Praeger replied, "give me all the accompanying papers. I will read everything before I sign."

And this was only the beginning. The new postmaster threw himself into the work with a passion that surprised—and occasionally disconcerted—the career bureaucrats. He took steps to modernize and reform the city's antiquated postal system, searching for ways to reduce cost and improve service. Obviously impressed, the postmaster general selected Washington as the site for the trial of an innovative automotive mail delivery system. Burleson's Republican predecessors had experimented with motor vehicles on urban postal routes, but had encountered stiff opposition from congressmen whose financial supporters held horsedrawn contracts. Contract postal truck service had been introduced in Washington in 1907; it ended four years later when the government failed to reach a satisfactory agreement with private transport companies. Burleson decided to try again, but this time with a government-operated service. He believed that the Post Office could do the job more efficiently and economically than private enterprise, and he expected Praeger to prove the point.

Praeger's enthusiasm and energy could be formidable when directed at a specific task. Ignoring pressure from automotive manufacturers with political influence, he selected trucks solely on the basis of merit. Praeger kept in close touch with every phase of the operation, carefully compiling statistics to demonstrate conclusively the superior efficiency of motor vehicles in government service. As a result of his success, Burleson extended the postal truck service to other cities, abandoning contract operations. By 1920 the Post Office had more than 2,600 motor vehicles on the road. "The growth of the Government-owned automobile service," one expert has pointed out, "is as striking as any record of U.S. postal development. . . ."[37]

Pleased with Praeger's work in this and other areas of reform, Burleson appointed him second assistant postmaster general on September 1, 1915, with responsibility for the delivery of all mails in the United States and its territories. Among the many items that came across Praeger's desk was a letter from the Alaska Engineering Commission indicating that aeronautical interests in the territory would be willing to initiate air mail service if a government contract could be secured. This came at the same time that promoters in Massachusetts were advancing plans for an air mail service between New Bedford and Nantucket. Praeger and Burleson decided to cooperate with these schemes. On February 12, 1916, the Post Office formally advertised for bids to carry air mail on seven routes in Alaska and one in Massachusetts.[38]

This was a bold move: the Post Office did not have funds to pay air mail contractors (although the advertisement did contain an escape clause that permitted the government to reject all bids). In order to obtain the necessary money, Praeger and Burleson decided upon a new tactic. Aware that the Senate was more sympathetic than the House toward air mail, Burleson wrote to Senator John H. Bankhead (Democrat, Alabama), chairman of the Post Office Committee, and asked that the Senate amend the House-passed postal appropriation bill to include $50,000 to contract for air mail. Burleson's maneuver worked. Bankhead's committee reported the amendment favorably, and in July it was accepted by both houses without debate.[39]

The Post Office now had its first funds for air mail. Unfortunately, the victory proved bittersweet. When bids had been opened on May 12, only one offer had been tendered, and this had been rejected because no bond had been posted. The promoters had decided that no aircraft could be obtained that was capable of coping with the severe weather conditions of the far north.[40]

Although this episode had no immediate result, it did excite the Post Office's interest in air mail. Before the end of 1916, the department was looking with favor on the possibility of contracting for a Chicago to New York service. This came in the wake of Victor Carlstrom's widely publicized Chicago–New York flight of November 2–3. Before Carlstrom's record-breaking trip, the last serious attempt to fly between the two cities had come in 1910 when Eugene B. Ely had had to abandon the effort after only thirty miles. Flying a Curtiss R biplane with a 200-hp engine, Carlstrom covered the 967 miles in eight hours and twenty-eight minutes of flying time (twenty-six hours elapsed time). En route, he broke the American cross-country nonstop record by flying 452 miles from Chicago to Erie, Pennsylvania. Delayed at Erie because of a loose connection on the gasoline intake pipe, he reached Hammondsport, New York, before dark. The next morning he flew the 315 miles from Hammondsport to New York, setting a new American cross-country speed record of 134 mph over the final leg of the trip.[41]

For some optimistic Chicago businessmen, Carlstrom's flight demonstrated the feasibility of a Chicago–New York mail service. Glenn Muffly, airplane engine manufacturer, and Walter L. Brock, consulting engineer for the Aero Club of Chicago, drew up elaborate plans to operate overnight service between the two cities. Airplanes would leave both terminals at 6 P.M. and follow a series of vertical searchlights to intermediate landing fields at Williamsport, Pennsylvania, and Napoleon and Niles, Ohio. They would arrive at their destinations at 9 A.M., carrying 500 to 1,000 pounds of mail.[42]

Burleson and Praeger accepted this visionary scheme at face value. Delighted to contract for an experimental mail service that would connect the nation's leading commercial centers, the postmaster general requested $100,000 for "aerial experimentation" in his *Annual Report* for 1916. Meanwhile, Praeger sought backing from the prestigious National Advisory Committee for Aeronautics.

Originally formed to oversee scientific inquiry into the problems of flight, NACA quickly had broadened its role to function as a general advisory board on all aspects of aviation. Its first interest in the air mail had come in October 1916 when Praeger attended NACA's annual meeting and discussed the Post Office's unsuccessful attempt to contract for service in Alaska. Now Praeger wanted NACA to endorse plans for a Chicago–New York contract operation.

Following discussions in late November between Praeger and H. C.

Richardson, a naval officer serving as secretary of the committee, NACA included a statement of support in its annual report to Congress, submitted on December 4. Air mail service was now practical, NACA argued. The committee therefore recommended to Congress "that the Post Office be authorized to establish one or more experimental routes, with a view to determining the accuracy, frequency, and rapidity of transportation which may reasonably be expected under normal and favorable conditions. . . ."[43]

Prospects for a Chicago–New York overnight mail service soon faded as the promoters realized that such an operation was far beyond the existing technical capabilities of aviation. NACA, in the meantime, had formed a subcommittee on aerial mail service that had been looking into the matter with more expert care than ever before. Headed by Maj. Gen. George O. Squier, the Army's chief signal officer, the subcommittee reached several important conclusions that brought the first note of realism to prospects for air mail after years of excessively optimistic statements by various promoters of aeronautics. It was not possible, the subcommittee announced, for the Post Office to locate responsible private companies to fly the mail. Instead, it recommended that the Post Office itself operate an experimental route between Washington and Philadelphia or New York.[44]

NACA's prescient recommendations came just as the United States entered World War I. Although the Post Office's plan for an air mail service was shelved temporarily, Burleson and Praeger were not prepared to abandon the scheme. In his memoirs, Praeger recalls a summons to Burleson's office during the winter of 1917–18. "It was a misty, dreary morning," he remembered, "the kind Washington is accustomed to in the winter months." Burleson was standing at the window when Praeger entered, looking out at the slush-filled streets and misting skies. He turned and asked: "Do you think that airplanes could operate in this kind of weather?" Praeger, whose only firsthand experience with aeronautics had been as an interested spectator during the experimental flights of the Wright brothers at Fort Myer in 1909, said that he did not know. Burleson told him to find out. *If* airplanes could operate dependably in marginal weather, the postmaster general stated, they should become a permanent part of the postal service. But, he warned, he did not want to start an air mail service and then be forced to abandon it.[45]

Following the meeting with Burleson, Praeger solicited proposals from three major aircraft manufacturers to operate for the Post Office a Washington–New York mail service. Curtiss showed no interest, citing large government war contracts, while L.W.F. Engineering suggested that the Post Office approach the Signal Corps and borrow six aircraft. The Standard Aero Corporation, however, submitted a detailed plan. Standard would supply five JR-1 aircraft with 150-hp Hispano-Suiza engines, five pilots, and two mechanics. Cost for the first month of operation—including aircraft ($68,000), spare parts, pilots, mechanics, hangars, and repair shops—would amount to $82,198.50. Operating costs for each subsequent month of service would be $3,973.75. Aircraft could be ready in seven weeks from date of order. Securing qualified aviators would be more difficult, and Standard suggested that the Post Office borrow pilots from the Army for the experiment.[46]

Praeger took the proposal to NACA for review. Congress, he said, had approved $100,000 for the current fiscal year (ending June 30, 1918) and another $100,000 for the following year to operate an experimental service. The Post Office would like to undertake the project, but Burleson demanded firm assurances "that the service, once established, will be a permanent feature." Based upon discussions with various aircraft manufacturers, Praeger said that he had reached the conclusion that "a dependable daily aerial mail service can be maintained." However, before presenting the scheme to Burleson for final approval, he wanted to know "whether your board can confirm this judgment."[47]

NACA assigned technical assistant John H. DeKlyn to examine Standard's proposal. Following discussions with officials from Standard Aero, he concluded that the aircraft and route were suitable for the experiment. "I fully believe," he informed NACA on January 29, 1918, "that the outline presented by Standard Aero, considering all the limiting factors of money, time, lack of previous experience or data to base the system on, present a good possibility of success." NACA adopted this position as its own.[48]

NACA's positive recommendation in hand, Praeger told Burleson that he was prepared to give the necessary assurances about the probable success of the project. Burleson, in turn, ordered Praeger to conduct an air mail service for the Post Office.

IN COMMITTING THE POST OFFICE to the air mail, Burleson had responded to an imperative as old as postal systems. Speed had been the objective of mail services since at least 500 B.C., when Persian postriders had driven their horses over 200 miles a day to maintain communications with the far corners of the empire. Indeed, as postal historian Wayne E. Fuller has pointed out, "so closely has speed been associated with the mails that much of the world's postal history can be written around the attempts to send the mail faster each day than it went the day before."[49]

But carrying mail by air posed a formidable challenge for the United States Post Office. In 1918 no nation in the world operated a scheduled air mail service. And despite the claims of enthusiastic aeronautical publicists and promoters, no such service ever had been conducted with regularity for any substantial period of time.

The decision to fly the mail came seven and a half years after Congressman Morris Sheppard had first suggested that the government study the feasibility of using aircraft to transport mail. During the intervening years, attention had focused on contract operations in remote areas. Fortunately, this experimental service had not been attempted. Operations in the far reaches of Alaska, Arizona, or Wyoming would have been a disaster. Aeronautics had not yet reached a point of technological development to permit such a hazardous undertaking. Engines were not reliable, bad weather flying techniques had not yet been developed, aeronautical compasses and other navigational instruments did not exist, and the requirements for a workable operational infrastructure were unknown. The inevitable failure of the experiment surely would have retarded plans for air mail by many years.

Thanks in large part to NACA's good advice, postal officials turned their attention to the possibility of a government-sponsored service over a shorter route, connecting Washington with a major business center. Although this route afforded a greater chance for success, Burleson remained cautious. The postmaster general shared the Populist view that government should own and operate such essential services of transportation and communication as railroads, telephone, and telegraph. He believed that efficient and inexpensive public operation of the air mail would lead to government ownership of other essential communications systems. While welcoming the opportunity to demonstrate what the government could do, he demanded assurance that the Post Office would not fall flat on its face.[50]

Otto Praeger was the key. The former newspaperman lacked a technical background in aviation, yet he had demonstrated impressive administrative skills in supervising postal modernization programs, especially in facilitating the transition from horses to motor vehicles in urban centers. Praeger said that the air mail could be flown with regularity, and Burleson believed him. The fate of this pioneering venture now lay in the hands of the second assistant postmaster general.

2 Into the Air

OTTO PRAEGER WASTED NO TIME in getting the air mail service underway. On February 12, 1918, the Post Office called for bids to construct five aircraft for a Washington to New York mail route. Tailored to Standard's earlier proposal, specifications provided for airplanes capable of carrying 300 pounds of mail at least 200 miles at a maximum speed of 100 mph. Bids were due in ten days, and aircraft had to be delivered no later than April 25. The Post Office stressed that the new mail route was not an experiment: "Once established, it is to remain a permanent service."[1]

If Praeger expected the opening of bids on February 22 to be a perfunctory, largely ceremonial exercise, he was in for a rude surprise. As bids were being unsealed, Col. E. A. Deeds of the Signal Corps appeared with a startling offer: the Army was prepared to operate the postal route with military airplanes and pilots. The Aviation Section of the Signal Corps (soon to be redesignated the Army Air Service) had just received a cable from headquarters in Europe, asking that pilots be given additional cross-country flying experience. Carrying the mail for the Post Office, he explained, would allow military aviators to obtain this necessary training. Praeger may have had reservations about Deeds's generous offer, but he had to accept. Not only had he been warned that it would be difficult to secure experienced pilots, but also he surely realized (especially with a name like Otto Praeger!) that it would be hard *not* to cooperate with the military in the midst of the patriotic fervor that was sweeping the country.[2]

Praeger and Deeds agreed on terms on March 1. The War Department would operate an air mail service for the Post Office for one year, beginning no later than May 15. The Post Office would be responsible for airfields, hangars, repair shops, clerical personnel, ground transportation, gasoline, and lubricants; the military would provide sufficient aircraft, pilots, mechanics, and spare parts *"to insure a dependable daily trip each way"* (emphasis added). Flights would be "in all respects under the control and operation of the War Department."[3]

Maj. Gen. George O. Squier, chief Signal Corps officer, immediately issued the necessary orders for six Curtiss R-4LM and six Curtiss JN-4H airplanes (specially modified with one of the usual two seats converted into a mail compartment), pilots, mechanics, and an officer-in-charge. All personnel and equipment had to be in place by May 15, he emphasized, to insure "the successful continuous operation of the project."[4]

Praeger assigned chief clerk George L. Conner to work with the Army in selecting airfields. Together with Capt. H. H. Salmon, Conner inspected a number of sites in the New York area, including Governors Island, Van Cortlandt Park, and Flatbush Gardens. None proved satisfactory. The two men finally settled on the infield of the Belmont Park racetrack on Long Island, a location used in the past for aircraft operations. Although owner August Belmont readily agreed to permit aircraft operations on his property, asking only a letter of appreciation, the Long Island Rail Road refused to run a special train from the racetrack to downtown Manhattan for less than $1.00 a mile. Praeger approved the arrangement only after Conner negotiated a lower rate.[5]

Next came Philadelphia, designated as a refueling and transfer point because the Curtiss airplanes did not have the range for a non-stop trip between Washington and New York. Conner and Lt. Gordon Dodge quickly settled on a field near Bustleton, located close to the railroad depot at North Philadelphia and a twenty-five-minute drive from downtown. Despite telephone and telegraph lines along the western boundary and a row of tall trees on the southern end, pilots would rate Bustleton as the best of the first air mail fields—this no high compliment. Conner leased the land for $800 a year and accepted bids for leveling, seeding, and other preparations.[6]

Not for the last time, finding an acceptable landing area in Washington turned out to be a challenge. Aviators preferred a spacious field at College Park, Maryland, but Conner objected that nine miles was too far from the main post office. He favored Polo Field, a grassy area between the Tidal Basin and the Potomac River that had been used at times as a landing field. This did not sit well with the military. Only 900 feet by 300 feet and surrounded by trees over six feet high, Polo Field posed a stiff challenge for experienced airmen even under ideal conditions. But with the air mail service inaugural date approaching, and with nothing else immediately available, the Air Service reluctantly agreed to use Polo Field while searching for something better.[7]

Friction between the Army and the Post Office began early in April when rumors reached Praeger "that certain officers of the Signal Corps were asserting positively that the mail route would not be flown every day but only on days of fair weather." Disturbed about a possible misunderstanding concerning the Post Office's requirements, Praeger called on Colonel Deeds and asked for assurances that the military was prepared to operate the mail service in all weather conditions. Deeds promptly complied. The air mail would not be "a pink tea flying affair," he told Praeger; it "would be flown daily, rain or shine."[8]

As Praeger would soon discover, Deeds—an industrialist (and non-flyer) who held a temporary wartime commission—did not speak for the Air Service. Many senior flying officers believed that it was a mistake to divert aeronautical resources to a civilian mail service in the middle of a war. If this had to be done because of a misguided decision taken by higher authorities, then they intended to emphasize the military training purposes of the original agreement. With regard to Praeger's concern about delays, Lt. Col. Thurman H. Bane advised General Squier that the Post Office "has the wrong impression with reference to the reliability of the aerial mail route service." The head of the air division's executive section pointed out that frequent interruptions could be expected, and he recommended that the postmaster general be informed "of the true state of affairs."[9]

Squier agreed with Bane. At his request, Secretary of War Newton D. Baker sent a letter to Burleson that explained the realities of flying operations. "The Signal Corps desires to make this experiment as thorough and representative as possible," he told the postmaster general, "but it is felt that unavoidable conditions are bound to arise which will interfere with the service, and which should be brought to the attention of your Department before the service is started." Interruption in mail service could be expected because of local storms or dense fog at points of departure; airplanes might be forced to land while en route because of approaching storms or engine trouble. Baker suggested a meeting between representatives of the Post Office and the Air Service to clarify possible misunderstandings.[10]

The meeting took place in late April, but it only added to the growing tension between the Post Office and the military. To talk to Praeger, Squier sent Lt. Col. L. E. Goodier, Jr., commander of the air division's operations section that had primary responsibility for the air mail. Goodier, in turn, brought with him a senior British military aviator and Maj. Reuben E. Fleet, newly assigned as officer-in-charge of the air mail. Goodier told Praeger in no uncertain terms that the Post Office had to give up the idea of daily flying regardless of weather. Conceding that severe storms and dense fog might create conditions of "utter invisibility" that would disrupt mail service, Praeger insisted "that flights should be made in rainy or fair weather and in fogs, so long as it was possible for an aviator to make out the . . . bounds of his fields for the purpose of alighting." Following a heated argument about the kinds of weather that would make flying impossible, Goodier suggested that it might be wise to abandon the entire project. Praeger insisted that the War Department live up to the terms of its agreement with the Post Office. At this point, the obviously agitated British officer blurted out: "Do you want us to lose the war?" Praeger responded that he failed to see how the outcome of the war hinged on six training planes. Goodier then turned to Fleet—who had remained silent throughout the meeting—and said: "Major, the job is yours." [11]

Fleet remained after Goodier and his British colleague departed and told Praeger that he would do everything in his power to see that the mail service operated with regularity, even if it meant flying in bad weather. While encouraged by Fleet's attitude, Praeger no longer trusted the military. He ordered six aircraft to be purchased from departmental funds and had plans drawn up for postal operation of the air mail should the Army refuse to fly in bad weather. [12]

Fleet, an experienced real estate and timber businessman with a limited flying background, had his work cut out for him. He quickly discovered that progress during the previous seven weeks had been confined to preparation of airfields. The only pilot detailed to the mail service, 1st Lt. Walter Miller, was at Hazelhurst Field at Mineola, Long Island, honing his skills in "stick control" and "flying by compass." Two newly commissioned officers whom the Post Office had asked to be assigned to the project, 2d Lts. George L. Boyle and James Clark Edgerton, were en route to Hazelhurst. As for aircraft, the Curtiss company had been instructed to convert six JN-4Ds to JN-4Hs, which involved substituting the more powerful 150-hp Hispano-Suiza engine for the 90-hp OX-5, and to install mail compartments in place of the forward cockpit. None had arrived. Fleet pressured Curtiss for prompt delivery of the airplanes. He urged the chief of training to expedite the assignment of three additional pilots and thirty-two enlisted specialists. And he continued his efforts to mend relations with Praeger by assuring him that "the primary object of this enterprise is to deliver mail with punctuality and regularity, with no interruptions. . . ." [13]

Despite Fleet's work, it appeared in early May that the failure of Curtiss to deliver aircraft would force a delay in the start of the mail service. Fleet asked for a postponement, but the Post Office insisted that the widely publicized starting date be met. Not until May 12, three days before the scheduled inaugural of service, did the pilots (except Boyle) and airplanes come together for the first time. Fleet's request for experienced personnel had left the training section unmoved. Two pilots (1st Lts. Miller and Torrey H. Webb) had had limited cross-country experience, while three others (2d Lts. Boyle, Edgerton, and Stephen Bonsal) had been flying for less than four months. Only 1st Lt. H. Paul Culver—an instructor at Ellington Field who had been teaching acrobatics to pilots destined for Europe—could be termed a seasoned airman, and he was bitterly disappointed at being assigned to the air mail instead of going overseas.[14]

The pilots were ready, more or less, but the airplanes were not. Although the JN-4Hs had finally been delivered by Curtiss, they arrived at Hazelhurst in crates. Fleet had less than seventy-two hours to assemble, test, and position them for the start of service. Edgerton recalled:

> *Picture the situation. The essential room for assembly was occupied by a mountain of crates. Before our new aircraft could emerge from their cocoons, butterfly fashion, there must be room to spread their wings. Each of the five pilots marked off the boundaries of his area by chalk. . . . My plane must be uncrated, assembled, serviced, checked, warmed up, tuned and flight checked. Wow! I staggered at the sheer audacity of this challenge.*[15]

With mechanics provided by Hazelhurst, the pilots started work. It took until sunset on May 13 to uncrate the aircraft, then the job of assembly began. Problems multiplied as the hours slipped away: the gasoline tank of one aircraft had a severe leak, fuselage wires of two aircraft were broken, the air pressure safety valve on all airplanes did not work, gravity tank feed pipes had to be replaced on all Jennies, control wires were either too short or too long, and so on.

The crews labored through the night and into the next day. Fleet needed four airplanes for May 15: one in Washington, one in New York, and two in Philadelphia, where the mail would be transferred and continue to its destination without delay. Edgerton—who had spent his off-duty hours at Ellington Field helping mechanics to assemble, rig, and tune aircraft—gave him the first one, and the veteran Culver provided a second. As Webb was making good progress, Fleet ordered him to continue work on his airplane, then fly it to New York. Edgerton and Culver would ferry their JN-4Hs to Philadelphia, accompanied by Fleet in a JN-4D borrowed from a squadron at Hazelhurst. Fleet would continue to Washington for the scheduled 11:30 A.M. departure from the nation's capital.[16]

The three pilots took off at 4:15 P.M., heading south in foggy weather. Edgerton and Culver soon lost sight of Fleet, who lagged behind in his smaller-engined Jenny. Landing at Bustleton without incident, they grew anxious when Fleet failed to appear at sunset.

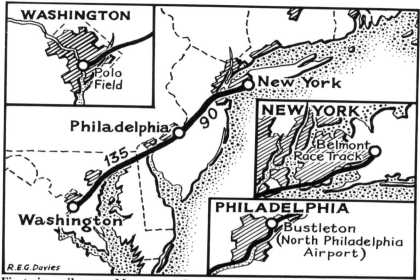

First air mail route, May 15, 1918.

Fleet had run into problems. Trying to find Philadelphia with an uncalibrated compass and a road map was not an easy task for a pilot with limited cross-country experience. Lost, he landed in a field and asked directions from a farmer. He took off and headed in the general direction of Philadelphia, but again became confused. Low on fuel, Fleet made a forced landing on a golf course several miles from Bustleton, smashing a landing gear wheel. Fleet got to a phone and reported the situation to Bustleton. Edgerton and Culver loaded a spare wheel on a field truck, and set out in the growing darkness to find Fleet. After some difficulty, they located the stranded major and fitted the spare wheel. Edgerton then drove back to Bustleton, where he persuaded passing motorists to stop and light the landing area with their headlights. The more experienced Culver flew the Jenny to Bustleton with Fleet as passenger, landing without difficulty. But Washington still lacked an aircraft, and nothing could be done until the next day.[17]

Fleet departed from Philadelphia in one of the JN-4Hs at 8:40 A.M., May 15, less than three hours before the first air mail was due to leave Washington. Following railroad tracks and prominent landmarks—the Delaware River, Chesapeake Bay, and Potomac River—he had no trouble finding his way and reached Polo Field at 10:35 A.M. Fleet or-

Polo Field, Washington, D.C., May 15, 1918. Persons shown are (*left to right*): Otto Praeger, Washington Postmaster Merritt O. Chance, Postmaster General Albert S. Burleson, President Woodrow Wilson.

dered the airplane refueled only to discover that there was no gasoline available. He was furious: Capt. Benjamin Lipsner, a nonflyer from the lubrication section of the Air Service's equipment division, had assured him that 1,000 gallons of gasoline would be delivered to each of the airfields by May 10. Fleet ordered a truck rushed to a nearby Navy facility to borrow gasoline. Meanwhile, he had the tanks of three aircraft—intended as escorts—drained of fuel.

As Fleet scurried to prepare the airplane and brief Boyle on the route, honored guests began to arrive. Thousands of spectators already lined the field, standing five and six deep behind ropes, while armed guards patrolled the perimeter. Not unmindful of the political benefits to be reaped from a successful air mail service that could be attributed to the efforts of a progressive Democratic administration, Burleson had arranged for an impressive turnout of high officials. Five hundred dignitaries jammed inside the small VIP enclosure, including Praeger, Secretary of the Navy Josephus Daniels and his youthful assistant, Franklin D. Roosevelt, members of NACA, Japanese Postmaster K. Kambara, members of Congress (including Morris

Sheppard who in 1910 had introduced the first bill pertaining to air mail), and assorted party stalwarts. Burleson even convinced President Wilson that it would be worthwhile to take time from affairs of state and make an appearance.

President and Mrs. Wilson arrived at 11:15 A.M. and received the cheers of the crowd. Five minutes later a truck from the central Post Office drove on the field and delivered four bags of mail (3,300 letters weighing 140 pounds). President Wilson opened one bag and deposited a letter from Burleson to Postmaster Thomas G. Patten of New York. Burleson then stepped forward, smiled, and without saying a word handed Boyle a bouquet of flowers. Wilson presented Fleet with engraved watches (courtesy of the Hamilton Watch Company) for himself and the six pilots. After a short delay while refueling was completed, Boyle climbed into JN-4H Number 38262 and started the engine. The crowd yelled their approval as the Jenny skimmed over the ground and rose into the air at 11:46 A.M.[18]

Given a road map by Fleet, the inexperienced Boyle had been instructed to follow the railroad tracks northbound out of Washington. Unfortunately, he became confused when passing over the jumble of

Maj. Reuben E. Fleet (*left*) briefs Lt. George L. Boyle on the route to Philadelphia, May 15, 1918.

tracks at the nearby marshaling yard and picked out a branch line that eventually took him south instead of north. Boyle's unreliable compass failed to alert him to the error. An hour after take-off, the lost pilot set down near Waldorf, Maryland (twenty-five miles south of Washington), to get directions. During landing, the propeller hit the ground and flipped the Jenny on its back, further embarrassing but not injuring Boyle.[19]

The southbound mail from New York fared better. A large crowd gathered at the Belmont Park racetrack to witness the historic event. At 11:20 A.M. two mail pouches (2,457 letters) arrived from Manhattan via the Long Island Rail Road. Clad in a leather jacket and headgear and accompanied by his wife of one year, Lieutenant Webb listened impatiently as Allan R. Hawley of the Aero Club of America told the audience: "This day will go down in history as marking the advent of a new epoch because the New York–Philadelphia–Washington aerial mail line is the forerunner of a network of aerial mail lines which will cover the entire world . . ." Promptly at 11:30 A.M., the *New York Times* reported, "Lieutenant Webb leaped into his seat and rose from the ground, leaving Mr. Hawley talking to an audience that had its eyes turned skyward."[20]

Webb reached Philadelphia one hour later, and transferred the mail to Edgerton. In Washington, Fleet greeted that excited pilot with a handshake and broad grin upon his arrival at Polo Field at 2:50 P.M. Then Elizabeth Edgerton presented her brother with an armful of roses. But Edgerton's thoughts were elsewhere. "As I scrambled out of the cockpit," he remembered, "I looked for the face which had haunted my dreams for long months. My heart skipped a beat. There she was, lovelier than memory, my fiancée and future wife, Mary Robinette."[21]

Meanwhile, word of Boyle's mishap had reached Culver in Philadelphia. Without the mail from Washington, Culver took off at 2:15 P.M., arriving in New York to a festive welcome at 3:37 P.M. *The air mail service had been inaugurated on schedule.*

Flights left Washington and New York without fanfare on May 16. The northbound schedule had no problems, but the southbound mail ran into trouble. Shortly after leaving New York, Lieutenant Bonsal encountered fog that grew worse with every mile, finally obscuring the ground. Disoriented and running low on fuel, he caught a glimpse of a field, descended, and prepared to land. At the last minute, he saw that the field was full of horses. When the sound of his engine failed to frighten them away, Bonsal had no choice except to set down among the milling animals. Luckily, he escaped injury when he had to swerve into a fence to avoid a horse in his path, but a broken propeller meant that the Jenny was through for the day.[22]

Lt. James C. Edgerton is greeted by his sister, Elizabeth, upon landing at Polo Field, Washington, D.C., May 15, 1918.

Bonsal had landed near Bridgeton, New Jersey, forty miles short of Philadelphia. A postal truck collected his mail and delivered it to Bustleton in the late afternoon. Miller loaded the delayed mail and took off from Philadelphia at 5:15 P.M., only to return twenty-five minutes later with ignition trouble. Faced with the possibility of a night landing at Washington, it seemed prudent to send the mail by train. But Edgerton, who had arrived earlier with mail from Washington, stepped forward and volunteered to make the flight, arguing that he had been over the route twice and that he had had instruction in night flying. "I had confidence in myself and my plane, and . . . I was thoroughly sold on the Air Mail," he later explained. Bustleton telephoned Washington and secured Fleet's approval for the flight.

Edgerton took off at 6:33 P.M. Navigating in the fading light was no easy task, while the possibility of a forced landing en route posed an even greater danger. Edgerton found his way without difficulty, and the Jenny's 150-hp Hispano-Suiza engine never missed a beat. Returning Edgerton's favor, Fleet had automobiles lined up to light Polo Field. Clearing the tall trees, the pilot squeezed into the tiny landing area, to the delight of Fleet and Praeger. Not everyone was happy with his performance: some Air Service officers complained about recklessness. To this, Edgerton replied: "What if men never took a chance? Anyhow, the flight fired the imagination of the entire service, morale was boosted—it was worth the gamble."[23]

Operations on Friday, May 17, got off to a bad start. Boyle again left Washington for Philadelphia. Carefully briefed by Fleet to keep the shoreline of the Chesapeake Bay on his left, he was escorted by Edgerton to the northern end of the Bay, just short of Havre de Grace. Edgerton then waved Boyle forward and returned to Washington. Faithfully keeping the now arcing shoreline on his left (and ignoring the position of the sun), the hapless Boyle was soon heading south, back down the Bay. Three hours and fifteen minutes after departure, Boyle ran out of shoreline and fuel at the same time and was forced to land at Cape Charles, Virginia. An exasperated Fleet summed up: "The Atlantic Ocean and lack of gas prevent[ed] him going further."[24]

Boyle purchased gasoline and oil, obtained directions, and once again tried to deliver the mail to its proper destination. Learning from experience, he managed to find Philadephia—but unable to locate the airfield at Bustleton, he flew around the city until he ran out of fuel. He came down on a golf course, breaking both right wings, the lower left wing, landing gear, center section of the fuselage, and numerous struts and wires. "The conclusion has been reached," Fleet informed his superiors, "that the best interests of the service require that Lt. Boyle be relieved from this duty. . . ."[25]

Saturday brought relief to the troubled mail service. Miller left Washington on time and flew to Philadelphia without incident. Bonsal, who earlier had arrived from New York with the southbound mail, continued the schedule to a successful conclusion, landing in New York at 2:52 P.M. At the same time, Culver left Philadelphia to complete the southbound route, arriving in Washington at 3:20 P.M. "The Postmaster General is very much pleased," Fleet sighed.[26]

Sunday was a scheduled day of rest that gave time to reflect on the first four days of operations. The *Air Service Journal* chose to look at the bright side. While the record of the air mail did not rival the railroad schedules on the route, "the outstanding fact of the service is its freedom from fatalities. . . ." And the *Journal* was not being facetious. On May 17 the *Washington Post* reported that twelve military aviators had been killed in training accidents in the United States during the previous two weeks, a tragic reminder that flying was a hazardous undertaking in 1918.[27]

But problems with the air mail could not be ignored. Operations had begun in haste. Despite the agreement of March 1, the Air Service had not directed Fleet to take charge until late April. Realizing that proper preparations had not been made, Fleet had wanted to delay the inaugural of service. The Post Office by this time distrusted the Army's commitment to the project and insisted that service begin as promised. Faced with poor fields, inadequate airplanes, and inexperienced pilots, Fleet had done the best he could. Thirteen of sixteen scheduled segments of the route had been completed. Lt. Boyle had had the most trouble, although he could hardly be held accountable. The Post Office had insisted that he be used to carry the mail; he was engaged to the daughter of Judge Charles C. McChord, interstate commerce commissioner who had championed the Post Office's parcel post service during attacks from private express companies. Boyle had less than sixty hours in his logbook. Assuming that he had followed the Army's usual training program, his cross-country experience would have been limited to a brief exercise that involved finding a field ten or fifteen miles from point of departure.[28]

Lt. E. W. Killgore replaced Boyle as the second week's service got underway, and Fleet faced the future with greater confidence. But flying between Washington and New York on a regular basis remained a pioneering undertaking, one that tested the limits of men and machines.

OPERATIONS BEGAN ON MONDAY on the usual sour note. Miller left Washington on schedule but became lost en route to Philadelphia. Recognizing Havre de Grace at the mouth of the Susquehanna River, he landed on the infield of a racetrack. Having refueled, he no sooner got into the air again when his engine began to cut out. Returning to the field, his aircraft turned over on landing. Miller walked away unhurt, but the Jenny was a wreck.[29]

Fleet had now lost two of his original six JN-4Hs. Fortunately for his efforts to maintain a schedule, the first of six Curtiss R-4LMs began to come into service. Pilots would grow fond of these "overgrown Jennies." Powered by a 400-hp Liberty engine, the R-4 flew faster (95 mph), had more range, and could carry a greater load than its smaller cousin. It did have one unpleasant quirk, as arm-weary pilots soon learned. The R-4 had a wide range of fore-and-aft trim, power on and power off, and it lacked an adjustable stabilizer. The aircraft was rigged tail heavy with power on to avoid a nose-heavy attitude on landing that could result in accidents. With a load of mail, pilots found that they had to exert a constant push of thirty to forty pounds on the wheel in order to keep the aircraft level. Three hours of such labor, one pilot recalled, could leave forearms "numb as blocks of wood."[30] But the R-4's good features more than made up for this flaw. Above all, it could land on short fields at slow speeds, a godsend for pilots who faced frequent—and often hazardous—forced landings.[31]

Tuesday, May 21, brought serious weather problems. Flying the southbound mail, Bonsal ran into a thunderstorm and returned to New York. Edgerton also encountered a line of thunderstorms between Philadelphia and Washington. Conventional wisdom dictated that he return to Philadelphia—taught to avoid clouds, pilots had been told that to be caught in a thunderstorm meant certain death— but the plucky Edgerton was determined to get through.

Edgerton challenged the line squall in northern Maryland. He tried to fly underneath but was rebuffed. Then he attempted to penetrate the storm at 6,000 feet without success. The frail biplane finally entered the boiling, black clouds at 10,500 feet. Edgerton remembered:

Here, in the heart of the storm, the turbulence and convection currents were spectacular, the electrical display awesome. One instant the plane became a tremendous elevator, to leap skyward hundreds of feet; promptly the bottom seemed to drop out, the dizzy fall to cover like hundreds of feet. Attacked by solid waves of air, the plane reared, slithered, and bucked.

Edgerton discovered that it was best not to fight the controls. He remained in the storm for nearly an hour before emerging on the other side. He no sooner reached clear air when a large sliver of wood flew off his propeller. He reduced power and made a long glide from 10,000 feet to Polo Field. He had to be helped from the cockpit after landing, as tension had locked his leg muscles. Staggering to the front of his plane, Edgerton assessed the damage:

The propeller was a sight to behold! The question was how it had held together. The fabric had frayed from the entering edge, slivers of wood had vanished and it was completely unbalanced. Paint was chewed off the leading edges of the wings, water streamed from the fuselage, flight and ground wires were slack, all mute witnesses to the stresses of the flight.

Edgerton had done what few men had done before: he had flown through a thunderstorm—and lived to tell about it. The experience, he reported, gave him confidence in his aircraft, and confidence in himself.[32]

Extensive fog covered the eastern seaboard on May 22, and three out of four flights had to be canceled. However, improved weather permitted all trips to operate on schedule during the next three days.

The third week of air mail service saw a change of command as

Capt. A. C. Weidenbach replaced Major Fleet, who had been on temporary assignment. Praeger was not pleased. "Major Fleet was just beginning to get some real results out of the pilots," he later wrote, "when he was called to other duties and in his place there was assigned an army officer who had been sent home from France under suspicion by the military intelligence service of having pro-German sympathies. This situation was widely known among military pilots and it did not tend to improve the interest of the army fliers in their work of carrying mail."[33]

It has not been possible to confirm Praeger's suspicions about Weidenbach. As often happens, memory may have changed rumor to fact. In any event, Weidenbach soon found himself in the middle of the festering controversy between the Army and the Post Office over the proper operation of the air mail service.

Following three days of uninterrupted schedules, fog shut down the air mail on May 30. The next day, after waiting for the fog to lift, Culver left Washington at 1 P.M., climbed to 4,000 feet, and headed for Philadelphia. He kept track of his progress through breaks in the clouds until fog obscured the ground at Baltimore, forcing him to navigate by an erratic compass. The veteran pilot waited until his estimated time of arrival over Bustleton, then descended through a cloud layer, breaking into the clear at 800 feet. He found himself over downtown Philadelphia—"a particularly dangerous position, as motor trouble would have necessitated landing in the city, which of course would be disastrous." Forced at times as low as 200 feet, Culver landed safely at Bustleton at 3:11 P.M. No other flight operated that day.[34]

Praeger was furious at the cancellations of May 30 and 31, which seemed to confirm his growing conviction that the Army was not committed to a scheduled mail service. Weidenbach tried to explain the realities of air navigation, but Praeger refused to listen. Edgerton, whom Praeger had grown to trust, decided to demonstrate the problems by taking the postal official for his first airplane ride on May 31. For over a half hour, Edgerton flew in and out of clouds, showing how easily a pilot could become disoriented. The lieutenant thought that he had managed to get his message across; he could not have been more mistaken.[35]

On Saturday morning, June 1, Praeger learned that an Army pilot not attached to the mail service had flown from Washington to New York on May 30, a day when mail flights had been canceled because of bad weather. A few hours later, he heard that Culver had canceled the day's New York–Philadelphia schedule because of weather at Bustleton. Looking at the clear skies outside his window, Praeger telephoned

Weidenbach and *demanded* that the Washington–Philadelphia route be flown. Believing that the fog at Philadelphia would clear during the afternoon, Weidenbach dispatched Edgerton with the mail. He got through without difficulty.

Praeger could barely contain his anger. "I am afraid that the officers who are flying these routes," he wrote to Weidenbach, "are laboring under the attitude of mind that this aerial mail service is merely for the purpose of carrying a handful of mail." They were mistaken, he said. "The prime purpose of the trips as the Post Office Department sees them is to establish a daily aerial movement in the face of weather obstacles, feeling confident that the necessities and exigencies of the situation will speedily devise means to overcome present obstacles to daily flights."

Unwilling to wait for his letter to be delivered on Monday, Praeger sent it to Weidenbach by special messenger. A covering note expressed his sense of urgency: "It seems to me as though we have about reached a crisis in the situation, which must be terminated."[36]

Weidenbach and Praeger met at 5 P.M. that same afternoon. Praeger complained that the mail service had been interrupted for the past three days because the pilots in charge at New York and Philadelphia had reported bad weather and canceled flight operations. They should have been ordered to fly. Weidenbach explained that he could not order pilots into the air in bad weather; flight operations were impossible when fog and mist reduced visibility. To Praeger's suggestion that pilots fly above the clouds and find their way by compass, Weidenbach replied that compasses used in aeronautics were unreliable. Even if a course could be maintained by compass, that would not solve the problem of locating an emergency landing field should problems develop while flying above the clouds. Furthermore, he stressed, "In fog or mists, an emergency landing can never be considered practical and safe. This is not due to the lack of skill of the pilots, but is due to the fact that aeroplane construction and aerial navigation have not reached a stage of reliability and safety."

Weidenbach finally agreed to originate flights regardless of weather, provided the destination was clear. But the air mail's commanding officer remained unhappy with the situation. He reported to his superiors that the meeting had failed to establish the principle "that the weather report of any landing field must be taken as final and binding." Until this was understood, "there will be no mutual satisfaction between Flying Personnel and the non flying officials of the Post Office Department." As Weidenbach did not believe that Praeger ever would accept this view, he concluded: "It is recommended, therefore, that the Post Office Department undertake the complete direction of the Aerial Mail Service and that all connection of the Army with the service be severed, that the Post Office Department furnish all flying equipment and especially the pilots and take complete charge of this service." Lieutenant Colonel Goodier, who had opposed the Army's participation in the postal scheme from the outset, forwarded Weidenbach's recommendation to higher authority with his warm approval.[37]

The first two weeks of June saw an uneasy truce between Weidenbach and Praeger. The Army officer urged his pilots to fly whenever possible; the postal official watched with suspicion and distrust, carefully noting each cancellation. At the completion of the first month of operations, the Post Office issued an optimistic press release, pointing out that the air mail service had carried 10,800 pounds of mail and flown over 1,000 miles at an average speed of 70 mph. Edgerton was singled out for his twenty perfect flights, "never having to make a stop en route, and without damaging a plane."[38]

Early June also marked the first air mail between New York and Boston. To demonstrate the potential of air mail, Postmaster Burleson authorized a special New York–Boston flight. In a gesture of Franco-American wartime solidarity, the Post Office selected Lt. Gustave Vannelle, a French military aviator, to make the trip. Unfortunately, he crashed on take-off on June 3, suffering minor injuries. Praeger then ordered Lt. Torrey Webb to fly the mail. Webb left Belmont Park at noon on June 6 in a Curtiss R-4. Battling rainstorms and stopping once en route for directions, he reached Boston shortly after 3 P.M. In landing at the Franklin Park Aviation School in Saugas, a wheel sank into a hole on the rain-soaked field, and the Curtiss flipped over on its back. Webb and mechanic R. Heck escaped without injury. Following several delays, Webb left Boston on June 11, carrying sixty-four pounds of mail for New York—and Boston Postmaster William Murray. The weather was rotten, and Webb had to dodge telephone poles all the way to Belmont. Postmaster Murray, making his first flight, seemed to enjoy the trip. "I have had a wonderful day," he told the press, "full of life, action, and thrills."[39]

The Post Office, at least in public, recorded Webb's New York–Boston adventure as another triumph. Privately, however, Praeger was far from content with the operation of the air mail service. For one thing, rosy predictions about the economic viability of air mail were proving false. In April Praeger had ordered the postmasters at Washington, Philadelphia, and New York to survey business houses about their expected use of the new service. The response had been enthusiastic. With the air mail postage set at 24¢ per ounce, Praeger envisioned revenues of $3,000 per trip.[40]

Reality set in shortly after flying began. While no company wanted to appear less than progressive on a postal questionnaire, few were prepared to pay 22¢ over first class postage to save a few hours (at best). Of the 10,800 pounds of mail airlifted during the first month of service, only 1,543 pounds carried the special surcharge; the balance consisted of first class mail. Daily loads were averaging less than fifty pounds, generating revenues of $50. In July the Post Office would reduce postage to 16¢ per ounce in an effort to attract business. By the end of the year, the rate would drop to 6¢. Finally, in July 1919, Praeger would eliminate the surcharge for air mail, leaving postal airplanes to carry a random selection of mail.[41]

Even more vexing to Praeger than these economic problems was his continuing unhappiness with military operation of the service. On June 20 he sent a lengthy memorandum to Burleson, reviewing the situation. As a postal proposition, he pointed out, the air mail "is unsatisfactory and will be certain to fail the public so long as the crucial difference between the Post Office Department and certain officials in the Army remains unsolved, namely: shall flights be made under substantially all weather conditions as is contemplated in the agreement between the two Departments, or shall the route . . . default whenever the aviator who is to fly decides that the weather is not propitious?" The Army inclined to the latter view. As a result, 15 percent of trips had been canceled.

Praeger was not surprised by this. The pilots, with one or two exceptions, had not wanted the assignment in the first place. "Their hearts," he observed, "are set on service in France." Furthermore, their superiors were sharply divided over the desirability—rather than the feasibility—of carrying out an agreement made by higher officials in the War Department. Under the circumstances, the Army either should live up to its original commitment and operate daily in all weather or else allow the Post Office to do it.

Should the War Department choose the latter course, Praeger assured Burleson that he would be able to begin operations by August 15: aircraft have been ordered, and civilian pilots are available "who will voluntarily sign an agreement to fly regardless of weather conditions." In any event, he warned, "we must settle this point now and definitely, else the aerial mail service will end in ignominious failure and will reflect alike on the Post Office Department and the War Department before the winter is over."[42]

Weidenbach also was writing pessimistic memoranda to his superiors. The air mail service, he noted, "was too hastily begun and there has been a continual shortage of the most necessary equipment." Young officers and inexperienced mechanics had caused problems;

however, the major difficulty was the attitude of the Post Office. Postal officials interpreted the original agreement with the War Department "as requiring an absolutely dependable daily service, and [object] that the decision as to whether flights are to be made or not should rest with the flying officers at each Landing Field, assuming that these officers are not sufficiently interested in their flights." The approach of fall and winter meant that the situation would get worse instead of better. Weidenbach again recommended that the Post Office "assume complete control of this Service." [43]

Focusing all its efforts on fighting a war, the Air Service had had enough of the air mail and its problems. The operations section advised Maj. Gen. William L. Kenly (Squier's replacement) that the air mail should be transferred to the Post Office. Kenly endorsed the recommendation and forwarded it to Chief of Staff Peyton C. March. Secretary of War Baker then wrote a diplomatic letter to Burleson, assuring the postmaster general that "having made this contract, I am very anxious to live up to it; but I do not want to have the execution of the contract a subject of controversy between our Departments." Under the circumstances, Baker suggested that it might be better if the War Department withdrew. Burleson concurred. After subordinates worked out the details of the transfer, the necessary orders were issued for the War Department to relinquish operation of the air mail service to the Post Office, effective August 12, 1918. [44]

WHILE AWAITING THE TRANSFER, Praeger kept a sharp eye on the Army's performance. He was especially pleased with Edgerton's continued enthusiasm. The lieutenant had secured his position because of political connections—his father was purchasing agent for the Post Office—but it had turned out to be a most fortunate arrangement. Edgerton led the way, flying in the worst weather and compiling useful in-flight logs. His experimental temperament resulted in numerous improvements in equipment. For example, the JN-4H carried a fire extinguisher that could not reach the engine, the most likely spot for trouble. Edgerton solved this problem by connecting a pipe fitting to the extinguisher nozzle, threading a pipe to the fitting, then extending the pipe past the mail compartment and into the engine space, ending at the carburetor intake. The pipe had fine spray holes for that portion inside the engine space, affording good coverage in the event of fire. Praeger prepared a letter of special commendation, signed by Burleson, praising Edgerton for his "judgment and courage as well in storms as in fair weather." This devotion to duty, the letter concluded, "should prove an inspiration to your co-workers as it has to the Post Office in its efforts to solve the problems attending the establishment of a dependable daily airplane service."[45]

Praeger was just as quick to criticize. In early July Lt. Gordon H. Dodge joined the small group of pilots assigned to the air mail. Two weeks later Praeger complained to Weidenbach (who had changed his name to Charles A. Willoughby)[46] that Dodge had made three forced landings due to thunderstorms in the course of eight scheduled trips. On one occasion, another mail pilot spotted Dodge's plane on the ground as he was flying the same route in the opposite direction. "It occurs to me," Praeger concluded, "that if the Lieutenant is permitted to continue on this run . . . our flying record will be sadly marred by the performance of one man." Dodge was reassigned.[47]

Despite the problems with Dodge, the Army's performance improved as pilots gained confidence in their ability to cope with bad weather. The record for July was outstanding: 98 out of 108 trips operated without interruption and only two flights were canceled because of weather (mechanical problems caused eight forced landings).[48]

Pilots now routinely flew through fog, haze, and rain to reach their destination. Lieutenant Killgore left Philadelphia for Washington at 1:25 P.M., July 31, despite a severe rainstorm at Bustleton. He flew southward through heavy rain, often losing sight of the ground, but he arrived on schedule. Flying the same route on July 25, Lieutenant Bonsal had encountered a severe storm near Laurel, Maryland. Instead of turning around or landing, he penetrated the heavy, dark clouds at 5,000 feet. After twenty minutes in and out of clouds, he descended. Bonsal broke out at 300 feet, located a landmark, and landed on schedule. Although *Aerial Age Weekly* was far too optimistic when it reported that "the mail aviators are demonstrating that it is possible to fly in any sort of weather," progress since May had been remarkable.[49]

Saturday, August 10, marked the Army's last day of mail flying. Burleson wrote to Baker and thanked him for the "valuable and whole-hearted co-operation" received from the War Department. He noted that the Army had carried 40,500 pounds of mail between Washington and New York, making 270 flights (421:30 flying hours) with only sixteen forced landings due to mechanical problems—"a high tribute to the Army's training planes and their engines." Burleson expressed appreciation for the assistance rendered by General Kenly, Colonel Henry H. Arnold, Major Fleet, Captain Willoughby (Weidenbach), and other officers connected with the mail service. He also commended the six Army pilots (Lieutenants Boyle and Dodge were not mentioned) who operated their aircraft "with courage and conscientious regard for duty." Burleson recorded their service:

	Trips	Forced Landings (mechanical)	Time
Edgerton	52	1	106:36
Killgore	39	5	85:50
Miller	48	4	60:50
Bonsal	38	4	74:33
Webb	41	1	44:49
Culver	36	1	47:52

"It is with pleasure," Burleson concluded, "that I have to advise you of the completion of the transfer of the equipment and flying operation of the Aerial Mail Service from the War Department to the Post Office Department on August 12th."[50]

DESPITE THE HIGH PRAISE in Burleson's letter of record, the Army's operation of the mail service had not been a happy experience for the Post Office. Using the air mail to facilitate military training had sounded like a good idea at a time when the nation was in the midst of war, but even before the first airplane left the ground, it had been clear that the Air Service and the Post Office harbored different ideas about the nature of operations.

To Praeger, it seemed that many Army officers disapproved of the project from the start and undertook it only with great reluctance. The Army had been slow to assign men and equipment to the service, and the caliber of both left a good deal to be desired. With one or two exceptions, pilots had not entered the air mail service with a commitment to solving the problems of daily scheduled flying. "They were detailed to it as a military routine," Praeger believed, "and their superiors do not feel like directing a flight after the fliers have declared the weather conditions unsatisfactory." Praeger was convinced that in many cases trips were canceled that should have been flown. Certainly, "they should have been attempted." He pointed with pride to Edgerton as an example of what could be accomplished with the proper enthusiastic spirit.[51]

Air Service officers saw things differently. They were convinced that Praeger did not understand the operational limits of flying. Few pilots had experience in cross-country flying, decent maps did not exist, and compasses were unreliable. There was no useful data on aeronautical meteorology, no accepted ways and means of coping with bad weather. Used to flying in good weather, pilots had been forced by the Post

Office to keep a schedule in the face of rain, fog, and storms. Praeger expected far too much, far too soon.

The arguments on both sides had merit. Lieutenant Colonel Goodier and many of his associates considered the air mail a wasteful exercise; it did not have a high priority. Most pilots were not as eager as Edgerton to explore the limits of their weather flying skills; if they had to risk their lives, they preferred to do so in combat in France. Praeger, on the other hand, failed to appreciate the technological limitations that prevented a daily scheduled air mail service. As the journal *Flying* noted, the military pilots were "doing pioneer work in an entirely new field, where there are no precedents to follow. . . ." It remained to be seen if the Post Office could do better.[52]

3 Lipsner Takes Command

PRAEGER SELECTED BENJAMIN B. LIPSNER to head the civilian-operated Air Mail Service. Lipsner accepted the assignment with confidence and enthusiasm. "I am looking forward to a rapid development in cross-country flying," Lipsner announced to the press following his appointment in mid-July 1918. He predicted—without the slightest factual basis—that experienced pilots would carry the mail "without hindrance by weather conditions." Furthermore, careful analysis of operational data would lead to increased engine life and greater reliability. The possibilities of the air mail, he concluded, "are almost immeasurable. . . ." [1]

Although not an aviator, Lipsner had a technological background that impressed Praeger. Born in 1887 in Chicago, where his father was a hay and grain merchant, Lipsner spent two years in medical school before deciding to study mechanical engineering at the Armour Institute (later, Illinois Institute of Technology). Developing an expertise in automotive fuel and lubrication, he had charge of motor equipment for Albert Pick and Company and, in 1915, the Texas Oil Company. Lipsner joined the Aviation Section of the Signal Corps in May 1917 and was assigned to the lubrication department. [2]

Despite Lipsner's initial failure to insure an adequate supply of fuel at Polo Field for the air mail's inauguration on May 15, by his tireless efforts to promote efficiency he had caught Praeger's attention. An admirer of scientific management techniques, the postal official had looked on with approval as Lipsner installed a comprehensive cost accounting and record system for the air mail. In many ways, Praeger tended to see airplanes as mechanical devices, not much different from motor vehicles, to modernize postal communications. He became convinced that what he earlier had done to bring trucks into the postal service, Lipsner could do now with airplanes. Praeger persuaded Lipsner to join the Post Office, secured his release from the War Department, and appointed him superintendent. [3]

When inquiries from prospective pilots had begun to arrive in June,

Praeger sent out a standard reply, indicating that the Post Office expected to use Standard JR-1 aircraft to operate an aerial mail route of 200 miles. The Post Office, he noted, was working with the Navy, National Bureau of Standards, and Weather Bureau to devise instruments that would "reduce the element of danger in flying during weather which shuts out visibility." Praeger stressed to all applicants: "To solve these problems the aerial mail service will be operated daily, regardless of weather conditions, *and only aviators who will agree to fly under such circumstances can be utilized.*"[4]

Max Miller was one of the first to respond to Praeger's challenge. An experienced flying instructor, he had more than 1,000 hours of flying time (an impressive total by the standards of 1918), including 200 hours of cross-country flying. "I've covered as much as 300 to 400 miles a day," he wrote, "only stopping for gasoline and oil or necessary repairs." For the past year, he had been working for the Army at Rockwell Field, San Diego, teaching everything from basic to acrobatic flying. "I have carefully considered the risks involved caused by bad weather conditions," Miller noted, "and I would be willing to do my best under those circumstances, and would be ready to go out at any time required." In return, he expected to be paid $3,600 a year, the same as senior civilian flying instructors with the military. Praeger placed Miller on the payroll as a mechanic on June 28. Promoted to aviator on August 1 at a salary of $3,600 a year (at a time when the average annual wage of a federal employee was less than $1,400), he took pride of place as the Service's first civilian pilot.[5]

Three other experienced airmen joined the Air Mail Service prior to mid-August. Robert Shank, a civilian instructor with the Army at Dallas, had accumulated 1,200 hours of flying time; Lipsner later described him as "a keen and practical pilot, who was punctual, reliable, and trustworthy." Edward V. Gardner, also from Dallas, had 1,450 hours—and a reputation as a ladies' man. Oldest of the trio at forty was Maurice A. Newton, a test pilot for the Sperry Gyroscope Company who had 1,000 hours in his log book. "I hired him in spite of his years," Lipsner recalled, "and he proved to be a wise choice. He was a steady, dependable pilot, and his knowledge of compasses and of the terrain over which we were flying proved invaluable."[6]

Lipsner hired Edward C. Radel as chief mechanic at a salary of $2,000 a year. Hard-working and enthusiastic (and a talented musician who played the saxophone and French horn), Radel put together a small staff of mechanics and riggers that included Henry Wacker, E. Neale Angle, Albert F. Cryder, Wilber O. Beaty, Charles C. King, Joseph A. Darneille, Edward C. Roll, and William C. Read.[7]

Men and machines came together at Standard Aero's factory at

Elizabeth, New Jersey, on August 6. Delivery of the six JR-1Bs that Praeger had ordered in April turned out to be a gala affair. President Harry Bowers Mingle of Standard began the day's activities by conducting a tour of the factory for postal dignitaries, military officials, and representatives of aeronautical organizations and publications. After inspecting Standard's facilities, the official party moved to the adjoining flying field and watched Gardner test one of the new "postal machines," a tractor biplane powered by a 150-hp Hispano-Suiza engine. He put on an impressive show, thrilling the audience with loops, figure eights, and other maneuvers. Returning to earth, Gardner reported that the aircraft had performed well—and he pledged "no more stunts" while flying the mail.[8]

Honored guests went back to Mingle's office for a buffet lunch. Then, at 2:30 P.M., Standard's 5,000 employees joined 5,000 spectators in a grandstand facing the flying field for the delivery ceremony. Mingle formally turned over the aircraft to Praeger, who accepted for the Post Office. President Alan R. Hawley of the Aero Club of America said a few words, then presented handsome watches crafted by Jacques Despollier & Sons to Praeger, Lipsner, Miller, Gardner, Newton, and Shank.

Lipsner made the major address. Aeronautics, he stressed, had passed "from poetry to mathematics." The romance of flight had given way to utilitarian concerns for the most effective commercial use

Elizabeth, New Jersey, August 6, 1918. Persons shown are (*left to right*): Harry L. Hartung, Otto Praeger, George L. Conner, L. Leroy Langley (reserve pilot), Edward V. Gardner, Benjamin Lipsner, Maurice Newton, Max Miller, Robert Shank.

of the airplane. The Air Mail Service should be seen as "the mechanical laboratory for the advancement of commercial aviation," a place where "the spirit of adventure is curbed down to the exactitude of routine performance." Lipsner promised to keep meticulous records, identify and correct defects, tabulate costs, and promote efficiency. In embarking on this pioneering venture, the Post Office would be taking "the first step toward the universal commercial use of the aeroplane."

Mingle distributed American flags to the four pilots, special mail was placed aboard their aircraft, engines were started, and "the planes took wing like eagles to their destinations." They arrived safely in Philadelphia after a flight of forty minutes.[9]

Civilian operation of the Air Mail Service began on August 12. As the Post Office had decided to abandon tiny Polo Field, Miller inaugurated the northbound route from College Park, Maryland, on the outskirts of Washington, D.C., leaving for Philadelphia at 11:35 A.M. Newton continued thence to New York, but a broken magneto shaft forced him down four miles short of Belmont Field. The mail was forwarded by truck, causing only a brief delay. Meanwhile, Shank and Gardner flew the southbound route without incident.[10]

The performance of the civilian pilots during the balance of August seemed to confirm Praeger's view that schedules could be maintained by experienced and enthusiastic airmen. "The operations for the month," the Post Office announced to the press, "were perhaps the most remarkable in the history of aviation." Besides Newton's mishap, only one other brief delay marred an otherwise perfect record, and even that delay testified to the skill and dedication the pilots brought to their task.[11]

Robert Shank had been scheduled to fly JR-1B Number 6 from New York to Philadelphia on the morning of August 27. As the aircraft's engine was being warmed up, the radiator sprang a leak. Mechanics rolled out a replacement, JR-1B Number 3. In preparing Number 3 for departure, they had to take the compass out of Number 6 and place it in Number 3. However, the mechanics did not have time to check or compensate the instrument without causing delay. Shank took off on schedule. Climbing to 500 feet, he encountered fog and low clouds. "Knowing that I had to go over quite a bit of water," he reported, "I thought it safer to go above the fog and trust my compass rather than fly below the fog and trust my motor." He broke out on top of clouds at 3,500 feet, and took up a compass course for his destination. After twenty minutes, however, he began to experience problems with his compass. First, it began to swing 180°, then it started spinning. Rather than become hopelessly lost, he descended through the clouds and tried to get his bearings. Unable to identify any land-marks, he set down in a field and asked directions from a farmer. He was soon on his way (he had not stopped his engine), and arrived in Philadelphia ten minutes later.

Shank was not at all happy to learn that Lipsner had blamed him for the delay. There were only two compasses at Belmont for three aircraft, he complained to the superintendent, "and these do not tal-ley [sic] with each other, neither do they read the same in different planes." Pilots could not be expected to make perfect records with in-adequate equipment. "With the above facts in view, and my explana-tion for this landing," Shank asked Lipsner, "do you still charge the fault to me? If so, what would you have done in like circumstances? So far my record has been 100% and I would like to maintain that stan-dard. Please let me hear from you." Lipsner charged the delay to the faulty compass.[12]

As Shank's experience revealed, compasses provided the sole means of point-to-point navigation when pilots lost sight of the ground. Offi-cials of the Air Mail Service placed great emphasis on finding a more reliable instrument for flight operations. The widely used Sperry model, developed from maritime compasses, tended to perform er-ratically, especially on northerly headings. The Post Office tested sev-eral models before selecting the Pentz compass. The Pentz departed from usual practices and suspended the entire compass system—card, bearing, and bearing post—in a liquid-filled spherical float chamber, thereby creating a damping effect that lessened the spin-ning tendency as compared to other models. Pilots found the Pentz superior to existing instruments. "I think this the best compass for aeronautical use that there is on the market," one air mail official concluded. After asking for minor changes in the spring and hair cushions, the Post Office ordered ten instruments.[13]

While pilots flew the mail and technicians tested instruments, Lipsner developed rules, regulations, and procedures to govern the operation of the Service. He took special pride in a dispatch board that displayed the location of aircraft and pilots, kept track of the progress of flights, and noted weather conditions. Detailed mechani-cal reports on all aircraft and engines were required as part of a sys-tem of meticulous record-keeping. Lipsner also issued a series of instructions to pilots: Do not carry passengers without written permis-sion from higher authority. Consult compasses at all times while in flight. Never perform stunts in mail planes. Fly over 5,000 feet when-ever possible.[14] (See Appendix C.)

And rules were enforced. One of Lipsner's first dictums specified that "any employee reported to be in intoxicated condition will be immediately dismissed from the Service." On the evening of August 15, reserve pilot W. Knox Martin was seen drunk in public. Although Marin was not on duty at the time, Lipsner promptly fired him. Martin pleaded for leniency, but the superintendent remained adamant, commenting that alcohol and aviation did not mix.[15]

Lipsner claimed that uncompromising rigidity toward subordinates served a good purpose. As he later wrote, "From the beginning of the service, I had been very strict in my discipline in order to maintain a high level of efficiency." Indeed, his stern action against Martin was in accord with the discipline that prevailed during the early years of the air mail. Born in the midst of war, the Service developed along quasimilitary lines. Pilots and other employees were expected to follow orders, or face dismissal.[16]

PRAEGER GAVE LIPSNER A FREE HAND to run the Service as he saw fit, at least at first. Content with the performance of the civilian pilots, Praeger concentrated on long-nurtured plans for a major expansion of the air mail. In late May, he had predicted the rapid development of a mail route to Chicago, followed by transcontinental service. This was far from idle speculation. Praeger, in fact, had decided that a longer route was necessary to demonstrate the advantages of aircraft over trains. The Washington–New York aerial route saved little time over rail transportation, even when the service operated on schedule. However, a link between the nation's two most important commercial centers, New York and Chicago, could cut by half the transit time for mail.[17]

Praeger planned to use the six aircraft ordered from Standard Aero for the projected New York–Chicago line. He needed, *and expected*, aircraft that could carry at least 300 pounds of mail over a distance of no less than 200 miles at a speed of 100 mph. In mid-August, Lieutenant Edgerton (whose assignment was extended at the special request of the Post Office) tested one of the new JR-1Bs. Taking off from Standard's field at Elizabeth, he noted a sluggish performance. At Bustleton, he had sandbags placed in the forward compartment to simulate a full mail load. Edgerton then tried to take off—and nearly cut short a promising career. With increased wing-loading, the aircraft refused to climb. Heading for the surrounding trees, he put the aircraft into a vertical bank and managed to squeeze through a small break in the tree line. Although the design flaw in the JR-1B was corrected by extending the wing tips so as increase the wing area, the airplanes never lived up to expectations. They could carry only 180 pounds of mail, and they flew at 80 mph. Adequate for the New York–

Washington line, they could not be used on the more demanding route to Chicago.[18]

The Post Office needed the more powerful Curtiss R-4s for the new route. Praeger had four of these, transferred by the Army when civilian operation of the air mail began in mid-August. But additional aircraft would be required to fly the schedule with regularity, and the only place to obtain them was from the unfriendly Army Air Service.

The Post Office bit the bullet on August 27. "In view of the uniformly successful operation of the aeroplane mail between Washington and New York," Postmaster Burleson wrote to Secretary of War Baker, "I am anxious to inaugurate, beginning October 1st, regular aeroplane mail service between New York and Chicago." With only six additional Curtiss R-4Ls, the Post Office would be able to reduce mail transit time from twenty-one hours by the fastest train to nine hours by air. Burleson concluded: "This is a gain to commerce operating at high pressure under war conditons which would fully justify the use of the comparatively small additional equipment needed."[19]

Secretary Baker promptly approved the request, and Chief of Staff General March instructed General Kenly, director of military aeronautics, to make the necessary arrangements. Kenly protested. The air mail had been turned over to the Post Office with the understanding that there would be no expansion during the war. "If this extension is made," Kenly argued, "it is not only a violation of this understanding but will hamper considerably war activities of the Air Service." A new route would require not only additional aircraft but also pilots and mechanics. He claimed that the Army Air Service already was short 50,000 mechanics and "a considerable number" of pilots. Furthermore, aircraft were not available. The R-4 no longer was in production. The Air Service had only eighteen older model R-4s, powered by 200-hp engines, that were assigned to the Second Reserve Brigade at Houston. This unit—"equipped and organized for possible service in Mexico"—was already six airplanes short of authorized strength and would be "completely disorganized" if six more were taken away. Kenly concluded: "I most urgently request that these facts be presented to the Secretary of War asking reconsideration of the action taken . . . and that no further extension of the aerial mail service be made until the close of this war."[20]

General March asked for a copy of the "so-called agreement" regarding nonextension of routes; he also wanted a definitive statement about the number of men who would have to be drawn from the civilian reserve to operate the New York–Chicago service. Kenly replied that a written agreement did not exist; nonextension was a "statement of policy" by the War Department at the time the air mail was transferred to the Post Office. (Although desired by the Army Air Service, there is no evidence that nonextension ever was a part—formal or informal—of the transfer agreement.) The new route, Kenly continued, would require fifteen pilots, fifty mechanics, and twenty-five aircraft. It would use 10,000 gallons of gasoline and 1,000 gallons of oil per month. Kenly's figures were not persuasive. March informed him on September 9 that the acting secretary of war, after considering all the facts, had confirmed the original decision: the six R-4s were to be turned over to the Post Office.[21]

While the War Department debated the fate of the R-4s, the Post Office went ahead with plans to open the route to Chicago. Beginning in late August, special representative John A. Jordan visited Bryan and Cleveland, Ohio, Chicago, and various intermediate points along the projected line to make arrangements for level fields of approximately seven square acres and hangars, all to be provided without expense to the government. Lipsner instructed Jordan to contact the postmaster at each city, secure introductions to officers of the Chamber of Commerce and wealthy businessmen, and arrange for newspaper publicity. "Bear hard on the great advertising the City will get from its selection as one of the first aero mail routes," Lipsner counseled, "and on the tremendous demand for faster mail service by bankers and business men." Jordan also was advised to cultivate "enthusiastic women of wealth; they are everywhere, and have in many cities the very fields we want, and as a rule are more quickly dealt with, if of the right caliber, than men."[22]

While Jordan wooed the ladies, Praeger scheduled a survey flight along the New York–Chicago route for early September. Aircraft flown by Max Miller and Edward Gardner would make the round trip, testing en route facilities and demonstrating the feasibility of the new route. The Aero Club of America prepared special sectional maps, showing landmarks, elevations, and compass courses along what it called the "Woodrow Wilson Airway." With refueling stops at Lock Haven, Pennsylvania (200 miles from New York), Cleveland (400 miles) and Bryan, Ohio (540 miles), plans called for the 750-mile trip to be completed in eleven hours westbound and ten hours eastbound.[23]

It all looked good on paper, but the reality left more than a bit to be desired. Taxiing out for take-off shortly after 6 A.M. on September 5, Gardner broke the tailskid on his Curtiss R-4. Miller, who had departed a few minutes earlier, returned to the field and awaited completion of repairs on Gardner's airplane. After one hour, Miller decided that he could delay no longer. He left Belmont at 7:08 A.M.

New York Postmaster Thomas G. Patten hands mail to Max Miller prior to departure for Chicago, September 5, 1918. *To the left* are Postmaster General Albert S. Burleson and Henry Woodhouse.

Encountering a bank of low clouds shortly after take-off, Miller placed his Standard JR-1B between cloud layers and took up a compass course of 284° for his first refueling stop at Lock Haven. He flew for two hours, hoping to find a break in the low clouds, but they remained solid beneath him. Miller decided to risk a descent and plunged into the billowy mass. Losing outside visual reference, he sat quite still and relied on his senses—the wind on his cheeks and the sound of the wire struts—to keep the airplane in a wings-level, nose-down attitude. Miller's apprehension grew as his altitude decreased. Finally, he broke out close to the ground. Landing to get directions, Miller discovered that he had come down near Danville, Pennsylvania, two miles off course. Lock Haven lay only forty-five minutes away, but across mountains whose peaks were obscured by clouds. Miller took off and again flew on top of the cloud deck. As he neared the mountains, his engine began to miss. Miller could only hold his course, hoping that he would not have to face the dubious prospects of a dead-stick landing in the cloud-covered, heavily treed mountains. Thirty anxious minutes later, he let down over what he estimated to be Lock Haven. *It was.* Spotting the airfield through a notch in the mountains, Miller made an uneventful landing. He remained on the ground only long enough to refuel, eat a couple of sandwiches, and have the spark plugs changed on his engine.

Departing at 11:45 A.M., Miller climbed out through the fog again and headed for Cleveland. He held a course of 283° for an estimated 100 miles. Having cleared all mountains, he came down to check his location. This third descent through clouds was almost his last. "The first thing I knew," he reported, "I hit the top of a tree." The airplane fortunately only grazed the treetop and kept flying. "That sure gave me a good scare," Miller continued. "I hustled back up into the fog, determined to get plenty of altitude and keep on going as long as my gas held out."

Fifty miles further on, the radiator began to leak. By this time, however, the clouds had begun to break up, enabling Miller to land without difficulty, refill the radiator, and check his location. Informed that he was at "Jefferson," Miller pulled out a map and located the town of Jefferson, Ohio, north of course. He took off and headed south to intercept his route. After an hour over unrecognizable terrain, he realized that "Jefferson" was not Jefferson, Ohio, but Jefferson *county,* Pennsylvania, placing him south, not north, of course. After a detour of 150 miles, Miller finally reached Cleveland at 9:20 P.M., just as darkness fell. Too late to continue his journey, the tired pilot stayed overnight.

Miller slept in the next morning while mechanics worked on his radiator. The weather was good when he left for Bryan at 1:35 P.M.; this was fortunate because the radiator again began to leak, and he had to make several stops in open fields to have it refilled. Reaching Bryan in midafternoon, Miller took on gasoline, oil, and water, and left at 4:35 P.M. He finally landed at Chicago's downtown Grant Park at 7:08 P.M., local time, thirty-seven hours after departing from New York.

Meanwhile, Gardner had been following in Miller's wake. Repairs on the tail skid delayed his departure from Belmont until 8:50 A.M., September 5. Flying the more powerful Liberty-engined Curtiss R and carrying mechanic Edward Radel in the front cockpit, Gardner encountered the same bad weather that had challenged Miller's piloting skills. Losing sight of the ground, Gardner flew by compass toward Lock Haven. At his estimated time over destination, Gardner descended through the clouds, broke out underneath, picked up landmarks, and landed at 1:50 P.M. After thirty-five minutes on the ground for servicing and repair of a broken gasoline line, Gardner headed for Cleveland. He ran into a heavy rainstorm over the mountains but managed to maintain a compass course until the weather cleared. He landed at Cleveland without incident and remained overnight.

Gardner left late afternoon the next day, reached Bryan at 5:15 P.M., refueled and took off for Chicago. The sun began to set as Gardner neared his destination. Unwilling to land at twilight on an unfamiliar field that would be crowded with spectators, he put down in nearby Westville, Indiana, to spend the night. He left the next morning at 6:39 A.M. and landed at Grant Park an hour later, having spent nearly forty-eight hours en route.

The pilots still had to get back to New York. Miller left Chicago at 6:26 A.M. on September 10. He had good weather along the route, but his radiator continued to give problems. Delayed at Cleveland while a broken connection was repaired, he was not able to leave until 4:30 P.M. He landed at Lock Haven too late to continue to New York. He took off at 7:20 A.M. the next day, reaching Belmont at 11:22 A.M., September 11.

Gardner and Radel already had arrived in New York by this time— but not in one piece. Leaving Chicago on the morning of September 10 with fair weather and tail winds, Gardner reached Cleveland and Lock Haven in record time. Spirits were high when he left Lock Haven at 5:51 P.M., climbed to 7,000 feet, and headed for New York. "I never thought that I could miss Belmont Park," Gardner reported, "but night came fast, and it was impossible to distinguish one place from another." He circled Long Island for two hours before a shortage of fuel forced a landing in a field near Hicksville, ten miles from Belmont. Public accounts of the incident noted that the pilot suffered slight injuries. In fact, the airplane had turned over and was wrecked. Radel, pinned under the aircraft, injured his arm and back; Gardner broke his nose, which only recently had healed from a break suffered in a previous rough landing.[24]

The New York–Chicago survey flight was hailed as a triumph. Miller, who had nearly lost his life among the treetops of Pennsylvania, pronounced the new route "entirely practical and feasible." With spare airplanes, Gardner agreed, "it will be possible in the very near future to make the trip [between Chicago and New York] in less than ten hours, probably in less than eight." *Aerial Age Weekly* spoke for the aeronautical community when it announced: "The pathfinding aerial mail flight to Cleveland and Chicago . . . has shown the thorough practicality of establishing a permanent aerial mail line between New York and Cleveland and Chicago, and such service is to be established within a month."[25]

If anyone made a realistic appraisal of Miller's and Gardner's heroic individual feats, no record of it has survived. As far as can be determined, the Post Office really *was* satisfied that the survey flight forecast daily, routine, scheduled operations along the route. Jordan continued his efforts to persuade local communities to provide fields and hangars, while Lipsner made arrangements to accept delivery of the six Curtiss R-4s that the secretary of war had ordered turned over to the Post Office.

Both men had their problems as the October 1 deadline drew near. Jordan's blandishments did work at Cleveland. The city donated land for an airfield at Woodland Hills Park and contributed $10,000 in public funds for construction of a hangar. Private benefactors provided the $8,000 needed to complete the facility. Chicago, on the other hand, proved long on good will and short on cash. The Chicago Association of Commerce agreed to raise $14,000 for a hangar, but local business houses had subscribed only $8,650. Work at other locations also lagged behind schedule as September slipped away.[26]

Obtaining the necessary aircraft proved equally difficult. On September 23 Lipsner and four pilots were in Houston to take delivery on the R-4s that the Army Air Service had been forced to relinquish. Miller, due out first, cut his throttle during take-off and ground-looped, damaging the aircraft. Climbing out of the cockpit, shaken but uninjured, he complained that the R-4, with a 200-hp Curtiss engine, was severely underpowered. Gardner decided to try with another aircraft, but he also cut his power prior to becoming airborne. The third pilot, Louis Gertson, managed to get off the ground, only to smash into trees at the end of the field. Gertson was not hurt, but the airplane was a wreck. At this point, Lipsner refused delivery of the R-4s. He returned to Washington and announced that the New York–Chicago route would have to be abandoned. As one student of the Air Service–Post Office controversy has noted, "the Army had temporarily stopped the extension of mail routes in wartime."[27]

The Post Office was left with the Washington–New York service. According to press releases, the air mail flew with "100 percent" performance during September, and with only two incomplete flights in October. Actually, these figures were deceptive. The Post Office recorded 100 percent if a trip was completed by airplane and not by train before the end of the day. Mail often arrived late, especially on the southbound route. Nor did the Post Office publicize a serious accident that took place on October 18. Flying between Philadelphia and New York, Maurice Newton's engine suddenly quit when he was north of Jamaica, Long Island. Unable to reach Belmont, he landed in a nearby field. The airplane ran into a deep hole that had been masked by grass and weeds, and nosed over. Despite serious bruises and cuts received when his head smashed into the windshield, Newton insisted on flying the next day. As fellow pilot Shank remarked, "Newton was a man who would keep injuries to himself, and assure one they were trivial, though perhaps serious. He always took this attitude because he felt the Department would think his age [40], and the fact that he wore glasses, hindered his flying." Newton persisted for the remainder of the month, but it was clear that his injuries were more serious than he would admit. Taken off flying status and assigned to ground duties in November, he resigned in January 1919. Less than three years later, he died, suddenly, after complaining of a headache. His widow filed for a government pension, claiming that the accident had contributed to his death. Although her claim was supported by officials of the Air Mail Service, the United States Employees' Compensation Commission turned down the request in the absence of direct medical evidence that connected the injury to Newton's death.[28]

Newton's determination to continue flying after his accident typified the spirit that the civilian pilots brought to the air mail service. But their efforts were not always appreciated. Praeger still harbored a suspicion, carried over from the time when the Army flew to mail, that pilots would cancel trips because of weather even when flying was possible. Given Praeger's—and Lipsner's—imperfect understanding of aviation's operational limits, a clash between the postal officials and the pilots came as no surprise.

Heavy fog blanketed New York on November 18. Gardner went up at 10:30 A.M. to evaluate weather conditions for the day's operations and immediately became lost in the fog. After thirty-five minutes, he managed ("by careful flying and good luck") to land in a field five miles from Belmont. While Gardner was in the air searching for a landing place, Belmont field manager H. Thomas received word that a test pilot for a nearby aircraft manufacturer had been killed while attempting to take off from the company field at Hazelhurst. As conditions showed no sign of improving, Thomas informed Washington that it would not be possible to operate the day's mail trip. Lipsner fired back: "Cannot understand the necessity for experimenting [Gardner's flight] when compass course is known. Every effort must be made to get mail on its way." He ordered Thomas to dispatch Gardner immediately. If there was a problem with Gardner, then Shank should be sent in his place.

Gardner and Shank informed Thomas that it would be suicide to fly in the heavy fog. Minutes after the harried field manager passed the information to Washington, a reply came back:

START THE MAIL SHIP WITHOUT A MINUTE'S DELAY.
PRAEGER

Both pilots refused to fly, Washington's fiat notwithstanding. Gardner did make an attempt to get through later in the afternoon, but a rainstorm forced him to return to Belmont. When he landed, he found that he and Shank had been fired.

The two men went to Washington the following day and tried to explain to Praeger the problems with the weather. Praeger refused to reconsider his action. He pointed out that they had agreed—in writing—to fly in all weather conditions, and they had refused. There was nothing more to be said.[29]

There was, of course, a great deal more to be said. Praeger's failure to appreciate the technological limitations of aeronautics, coupled with his dogged determination to operate a scheduled mail service, made inevitable a continuation of the struggle between postal officials and pilots. But that lay ahead.

EVEN IF ONE ALLOWS for the Post Office's tendency to exaggerate, performance had been impressive on the Washington–New York route during the first three months of civilian operation. Until the problem with Gardner and Shank, Praeger had had nothing but praise for his pilots. They had flown over 30,000 miles in rain and shine, often risking their lives to make sure that the mail got through. In fact, it was their skill and determination that convinced Praeger that the air mail could succeed. Realizing that a longer route would be needed to demonstrate the full potential of aerial transportation, Praeger envisioned a major expansion of service. Although the attempt to reach Chicago had suffered a series of frustrating setbacks, he refused to admit defeat. "The New York–Chicago route will be established by the Post Office Department this winter," Praeger informed *Aerial Age Weekly* in mid-October. Then came the momentous event of November 11, 1918.[30]

4 Post–Armistice Blues

THE ELEVENTH HOUR of the eleventh day of the eleventh month of the year 1918 marked the end of more than four years of horrendous bloodshed. The Great War was over, and people throughout the world rejoiced. For a brief period following the Armistice, a kind of "cosmic optimism" pervaded the United States. This euphoria would not survive the new year: 1919 would bring strikes, inflation, racial unrest, and controversy over the Versailles peace settlement. But it was impressive while it lasted.[1]

Aeronautical enthusiasts led the way. Although the war caused many intellectuals to question the relationship between man and technological progress, the Manufacturers Aircraft Association spoke with buoyant optimism. Wartime developments in aeronautical technology, it claimed, represented another advance in mankind's never-ending quest for scientific truth. Aviation had freed man from "the old belief in his limitations, from the cramped power of one who is a creature of the earth and subject to it. Now, neither earth's mountains, nor deserts, nor storms are obstacles to his passage. Not only the world but the sky has been given to man's dominion."[2]

The potential of the airplane in a time of peace seemed boundless. It could be used in mining operations to transport workers to and from isolated locations, to guard the nation's forests against fire, to explore remote areas and search out the earth's secrets. However, in no area did the opportunities appear more promising than in the postal service. As one group of prominent aeronautical promoters telegraphed President Wilson on Thanksgiving Day:

> A new epoch has dawned for the commerce of America and the whole world. We all join in Thanksgiving for the stupendous victory achieved and for the realization of our hopes, which we confidently believe will be soon followed by results of the utmost benefit to civilization when the marvelous developments in military aeronautics are turned to utilitarian purposes and aerial mail service is established throughout the United States.[3]

Otto Praeger was ready. Throughout the summer of 1918, he had been formulating plans for a breathtaking postwar expansion of air mail service. His scheme involved two major domestic trunk routes. A coast-to-coast route would connect New York to San Francisco via Cleveland, Chicago, Cheyenne, and Salt Lake City, with feeder lines running south from Chicago to St. Louis and Dallas, and north to Milwaukee and Minneapolis. A second truck line would link Boston and Key West via New York, Philadelphia, Washington, and Atlanta, with feeder lines extending to Pittsburgh, Cincinnati, and New Orleans. Two international routes would originate at Key West, one going to Panama via Cuba, and the other to South America via the West Indies. Whatever Praeger's shortcomings, timidity was not among them![4]

Although earlier thwarted in his attempt to begin the New York–Chicago route, first link in the nationwide mail service, Praeger redoubled his efforts at the end of the war. On November 15, with cheers for victory still ringing in the air, he ordered Maurice Newton to organize rural foresters and engineers in central Pennsylvania and survey proposed emergency landing fields along the New York–Chicago line. Five days later, Praeger and Postmaster General Burleson met with Secretary of War Baker to discuss the availability of airplanes. Under the appropriation act for the current fiscal year, the secretary had authority to transfer to the postmaster general aircraft that were not suitable for military purposes but could be used in the postal service. Baker said that one hundred de Havilland 4 (DH-4) biplanes, powered by 400-hp Liberty engines, could be made available at once. Also, twelve twin-engine Handley-Page machines could be delivered at the rate of one every ten days, while twelve twin-engine Martin bombers would be ready at the rate of one or two a month.[5]

A delighted Praeger appeared before the House Post Office Committee on December 4 and announced that service to Chicago would begin on December 15. Six Curtiss R-4s and nine DH-4s would be used to open the route. By the end of the month, four giant Handley-Pages, each capable of carrying 4,000 pounds of mail, would be introduced into service. Even more wonders lay ahead. The Post Office planned to use twin-engine Martins to carry the mail *at night*. The transcontinental route would be extended to San Francisco, followed by service to St. Louis, Memphis, Seattle, New Orleans, and other cities. Prospects for expansion of the air mail seemed limitless.[6]

Two days after Praeger's optimistic testimony, Lipsner dropped a bombshell by angrily and publicly resigning from the Air Mail Service. In his letter of resignation to Burleson—which was released to the press and carried on the front page of the *New York Times*—Lipsner charged that the Post Office intended to spend tens of thousands of dollars in "unnecessary expenditures" for new aircraft and for modification of existing planes. He opposed this wasteful use of public money. Also, he had grown fearful that planned extensions of the mail service would be delayed "if so-called technical men and novices lacking experience in this new field should be permitted to interfere in the handling of the aerial mail service and its equipment."

Lipsner's decision to resign ("to keep my record as first superintendent of the air mail service spotless") was reached on December 5, he revealed, after a conference with Praeger. Lipsner had tried to discuss these disturbing developments with his superior, but he had refused to listen. "He cut me short," Lipsner told the press, "and stated that these were the conclusions he had reached and that they would be carried out regardless of what I thought or said."[7]

Forced into public dialogue, Burleson sent a blistering reply (no doubt drafted by Praeger) that also was released to the press. "Your letter," Burleson wrote, "from beginning to end is a tissue of misstatements about matters of which you should have been fully conversant. . . ." The Post Office had no plans to purchase new aircraft. Modification of airplanes acquired from the War Department had been done with Lipsner's knowledge and at his request. The charge that "novices" would "interfere" in the operations of the Air Mail Service was absurd. Moreover, Burleson concluded, "the achievements of the aerial mail service were accomplished not by you, but by Second Assistant Postmaster General Otto Praeger, who has directed its movements from its inception to the present time in all its details."[8]

In his autobiography, published in 1951 (after Praeger's death), Lipsner developed at greater length the circumstances surrounding his resignation. Political interference, he claimed, had prevented him from doing his job: "Men were hired and fired over my head and the reason for each action was political." His anger "reached a peak" when he returned from a trip to Minneapolis in mid-November to find that Praeger had fired Gardner for refusing to fly the mail in bad weather. "I was furious at the whole thing," Lipsner recalled, "and thoroughly digusted at this interference." In addition, he had "strongly opposed" as unsafe Praeger's plans to begin the New York–Chicago service in the middle of winter. "I saw more and more clearly with each passing day," he continued, "that there was only one thing for me to do. And that was to give up my cherished hopes of making an outstanding success of the service." In the meeting with Praeger on December 5, Lipsner had made a final effort to correct the worsening situation, warning about the dangers of outside political interference and voicing his opposition to "the wholesale expenditure of funds" for new airplanes when so many surplus military aircraft were available. In particular, "I objected to the proposed plans of opening the New York–Chicago route before spring." But when Praeger had refused to listen, Lipsner knew that the time had come to resign.[9]

For the most part, available documentary evidence does not support Lipsner's interpretation of events. Praeger did fire Gardner—and Shank—for refusing to fly in bad weather (as related above, in Chapter 3), but Lipsner was in Washington at the time and *participated* in the decision. Lipsner himself was telling the press in November that within three years giant airplanes would be carrying the mail from coast to coast and from Canada to Mexico, flying in all weather and at night. As late as December 3 Lipsner was pushing the modification of military aircraft in order to inaugurate the route to Chicago by December 15. There is no evidence in Post Office records, in Lipsner's personnel file, or in his surviving personal papers that he had been expressing doubts about winter operations to Chicago—or that he was seeking to delay the opening of the route. (As events turned out, he should have.)[10]

Yet there had been considerable "political interference"—of a kind. Praeger's confidence in Lipsner had evaporated during September's abortive attempt to extend mail service to Chicago. Praeger had become his own superintendent, using Lipsner only to attend to details of plans that he had neither made nor approved. Praeger, for example, had *ordered* Lipsner to use Newton as his assistant, to arrange modifications of the Handley-Pages, to hire a chief mechanic, to place Pentz compasses in all new aircraft. Harried, puzzled, and hurt, Lipsner had sought an interview with Praeger on December 5 to clarify his authority, only to learn that he had none.[11]

While the public debate over Lipsner's resignation raged, Praeger reorganized the Air Mail Service. He abolished the office of superintendent and created two new sections, which would report to him directly. An operations department would be responsible for day-to-day flying activities, while a maintenance section would perform all repairs and inspections, and purchase all supplies.

Praeger picked Louis T. Bussler to head the maintenance section. A physician who as chief sanitary inspector of the Army's southern department had accompanied General Pershing to Mexico in 1916, Bussler also had an extensive aeronautical background. He had been a qualified pilot and adjutant of the West Virginia Flying Corps until an accident ended his flying career in 1917. Hired by the Post Office in August 1918 to organize a civilian mechanical staff and supervise maintenance work, Bussler's new title—chief of maintenance—only acknowledged his existing responsibilities.[12]

Praeger's choice for chief of flying came more as a surprise. On De-

Air Mail Service office, 1918. Persons shown are (*left to right*): Marie Miller, May Helms, James B. Corridon (of the Division of Railway Adjustments), George L. Conner, Benjamin E. Buente, Marjorie H. Spurlock, an unidentified man, James C. Edgerton, Wanda Orynski.

cember 6, within hours of Lipsner's resignation, he telephoned Lieutenant Edgerton and offered him the position. Praeger's favorite Army flyer had been ordered to Bolling Field after the Post Office took over the air mail. Edgerton enjoyed the assignment, ferrying high-ranking officers around the country, working with Col. C. C. Culver on ground-to-air radio experiments, and testing new navigational instruments. Air Service officers held out to him the possibility of a captaincy in the peacetime Army. While tempted to remain in the military, Edgerton decided that family responsibilities took priority: $3,600 a year— more than double his military pay—was too much to turn down with a first child on the way. He called Praeger the next day and accepted the job.[13]

Completing the reorganization, Praeger put Chief Clerk George Conner in charge of records and maintenance, and detailed John A. Jordan to oversee the New York–Chicago operation from his headquarters in Cleveland.[14]

The turmoil caused by Lipsner's departure did not deter Praeger from his intention to inaugurate service to Chicago on December 15. But problems multiplied. Jordan reported on December 9 that the hangar at Cleveland would not be ready for two weeks, while Standard Aero, hired to make minor modifications in the military DH-4s, failed to meet promised delivery dates. With no choice, Praeger had to postpone the start of service until December 18.[15]

While waiting for preparations to be completed, Praeger received a solemn reminder of the hazards of flight when the air mail suffered its first fatality on December 16. Carl B. Smith, one of fourteen new pilots hired in early December, was at Standard's field in Elizabeth, testing one of the modified DH-4s and demonstrating his flying proficiency. He pulled up sharply at an altitude of 400 feet, the DH stalled, went into a tail spin, and crashed. Edgerton, sent to investigate the accident, blamed pilot error.[16]

Against this somber backdrop the New York–Chicago route opened for business on December 18. Praeger watched as Leon D. Smith took off from Belmont at 6:20 A.M. with 224 pounds of mail. "The whine of the motor had scarcely died away," one newspaper reported, "when it came again to the ears of those on the field." Smith landed a few minutes later and complained that the Liberty engine of his DH-4 was overheating. Mechanics prepared another aircraft, mail was transferred, and Smith departed again at 7:20 A.M. Becoming lost en route to his first refueling stop at Bellefonte, he landed near State College, Pennsylvania, twelve miles from his destination. By this time, Edward A. Johnson had left Bellefonte on schedule at 9 A.M., without the mail. Unable to find the airport at Cleveland, he set down ten miles short of the lakeshore city and spent the night.[17]

The eastbound service from Chicago fared even worse. Officials showed up for the scheduled 10 A.M. departure from Grant Park to find only embarrassed air mail supervisors: no aircraft was available to carry the mail. Lyman W. Doty had left Elizabeth with a ferry aircraft the previous day, but had been unable to complete the trip. While he was landing at Defiance, Ohio, en route from Cleveland to Chicago, a woman with a baby in her arms ran out on the field and into his path. Doty swerved to avoid her and crashed into a fence.

An aircraft finally managed to reach Chicago on the afternoon of December 18, long after the dignitaries had gone home. Mail was placed aboard the DH, and Carroll C. Eversole took off at 4:07 P.M. He did not get far. With darkness approaching, he landed at Ashburn Field on the outskirts of Chicago to spend the night. "All that remains of the New York to Chicago air mail service, which began life fresh and full of vigor yesterday morning," the New York *Tribune* mourned, "is a trail of broken or lost aeroplanes across the country from Belmont Park to Defiance, Ohio."[18]

The next two days brought no relief to the beleaguered service.

Two aircraft left New York on December 19, but neither managed to reach Cleveland by sunset. Meanwhile, Eversole crashed on take-off from Ashburn Field. If anything, the situation got worse on December 20. Again, two aircraft took off from Belmont at dawn, only to return with engine trouble. Johnson—still trying to reach Chicago after leaving Bellefonte on schedule two days earlier—departed from Cleveland with mail for Chicago but got no further than Bryan; the mail went by train. Failure of aircraft to reach Chicago wiped out the possibility of operating the eastbound service on those two days.[19]

The Post Office attempted only one flight on December 21. Dean I. Lamb flew from New York to Bellefonte without incident. Having never been over the Bellefonte–Cleveland segment, he asked field manager Carleton Kemper for a map. Kemper said that he did not have one; he had asked Washington for maps several times in the past, but none had been provided. Lamb took off, trusting to his compass and general sense of direction. Not surprisingly, he failed to reach Cleveland.[20]

At the end of the fourth day of operations, Newton (in charge of the Cleveland–Chicago portion of the route) reported a chaotic situation. Aircraft were scattered all over the landscape; not a single airplane had reached Chicago since Eversole's ill-fated adventure. "I am all at sea as to what to do," he confessed, "because of the planes not getting where I send them." Facing reality, Praeger suspended service for ten days.[21]

In reviewing the situation, Praeger ignored the haste and lack of planning that had contributed so heavily to the four-day fiasco, and placed a major share of the blame on faulty engines. He did have a point, as overheating had caused numerous delays. Inspections ordered by Praeger revealed that the Liberty engines had been carelessly assembled; in one case, a piece of cardboard was found in the bowl of a carburetor. Praeger gave instructions for the meticulous examination of every aircraft and engine, followed by at least four and a half hours of test flying, prior to resumption of service.[22]

This testing program, which should have been done before attempting the New York–Chicago route, revealed serious problems not only with engines but also with airframes and other components. Complaints about the DHs began to pour into Washington. The material and construction of the aircraft, one pilot reported, were "very poor," with soft white pine used for longerons (the main structural members of the fuselage). Another pilot wrote: "The whole plane in general is constructed of the cheapest material I have ever seen used in the manufacture of an airplane. Soft wood such as pine has been used where ash or some other equally as strong wood should have been used. Holes have been drilled through the longerons and other parts of the [airplane] for bolts and fittings thus weakening the machine to a great extent." One can only wonder what would have happened had these airplanes reached their intended destination on the western front.[23]

Experience also demonstrated that the landing gear of the Standard-built DHs could not withstand even moderately hard landings. Lyman Doty made this point in painful fashion on December 28. While landing at Belmont, the right axle of his DH snapped, the struts gave way, and the aircraft slid along the bottom of its fuselage before collapsing in a heap. Doty suffered serious injuries. Two days after the accident, the Post Office announced that resumption of the New York–Chicago route had been postponed indefinitely.[24]

THE ABORTIVE EFFORT to establish service to Chicago was only one of many problems faced by Praeger during a troubled December 1918. In fact, his battle against an attempt by the Army Air Service to take over all air mail operations made his other woes pale in comparison.

On November 7, four days before the Armistice, Col. A. L. Fuller and Lt. Col. Benjamin F. Castle met to discuss postwar prospects of the Air Service. They agreed that control of the air mail would be one important way to maintain the momentum that the war had imparted to military aeronautics. The Air Service, Fuller suggested, should at once order three small dirigibles from England; they could be delivered within a short space of time. The equipment would be a powerful argument for military operation of the longer mail routes, such as New York to Chicago. Castle agreed. "Now is the time to put this [dirigible] project into execution," he recommended to his superiors, "as the Air Service has the funds and there is no question as to the possibility of acquiring the equipment if immediate steps are taken to do so."[25]

Although the dirigible scheme was not approved, Air Service interest in the air mail remained undiminished. Castle met with Praeger the day after the Armistice to explore possibilities for "cooperation" between the military and the Post Office. Army operation of the air mail between May and August 1918, Praeger observed, had not worked because the military allowed individual pilots to decide whether or not weather conditions permitted flying. Castle assured him that this time things would be different. Mail flying, he said, would be an important part of peacetime training, "simulating to the closest possible degree conditions of actual service." Indeed, operating in all kinds of weather would have a disciplinary effect "analogous to hazardous flying under war conditions."

Unconvinced, Praeger pointed out that existing legislation directed the Army to supply surplus aircraft to the Post Office. With these planes, flown by skilled pilots obtained from the ranks of demobilized Air Service personnel, the Post Office would not need the Army's help to deliver the mail. Castle blithely disagreed. The Army would need for training purposes "all available airplanes and those now on order." And it would be difficult to attract experienced pilots who would be willing to trade their commissions for the civilian status of "a mere mail carrier." Would it be possible, Praeger asked, to *detail* the necessary personnel to the Post Office? That was "entirely possible," Castle replied. On that tentative note, the two parted with a promise to exchange drafts of their views.

Reporting the meeting to General Kenly, Castle urged that Kenly and Assistant Secretary of War John D. Ryan seek a conference with Postmaster General Burleson the following morning, and if possible obtain Burleson's "definite approval of the policy of depending on the Army for equipment and personnel in the operation of the Aerial Mail." Praeger should not be regarded as an obstacle. After all, sniffed Castle, he was only a "subordinate who is engrossed more with details and who possibly has been side-tracked by pet hobbies. He is now at the point where he will willingly be converted to a complete agreement with the Air Service view if the policy is decided by Mr. Burleson."[26]

Kenly enthusiastically embraced Castle's scheme as sensible in terms of economy and efficiency; also it promoted fundamental national objectives. "America must be supreme in the air as England has the mastery of the seas," he wrote to Secretary Ryan. "To attain supremacy of the air, all aerial activities in the United States, in peace or war, should be under the control of a single Air Service." Deploring the existence of separate air components in the Army, Navy, and Marine Corps, Kenly argued that an air service run by the Post Office would not serve the national interest. A conference with Burleson should be "immediately arranged" to discuss arrangements for military "cooperation . . . in the operation and control of the Aerial Mail."[27]

While Praeger could hardly ignore the Army's offer to cooperate, he was determined to insure that any joint venture to fly the mail would be on terms favorable to the Post Office. The key would be control. In his promised draft to Castle, Praeger suggested that the Army provide aircraft, landing fields, hangars, parts, tools, and equipment for a nationwide mail service. Every ninety days, the Air Service would detail to the Post Office 1,000 pilots and 3,000 ground personnel for cross-country training in connection with air mail operations. All individuals, Praeger stressed, would be subject to the direction of the Postmaster General.[28]

There are indications that Lieutenant Colonel Castle might have accepted such an arrangement, but General Kenly demurred. The director of military aeronautics believed that there was no more reason for the Post Office to control operation of the air mail than to run the steamship companies and railroads that carried surface mail. His assistant, Col. Arthur Woods, informed Praeger that the Army wanted to fly the mail, but only under arrangements similar to those that the Post Office had with other contract carriers. Praeger, firmly supported by Burleson, rejected the idea.[29]

If postal officials thought that the matter had been settled when Secretary of War Baker agreed on November 20 to transfer surplus aircraft to the Post Office, they were mistaken. In December the struggle for control of the Air Mail Service moved into Congress. The House Post Office Committee, in a burst of post-Armistice largess, had recommended an appropriation of $2,185,000 for fiscal 1920 (July 1919 to June 1920) to operate a nationwide air mail service. When the measure reached the floor of the House on December 17, friends of the Army Air Service, led by Fiorello H. La Guardia (Republican, New York), tried to reduce the appropriation to a token amount and have the military fly the new mail routes.

Congressman La Guardia spoke with an authority that most of his colleagues respected. An early aeronautical enthusiast and pilot who had commanded American air units on the Austro-Italian front during the war, La Guardia had just returned to his seat in the House following fifteen months in the Army. The feisty politician did not hesitate to trade on his reputation as an aeronautical expert in order to promote a united air service. While he supported air mail, La Guardia argued that the Post Office should leave flying to the military. "Let us not repeat the errors of 1917," he cautioned, "and give a million dollars to everybody who wants to come in and try to experiment on aviation." A House keenly aware that America's wartime air effort had turned out to be an expensive fiasco broke out in applause.[30]

Congressman Joseph W. Fordney (Republican, Michigan) spoke in support of La Guardia's contention that postal operation of the air mail would be a needless expense: "I believe that the time for spending the people's money extravagantly, without questioning the purpose for which it is raised and spent, is nearly at an end." Former Speaker Joseph G. Cannon voiced his fear that the Post Office's interest in the air mail was part of a larger scheme by Burleson to acquire permanent control over railroads, telegraphs, and telephones. "He is a radical Government-ownership man," Cannon warned. Following two days of debate, the House voted 92 to 82 to reduce postal appropriations for the Air Mail Service to $300,000—enough to continue the Washington–New York route—and require that additional routes "shall be operated and maintained by personnel of the Army Air Service, under the direction of the Postmaster General."[31]

In the wake of this stunning defeat, and at a time when attempts to operate the New York–Chicago route were driving postal officials to distraction, Lispner renewed his attacks on Praeger and Burleson. In a letter to Senator Lawrence Y. Sherman (Republican, Illinois), the former superintendent blamed the disastrous New York–Chicago operation on mismanagement by inexperienced people like Edgerton and Bussler. Furthermore, Lipsner claimed that Praeger had told him that the real reason why the Post Office wanted large sums of money from Congress for the air mail was because it planned to buy aircraft from the Glenn Martin company, in which Burleson had a sizable financial interest. Senator Sherman informed the press on December 20 that Lipsner's letter would be turned over to the Military Affairs Committee, raising the possibility of a congressional investigation.[32]

Furious, Praeger decided that the time had come to settle with Lipsner, once and for all. First, he denied that he had ever spoken to Lipsner about purchase from the Martin company (Burleson disclaimed any financial interest in the organization). Next, he ordered postal inspectors to investigate Lipsner's expense account. The inquiry took only three days. It revealed that the former superintendent had charged the government (up to $5 per diem) for hotel and meals while staying in Chicago with his father-in-law. "The evidence conclusively shows," the inspectors wrote on December 24, "that Lipsner violated section 35 of the criminal code. . . ." The report went to Praeger instead of the United States Attorney, as normally would happen. The historical record ends at this point, but Lipsner was not prosecuted (the report went into his personnel file), and his hostile public comments ceased—until after Praeger's death in 1948.[33]

With Lipsner silenced, Praeger could turn his full attention to the more important task of thwarting the Army's designs on the air mail. In early January 1919 he appeared before the Senate Post Office Committee and testified at length about the problems with a military-run air mail service. "The Army," he said, "will not operate a mail service on schedule." As demonstrated during the past summer, the military's first priority was training, and this would not change. Nor would the air mail cost less under the Army, which tended to be more lavish in the use of men and materials than did nonmilitary enterprises. The

Post Office by contrast, with only $2,000,000, could undertake a major expansion of air mail service. Praeger estimated that $1,600,000 would be needed to develop routes from New York to Omaha (en route to San Francisco) and from Boston to Atlanta. Feeder routes to these trunk lines would cost $400,000. He predicted that revenue from mail carried on the routes would equal operation costs within a short period of time. Civilian development of the air mail, Praeger stressed, not only would result in untold postal advantages but also would "inspire the commercial use of the aeroplane."[34]

Praeger's testimony persuaded the committee to support civilian control of the air mail service, but then it recommended only $850,000 for postal operation of either the New York–Omaha or the Boston–Atlanta line. When this version of the postal appropriations bill reached the floor of the Senate on January 31, Senator Harry S. New (Republican, Indiana), member of the Military Affairs Committee and outspoken supporter of a unified air service, led the opposition. New, himself destined to become postmaster general in 1923, favored the House-approved bill: "This is not the time or place to indulge in what I think is an extravagant experiment by the Post Office, which is not equipped at present to carry out any extended operation of that character."[35]

Nonetheless, after Democratic senators Bankhead (Alabama), McKellar (Tennessee), and Swanson (Virginia) spoke out in defense of the Post Office, the Senate adopted its committee's bill. The House-Senate conference committee went along with the Senate's version. Although House acceptance of the conference report was a foregone conclusion, Congressman La Guardia put in a final word. Taking a jab at Praeger, he complained that the testimony of postal officials on aviation matters "is pathetic in their ignorance of the subject." The Post Office had not yet carried a single letter between New York and Chicago, and it would not be able to do so during the coming year. "The aero mail of this country," he predicted moments before the House approved the conference report, "is doomed to failure."[36]

THE AIR MAIL SERVICE had gone through turbulent times following the Armistice. At first, Praeger had believed that the moment was opportune to implement a far-reaching program of expansion. All looked rosy in early December: the War Department had agreed to supply aircraft, the House Post Office Committee had approved over $2,000,000 for the air mail, and preparations were under way to inaugurate the New York–Chicago route. Then, the bottom had fallen out.

Lipsner's angry and carefully publicized resignation was the first in a series of shocks that nearly brought the Post Office's Air Mail Service to a premature end. As Praeger struggled with organizational problems, inauguration of the New York–Chicago service turned into a public debacle. "This was a premature operation," Edgerton later pointed out, "plagued by atrocious or non-existent landing fields. Hangars, tools, and spare parts were in short supply, and worse still— a dangerous deficiency—our war surplus DH-4 planes were a deadly liability."[37]

In the midst of these troubled times, Praeger faced a dangerous challenge for control of the Air Mail Service by the Army and its supporters in Congress. The low point had come in mid-December when the House voted to place postal expansion in the hands of the Air Service. Praeger had had to bring to bear all his public relations and lobbying skills to defeat the military's determined effort to fly the mail.

Praeger had saved the Air Mail Service. But it would be an empty victory if La Guardia's prediction of failure proved accurate. The ability of the Post Office to operate a scheduled air service to Chicago remained to be seen.

5 From New York to Chicago

O N JANUARY 4, 1919, A RESOLUTE Otto Praeger again made a
pledge to open an air mail route between New York and Chicago. Unlike his previous statements, however, this one contained a
note of realism. "Very few people realize what an undertaking this is,"
he pointed out. The Post Office would be making daily round trips of
more than 1,500 miles, flying over mountainous terrain that afforded
few landing areas. "When you consider that this is being done with a
single-motor plane," Praeger stressed, "the task is stupendous. This
has never been attempted, either in America or in any other country
of the world. . . ." Praeger refused to give a firm date for the start of
operations, but he hoped that it would be possible to begin within "a
few months." [1]

It would be too much to say that the disastrous first attempt to extend service to Chicago had taught Praeger to be patient; at best, the
experience had brought home to him the need for careful preparation. Pilots had to be hired and trained, and suitable aircraft had to
be found. Above all, an airway had to be built. This meant that adequate landing fields had to be prepared, hangars erected, spare parts
shipped, communications arranged, and a thousand and one details
attended to before a flight between two points could become a routine
operation instead of an individual adventure.

Edgerton had primary responsibility for putting together the pilot
staff. With flying jobs few and far between after the war, qualified applicants abounded. Also, the Post Office paid extremely well: a pilot
started at $2,000 a year, with raises of $200 for each thirty hours of
successful flying up to $2,800, plus special merit increases to a maxi-
mum of $3,600. Not surprisingly, the Air Mail Service had a waiting
list of 300 applicants, mostly former military pilots. Edgerton could
select from the best aviators in the country. [2]

The first man hired by Edgerton was Charles I. Stanton. Although
short of flying hours (normally, pilots had to have at least 500 hours),

this future head of the Civil Aeronautics Administration (1942–44) proved a wise choice, bringing needed technical skills and administrative ability to the Service. Graduating from Tufts University in 1917 with majors in engineering and history, Stanton had passed the difficult Massachusetts examination in engineering before enlisting in the Army Air Service. Following flight school, he was assigned to the 122d Aero Squadron at Camp Alfred Vail (later renamed Fort Monmouth), New Jersey, where he tested experimental radio-equipped aircraft. "Lieutenant Stanton is not only a pilot of exceptional ability," his commanding officer wrote to Edgerton, "but he is also a very capable and thorough aeronautical engineer." Edgerton placed Stanton in charge of testing postal aircraft and flight instruments.[3]

Termination by the Army Air Service of the civilian flying instructors program in December 1918 gave Edgerton the opportunity to hire Ira O. Biffle, E. Hamilton Lee, and Leon D. Smith. All were highly experienced. Lee, for example, had 1,500 hours, including extensive cross-country flying. "I have never been injured or had a crash in flying," he wrote; "I am a married man with a family. Positively do not drink. I am a responsible party, and a North Dakota wheat farm owner." Also, with Praeger's permission, Edgerton rehired Gardner and Shank.[4]

Edgerton was younger and less experienced than his pilots, but this did not prevent him from keeping a close watch on them. "It has been reported to me," he wrote to Leon Smith, "that during the trip from New York to Bustleton last week you cut your motor at the altitude of 5000 feet and spiraled and dove to a landing without ever clearing your motor from a position over the field." Reminding Smith that this unsafe practice led to fouling of spark plugs as well as rapid and irregular engine cooling, Edgerton directed that henceforth glides should be started close enough to the field to allow an approach under power. "You will be held responsible for such conduct in the future," he warned.[5]

In the wake of this incident, Edgerton required all field managers to submit weekly efficiency reports on pilots. They were to note any pilots' mishandling of aircraft or engines on the ground or in the air, punctuality in reporting for duty, conduct that merited commendation, and the "amount of interest displayed in matters which concern their work." There followed a series of "General Orders for All Aerial Mail Pilots," eventually codified as *General Directions to Entire Personnel*. This document went much further than the instructions issued earlier by Lipsner (see Appendix C) and even included rules to be followed in starting a Liberty engine:[6]

1st   Close radiator shutters.

2nd   Retard spark and close throttle.

3rd   Turn on gasoline.

4th   Pump up three pounds pressure.

5th   Prime motor; i.e., turn on gasoline pet-cock to priming pump, pull plunger out *slowly* and *discharge quickly*; THREE times for COLD motor and ONCE ONLY for WARM motor.

6th   CLOSE gasoline petcock to priming pump.

7th   Turn motor over four times.

8th   Crank motor with ONE switch ONLY (SEE NOTE).

9th   After starting, open throttle slightly and advance spark about half way.

10th Run motor at 450 to 500 RPM until water is at 40 to 45 degrees centigrade and oil pressure is about 10 lbs. Then run at 1000 RPM until water is at 60 to 65 degrees and oil pressure about 20 lbs. (SEE NOTE).

11th Test ignition through each switch. Determine setting of spark for maximum RPM.

12th Open the shutters.

13th Use spark setting determined above for climbing.

14th Never run motor 1400 RPM on ground longer than necessary to read tachometer for determination of spark setting.

NOTE: Generator reaches voltage at about 750 RPM. NEVER use two switches below 750. ALWAYS use two switches about 750.

The Air Mail Service, in short, was developing what later would be known as an airline operations manual—that is, a systematic body of rules and regulations to insure safe and efficient operations. These rules were not arbitrary, but rather were the product of experience. For example, on February 5 reserve pilot Frank McCusker was ordered to test fly an airplane following an engine change. Coming in for a landing, he stalled when thirty feet off the ground and slammed into the field, damaging the landing gear and propeller. "This was the first time I have been in the air since Dec. 28th," McCusker explained to Edgerton, "and everything seemed strange." The young chief of flying did not discipline McCusker for the bad landing; instead, he issued orders that all pilots must receive dual instruction after thirty days on the ground before they would be allowed to fly alone.[7]

Infractions of rules, however, were taken seriously, with punishment ranging from dismissal to loss of "satisfactory" flying hours that pilots needed for salary increases. Charles H. Anglin learned this when he ignored the landing tee at Bellefonte, landed downwind, ran out of real estate, and smashed into a fence. The uninjured pilot was "derated" five flying hours and informed that "this is regarded as an extremely light penalty."[8]

While Edgerton recruited pilots, Praeger searched for an "ideal mail plane." He wanted multi-engine aircraft for the Air Mail Service, but none was immediately available and he had to make do with the de Havillands provided by the War Department. By January 1919 the Post Office had taken delivery on sixty-four of the promised one hundred de Havillands; however, as Praeger had learned in December, these biplanes were too frail for sustained cross-country operations. The Post Office had asked three aircraft manufacturers to devise methods of strengthening the airplanes. L.W.F. Engineering Company of College Point, New York, came up with the most promising solution. L.W.F. wanted to move the pilot's cockpit to the rear (observer's) compartment and install a new gasoline system, thereby eliminating the possibility of the pilot's being crushed between the gasoline tank and engine in crash landings. The fuselage would be rebuilt, using steel strips and plates at key points to increase structural integrity, while the landing gear would be fitted with a heavy axle and larger wheels, then moved eleven inches forward to remedy the nose-heavy characteristics of the military aircraft. In all, there were seventeen major changes. On February 26 the Post Office accepted L.W.F.'s bid to modify sixty DH-4s at a cost of $1,462 each.[9]

Impatient as usual, Praeger wanted the first six airplanes within four weeks, but L.W.F. was unable to meet this schedule. Although irritated by the delay, Praeger had no cause to be displeased with the results of L.W.F.'s work. During the testing program, two modified DHs crashed at Belmont Field after their engines failed. "In both instances," Praeger reported, "nothing but the stick and radiator and wing trouble resulted. The fuselage seemed to hold like a Pennsylvania [Railroad] steel car."[10]

Praeger decided to open the New York–Chicago route in stages, as modified aircraft became available. First would come Cleveland–Chicago, followed by the mountainous New York–Cleveland section. In early April he dispatched pilots and modified DHs to Cleveland for a planned May 1 inauguration. "When you get the flyers," Praeger instructed divisional superintendent John A. Jordan, "insist that they fly regardless of weather. Will give you six to start with and will hold more in reserve here so that you can replace them as fast as you fire them, or lay them off for failure to fly." Jordan assured Praeger "that flyers on this division will fly, and if they do not I shall ask you to relieve me of their presence. . . ."[11]

Apparently a winter's experience on the New York–Washington route had not given Praeger any greater appreciation of the limits imposed by weather. In fact, a mild winter, combined with the determination and skill of the air mail pilots, had produced a fortuitously impressive record. Praeger took special note of the heroic performance of reserve pilot John N. Miller. On March 28 a severe northwest gale hit the east coast, tearing roofs off houses and uprooting trees in cities from Boston to Washington. Despite the storm, Miller tried to fly the mail from Philadelphia to New York. He took off from Bustleton in a Liberty-powered Curtiss R-4 against a 43 mph surface wind and had to battle turbulent air all the way to New York. As he neared the city, Miller ran into a heavy snowstorm that obscured the ground and forced him to navigate by compass. Although he managed to pinpoint his position when he spotted the Woolworth Tower—the world's tallest building at 792 feet—rising out of the clouds, Belmont still lay hidden, twenty miles away. Miller finally set down in an open field near Great Neck, Long Island, at a time when the weather bureau in New York was reporting winds with an average velocity of 62 mph, with gusts to 92 mph. "The performance of this flight for courage and successful handling of an aeroplane," Praeger informed Burleson, "has never been surpassed, perhaps never equalled."[12]

MAY 15, 1919, WAS A DOUBLY auspicious day for the Air Mail Service: the Post Office celebrated one year's successful operation of the New York–Washington route, and it inaugurated the long-delayed Cleveland–Chicago schedule.

At College Park, just outside Washington, Postmaster General Burleson, Army Air Service chief Charles T. Menoher, British air attaché L. E. O. Charlton, and other notables joined with Praeger to mark the air mail's first anniversary. The Post Office proudly announced that the "practical commercial utility of the airplane" had been demonstrated. Out of 1,261 possible trips on the route, only fifty-five had defaulted because of weather. There had been "only" fifty-one forced landings caused by weather and thirty-seven by engine trouble. Pilot Dana C. DeHart had the best record with 191 successful trips (21,360 miles), seven forced landings, and five uncompleted schedules. "One of the lessons learned . . . during the year," Praeger pointed out, "is that the element of danger that exists in the training of aviators in military and exhibition flying is almost entirely absent from commercial flying. . . . No airplane carrying the mail has ever fallen out of the sky, and there has not been a single death of an aviator in carrying mail." [13]

May 15 also saw the inauguration of the long-delayed Cleveland–Chicago route. The fiasco of December now in the past, this time careful preparation and spring weather had reduced the service to routine operations. Trent C. Fry flew a freshly modified DH with 450 pounds of mail from Chicago to Cleveland (325 miles) in 3 hours 13 minutes, including a brief stop at Bryan, Ohio. Edward Gardner covered the westbound segment without incident in 3 hours 50 minutes. [14]

Edgerton inspected the route during the first three days of operations, reporting strengths and weaknesses to Praeger. The main problem at Chicago's Grant Park, he observed, was the presence of unmanageable spectators who arrived fifteen minutes before arrivals and departures; he recommended that at least four mounted policemen be assigned to control the crowds. Edgerton disliked the approaches to the field at Bryan, especially the telephone wires on the west end; also, poor drainage made the landing area treacherous after heavy rain. Mechanics, while inexperienced, "could be whipped into shape eventually." He was most impressed with Bryan field manager Warren E. ("Dad") LaFollette. "He is taking hold in a very thorough manner," Edgerton wrote, "and I feel sure will produce results." Cleveland was in best shape of all, with a good field and trained staff. Edgerton considered field manager W. J. McCandless a "very bright, energetic man who will undoubtedly make good." Divisional Superintendent Jordan had seven experienced pilots—Biffle, Gardner, McCusker, and Lester F. Bishop based in Cleveland, and Fry, John Miller, and Max Miller assigned to Chicago—and an adequate number of modified DHs. Although minor interruption of service could be expected as pilots and mechanics gained experience, Edgerton concluded: "I believe that success will certainly follow." [15]

The first week of operations bore out Edgerton's prediction. Out of thirty scheduled trips, only two were canceled because of weather, and there were no forced landings. But the second week brought tragedy. [16]

Frank McCusker, hired by Edgerton in December, had served during the war with the Royal Canadian Flying Corps and later worked as an inspector of de Havillands for the Standard Aero Corporation. He was an experienced pilot, with over 1,100 hours in his logbook and extensive cross-country experience. Shortly after McCusker took off from Cleveland on May 25, observers noted smoke coming from his aircraft. He tried to fight the fire (his Pyrene extinguisher was found empty), but without success. At a time when parachutes were not a part of a pilot's standard equipment, McCusker faced the choice that all aviators dreaded: burn or jump. At 200 feet he jumped, fracturing his skull and neck on the stabilizer. He died before he hit the ground.[17]

Divisional Superintendent Jordan promptly blamed pilot error. On the basis of slender evidence, he speculated that McCusker had disobeyed orders and ran his engine above 1,500 rpm, causing it to overheat. Furthermore, the absence of burns on McCusker's body led Jordan to the conclusion that the pilot "contributed largely to his own death in jumping from the ship many seconds before it was necessary to leave. . . ." McCusker of course could offer no defense. There was no further investigation.[18]

The records indicate, perhaps unfairly, that there was greater concern over the bank mail lost in the fire than over McCusker's death. Banker J. W. Harriman reported that $63,000 in checks and drafts had been destroyed. This was a "high-handed outrage," he cried; bank mail should not be carried in "experiments." Congressman Steenerson, chairman of the House Post Office Committee, introduced a resolution calling upon Burleson to provide information on the loss of the mail, and to clarify the authority under which such valuable cargo was carried in the first place.[19]

Congressional complaints led to the adoption of devices to protect the mail. The Post Office equipped all aircraft with asbestos fire walls that enclosed the mail compartment, replaced hand fire extinguishers

Pilot Trent C. Fry delivers the mail to Chicago on time but not without incident, June 16, 1919.

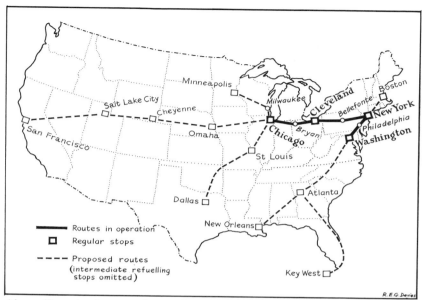

Air mail routes in operation and proposed, July 1, 1919.

with a compressed air spray system of chemical extinguishers, and pushed development of a noninflammable mail bag. The mail would survive a fire even if the pilot did not.[20]

Loss of the first pilot in mail operations failed to restrain the Post Office's enthusiasm over performance on the Chicago–Cleveland route. On June 21 Praeger announced that fifty-eight consecutive trips had been completed without a single forced landing because of weather or mechanical trouble. Engines and planes "had performed faultlessly," Praeger crowed, and pilots had displayed considerable navigational skills.[21]

On July 1 the Post Office opened the New York–Cleveland portion of the route to Chicago. Earl F. White left Belmont Field at 5:15 A.M. EDT and flew without incident to Bellefonte, Pennsylvania (215 miles). Max Miller went on to Cleveland (215 miles), where Ira Biffle took over and completed the trip to Chicago (325 miles), arriving at 12:58 P.M. CDT. Again, what had seemed so difficult six months earlier, now was accomplished with apparent ease.[22]

Determined to maintain schedules, Praeger kept up pressure on the pilots to perform. On July 5 Superintendent Jordan reported to Praeger that Biffle had gotten "cold feet" in fog while en route from Cleveland to Chicago and had landed thirty miles short of his destination. After waiting for the weather to improve, Biffle took off and reached Grant Park one hour and thirty minutes behind schedule. If extra pilots were available, Jordan said, he would ground Biffle for thirty days without pay.[23]

"You have authority to act in Biffle case," Praeger replied. Extra men would be sent, if necessary. "Pilots either must fly or resign," he commanded. "Everybody must understand that the route must operate or the service [be] suspended until we can fly on schedule. Situation too serious to play with. Act promptly in all cases."[24]

Jordan needed little prodding. A few days later, Biffle again encountered fog, landed at Hammond, Indiana, and was fifty-five minutes late reaching Chicago. Jordan promptly suspended him without pay. Biffle complained to Edgerton: "Myself and other pilots discouraged and do not consider this just treatment." After Edgerton explained the circumstances, Praeger relented (as he often did in individual cases) and reinstated Biffle. But this did not mean that his attitude had softened.[25]

The demands of postal officials, combined with the pilots' professional pride, took airmen into weather conditions that tested the limits of their skill. Shortly after noon on July 10, Charles Anglin was en route from Bellefonte for New York when he ran into low clouds and heavy rain over the Alleghenies. Unable to get through underneath, he climbed on top of the clouds and attempted to fly by compass. After forty minutes, he descended over lower ground to check his location. Anglin broke out at 700 feet, could not recognize any terrain features, and landed to ask directions. He was near Sellersville, Pennsylvania. While attempting take-off, Anglin hit the top of a row of bushes and turned over, smashing the propeller, radiator, and rudder, and damaging both upper wings and the left side of the landing gear. Anglin was not injured.[26]

Robert H. Ellis had a narrow escape five days later when he became trapped in a heavy rainstorm while en route from Bellefonte to Cleveland. With visibility reduced to a few feet and mountains all around, Ellis tried to set down in a small field on the top of a hill. Pilots would term it a good landing: the airplane was demolished but Ellis walked away without a scratch.[27]

Fate was not as kind to Charles W. Lamborn, who took off from Bellefonte at 10:20 A.M., July 19, with 404 pounds of mail for Cleveland. The weather was unsettled, with fog and low clouds masking the tops of surrounding mountains, and occasional heavy rain showers. Lamborn stayed low after take-off, ducking under clouds and passing through a gap in the range of mountains that runs from Bellefonte to Milesburg. Crossing the Snowshoe Mountains, however, he was forced to enter clouds. Lamborn lost outside visual reference and became disoriented. Witnesses on the ground saw his DH appear through the clouds at 400 feet, pointing nose down. Unable to recover in time, Lamborn smashed into the ground, breaking both legs and ankles, ribs, and collar bone. He died en route to the hospital. The Alleghenies had claimed their first victim.[28]

A confrontation between Praeger and the pilots was inevitable, and it occurred on July 22. Leon Smith was scheduled to leave New York for Washington at 11:40 A.M. in a Curtiss R-4. With rain, low clouds, and visibility less than 200 feet, Smith complained that the aircraft was too dangerous to use in bad weather because its Liberty engine overheated at low altitudes. Instead, he offered to fly a Curtiss JN-4H with a 150-hp engine. Belmont field manager Harry W. Powers passed the information to Washington (where the weather was clear). Praeger replied: "Smith must fly R-4 or tender resignation effective today."

Smith's resolve matched Praeger's: he would not fly the R-4. Powers turned to reserve pilots Walter H. Stevens and Clifford L. Webster. Both men sided with Smith. He then telephoned the only other pilot in the area, E. Hamilton Lee. Although Lee was not due out for three days, Powers ordered him to report to the field. By the time he arrived, weather conditions had gotten worse. Lee also refused to fly the Curtiss R-4, but offered to take the JN-4H. Powers had run out of pilots.[29]

Praeger ordered Carl Egge, assistant superintendent of the Railway Mail Service (who was in New York) to investigate whether there had been a "collusion to delay the mails." Egge reached Belmont at 3:40 P.M. He found Powers in his office and the four pilots gathered in front of the hangar. After talking with Powers, he asked the pilots for written statements setting forth their reasons for refusing to fly. Stevens and Lee were temperate. Stevens pointed out that he had never flown the route before, while Lee noted that the high-compression Liberty engines on the Curtiss R-4s tended to overheat at low altitudes. Webster was not as cautious. On three of the six trips he had flown, Webster complained, "I have been compelled to fly close over the housetops of thickly settled cities for a considerable distance, in order to find my way through. As under these conditions a motor failure would probably result in the injury or death of people upon the ground, I consider it would be little less than criminal to take such chances." Arguing that the Post Office required pilots to take "unreasonable risks," he concluded: "I believe that only exceptional good fortune has kept the death rate as low as it is. Unless there is a change of policy I do not think I shall care to remain in the Aerial Mail Service very long."[30]

Leon Smith used the occasion to deliver a scathing personal attack on Praeger, accusing him of placing Curtiss R-4s on the Washington–New York route "through ignorance of the flying game." For months, pilots had been complaining about the situation, but their protests had been ignored. Smith blamed Praeger:

> *It is mighty easy Mr. Praeger for you to sit in your swivel chair in Washington and tell the flyers when they can fly. . . . Pilots have been killed and only last week one of the best flyers in the United States lost his life when he tried to obey your orders and come through with the mail. Mr. Lamborn is the man I refer to. You do not regard a man's life worth the least of respect, nor do you stop to consider the number of planes that have been smashed up with a big expense to the Government. It matters very little as long as you can run things in your own way. I think Mr. Praeger that it is long past the time that a man with as little knowledge as you have of the flying game . . . should be at the head of as large a proposition. It is not fair to the pilots, or to the public in general, and you may rest assured that I for one shall give you all the publicity I can.*[31]

Egge reported to Praeger that he could find no "collusion." Smith was the "cause of all the trouble," being the senior pilot and having done most of the complaining. "It is my opinion," Egge stated, "that Smith and possibly the other pilots have lost their nerve, and the morale of the pilots and perhaps the employees of the field is below par." Praeger fired Smith and Lee, and he ordered Divisional Superintendent Stanton to investigate further the cases of Webster and Stevens.[32]

The following day, July 23, all four scheduled trips of the Eastern Division operated on schedule—but not without trouble. Stevens and Merrill K. Riddick were scheduled out of New York at noon, Stevens to Bellefonte and Riddick to Washington. When Riddick agreed to fly a Curtiss R-4, Stevens and Riddick exchanged words, then punches. After they departed (on schedule), the pilots at Belmont continued the discussion. After contacting pilots at other fields, they sent the following telegram to Praeger:

> *The summary dismissal of Pilots Lee and Smith without investigation or justification is considered a direct attack on every pilot in the aerial mail service inasmuch as it was merely their misfortune to be the ones in position to have to refuse to fly in order to protect their lives. Their reinstatement pending such investigation is requested. In order to be fair we will defer action for twenty-four hours. The everlasting fly regardless of weather conditions or resign must cease as we are as human as the rest.*
> *Pilots of the Aerial Mail*[33]

Egge returned to Belmont on July 24 and was informed by Charles Anglin, who had emerged as spokesman for the pilots, that unless a favorable reply to yesterday's wire to Praeger was received by 5 P.M., no mail planes would fly on July 25. The New York newspapers, he continued, supported the pilots; if Smith and Lee were not reinstated, stories adverse to the Post Office would appear the following morning. Finally, Anglin warned that "certain Congressmen" would be pleased to receive information that thousands of dollars worth of airplanes had been destroyed during the past ten days.[34]

While Anglin was laying down the pilots' demands, a telegram arrived from Praeger. Smith and Lee would not be rehired. Pilots must carry out the orders of the Post Office or resign. "Every pilot," Praeger stated "is expected to carry out his duty in accordance with his oath and sense of loyalty to the service and to aviation in general." He concluded by calling attention to the conspiracy provisions of federal law.[35]

Egge explained to Anglin that conspiracy against the government was punishable by a fine of up to $10,000 and up to two years in prison. Anglin promptly picked up the phone and called the Associated Press. Praeger, after hearing from Egge about the day's events, ordered postal inspectors to investigate for possible violations of federal law.[36]

The next morning, Egge and a team of postal inspectors accompanied the mail to Belmont Park, arriving at 4:40 A.M. The mechanic on duty placed the mail onboard an airplane for the scheduled 5 A.M. departure for Bellefonte, but no pilot appeared. Field manager Powers did not turn up until 8 A.M. He explained that Anglin, the scheduled pilot, had called the previous evening and claimed that a "lame back" would not permit him to fly. Powers had called backup pilot Webster; he said that it was not his day to fly. Powers told Egge that he had not bothered to contact anyone else.[37]

As the morning wore on, Divisional Superintendent Stanton and a group of pilots gathered at the field. At noon, Randolph G. Page, a recently hired pilot, flew in and landed with the mail from Washington. Asked by his peers why he had flown the trip, Page said that he could not get any information in Washington so he decided to fly to Belmont to see what was happening. About this time, Riddick showed up for the southbound schedule. He was ready to fly, he told Stanton, but the previous evening he had received an anonymous phone call from a woman, warning that it would be dangerous to make the trip. Stanton said he would not require Riddick to fly lest an accident be blamed on sabotage by dissatisfied pilots or mechanics. Meanwhile, flights operated without incident between Chicago and Cleveland.[38]

As Anglin had warned, the New York press took the side of the pilots. The stories that appeared on July 25 portrayed the Post Office as ignorant and insensitive in its conduct of the air mail. Pilots were being forced to risk their lives in all kinds of weather "for a two-cent stamp." They were being ordered to fly airplanes that were too heavy and too fast. The airplanes that they used could not go slower than 100 mph, causing landing problems. High compression engines overheated at low altitudes and were dangerous. Requests for lighter and slower aircraft had been ignored. Attempts to obtain "stabilizers" (turn indicators) that would show if they were flying on an even keel in fog had been denied on the grounds of expense; besides, pilots had been told, they could always steer by compass. There had been fifteen accidents between July 15 and 22, and two pilots had been killed in aircraft that they had advised their supervisors were unsafe. The firing of Smith and Lee was an insult to every pilot in the Air Mail Service.[39]

Praeger issued an immediate point-by-point denial. The charges were not true. In fact, there had been no complaints before the dismissal of Smith and Lee, and nothing would have been said if he had reinstated the two pilots. Furthermore, the Curtiss R-4 was not unsafe. Statistics gathered during the past year showed that the Liberty-engined R-4 was not "more dangerous and liable to forced landings in bad weather than the small JN-4H plane with a 150 H.P. Hispano-Suiza motor." Also, its engine had to be pushed to the limit to achieve 100 mph, and its landing speed of 55 mph was only 5 mph greater than a JN-4H's. Moreover, the sturdier construction of the R-4 made it safer in forced landings than a JN-4H. The Post Office had not refused to supply turn indicators; these new devices had been ordered but the manufacturer had said that none would be available for at least two months. There had not been fifteen accidents during the previous week, and McCusker had died two months previously in an accident unrelated to weather. The safety record of the Air Mail Service stood as proof of the Post Office's "ceaseless attention" to supplying safe aircraft to the pilots.

Safety was not the real issue, Praeger claimed. At stake was the matter of control. The Post Office "cannot leave the question of when to fly and when not to fly in each instance to the judgment of a dozen different aviators. If this were done, it would be impossible to operate the mail schedule with any degree of dependability and the Air Mail would have to be abandoned." There were other pilots readily available to do the job, Praeger warned, if the current group was not prepared to follow orders.[40]

As the conflict escalated and positions hardened, Stanton moved into the role of peacemaker. Throughout the afternoon of the 25th, he held discussions with the pilots at Belmont, searching for an acceptable compromise. The pilots finally agreed to have a representative meet with Praeger. With threats of congressional investigations in the air, Praeger also agreed, suggesting only that "for the purposes of harmony" the pilots select someone who was not directly involved in the controversy of July 22. The pilots picked Anglin. He told the press that the strike was temporarily called off, but issued a defiant statement. "We will insist that the man who risks his own life be the judge [of when to fly], not somebody on the ground [who] risks other people's lives. If this is not granted the strike will be resumed again."[41]

The meeting began at 3:45 P.M., Saturday, July 26, in Praeger's office. Present were Praeger, James B. Corridon (superintendent of the Division of Railway Adjustments), Edgerton, Stanton, and Anglin. Benjamin E. Buente, a clerk in Praeger's office, took notes but did not participate.[42] The meeting lasted until 5:40 P.M., then continued the next day at 10:40 A.M. Equipment problems, supposedly the reason for the strike, were not even discussed; however, the transcript of the meeting indicates that an understanding—of sorts—was reached regarding orders to fly in bad weather:

> Anglin: *"Do I understand correctly when I say that new orders will be issued covering flights which will provide that when a pilot believes it unsafe to start that the field manager will be the proper authority whether flight shall be begun or not?"*
>
> Praeger: *No new orders are necessary because the field manager already has such authority:* "The pilot has never been held responsible or disciplined if he did not fly when the manager told him he can wait, or when he told him he can use his own judgement. This has been the practice at all times."
>
> Anglin: *"As far as I am concerned, that settles the question of flying regardless of weather conditions, resign or be fired."*
>
> Praeger: *"You of course understand that if the field manager directs a pilot to fly, he must fly."*
>
> Anglin: *"We don't believe that the manager of a field will order a pilot to take [to] the air under such conditions when he would be afraid to fly himself. If the question is in doubt, he will be invited to take a ride."*

Discussion of the issue ended on this puzzling and ambiguous note.

The conferees then took up the dismissal of Smith and Lee. Praeger defended his actions as "fully justified," but agreed that both men could apply for reinstatement. Although Anglin pressed Praeger for a commitment to rehire the men if they did apply, he refused.[43]

The meeting adjourned at 1 P.M. so that Praeger would have time to consider the reinstatement applications (which Anglin had supplied). At 4:30 P.M. he announced his decision. Smith, who had sent the abusive telegram of July 22 to Praeger (an action not condoned by the pilots), would not be reinstated. Lee, after pleading his case in person—he told Praeger that he "probably" would have flown on the 22d if the other three pilots had been asked to resign or been removed—received more sympathetic treatment. Praeger agreed that field manager Powers had made a mistake in handling the matter; he should not have asked the inexperienced Stevens or Webster to fly. After defending the use of the Curtiss R-4 and the right of management to control flying, Praeger concluded regarding Lee: "In view of these conditions, particularly in view of the fact that your satisfactory flying and your interest in having the air mail flown in conditions of bad weather, as well as fair days, your application for reinstatement is hereby granted. . . ."[44]

This settled the dispute. Praeger told the press that the chief factor in reaching an agreement was Anglin's fair attitude and the desire by all pilots to see the Air Mail Service operate with the highest possible degree of efficiency. Anglin, in turn, praised Praeger for his consideration and courtesy.[45]

The press claimed victory for the pilots. The *New York Times* reported that the field manager now would decide whether or not to fly when the weather is bad. If the pilot still refused to fly, "the manager will himself take a plane and go aloft, thus demonstrating to the pilots that the weather is safe."[46] But the *Times*—and later historians[47]—misunderstood the results of the strike. Anglin may have thought that he had secured an important concession from Praeger, but the postal official saw things in a different light. Praeger continued to insist that pilots fly in bad weather, and in aircraft designated by the Post Office. Field managers, most of whom were not aviators, were not required to go aloft to assess the weather. Furthermore, the pilots did not challenge Praeger on this during his remaining twenty months in office. Praeger's modification of the standard employment form for pilots put his position clearly:

> *I hereby make application for position of pilot in the Aerial Mail Service and hereby agree, if appointed, to fly whenever called upon and in whatever Aerial Mail plane that I may be directed by the Superintendent of the Division to which I am assigned,* or his representative on the field, *and in the event of my refusal to fly, such refusal shall constitute my resignation from the service, which you are hereby authorized to accept.*[48]

As he had threatened, Webster left the Air Mail Service in August. Anglin departed shortly thereafter, but when his new job failed to work out he telegraphed Praeger and asked for reinstatement. Praeger wrote on top of the telegram: "Wire Anglin *NO* & we are full up on fliers." Leon Smith barnstormed until August 1922, then applied unsuccessfully for a job with the Air Mail Service. Lee would go on to a distinguished career with the air mail and United Air Lines. As for Praeger, his reputation for calloused insensitivity in dealing with pilots would follow him to his grave—and beyond.[49]

THE POST OFFICE HAD LAUNCHED a monumental undertaking during the first half of 1919. The 755 miles of the New York–Chicago route, equivalent to the distance from London to Madrid, was a pioneering venture of the first magnitude. Never before had anyone, anywhere in the world, attempted to operate a scheduled airplane service over such distances. As the National Advisory Committee for Aeronautics noted in its *Annual Report* for 1919, the Air Mail Service was making a "substantial contribution in the practical development of commercial aviation."[50]

Careful preparation had been the key to success. Unlike the hasty effort to begin service the previous December, this time the Post Office had made sure that experienced pilots, suitable aircraft, and proper ground facilities were in place before attempting to fly the route.

Many individuals had contributed to the success of the operation, including Edgerton, Stanton, Jordan, and a group of skilled and determined pilots. But, as Stanton pointed out, the "driving force" behind the Air Mail Service was Praeger. The air mail had become Praeger's passion. He supervised every detail, from pilots to spare parts. Stubborn and persistent, he drove his subordinates to achieve goals that they had thought impossible. Praeger, Edgerton later explained, was "invaluable to our success—he lived, ate and slept Air Mail. His favorite weekend was to have Stanton and me, with the frequent addition of [chief clerk] George Conner, spend Sunday mornings in executive sessions. . . . There we would sit in his private office, coats and ties off and feet propped on his huge desk—at least huge in comparison to his own short, rotund proportions—as we threshed out Air Mail improvements."[51]

Praeger's weak spot was his inability to believe that most of the pilots cared as much about the success of the air mail as he did. Praeger was not fanatical about flying in all kinds of weather. In a report to Burleson in May 1919, Praeger stated: "A year's flying of the aerial mail with all types and temperaments of aviators establishes the fact that 200 feet visibility from the ground is the limit of practical fly-ing. . . ." Trips often were canceled in bad weather. However, Praeger distrusted his pilots; he insisted that they at least *try* to fly in mar-ginal weather conditions. Also, he strongly believed that subordinates should obey orders—or quit.[52]

Given Praeger's attitude, a confrontation with the pilots had been inevitable. No one came off well during the short-lived strike of July 1919. Leon Smith alienated potential allies with his vicious personal attacks on Praeger, Anglin was not an effective spokesman, and the pilots lacked solidarity. Praeger may have won, but it was a hollow vic-tory, one that damaged the reputation of his beloved Air Mail Service.

6 On the Frontiers of Aeronautics

THE ROUTE TO CHICAGO represented only the first step in Praeger's grand scheme for nationwide air mail service. The day would come, he predicted in August 1919, when all important cities in the country would be linked by air. Looking to the immediate future, he said that the Post Office was ready to use multi-engine aircraft, guided by radio beams, on routes between New York and San Francisco, and from Boston to Havana, as soon as Congress approved the necessary funds. "Commercial aviation has arrived," Praeger announced, "and it cannot be stopped."[1]

Praeger earlier had concluded that multi-engine aircraft would be required for safe and reliable operation of mail routes, especially over the high mountains of the West. He knew that there had been twenty-three forced landings because of mechanical problems during the first nine months of operation. Spark plug fouling led the list with six incidents, followed by radiator leaks (five), oil leaks (four), and ignition system trouble (four). Solutions to specific problems were being sought: the Air Mail Service supported the development of a ceramic and mica spark plug that promised long life and freedom from fouling, installed duplicate ignition systems on all aircraft, and relocated radiators to reduce vibration. But engines continued to fail at a high rate. "A study of the motor troubles causing forced landings," Praeger concluded, "points irresistibly to the multiple engine as a solution."[2]

The Post Office tested British twin-engine Handley-Page bombers that were being built under contract in the United States by the Standard Aero Corporation, but found that these big crates were too slow (70 to 90 mph) and could not maintain altitude with a single engine. Caproni trimotors being built by General Motors also proved unsuitable. After polling air mail pilots on their requirements for an "ideal mail plane," consulting with aeronautical engineers, and discussing various possibilities with aircraft manufacturers, Praeger issued a set of specifications and called for bids.[3]

The Post Office wanted an aircraft with two or more engines, capable of carrying at least 1,500 pounds of mail at 90 to 100 mph, with an endurance of six hours and a service ceiling of at least 15,000 feet. Bids would be opened on June 2, with delivery within six months of letting the contract.[4]

Praeger received an enthusiastic response from airplane manufacturers who had been wondering where orders would be coming from in the postwar years. Thirteen companies submitted bids; the Post Office accepted three.[5]

The Thomas Morse Aircraft Corporation received a contract ($106,000) for four twin-engine biplanes, powered by opposing (one tractor, one pusher) Hispano-Suiza engines. With a length of 26'6" and a wingspan of 46'6", the Thomas Morse had a fully loaded weight of 5,700 pounds and would carry 1,500 pounds of mail at 100 mph for five and a half hours. L.W.F. agreed to deliver four giant trimotors for $140,000. More than twice as large as the Thomas Morse, the L.W.F. "Owl" was 56'9½" long and had a wingspan of 105'. Its three Liberty engines lifted a maximum weight of 18,500 pounds and would carry 2,000 pounds of mail at 105 mph for ten hours. The Glenn L. Martin Company's design fell between the Thomas Morse and the L.W.F. The Martin twin-engine biplane was 44'10" long, had a span of 71'5", a maximum weight of 9,500 pounds, and proposed to carry 1,500 pounds of mail for five and a half hours at 90 mph. The Post Office ordered six Martins for $189,000.[6]

In September Praeger predicted that by winter the L.W.F. trimotors would be flying nonstop between New York and Chicago, while the Martin and Thomas Morse aircraft would be operating New York–Cleveland–Chicago "with great speed and regularity." The Post Office would expand service in the spring from Chicago to Minneapolis, Omaha, and St. Louis, with further extensions as funds permitted.[7]

November brought a measure of reality when Praeger learned that two of the manufacturers had produced duds. The Thomas Morse airplane with tandem engines fell painfully short of expectations and could not be used to carry the mail; the Post Office eventually turned them over to the Army Air Service for additional testing. The giant L.W.F. trimotors also turned out to offer more promise than performance and did not go into service.[8]

Delivery of the six twin-engine Martins, however, gave some cause for optimistic expectations of performance. Similar in general specifications to the Martin bombers then being used by the Army Air Service, the airplanes at least *looked* impressive. Painted blue-black (with a

The Thomas Morse MB-4, one of several airplanes that failed to meet Praeger's expectations for use in the Air Mail Service.

final coat of varnish to give the appearance of patent leather), they had U.S. MAIL and the aircraft's number (201 to 206) emblazoned on the side of the fuselage in white with red shading. The aircraft featured a bullet-shaped nose, held in place by four bolts. Thus, the nose quickly could be detached and replaced should it be damaged in a forced landing. There were five mail compartments, four of which had trap doors that permitted mail to be dropped by parachute.[9]

Initial performance delighted Praeger. Two aircraft were ferried nonstop from the Martin factory in Cleveland to New York in 3 hours 31 minutes and 3 hours 50 minutes, each carrying over 1,000 pounds of mail. On November 18 a Martin flew nonstop from New York to Washington in 3 hours 10 minutes with 746 pounds of mail. The Post Office, it seemed, had found the ideal mail plane.[10]

Unfortunately, the Martins came into service at the beginning of what turned out to be the severest winter in half a century and at a time when the Post Office was operating from marginal airfields. The fields at Chicago (Grant Park) and Cleveland (Woodland Hills) were barely adequate for DHs; they could not accommodate the larger Martins. Aware of the problem, the Post Office planned to use Checkerboard Field in the Chicago suburb of Forest Park, where an 80' × 100'

A Martin mail plane.

hangar was being built specifically for the Martins. Also, Praeger secured access to Glenn Martin Field in Cleveland, at least temporarily.
But the situation in New York proved more difficult to resolve.[11]

After August Belmont withdrew permission for the use of his race-
course, the Post Office arranged with the city of Newark to operate
from a newly constructed airfield. Newark provided, free of charge, a
tract of land adjacent to Tiffany's silver factory in what became Branch
Brook Park. The city also appropriated $25,000 to clear the property
of 1,200 trees and stumps. The financially strapped Air Mail Service
jumped at the opportunity to use this free airport. But Praeger—and
he must bear ultimate responsibility for the decision—had blundered.
Heller Field turned out to be a pilot's nightmare. Wedged in rough
terrain between a fork in the Erie Railroad tracks, it afforded only 900
feet of landing area. And obstructions abounded. Two eighty-foot factory chimneys rose at the north end of the field; there was a canal at
the south end. Under prevailing winds, pilots had to approach the
field by flying between factory buildings, make a sharp bank over a
gully filled with stumps and debris, then settle down quickly at the
end of the small landing area. With only a tailskid for braking, it was
easy to run out of field. Employees would line up on the ramp to observe the first landing by new pilots, expecting the worst.[12]

On December 3 Walter H. Stevens brought the first Martin into
Heller Field. He made a difficult landing, barely avoiding disaster. As

Stevens taxied to the hangar, twenty to thirty children ran out on the field (no fences or chains restrained spectators) and into the path of the aircraft. Stevens swerved the brakeless plane to the right, clipped a construction pole with a wingtip, and veered toward the railroad embankment. Another group of boys—fleeing the embankment to escape the oncoming plane—crossed in front of the giant Martin, and one was struck by a propeller and killed. "We will have more or less trouble landing large planes on this field at all times," Stevens informed Praeger following this incident.[13]

Time only deepened Stevens's passionate aversion to Heller, a feeling shared by all air mail pilots. In January he complained that taking off from Newark was "extremely dangerous." He had barely managed to get the large Martin off the ground, he said, by bouncing it into a stall, leveling off, and clearing the canal by five feet. The Post Office filed Stevens's letter in his personnel file, and business went on as usual.[14]

Heller Field was only part of the operational problems faced by the Martins. In mid-January it took Paul S. Oakes three days and five forced landings to fly Martin Number 205 from Cleveland to Chicago. He arrived with a broken tailskid, inoperative ailerons, holes punched in the wing coverings, a hole where someone had stepped through the cover of the rear mail compartment, and with both engines running rough. When James H. ("Jack") Knight arrived at the field on the morning of January 17 to take Number 205 back to Cleveland, mechanics were still working on the engines. Several hours later they judged the aircraft ready for service. Knight had his doubts: neither tachometer was working, and the left engine "sounded awfully sour." The field manager insisted that he fly, and Knight obeyed. He managed to get off the ground, but not much further. He lost aileron control at 50 feet; at 200 feet the left engine died, and the Martin began to settle toward the roofs of factories north of the field. Knight nursed the aircraft to 800 feet and made a skidding turn toward open country. Then his right engine quit. Trying to stretch the glide to reach the nearest open field, he landed short, breaking the tail-skid and bending the strut on the landing gear.[15]

Four days later Oakes and mechanic Edward F. Doty made a forced landing near Black Oak, Indiana, in Number 205. During an attempt to restart the engine, the Martin caught fire and burned. An investigation revealed that the drain pipe had been disconnected from the drain bowl under the carburetor of the right engine. In priming for a start, the carburetor flooded, fuel had drained around the engine, and a mild backfire had ignited the gasoline. Also, the aircraft's pressure fire extinguisher system had not been connected and no hand

extinguishers had been carried. Starting the engine with a disconnected drain pipe, Praeger wrote, "indicated gross ignorance or negligence, or both."[16]

What could go wrong with the Martins did go wrong. By the end of
1920, four of the large airplanes had been lost in accidents (with one
fatality, mechanic N. C. Montis). The Post Office transferred the two
surviving Martins to the Army Air Service.[17]

ATTEMPTS TO USE RADIO as an aid to navigation also proved
abortive, but the Post Office did sponsor a number of interesting and
important experiments in this area. From the beginning, Praeger
had hoped that radio might solve the problems of navigating in bad
weather. In August 1918 he had asked the National Bureau of Standards to investigate the possibility of employing radio signals to mark
the location of landing fields. Frederick A. Kolster—considered by
historian Rexmond C. Cochrane to be "one of the most inventive mechanical geniuses ever to work at the Bureau"—took charge of the
project. By early November he was ready for an experiment. He
wrapped a transmitting coil (six turns of insulated no. 12 copper wire)
around the edge of the new Radio Building at the Bureau's testing facilities in northwest Washington, D.C., and used low-frequency alter-
nating current (24 amperes of 500 cycles) to produce a localized signal
that was strong near and above the building but faded rapidly with
distance. An air mail JN-4H was fitted to receive the signal through a
"searching coil" (forty turns of magnetic wire in a large loop on each
side of the lower wing); a three-stage amplifier boosted the signal
strength in the pilot's headphones. On Armistice Day, November 11,
1918, the airplane flew over the Radio Building and clearly heard the
signal at 3,000 feet for five seconds.[18]

Encouraged by these results, the Bureau moved the experiment to
the airfield at College Park, installing the transmitting coil around the
edge of the landing area (1,500 feet by 2,000 feet). Edgerton assigned
Stanton to work with the Bureau. Using a Curtiss R-4, he was able to
hear the signal at 1,500 and 2,000 feet. He could almost circle the
field within range of the signal. By May 1919 the scientists had devised an antenna that radiated a localized signal over the field in the
form of an inverted cone with a hollow center (where no signal could
be heard). Although these experiments eventually would lead to the
perfection of the radio marker beacon, an important aid to navigation
in the electronic airway of the future, this preliminary work never
reached a point where the Post Office could apply the device to current operations.[19]

Praeger had even higher hopes for development of a radio direction finding (RDF) system. The Post Office began work on this project in February 1919. With the cooperation of the U.S. Navy, a direction finder was installed on Stanton's Curtiss R-4. Two large loops of rubber-covered wire ("A" and "B" coils) were wound around the aircraft at right angles to each other, then connected to batteries, a six-stage amplifier, and a variable condenser. The pilot switched to the loop parallel to the line of flight (A" coil) and flew toward the transmitting station by following the maximum signal strength. Nearing the station, he switched to the "B" or minimum strength coil (null) for greater accuracy.[20]

Early experiments were plagued by interference from engine ignition. Attempts to shield the ignition circuit failed, as did efforts to shield the RDF circuit. The best that could be done was to move the loops as far as possible from the engine. By summer 1919 results were so promising that Praeger established a radio laboratory at College Park, Maryland, under the direction of John A. Willoughby.[21]

Pilot Kenneth McGregor later recalled the summer day in 1919 when he was ordered to report to the "dirt-floored lean-to which we called a hangar" at College Park where he was introduced to Willoughby. "With his sandy hair and a quick grin," McGregor remembered, "he could have passed for a cowboy." Willoughby explained that they would be trying to follow a radio signal to Philadelphia. McGregor took off as instructed, flew above clouds, and waited for hand signals. Willoughby sat in the mail compartment on a stool latched to the floor, radio receiver on his lap, and earphones over his head. McGregor flew as directed for an hour and forty minutes. Low on fuel, he saw a clear field below the aircraft and landed. "Where's Philadephia?" McGregor asked a farmer. "I dunno," the farmer replied, but "Norfolk is right over there." McGregor had flown ninety miles in the opposite direction, and Willoughby had learned an early lesson in signal ambiguity.[22]

The Post Office wanted to use the RDF equipment on the new Martins, but the coil or Robinson method (after Dr. James Robinson of England) had to be abandoned because of the size of the aircraft and the increased ignition interference from the second engine. Instead, a small rotary coil was mounted inside the fuselage near the tail, and connected to a forward radio compartment. The Martins carried a radio operator and complete radio installation, including a transmitter (Navy model SE-1310 airplane spark set) for wireless telegraphy, all-purpose receiver (Navy type 1605-B), trailing wire antenna, and radio direction finder.[23]

Experiments with the radio equipment had produced such encouraging results, Edgerton informed Praeger in 1920, that the remaining problems "can be successfully and readily worked out." Radio navigation, he stressed, "is the only possible way in which long distance flights can consistently be made under varying weather conditions." Impressed, Praeger created a Radio Division and put Edgerton in charge. But operational problems that took the Martins out of service, together with pressure to begin transcontinental service, soon shifted Edgerton's attention to the establishment of a point-to-point radio communications network and brought an end to RDF work.[24]

WHILE THE POST OFFICE SEARCHED for radio-guided, multi-engine aircraft for a transcontinental route, the Army Air Service provided a dramatic demonstration of the hazards of cross-country aviation with existing equipment and facilities. In order to mobilize public opinion behind legislation that would join the aviation sections of the Army and the Navy in a "unified" air force, Brig. Gen. William ("Billy") Mitchell had drawn up an imaginative plan for his airmen to fly en masse across the North American continent. Mitchell insisted on the official designation of "Transcontinental Reliability and Endurance Test," but no one harbored illusions about the true nature of the event. As the *New York Times* announced in October 1919, Americans were about to witness the "greatest air race ever attempted."[25]

Air Service officers selected a route that would run from New York to Buffalo, skirting the Appalachian Mountains, then along Lake Erie to Cleveland before turning westward to Chicago and Omaha. Aviators would pick up the tracks of the Union Pacific Railroad at Omaha, continuing to San Francisco via Cheyenne, Salt Lake City, Reno, and Sacramento. The railroad route was compelling: it followed favorable terrain, supplies and equipment could easily be moved by rail to intermediate points, and tracks ("iron compass") would serve as the primary navigational aid from Omaha to San Francisco.

Mitchell's planners established twenty refueling or control points along the 2,701-mile route. Contest rules called for a minimum stop of thirty minutes at each point. Also, in the interests of safety, flying was restricted to daylight. Originally conceived as a one-way crossing, with contestants starting simultaneously at New York and San Francisco, the Air Service responded to criticism and changed the event to a round trip, thus neutralizing the possible advantage of prevailing westerly winds. This also doubled the distance, a fact that passed without much notice.[26]

October 8 dawned clear and cool with a fresh northeasterly wind. More than 2,000 spectators showed up at Roosevelt Field, Long Island, for the day's festivities. The 22d Infantry Band provided music, while ladies from the War Camp Community Service passed out sandwiches and coffee to contestants and guests. Assistant Secretary of War Benedict Crowell, a supporter of unification, was on hand. Billy Mitchell arrived from Washington, where he had been testifying in support of a separate air force before House and Senate committees.[27]

Shortly before 9 A.M., the throaty roar of a dozen engines caught the crowd's attention. Starting honors went to Air Commodore L. E. O. Charlton, British air attaché, who was participating as a courtesy. Unfortunately, Charlton's Bristol fighter developed engine trouble. Lt. J. B. Machle, next in line, took off first at 9:13 A.M. Conforming to the rules, Machle rose to 1,000 feet and circled the field before setting course for the first control point at Binghamton in upstate New York.[28]

Departures were routine until it came time for Lt. Belvin W. Maynard to take off. As he started the Liberty engine of his DH, the flyer's dog Trixie ran up to the airplane, barking and jumping with excitement. Maynard climbed down, picked up the Belgian police dog, and hopped back onboard. He took off with the obviously delighted Trixie hanging over the side of the open cockpit. The crowd cheered with pleasure.

Secretary Crowell took advantage of a lull in the proceedings to speak with the press. "It is beyond dispute," he said, "the greatest aerial contest in the world." Pointing out that the United States lagged sadly behind Europe in the development of aeronautics, Crowell voiced the hope that the race "will awaken people" to the need for increased American effort in this critical area. Deciding to get into the spirit of things, the secretary asked to be taken up for a ride. Mitchell promptly made the necessary arrangements. Sporting borrowed goggles and leather coat, Crowell waved to the crowd as he clambered into the cockpit of a Curtiss biplane. The aircraft taxied to the edge of the field, turned into the wind, and began its take-off run. Just as the wheels left the ground, the engine failed. The Curtiss stalled to the right, a wingtip struck the ground, and the aircraft turned over on its back. After a moment of stunned silence, a crowd rushed out onto the field to find Crowell and pilot M. G. Cleary shaken but uninjured. "That's the shortest flight on record," Crowell quipped to reporters. The secretary said that he was ready to go up again; unfortunately, a "pressing appointment" in the city prevented another flight. He assured Capt. Cleary that the accident was not his fault, and posed for a photograph with the embarrassed aviator before leaving the field.[29]

There was far less excitement in San Francisco. Even the weather— seasonal low clouds and fog—seemed in keeping with the subdued mood. The West Coast contingent of fifteen might have been few in number compared to New York's forty-eight starters, but it did boast several noted flyers, including Maj. Carl Spaatz (assistant air officer for the region), Maj. Dana Crissey (commander of Mather Field at Sacramento), and Capt. Lowell H. Smith (who had flown for Pancho Villa in the early phases of the Mexican revolution). Col. Henry H. Arnold, in charge of military aviation on the Pacific coast, joined a small group of local officials to bid farewell to the departing airmen.[30]

The end of the first day saw Lt. Maynard—dubbed the "flying parson" by the press because he had left a Baptist seminary in 1917 to join the Air Service—clearly in front. Maynard reached Chicago by dark, a distance of 810 miles from New York, while his three nearest competitors spent the night in Bryan, Ohio. Eighteen flyers failed to get beyond Buffalo. These were the fortunate ones.[31]

The eastern half of the transcontinental route, in fact, lay strewn with debris. Commodore Charlton wrecked his Bristol fighter during an emergency landing near Ithaca, New York. Lt. George McDonald's DH-4 suffered a similar fate when he was forced down in Pennsylvania. Lt. D. G. Gish and Capt. Paul de Lavergne, French air attaché, narrowly escaped death when their aircraft caught fire over Livingston County, New York; Gish managed to crash land the DH before flames reached the cockpit. The most serious incident occurred when Col. Joseph Brant crashed during an emergency landing at Deposit, New York, killing his observer, Sgt. W. H. Nevitt.

Meanwhile, the racers from San Francisco had managed to cross the treacherous Sierra Nevada Mountains without incident. Eleven of the fifteen flyers reached Salt Lake City by the afternoon of October 8; they were held there overnight because of poor field conditions at the next control point. Among the last to reach Salt Lake City were Major Crissey and Sgt. Virgil Thomas. Crissey circled the field, waving to the crowd that had gathered to greet the airmen. All seemed in order until the final approach. Crissey came in at an abnormally steep angle; the aircraft stalled, then smashed into the ground. Both occupants were killed.

Maynard left Chicago at first light on Thursday, October 9. Encountering severe turbulence en route to Des Moines, he became airsick for the first time in his flying career. At North Platte, Nebraska, he met and exchanged greetings with the eastbound leader, Capt. Lowell Smith. Maynard continued to Cheyenne, while Smith spent the night in Omaha. The "flying parson" ended the day with a 236-mile lead over Smith, or a little more than two hours flying time.

Casualties continued to mount behind the leaders. Rainstorms east of the Mississippi River caused numerous forced landings, and four aircraft suffered major damage. Lt. A. M. Roberts and his observer survived an especially close brush with death. In an effort to make up time between Buffalo and Cleveland, Roberts elected to fly the direct route, across Lake Erie. His engine failed, and he had to ditch in the water. Luckily, a passing freighter saw the crash and picked up the two men.

Snowstorms over Wyoming led to a fatality in the west. E. V. Wales and William Goldsborough were en route from Rawlings to Cheyenne, flying close to the ground below low clouds, when they encountered a snowstorm. Wales lost forward visibility. Suddenly, a mountain loomed ahead. Wales threw the aircraft into a violent turn, stalled, and dove into the ground. Lieutenant Goldsborough emerged from the wreck with serious injuries, but he managed to walk three painful miles for help. When rescuers reached the wreckage, Wales was dead.

The third day of the race, October 10, began with problems for Lieutenant Maynard, who had hoped to reach San Francisco by sundown. Frosty overnight temperatures at Cheyenne resulted in an ice-clogged overflow pipe that caused the engine to overheat upon starting, damaging the radiator. Sgt. William E. Kline, Maynard's observer-mechanic, made the necessary repairs, but the job took five hours. Maynard ended the day at Saldura, Utah, three control points and 518 miles from his final destination.

Captain Smith continued to lead the eastbound contingent, with Major Spaatz and Lieutenant Emil Kiel in hot—and acrimonious—pursuit. Kiel arrived at Des Moines twenty-four minutes before Spaatz. When the major landed, he protested that Kiel had left the previous control point two minutes before the required thirty minutes for stopovers. The officer-in-charge honored Spaatz's complaint and forced Kiel to wait an additional two minutes at Des Moines. Shortly before nightfall, Spaatz and Kiel caught up with Smith at Bryan, Ohio. New York lay only 560 miles away, and they would have the advantage of the rising sun. Maynard's lead had vanished.

October 10 also saw three serious accidents and one fatality. Maj. A. L. Sneed made an especially hard landing at Buffalo while short of fuel. The DH-4 bounced high in the air, then smacked down on its nose. Sneed's observer, Sgt. Worth C. McClure, catapulted out of his seat, suffering a broken neck which killed him.

Saturday, the end of the first phase of the transcontinental air race, proved anticlimactic. Maynard left Saldura at first light, found ideal weather en route, and arrived in San Francisco without incident at 1:12 P.M. Major General Menoher, Colonel Arnold, and a small group of officials and spectators were on hand to greet the slender, bespectacled aviator, who had just set a new transcontinental speed record.

The eastbound flyers had run into trouble. Smith, Spaatz, and Kiel left Bryan at dawn and headed straight into bad weather. Smith battled rainstorms to Cleveland, but he could not find the airfield.

Coming down to ask directions, he damaged the landing gear and propeller of his DH. Repairs took five hours, putting him out of contention.

Spaatz and Kiel located the field at Cleveland without difficulty, but minor mechanical problems plagued their journey. In late afternoon, Spaatz reached Binghamton where he encountered a brief mechanical delay. Kiel, who landed shortly after Spaatz, was asked to delay his departure until ten minutes after the major left, in deference to his senior. Kiel refused, and both men took off at the same time. Spaatz gained the lead en route to New York, but he landed by mistake at Hazelhurst, adjacent to Roosevelt Field. Discovering his error, he left immediately. But he was too late. Kiel beat him to Roosevelt by twenty seconds.

October 12 was a Sunday, twenty-four hours of rest under contest rules, and time to take stock of the past week's events. A majority of contestants had yet to complete a one-way crossing of the continent, and the race already had claimed five lives (seven, if the death of two flyers en route to the starting point are counted), not to mention numerous injuries. The New York *Tribune*, which earlier had attacked Praeger for unnecessarily risking the lives of air mail pilots, tended to be philosophical about these losses. "Man," an editorial in the *Tribune* announced, "is compelled to pay the toll to a nature which is jealous of his progress." Some of the participants took a less detached view. Major Spaatz (who in 1947 would become the first chief of staff of the United States Air Force) opposed continuation of the race, arguing that no useful purpose would be served by going ahead. If the War Department insisted, he said, then the flyers should return at a leisurely pace via a less hazardous southern route. Lieutenant Kiel was even more outspoken. "No one," he told a reporter, "can make me race back to California. . . . The train will be good enough for me."

Lieutenant Maynard resumed his flight in accordance with contest rules (forty-eight hours, not counting Sunday, after arrival) on Tuesday afternoon, October 14. Spaatz got underway from New York the next morning, followed by Captain Smith. Lieutenant Kiel, who did not receive a train ticket, complained that his aircraft needed extensive repairs and delayed his departure.

Resumption of the race brought a resumption of fatalities. On October 15, Stanley C. Miller died in an attempted emergency landing following engine failure near Evanston, Wyoming. This produced the first severe public criticism of the race. The *Chicago Daily Tribune* led the way, terming the contest "rank stupidity." Even such staunch supporters of the Air Service as Congressman La Guardia spoke out in opposition. But the War Department remained unmoved, and the race continued.[32]

Fate turned against Lieutenant Maynard on October 16, when a broken crankshaft forced him down forty miles west of Omaha. The "flying parson" needed a new engine. Even if he could find one, it normally took about three days to make the necessary repairs. But Maynard was a resourceful and determined young man. He located a Liberty engine in Omaha, courtesy of Captain Francis whose Martin bomber had crashed earlier in the week. Although the Martin had been demolished, one of the engines had escaped damage. Francis had it trucked to Maynard, then arranged for searchlights so the repair crew could work through the night. Sergeant Kline performed a minor miracle, and had the airplane ready to fly in eighteen hours.

An equally determined Smith had become the westbound leader, but he also ran into problems. On the evening of October 15 his aircraft was destroyed by fire in Buffalo when lanterns being used by mechanics ignited a wing. Although he received permission to continue the race if he could find a replacement aircraft, prospects seemed dim until Spaatz arrived on the 17th. It took only a little pleading before Spaatz happily agreed to bow out of the race and turn over his DH to the eager captain. Displaying the resolve that would make him leader of the first round-the-world flight in 1924, Capt. Lowell H. Smith became the first West Coast flyer to complete the round trip, arriving in San Francisco on October 21.

By then, Maynard had already won the race. The lieutenant had no serious problems after Omaha, and he landed at Roosevelt Field in the early afternoon of October 18. Only 1,000 people turned out for the victory ceremony, including the aviator's wife and two young daughters. The girls seemed especially happy to see Trixie, surely the first dog to make the double crossing of the North American continent by air. When asked to explain his success, Maynard credited Sergeant Kline's mechanical feats, good luck, and the fact that he had relied extensively on his compass for point-to-point navigation. General Mitchell took the opportunity to announce that Maynard's arrival marked the end of America's isolation. The race, he said, amply demonstrated the capability of air power. Maynard collected his family and Trixie and went home. Three years later, on September 7, 1922, he met his death while stunt flying at a county fair in Rutland, Vermont.[33]

Although the transcontinental air race disappeared from the front pages of the nation's newspapers with Maynard's arrival in New York, weary contestants kept going until October 31. Thirty-three aircraft completed one-way crossings; only eight managed the round trip. While accidents continued during the final stages of the race, there were no additional fatalities.

Even at a time when flying was a hazardous occupation, Billy Mitchell's great adventure had been costly. The seven fatalities in the race occurred at the rate of one death every 180 flying hours; the Air Service lost seventy-four aviators in cross-country operations during 1919 at the rate of one man killed per 274 flying hours. The announced purpose of the contest was to test the reliability and endurance of equipment. It surely demonstrated that the aircraft of 1919 were far from reliable, and that endurance was more human than mechanical.[34]

The race failed to generate support for the Post Office's planned transcontinental service, as Praeger had hoped. The New York *Sun* led the way in criticizing the proposed coast-to-coast schedule. Taking the accident figures from the race, it calculated that air mail operations would cost the lives of three or four pilots a month. "The Praeger scheme is not progress," an editorial proclaimed; "in light of what happened in the recent race, it is more like homicidal insanity."[35]

Praeger had no choice but to put the best face possible on the Air Service's misadventure, ignore the fatalities and accidents, and hail the race as the forerunner of regular transcontinental operations. "Thanks to the activity and initiative of the Army," he announced, "we have obtained the necessary information as to meteorological conditions, landing fields, and, more than all, as to the intense interest of the people." Actually, the Post Office had learned little of operational value from the military exercise.[36]

CASUALITIES IN OCTOBER were not confined to the Army Air Service. On the 14th, as the military flyers continued their aerial trek across the continent, the Post Office lost one of its most experienced and determined pilots, Lyman W. Doty.

Graduating from the Christofferson School of Flying in 1916, Doty became a professional acrobatic pilot, joined the Army Air Service in 1917, instructed at Kelly Field, and later served as a test pilot. Impressed with his 1,500 hours of experience, Edgerton hired Doty on December 6, 1918. Three weeks later, Doty left New York on the regular mail flight to Washington in an unmodified DH-4. His engine began to miss over Brooklyn, and Doty returned to Belmont. The DH's faulty axle gave way on landing, and the fuselage crumpled. Doty, sitting in the front compartment, was crushed between the gasoline tank and engine. He was unconscious for three days from a skull fracture, and he suffered partial amnesia for another two weeks. Discharged from the hospital in February, Doty took three months to recuperate. In May he failed a flight physical because fractured nasal bones had caused a deviated septum, with possible pressure on the right eyeball that affected distance judgment. Doty sought an operation. It succeeded, and he returned to flying in July.[37]

On the morning of October 14 Doty was en route from Washington to New York, when a caretaker at the Rolling Road Golf Club, Catonsville, Maryland, saw an aircraft flying very low in thick fog. As he watched, it hit the top of a tree, plunged to the ground, turned over, and caught fire. Flames prevented the caretaker from reaching Doty.

Doty's remains were shipped to his home in California, accompanied by pilot Samuel Eaton. Praeger wrote to the young airman's father: "He was dependable, courageous and of the highest integrity, and died at his post of duty. His career is worthy of emulation, and no doubt must be a source of pride to his family." Mr. Doty thanked Praeger "for the kind consideration shown in the hour of trouble, and the courteous care of all that was mortal of my boy." The bereaved father concluded: "He was all I had."[38]

Two weeks later John P. Charlton, Jr., was killed in similar circumstances. Charlton had been with the Air Mail Service for only five days when he took the Washington–New York schedule on October 30. At 2 P.M. inhabitants of Long Valley, New Jersey, heard an airplane approaching from the west. The valley was clear but fog lay on top of the nearby Schuley Mountains and along an elevated ridge to the north of town. The drone of the engine coming out of the fog passed to the east, circled back to the north and west, then stopped abruptly. A search party found the aircraft on the top of the mountain, inverted, tail in the air, and with Charlton's lifeless body strapped into the smashed cockpit. Stanton investigated the accident, concluding "that the pilot lost his bearings in fog and rain, then lost control of the plane and plunged to the ground either in a dive or spin, too steeply to be able to level out in time to avoid crashing to earth."[39]

The bad weather that caused the deaths of Doty and Charlton grew worse as winter approached. December brought to New York the lowest temperatures in fifty years, while January saw unprecedented snowfall throughout the northern part of the country. Radiators and water pumps froze, congealed oil overflowed, and pipes burst. Pilots faced temperatures of $-25°F$ in open cockpits and tried to prevent ice from forming inside their goggles. Performance plummeted from the 98 percent of summer to 73 percent in December (thirty-one trips defaulted) and 69 percent in January (forty-six trips defaulted). Never before had scheduled air operations been conducted in such adverse conditions.[40]

On January 12, 1920, Paul W. Smith left Newark in DH Number 108 for Bellefonte. Noticing a drop in oil pressure, he landed at Laurelton, Pennsylvania, bought five gallons of oil, then took off. As the plane was climbing to 3,000 feet in order to clear the first range of mountains west of Laurelton, Smith's engine quit just as he entered a snow squall. He glided into a tree-filled valley, searching in vain for an open field. Smith cut his switches, turned off the gas, removed his goggles, then stalled over the trees, actuating his pressure fire extinguisher system at the last possible minute. The right wings broke off at first contact with the trees, then the left wings hit. For a brief moment, the DH lay suspended in the trees, twenty-five feet off the ground. Then the nose dropped, and the aircraft slid the remaining distance to the valley floor. Smith jumped clear with two cracked ribs and numerous bumps and bruises; he walked three miles through snow and sleet to the nearest farmhouse.[41]

Edgerton complimented Smith for his remarkable landing. "Such emergencies," he wrote, "mark the line of success or failure as a pilot very clearly and your work on this forced landing displays all the elements for quick and accurate thinking." Take heart, Edgerton concluded, "Spring will soon be here and better times are coming."[42]

But the times did not get better even when winter finally loosened its grip on the land. On March 10 Clayton W. Stoner was en route from Chicago to Cleveland when he flew into a tree during heavy fog and was killed. Twenty days later, Newark's Heller Field claimed a victim when Harry C. Sherlock smashed into Tiffany's brick smokestack. On April 10 Mark C. Hogue was ferrying a Curtiss R-4 to Washington with pilot Richard W. Wright in the mail compartment when the engine threw a rod and caught fire. Wright crawled out on the right wing and tried to fight the flames with a hand extinguisher. Two hundred feet off the ground, Wright either lost his hold or jumped. He landed on his feet in sand, fracturing both thigh bones. The aircraft smacked into a tree, throwing Hogue clear of the burning wreckage. Wright died two days later; Hogue survived.[43]

Nor was this all. On April 11, as Wright lay dying in the hospital, Frederick A. Robinson was thrilling thousands of spectators at Heller Field with his usual—and unauthorized—Sunday afternoon exhibition of stunt flying. Mail clerk Clarence Stapleton, who had never flown before, asked to go along, and Robinson agreed. During the performance, Robinson lost control of the aircraft when Stapleton either fainted or in panic grabbed the control stick of the dual-control JN-4H. The Jenny spun into the ground, striking the Erie Railroad tracks. Stapleton died forty-five minutes later of a fractured skull.

Robinson survived minor injuries to his nose and leg, only to die five months later in another aircraft accident.[44]

"The mail service is almost paralyzed by all of the accidents," pilot Wesley L. Smith wrote in his diary on April 12. "I had to rush out to the field [College Park] at the last minute to fly the mail but [E. Hamilton] Lee showed up just ahead of me and went up. [Randolph] Page came down with the mail [from Newark] after an hour's delay in starting due to nerves. . . ."

Page was not the only one with a case of the "nerves." Later in the week Paul Smith informed Edgerton that he no longer intended to fly. "Due to the several fatal accidents we have had in flying activities lately," he explained, "my wife has insisted that I cease flying at once as the nervous strain to which she is subjected is too much for her to stand." Smith asked for—and secured—a ground position.[45]

Other pilots left the Air Mail Service during this time of troubles, but most stayed on the job. On April 27, when approaching Newark with mail from Washington, Wesley Smith flew into a fog bank and lost sight of the ground. Forced to climb over the fog, he followed a compass course to Heller Field, dipping down through the thinner patches of fog from time to time in an effort to recognize landmarks. After narrowly averting a collision with a church steeple, Smith plowed into trees at the crest of the Orange Mountains. The aircraft caught fire, but Smith managed to crawl free of the wreckage, wrenching his left shoulder, bumping and scratching his head, and knocking the skin off various patches of his anatomy. Four days later, he took his regular turn on the mail run.[46]

Jack Knight was made of the same stuff. En route from Chicago to Cleveland on May 4 when his engine quit, Knight spotted a small field and began to glide toward it. When he was about a hundred yards from the field, a sudden downdraft caused him to lose forty feet of precious altitude. Realizing that he could not make it over a string of telephone and telegraph wires that bordered his chosen landing area, Knight tried to turn around and squeeze into a smaller field that lay directly underneath. The aircraft sideslipped into a crash, tearing the engine loose, breaking the fuselage in half, and badly damaging the wings. Knight smashed his head on the cowling and lay unconscious for five minutes. Luckily, the airplane did not catch fire (Knight had turned off the gas and cut the switches). When Knight came to, he hired a watchman to guard what was left of the airplane, arranged for a train to stop and pick up his eight sacks of mail, then took a trolley car to nearby Cleveland so that he could fly the next day's mail to Chicago.[47]

ON MAY 15, 1920, THE POST OFFICE celebrated the second anniversary of the air mail with a self-congratulatory press release. When operations began, it read, aeronautical experts had been sharply divided about the possibility of operating a regular schedule under all weather conditions. But the air mail's "phenomenal success" had put an end "to skepticism as to the practicality of air transportation." This past winter—"the most severe in some time"—had provided convincing proof that commercial aviation had come of age. Pilots had landed in New York "in gales and snowstorms which tied up harbor shipping" and had flown into Chicago and Cleveland when all other forms of transportation had been paralyzed. Furthermore, the Post Office boasted, "only six pilots have lost their lives while transporting mail." Two successful years of flying the mail meant that transcontinental service was feasible, the Post Office concluded; the route between Chicago and San Francisco would be opened by the end of the summer.[48]

Public relations aside, the Air Mail Service had compiled a remarkable record. Unfortunately, its accomplishments soon slipped from memory. If people recall anything about aviation in the period immediately after the First World War, it is most likely to be the heroic nonstop flight across the Atlantic Ocean by Alcock and Brown (forgetting the U.S. Navy's earlier conquest of the Atlantic in an NC-4 flying boat). Certainly, the transatlantic flights deserve attention—but as harbingers of the future, not as part of a continuing line of development. Historians of commercial aviation emphasize the beginning of passenger service between London and Paris. The importance of the London–Paris service is undeniable; however, this achievement pales in comparison to that of the air mail. George O. Noville, who served as superintendent of the Eastern Division during the winter of 1919–20 and then left for a position with the French company Messagerie Aerienne, was in a position to compare developments in Europe and the United States. "This Paris to London flight," he wrote to Praeger in July 1920, "is child's play, compared to what we went through last winter. . . . I know positively that we have the world beaten as a mail carrying proposition."[49]

7 Transcontinental Air Mail

WHILE AIR MAIL PILOTS battled wind and weather during the winter of 1919–20, Praeger fought the annual battle for appropriations on Capitol Hill. The previous year Praeger had had his hands full with the lame ducks of the outgoing Democratic-controlled Sixty-fifth Congress; this time he had to contend with a Republican majority. The GOP had triumphed in 1918, winning the House by a margin of 240 to 190, and controlling the Senate, 49 to 47. And the Republicans were out for blood. Preparing for the presidential election of 1920, they were intent on discrediting the Wilson administration and all its works.[1]

Praeger bent with the political winds. Appearing before the House Post Office Committee on December 10, he appealed for funds by stressing the economic advantage of the air mail. The Post Office wanted $3,000,000 to operate routes from New York to San Francisco, Pittsburgh to Milwaukee, New York to Atlanta, and St. Louis to Minneapolis via Chicago. Praeger admitted that this might seem like a good deal of money during times of financial stringency, but he pointed out that railway mail service along these routes would cost only $500,000 less. Asked about the ultimate purpose of the air mail, Praeger tacitly acknowledged that Postmaster General Burleson's plans for a permanent government-run service had been abandoned. "We simply want to develop aviation to that point where corporations will come in and run the lines," he told the private-enterprise enthusiastis who now controlled the committee. "Then we will make contracts with them as we do with power boat or steamship lines."[2]

His arguments fell on deaf ears. In early January 1920 the committee voted not to increase appropriations for the air mail beyond the current level of $850,000. If Congress sustained this action, Praeger explained to a friend of the air mail, no extension of current routes would be possible.[3]

Worse lay ahead. During consideration of the postal appropriation bill in the House, Congressman Jasper Napoleon Tincher (Republican, Kansas) raised a point of order. Congress, he said, had never passed a law that authorized the Post Office to operate an air mail service. Technically, appropriations for such an activity were illegal. The presiding officer shocked supporters of the air mail by agreeing with Tincher. He sustained the point of order, and the $850,000 for air mail was stricken from the postal appropriation bill.[4]

The fate of the air mail now rested in the Senate. The Post Office Committee, Praeger knew, was the key. If he could secure its support, the full Senate likely would go along. Also, there was no danger of a point of order because the Senate's rules did not permit such a parliamentary ploy. Once the matter reached the House-Senate conference committee, Praeger expected the wishes of the upper house to prevail, as had happened the previous year.[5]

In testimony before the Senate Post Office Committee on January 29 and again on February 9, Praeger expanded the arguments that he had made to the House committee. Because private capital was not yet available for investment in commercial aviation, he explained, the Post Office was doing the necessary experimental work that would prepare the way for private enterprise. He then produced impossibly optimistic figures to show that mail could be transported by air at less expense than by train! Praeger pointed out to the silent legislators that it would cost $1,043,363 to operate the air mail route from New York to San Francisco for one year. When car space, distribution, clerical and other expenses were taken into consideration, the sum required to move the same amount of mail by rail came to $1,222,803. And there was the matter of speed. Mail would travel by air from coast to coast in fifty-six to fifty-nine hours by daylight flying, and thirty-six to forty hours when night flying was introduced; the fastest rail connections were ninety hours eastbound and one hundred and two hours westbound.[6]

Praeger did not get the $3,000,000 that he wanted, but the Senate did approve $1,375,000 for the New York–San Francisco service. It also authorized the Post Office to contract with private individuals to carry mail by air at a cost (to be funded out of railroad appropriations) not to exceed the cost by rail, and it made available $100,000 to carry foreign mail by air. The House, as expected, approved the Senate version without debate.[7]

The Air Mail Service would survive for another year. Although it seemed for a time that limited appropriations would force the Post Office to abandon the New York–Washington route and defer plans for expansion, Burleson and Praeger were not so easily thwarted. They decided to make an end run around Congress. Section 3 of the Appropriations Act for fiscal 1921 not only instructed the secretary of

war to turn over to the Post Office surplus equipment (including aircraft) that could be used in postal operations, but it also authorized
the postmaster general "to pay the necessary expenses thereof . . . out
of any appropriation for the service in which such vehicles or aeroplanes are used." Since surplus aircraft augmented railway and other
mail service, the Post Office argued that it would be perfectly legal to
spend funds on the Air Mail Service that Congress had appropriated
for railway transportation. Using this rather strained interpretation of
the law, the Post Office would take $1,275,271 out of railway appro-
priations during fiscal 1921 (July 1920–June 1921) to operate the
New York–Washington service and open new routes from St. Louis to
Minneapolis via Chicago. Congress, in time, would have a good deal to
say about this legalistic sleight of hand.[8]

THE GROUP CHARGED WITH PREPARING the Chicago–San
Francisco section of the transcontinental route was a familiar one.
Stanton had returned from field assignment to become chief of maintenance and supplies when Bussler resigned in March; Edgerton remained chief of flying, although he tended to fly less himself (rumor
had it that his wife objected); Jordan—now sporting the title of chief
of construction—retained responsibility for finding and preparing
suitable landing fields; and chief clerk Conner continued to supervise
administrative details with his usual efficiency.[9]

There was only one significant addition to Praeger's "inner circle."
In January Praeger had hired Leon B. Lent as his adviser on aeronautics. A graduate of Stevens Institute of Technology (1897), Lent
had spent twenty years as a mechanical engineer, designing, con-
structing, and operating steam and gas plants, including the huge gas
power plant at the Detroit factory of the Ford Motor Company. In
1915 he formed his own business and produced fire engines. Enlisting in the Air Service in 1917, Lent learned to fly (at age 42), and went
on to command the 122d Aero Squadron at Camp Vail. He was in
charge of Roosevelt Field on Long Island when recruited by Praeger.[10]

By February, Lent (whom Stanton considered the "smoothest talking fellow I ever knew") was general superintendent of the Air Mail
Service, the first to hold this position since the Lipsner imbroglio. His
title, however, tended to be more impressive than his responsibilities.
From his desk outside Praeger's office in the Post Office Building, Lent
gave advice on technical matters and coordinated daily operations,
but Praeger kept him—and everyone else—on a short leash. "He
[Praeger] knew the name of every pilot, mechanic and other employee
down to the watchman," Lent later wrote. "He knew the location and
the condition of every ship in the service. The pile of daily telegrams

which came into the office reporting operations were read by him before finally leaving the office." Conferences about the Air Mail Service were held in the evening. "I can see him now," Lent recalled, "sitting in his office chair behind a desk piled high with papers, with one or both of his feet tucked under him . . . going over the events of the day and planning for the morrow. When he said, 'By Golly, that's what we'll do,' there was no appeal from this decision." That was fine with Lent since he found that Praeger's decisions "were rarely, if ever, in error."[11]

The most challenging tasks faced by Lent and his associates in spring 1920 centered on the continuing search for decent airfields and aircraft. Although the eastern end of the transcontinental route was in fairly good shape (the Post Office had moved in January 1920 from Chicago's Grant Park to more spacious facilities at Checkerboard Field in suburban Maywood, and it had abandoned Cleveland's Woodland Hills Park in March in favor of Glenn Martin Field), preparations to the west lagged far behind schedule. In May Jordan visited Cheyenne, met with the Chamber of Commerce, and outlined plans for the coast-to-coast mail service. Owing to a shortage of funds, he explained, the Post Office expected cities along the route to provide (at their own expense) suitable fields and hangars. The Post Office wanted to stop at Cheyenne, which surely would benefit from its position as a terminus on the air route; however, discussions also were taking place with officials in Laramie, who already had agreed to provide the necessary facilities. Jordan's carrot-and-stick approach worked wonders. In a burst of civic pride, the city fathers of Cheyenne appropriated $15,000 for the privilege of becoming an air mail station.[12]

Jordan went to Reno on May 10 to make his sales pitch. This time he used Carson City to frighten the town's leaders. He even gave them a deadline of September 1 to complete all work. Reno promptly fell in line to the tune of $29,000. Salt Lake City came next. After listening to Jordan's blandishments, the city approved $27,000 for facilities lest Ogden make a deal with the Post Office and reap the economic benefits and prestige that were rightfully Salt Lake City's![13]

For a time, at least, a solution to the aircraft problem seemed at hand. Although the twin-engine Martins that had been introduced on the eastern routes during the winter of 1919–20 were not working out, the Post Office had an alternative—and a far less expensive one. In December L.W.F. Engineering Company turned over to the Air Mail Service the first twin-DH. Working with $18,000 of Post Office funds, L.W.F. had consulted some of the leading aeronautical engineers in the country (including Alexander Klemin, Jerome C. Hunsaker, and Col. Virginius E. Clark) to produce what one pilot later termed "a dreadful abortion of a plane." At the time, however, it appeared impressive. L.W.F. had used parts from surplus DHs to build a twin-engine aircraft that could fly faster and carry twice the mail as the standard DH—or so it seemed.[14]

Initial tests of the twin-DH left postal officials ecstatic. On December 2 Samuel C. Eaton, Jr., flew the prototype on the regular mail run between Washington and New York. Carrying 630 pounds of mail, he made the trip in a record 1 hour 34 minutes (averaging 138 mph); the previous record was held by a DH that had carried 300 pounds of mail at 123 mph. The Post Office hailed the twin-DH as the "greatest forward step made in the development of a small weight-carrying plane." Not only could the aircraft maintain altitude at full weight with a single engine, but it also had a positive rate of climb. No other twin-engine aircraft in the world could boast such performance.[15]

Praeger could hardly contain his enthusiasm. The twin-DH virtually eliminated forced landings for mechanical reasons. It could be used on high altitude routes in the west, and was economical to operate, cutting ton-mile costs in half. Also, conversions cost only $7,000 each, far less than a Martin ($31,600 each). Terming development of the twin-DH the "single greatest contribution during the year, commercially as well as mechanically, of the Air Mail Service to commercial aviation," he ordered fifteen of the fabulous planes.[16]

L.W.F. scarcely had started work on the contract when an even more dazzling aircraft appeared on the scene. In early June Lent received a telegram from an old friend, aircraft designer William B. Stout: "Do not fail to investigate Junkers planes now at Mineola. Performance

The twin-DH: "a dreadful abortion of a plane . . . ."

nearly twice that of present ships. Had marvellous flight Friday." Stout's telegram announced the arrival in the United States of the world's first all-metal airliner.[17]

Hugo Junkers pioneered the development of all-metal construction, producing a series of "armored" ground attack airplanes for the German Air Force during the First World War. After the Armistice, Junkers switched to civilian projects. His F.13—far ahead of its time in structural and aerodynamic design—first flew on June 29, 1919. In place of the linen-covered wooden frame and externally braced wings of traditional biplanes, Junkers designed a cantilever monoplane with a duraluminum structure that was covered with corrugated dural skin. The F.13 featured a semi-enclosed cockpit with dual controls and an enclosed cabin that could seat four passengers. Powered by a single 185-hp B.M.W. IIIa six-cylinder, water-cooled, inline engine, it cruised at 87 mph and had a maximum speed of 110 mph.[18]

Aware of this advanced German technology, former munitions manufacturer John M. Larsen hoped to make a good deal of money by exploiting it. Early in 1920 the Danish-born American citizen left for Europe with consultant Charles B. Kirkham, a noted aeronautical engineer and designer for Glenn Curtiss. After visiting the Junkers works at Dessau, Larsen purchased the American patent rights to the F.13. He planned to import several planes, then manufacture them in the United States under the designation JL-6.[19]

In May Larsen displayed two imported JL-6s at the Pan-American Aeronautical Congress in Atlantic City. Their clean lines and all-metal construction placed them in a class apart from all contemporary airplanes. At one point, a JL-6 flew from Atlantic City to New York (130 miles) with five passengers and baggage in eighty minutes. Not only did the aircraft demonstrate remarkable performance, but it also seemed to promise a new level of safety. "These metal machines," Larsen announced, "eliminate the aviator's greatest fear—fire."[20]

Word of the unique airplane quickly spread. Maj. William C. Ocker inspected a JL-6, hailed it as the "airplane type of the future," and recommended that the Army Air Service purchase one for further investigation. Lt. Col. Harold E. Hartney, chief of training and operations, flew a JL-6 at Bolling Field and came away properly impressed. "This should be a very successful plane," he wrote to his superiors, "for night bombardment, day bombardment, high altitude photography, night pursuit and especially low bombardment." The general opinion of knowledgeable airmen, *U.S. Air Service* summarized, "is that the metal monoplane has greater speed, less fire risk and greater inherent invulnerability; in short, that it will have a far-reaching, if not revolutionary, effect on flying."[21]

Brig. Gen. Charles T. Menoher, chief of the Army Air Service and chairman of the Interservice Aeronautical Board, became a strong advocate of the marvelous metal flying machine. "There can be no question," he wrote to Larsen, "that the all-metal plane is here and it behooves the rest of us to get busy in the near future if we hope not to be left entirely behind in the race." Wearing his Aeronautical Board hat, Menoher recommended that development of the all-metal aircraft "be rapidly proceeded with by both services." The Army and the Navy promptly purchased six aircraft from Larsen.[22]

Was it any wonder, Lent recalled, "that we soon found ourselves thinking of this remarkable plane in terms of its use in the mail service?" He recommended to Praeger that the Post Office purchase several JL-6s to try on the eastern half of the transcontinental route. If they proved satisfactory, he planned to shift them to the west in order to take advantage of their high-compression B.M.W. engines (Lent believed that a fully loaded JL-6 "could easily climb 18,000 to 20,000 feet"). With the beginning of the fiscal year approaching (July 1), Praeger had enough money to strike a deal with Larsen. For the bargain price of $200,000, the Air Mail Service acquired eight JL-6s, four additional engines, and a long list of spare parts.[23]

Impatient as ever, Praeger decided to begin service on the Chicago–Omaha segment of the transcontinental route while waiting for the new aircraft to appear and new facilities to be constructed further to the west. On May 12 newly hired pilot Homer W. Johnston was returning to Chicago after a survey flight to Omaha, carrying divisional superintendent William J. McCandless as passenger, when he became lost. While Johnston was attempting to land near Oskaloosa, Iowa, to get directions, a strong gust of wind blew the aircraft onto its back, slightly injuring Johnston but crushing McCandless's skull.[24]

Despite the death of McCandless, the Chicago–Omaha route opened three days later, on schedule. Lack of aircraft, however, caused constant interruptions. "Please get ships immediately and as fast as possible to Chicago for the Omaha Division," Praeger wrote in June to chief of maintenance Carleton A. Parker. "We *must* reestablish and keep up that service."[25]

In July Praeger fixed September 1 as the starting date for the transcontinental route. The Post Office leased Hazelhurst Field, Hempstead, Long Island, from the Curtiss Aeroplane & Motor Corporation to serve as the eastern terminal of the service (Newark's Heller Field remained the terminal for the New York–Washington route). Praeger selected Andrew R. Dunphy, a tough former Marine, to head the Omaha–Salt Lake City division (with headquarters at Cheyenne), and named Jordan as superintendent of the Salt Lake City–San Francisco section. The two men had only a few short weeks to complete preparations for fields, requisition and arrange shipment of spare parts from the air mail warehouse in Newark, coordinate schedules with postmasters along the route, assign mechanics, helpers, and pilots, and look after the numerous minor items that so often spell the difference between success and failure.[26]

Praeger told Edgerton to set up a point-to-point radio network along the route, instructing him to keep within a budget of $20,000. Together with Eugene Sibley, a former Navy radio operator now in charge of radio operation and maintenance, Edgerton plotted a tentative network on a map. The Post Office already operated stations at New York, Bellefonte, and College Park, and the Navy likely would allow the use of their stations at Cleveland, Chicago, and San Francisco. Eight new stations would have to be established at St. Louis, Omaha, North Platte, Cheyenne, Rock Springs, Salt Lake City, Elko, and Reno—and at a cost of no more than $2,500 each.[27]

Edgerton began by trading airplane linen for 6-KW generators. Then he and Sibley located a supply of surplus 2-KW arc transmitters (intended for shipboard use) and SE-1420 receivers. Tests proved that the mismatched 2-KW transmitters could withstand the full 6-KW input and produce a powerful signal. "They were perfect for our purpose," Edgerton observed.[28]

Edgerton next started on a tour of cities. Armed with blueprints, he attempted to persuade city officials to provide land and a building free of charge in return for potential emergency communications. At his first stop, Omaha, the enthusiastic mayor called a meeting of the city council, which promptly voted to erect a building on city land. Edgerton selected the site, then worked with the city engineer and power company to make sure that the project got underway without delay. Although the visit cost "two precious days," it was well worth the time. Word of what had happened at Omaha quickly spread to other cities. "Each success induced others," Edgerton recalled. "In what had become a triumphal procession, the publicity proceeded me as my journey took me from city to city along the transcontinental [route]. Within ten days all work was in progress."[29]

Meanwhile, Sibley was recruiting operators, drawing up operation manuals and station instructions, and testing frequencies. He moved the station at College Park to the Post Office Building at 11th Street and Pennsylvania Avenue in downtown Washington. An antenna covered the entire roof of the hugh structure, while a complete radio station was installed in the outer room of a new suite of offices high up in the northeast tower. "Gradually," Edgerton noted, "order appeared out of chaos." It was a great day when all stations checked in, their dots and dashes spanning the miles. The network was rough in spots, but it *was* in commission—and within budget.[30]

Edgerton recalls Praeger's smiles when he reported the network in operation. The postal official pored over the financial statements, savoring the details. "He fidgeted in the elevator en route to the new radio station," Edgerton wrote, "examined the apparatus with awe, then scribbled out a message of congratulations to all stations. I will never forget the little man as he rubbed his hands in glee." Only later did Praeger tell Edgerton that he originally had grave doubts about the success of the project because of the lack of time and money.[31]

Praeger had less cause for glee as the new airplanes came into service. Trouble began when Walter Stevens left Chicago for Cleveland in a twin-DH on August 11. Starting a turn, about seventy-five feet off the ground, Stevens felt something snap on the right side of the aircraft. The twin-DH whipped over to the right, then dove for the ground. Stevens survived a controlled crash with a "slight cut on the end of my already badly scarred nose," but the aircraft was demolished.[32]

The next day, as officials were looking into the cause of Stevens's crash, Frederick Robinson reported serious problems with his twin-DH. Both engines vibrated excessively, and climb performance was "extremely poor." The airplane—which was supposed to climb on one engine—"has not enough reserve power [with both engines] to be safe in bad air conditions."[33]

The unwelcome news continued. Oscar B. Santa Maria was cruising at 2,000 feet in a twin-DH when something gave way. There was terrific vibration from the left engine, the left wing dropped, and the aircraft settled into an involuntary spiral. The left wingtip hit the ground, the twin-DH turned over, and was wrecked. Santa Maria escaped serious injury.[34]

Stanton had seen enough. From recent reports, he informed Praeger on August 23, "it would seem . . . that there is something radically wrong in the construction of this ship." He recommended that the twin-DHs be withdrawn from service and thoroughly tested. Praeger could only agree.[35]

The Junkers JL-6s also made their eagerly awaited appearance in August. Max Miller flew one of the first aircraft and came away disappointed about its performance, finding it "rather a slow ship" that was hard to fly at maximum speed because of excessive vibration. Even more serious problems surfaced during the last two weeks of August. JL-6s made at least nine forced landings during this period—four because of radiator leaks, three because of fuel leaks, and two because of clogged fuel strainers.[36]

The ill-fated JL-6.

On August 31 Wesley L. Smith and Edward M. Haight left Chicago for Cleveland in a JL-6. It was a clear morning, and there was a good tail wind. Smith climbed to 8,000 feet, where the high compression engine (with fixed propeller) performed best. One hour out of Chicago, a fuel leak developed. As it did not seem serious, Smith decided to continue to Cleveland. Forty-five minutes later, just south of Toledo, the engine quit. Thinking a tank had run dry, Smith was in the act of switching tanks when his feet were engulfed by flames that had burned through the metal floor. He describes what happened next:

We had no parachutes so I turned the fuel off and put the airplane into a vertical sideslip to the right, since I was in the left seat and the flames were coming from the vicinity of the carburetor on the left side of the engine. We had lost 1500 feet before the flames subsided so that I could see anything and the airplane was in a vertical dive then. The Junkers had no adjustable horizontal stabilizers and were normally balanced in flight by pumping fuel into or out of a tank located in the tail section and by moving the mail forward or backward in the cabin. The elevators were blanketed by the thick monoplane wing at that speed so they were ineffective but I managed to get the airplane into a spiral by violent action on the ailerons and rudder. This reduced the airspeed until I had elevator action again and I was able to flatten the airplane's path to a normal glide at 4000 feet.

All the fields within gliding distance were covered with either standing corn or shocked corn so I chose a field of standing corn as one that would damage the airplane least in the forced landing. Haight was uninjured so I sent him into the cabin to move all of the mail sacks to the rear . . . and to stay there himself to help hold the tail down when we landed. The airspeed indicator had been wrecked by that initial fast dive but I managed to stall the airplane safely into the standing corn which was about six feet high. The propeller stopped horizontal and was not damaged when the airplane finally went up on its nose as it skidded to a stop and then settled back to its normal upright position amidst the standing corn. The tires were the only casualties beside the fire damage.

Thanks to his leather gear—helmet, long coat, and puttees—Smith's injuries were confined to nasty facial burns. Haight flagged down a passing car, and Smith was taken to a nearby town for treatment.[37]

The next day, Max Miller and Gustav Reierson left Hazelhurst Field, New York, for Cleveland at 5:30 A.M. in JL-6 Number 305, carrying eighteen pouches (600 pounds) of mail. Inexplicably, two hours later the airplane was observed over Morristown, New Jersey—only twenty miles distant—by Postmaster W. B. Haley of nearby New Vernon. As it passed from view, Haley noted that the plane was flying low and that its motor was cutting out and backfiring. Minutes later, farmers saw flames coming from the front of the aircraft and someone (Reierson?) throwing out mail sacks. The flames then billowed out, engulfing the entire front end of the JL-6. The aircraft nosed over and dove into the ground. The gas tanks exploded, blowing the wings off. Fire consumed the fuselage until it collapsed in a broken heap of metal. The bodies of Miller and Reierson were found inside the pyre, horribly burned.[38]

If Praeger had a favorite pilot, it was Miller. Born in Norway in 1893, the son of a Norwegian mother and English sea-captain father, he was raised in England until age eleven, and then came to the United States. He joined the Army at eighteen and served two three-year enlistments. A civilian flying instructor at San Diego during the war, he was the first civilian pilot hired by Praeger in 1918. Tall, slender, with curly blond hair and blue eyes, Miller did not drink but constantly smoked cigarettes. He loved to ride horses, and he could sit for hours and watch the flight of birds. He quit the air mail after Lipsner's resignation but rejoined a few months later. In February 1919 he married Daisy Marie Thomas, who worked in Praeger's office.

Max Miller.

A superb airman, skilled and determined, he set the standard for other pilots—and won Praeger's respect and admiration. Upon learning of his death, Praeger told the press: "Max Miller was the best pilot who ever sat in a plane." [39]

The New York *Sun*, fierce opponent of the air mail, had a field day with a tragedy. "Mr. Burleson's most spectacular fad continues to be indulged in at ghastly expense," it announced on September 3. The death of the two men was simply another example of the Post Office's "great mistake." The small savings in time to advance the mail was not worth the human price; the air mail, in fact, amounted to nothing but publicity for Burleson. The *New York Times*—and most other newspapers—took a less extreme position. The accident did not prove that aviation was unsafe, the *Times* remarked; however, it did demonstrate that the all-metal airplane was not the answer to fire aloft. [40]

The transcontinental air mail route, already postponed until September 8, could not have started under less favorable conditions.

Praeger nevertheless was determined to begin without further delay. With the twin-DHs and the JL-6s grounded, the trusty DH-4s would have to do.

Randolph Page took off from Hazelhurst Field at 6:41 A.M., September 8, on the first leg of the new coast-to-coast air mail service. There had been a short delay because the 400 pounds of mail (16,000 letters) for the inaugural flight would not fit into the fuselage compartment of the DH. Page had solved the problem by filling a suitcase with the excess and strapping it to the wing of his aircraft. Through an operation like an airborne Pony Express, with relays of several planes and pilots, the mail reached Iowa City by dark. The next day it arrived in Cheyenne. On September 10 James P. Murray carried the mail over the Rockies, arriving in Reno as the sun set. Edison E. Mouton completed the trip on September 11, landing at San Francisco's Marino Field at 2:33 P.M. The Post Office's schedule had called for a coast-to-coast transit in fifty-four hours; the first trip had taken nearly eighty-three hours. But this was a minor disappointment. As *Aerial Age Weekly* announced: "September 8, 1920, will go down in history as the great day when the epoch-making event, the first trip of the transcontinental aerial mail, took place."[41]

PRAEGER HAD A RIGHT TO BE PROUD of the Post Office's great accomplishment. In January he had faced hostile congressmen and fought for the continued existence of the Air Mail Service. Winning that battle, he had prodded, cajoled, and encouraged a group of talented subordinates into building an airway from Chicago to San Francisco across 1,900 miles of prairies, deserts, and uncharted mountains. His search for safe and efficient aircraft had been a bitter disappointment, but he had persevered where lesser men would have surrendered. While the development of the New York–San Francisco airway was the result of the combined efforts of many dedicated, hard-working individuals, it is difficult to believe that there would have been a transcontinental air mail as early as 1920 without Otto Praeger.

But Praeger had no time to rest on past laurels. Establishing the transcontinental route had been one thing; making it into a successful operation would be another. In many ways, as Praeger soon found out, the easy part was behind him. Winter lay ahead.

8 End of an Era

THE JUNKERS MONOPLANES that were grounded after Max Miller's crash soon were back in service, their fuel system problems apparently eliminated. On September 14, 1920, Walter Stevens and mechanic Russell Thomas were flying between Cleveland and Toledo in JL-6 Number 308. The two men were in a festive mood: Stevens had just signed a contract to work for the Glenn L. Martin Company and was on his last trip for the Post Office, and Russell had been married four days earlier. Stevens was known as a careful pilot. Perhaps it was because he was older than his brother airmen; at age thirty-seven he was considered an "old man" by the youthful flyers of the Air Mail Service. He had once worked for the railroad in his native Colorado (and had lost a finger in an accident); he had been a policeman, a prospector, and he had taught himself to fly. Joining the Army as a private at the outbreak of the war, Stevens gained a commission and became a flying instructor. He knew engines, and he knew how to rig an airplane. He used to teach his students how to calculate drift on cross-country flights by watching the shadow of the airplane's wings over the earth. "He took his work seriously," one former student recalled, "though not himself; he had no use for the 'lunatic fringe' which, he believed, retarded the country's flying progress." Employed by the Air Mail Service in June 1919, Stevens quickly gained the respect of his superiors and was selected to fly the new Martins. He was a natural choice for the troubled Junkers.[1]

As the flight neared Pemberville, Ohio, observers on the ground saw the JL-6 overhead at 1,000 feet and heard its engine cutting in and out. Suddenly, it burst into flames. The airplane continued level for about a half mile, then plunged into a clover field at a 45° angle and blew up. The largest remaining piece of the Junkers measured three feet by eight feet. The charred bodies of the two crew members were identified by the respective sizes of their torsos.[2]

The second fatal Junkers accident in two weeks provoked widespread criticism of the Post Office. Even such supporters of the air mail as the *New York Times* called for an inquiry into the situation. "While it is gratifying to know that the Post Office is doing remarkable things in establishing long-distance air mail routes," the *Times* noted, "success at an unnecessary cost of life would be deplorable."[3]

Responding to the growing public outcry, Praeger created a new engineering section and placed Lent in charge. With headquarters in New York and reporting directly to Praeger, Lent had a mandate "to design, devise and create improvements of all characters in the planes, equipment and aviation facilities used by the Air Mail Service, for the safer, more effective and more economical operations of Air Mail planes." His most pressing task was to look into the problem with the Junkers.[4]

Working with experts from the Air Service, Lent concluded that the Junkers accidents had been caused by a defective fuel system. There being no octane gasoline in 1920, the JL-6 burned antidetonation benzol that had to be piped through rigid lines and connections because it would burn through rubber. The engine vibrated badly, causing fuel leaks. As no provision had been made for the leaking benzol to escape, fuel and fumes collected beneath the engine. Fuel starvation caused the engine to backfire, exploding the benzol that had accumulated in the engine compartment.[5]

Lent came up with four major modifications. He wanted a scoop to carry the carburetor intake ouside the fuselage, new fuel lines with flexible hose connections, a venting system to allow fuel to escape from the bottom of the fuselage, and an improved ignition system to prevent short-circuiting and the discharge of sparks within the engine compartment. "These recommendations are being put into effect as rapidly as possible," the Post Office announced on October 1, "and the machines should be ready for flying again very shortly."[6]

But casualties continued to mount, even without help from the trouble-plagued Junkers. On September 27 Frederick Robinson was carrying mail on the New York–Chicago route, flying low in bad weather, when he struck heavy cables that spanned the Susquehanna River at Millersburg, Pennsylvania. The DH-4 slammed into the riverbank, killing Robinson. On October 15 Bryan McMullen departed from Chicago for Omaha in poor weather that got worse as he flew westward. Forced down near Batavia, Illinois, he stalled while trying to squeeze into a small field, and spun into the ground. McMullen died when the gas tanks exploded.[7]

While Praeger and Burleson fended off public criticism over the escalating human cost of carrying mail by air, Stanton struggled to keep the far-flung aerial routes in operation. Since taking over as superintendent of operations following Lent's reassignment, Stanton had had to deal with the problems caused by too rapid expansion. With only forty-eight airplanes and fifty pilots (up from twenty-one in May), maintaining scheduled service was no easy task.[8]

The Newark–Washington line caused the least problems, operating at nearly 100 per cent. "Too much praise cannot be given the pilots," Stanton wrote to Praeger on October 18, "as the weather has been just as bad on this route as on others." The new route from Chicago to St. Louis, opened on August 16, was another bright spot. Using seven Curtiss JN-4Hs that had first flown between New York and Washington in 1918, divisional superintendent Carl F. Egge had compiled an impressive record under difficult circumstances. Although only 270 miles separated Chicago from St. Louis, the short-range Jennies required a refueling stop at the Army field at Rantoul, Illinois. Also, the St. Louis landing area, located in a city park (Forest Park), was small and soft; in rainy weather, Egge had to move to Scott Army Field at Belleville, Illinois, twenty-six miles to the south. The aging airplanes were constantly breaking down and spare engines were in short supply. Stanton recognized these problems, and he planned to replace the JN-4Hs as soon as better equipment became available.[9]

The transcontinental route caused the most headaches. Bad weather and equipment shortages caused by sending aircraft to the Mountain

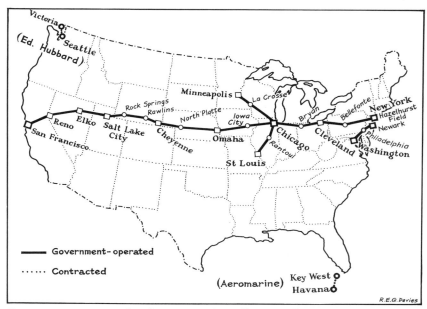

Government-operated and contract air mail routes, January 1, 1921.

and Pacific divisions hampered performance east of Omaha, although Stanton was not displeased with overall results. On the western routes, however, a series of accidents conspired to put aircraft out of service faster than they could be shipped from the east. In mid-October only nine of twenty assigned airplanes were available to fly sporadic schedules between Cheyenne and San Francisco.[10]

Part of the explanation for the poor performance of the two western divisions lay in the nature of flying conditions. Daily operations over such forbidding terrain had never before been attempted, with the Cheyenne–Salt Lake city segment posing an especially difficult challenge for men and machines. Leaving Cheyenne (6,000 feet above sea level), pilots had to climb to 9,000 feet immediately after take-off in order to cross the Laramie Range, only twelve miles away. They then flew over the Continental Divide, following the Union Pacific tracks through the Laramie Valley and across the Medicine Bow Range to a refueling stop at Rock Springs, 231 miles from Cheyenne. The worst part of the trip—the rugged Wasatch Range—now lay ahead. Looking at what was described by geologists as a "maturely dissected complex mountain area," pilots saw a maze of canyons, deep narrow defiles, and sharp crested ridges that offered little hope of a survivable forced landing. Coaxing their DH-4s to 12,000 feet, postal airman often faced the worse weather in the country, including sudden snowstorms, treacherous mountain waves, subzero temperatures, and near-jetstream winds. James F. Moore expressed the feelings of many fellow pilots when he wrote to chief of flying D. B. Colyer (who had replaced Edgerton): "Would like to say that [route] from here [Cheyenne] to Salt Lake City is a good one to kill the men that you seem to have a grudge against or want to see out of the way."[11]

James P. Murray could testify to the hazards of the route. He left Salt Lake City on the afternoon of October 18 on the regular mail run to Cheyenne. Crossing the Wasatch Range without difficulty, he followed the Union Pacific tracks from Rock Springs to Wolcott. Ahead lay Medicine Bow Range, cloud-covered except for the top of 12,000-foot Elk Mountain. A gap in the clouds lured Murray to the south. He tried to slip through the mountains to the Laramie Valley, but the gap closed, and he found himself in the middle of a blinding snowstorm. Unable to turn around, he had to continue eastward, hoping to clear the range and reach lower ground. He could see nothing but trees directly below and a white wall ahead—and the trees kept getting closer. "I gradually climbed the machine full engine," Murray reported, "until I felt it stalling and the treetops not more than fifty feet away." Finally, he had no option except to cut the switches and pancake into the treetops. The aircraft was a complete write-off but

Rock Springs, Wyoming, 1920. Pilot James P. Murray on the first transcontinental flight.

Murray crawled out of the wreckage with only minor cuts and bruises.

The accident took place at 4:45 P.M. Murray decided that he would have to walk to safety. With the aircraft's compass smashed, he used the setting sun as a reference and trudged eastward for an hour through two feet of snow until he reached a frozen lake. With snow still coming down, and darkness approaching, Murray took refuge under a cedar tree for the night. The next morning he found an abandoned cabin but no food. Walking into the rising sun, he came across a road with a signpost pointing to Arlington, fourteen miles distant. "The first eight miles seemed endless," Murray wrote, "with not much perceptible thinning out of the snow." Eating occasional handfuls of snow, he continued on his way. The tired and hungry pilot reached Arlington at 2:45 P.M., having walked eight hours to cover the fourteen miles.[12]

John P. Woodward was not as lucky. Flying DH Number 178 on November 7, he ran into a snow squall near Tie Siding, forty miles west of Cheyenne. Blinded by the storm, he smashed into the side of a hill and was killed.[13]

Conditions on the Pacific Division, if anything, were worse. The route from Salt Lake City to Elko consited of 204 miles of swampland, stunted sagebrush, alkali, and desert. Nearing Elko, pilots had to locate Secret Pass in the East Humbolt Range in order to cross over the mountains at 9,500; terrain on both sides of the pass rose up to 13,000 feet. The landscape along the 233 miles between Elko and Reno was no better; in fact, half the route passed over the most desolate and uninhabited stretch on the entire coast-to-coast route, with the nearest human being often more than seventy-five miles away. Leaving Reno, pilots headed southwest and climbed to 10,000 feet, or higher, before turning west to cross the mighty Sierra Nevadas. For ninety miles, a contemporary noted, pilots flew over a "genuine no man's land of mountains, cliffs, canyons, small lakes, creeks, and trees, and general rotten flying territory—the most dangerous on the Transcontinental route." Descending into the Sacramento Valley, pilots then had to contend with the fog that so often blanketed the San Francisco Bay area.[14]

Rugged terrain and bad weather were not the only problems on the Pacific Division. Lt. R. N. Kelly of the Air Service had been asked by Superintendent Jordan to pass on the flying ability of applicants for positions with the division. Kelly found that half had not flown an aircraft within the past year, and some had never been in a DH-4. Furthermore, he reported to his superiors in Washington, the new pilots were sent out without proper training, and they lacked such basic equipment as suitable maps that showed terrain contours. Ground facilities also left a good deal to be desired, with the field at Reno unsafe even for experienced DH pilots under ideal conditions.[15]

Despite a series of accidents (none fatal) and frequent delays and cancellations, Praeger retained his faith in Jordan. Chief clerk Conner, however, took a different view, reminding Praeger that it was Jordan who had insisted on starting service on the Pacific Division before preparations were completed. Now, in the wake of criticism for the division's failings, he was telling newspaper reporters how he had begged in vain for a two weeks' delay. "I am sorry not to share your opinion of Jordan," Conner concluded. "I think he is an excellent promoter but a very poor administrator."[16]

Praeger no doubt appreciated Jordan's firm attitude toward the pilots. "You will please understand," Jordan informed all personnel of the Pacific Division, "that we are here to fly the mail, and that we do not allow weather to interfere with us." This was Praeger's position, but with important differences. Praeger would listen to Stanton and Edgerton, and he often softened his attitude; Jordan lacked—or failed to heed—such counsel. Also, Praeger never held his pilots in contempt; Jordan did. "Sometimes a flyer will not fly," Jordan explained to a congressional committee, "and very often they are bilious or have been up the night before, they will not fly. They would attribute it to the weather or something else. They are as temperamental as a lot of chorus girls, and about as easy to handle."[17]

The new year, 1921, opened with more trouble on the Pacific Division. On January 4 Stanhope S. Boggs took off in fog from San Francisco's Marino Field, bound for Reno. He was seen in and out of fog as he spiraled upward. At 2,000 feet his engine quit, forcing Boggs to put his aircraft into a flat glide. He broke out of the fog at fifty feet, directly over the center of the city. Attempting to land on Gough

Street, in the block between Hay and Fell, he hit trolley wires and nosed into the ground. Fire broke out as Boggs tumbled out of the cockpit, uninjured. He ran to the nearest fire alarm box, about a hundred feet away, and pulled the lever.[18]

Faced with extensive—and adverse—publicity caused by the accident, Jordan promptly convened a Board of Inquiry. Its members included three employees of the Air Mail Service, Maj. Henry H. Arnold (Air Officer of the Ninth Corps District), and Supervisor R. J. Welch of San Francisco. The Board met in San Francisco on January 5, examined Boggs and other witnesses, and issued their findings at the end of the day. The Board held Boggs responsible, criticizing his judgment for attempting to fly in unsuitable weather. The report continued: "This condemnation, however, is greatly modified by the fact that the traditions of the United States Mail Service makes the expedition of the mail imperative at all times, and the Board believes that Pilot Boggs had this idea strongly in mind when he started on his flight."[19]

Boggs immediately attacked the Board's findings. His father, Edward M. Boggs, went even further and fired off a telegram to Postmaster General Burleson that charged Jordan with "incompetence and culpable mismanagement." Pilots on the Pacific Division, he claimed, were required to fly unsuitable and defective aircraft in dangerous weather. Jordan's "profane and insulting abuse of pilots who fail to perform the impossible," the senior Boggs concluded, should make it clear that he was "temperamentally unfit" for the job. He demanded an immediate investigation. Frank M. Silva, U.S. District Attorney in San Francisco, agreed. The situation, Silva informed Attorney General A. Mitchell Palmer, warranted a "thorough investigation" by the Justice Department.[20]

Jordan leapt to his own defense. "I understand some hysterical gentleman wants me investigated," he telegraphed Praeger. Jordan freely admitted that he compelled pilots to go out in bad weather, and he assured Praeger that he would continue to insist that they fly under such conditions "when there is a chance of going through." He pointed out that there had been no injuries to pilots on the Pacific Division. Engine trouble of course would continue "so long as gas engines are used."[21]

Jordan did not lack supporters. Edward M. Barber, field manager at Elko, said that the criticism of Jordan was not justified. No airplanes had been dispatched from Elko in impossible flying weather. Furthermore, 70 percent of the forced landings on the division had been due to the bad judgment of pilots or carelessness of mechanics. Jordan, in fact, "deserves commendations for maintaining schedules under most

Dressed for winter operations, pilot Paul P. Scott stands in front of his DH at Salt Lake City, Utah.

difficult conditions." Arlen C. Nelson, field manager at Salt Lake City, agreed, terming Jordan's supervision at all times "efficient and agreeable." No pilot, however, sang his praises.[22]

Burleson declined to launch an investigation. The Justice Department ruled that the matter fell within the jurisdiction of the Post Office. Praeger sustained the findings of the Board of Inquiry and directed that "necessary disciplinary action" be taken against pilot Boggs for his public statements attacking the Board and its conclusions.[23]

THE BOGGS INCIDENT CAME in the midst of Praeger's annual battle for appropriations. The outlook for the air mail was far from promising during the winter of 1920–21. Republicans controlled both houses of Congress, and a lame-duck President occupied the White House. Warren G. Harding's victory in November meant that Praeger was a member of an outgoing administration; he was fighting for the money that his Republican successor would spend. One other factor complicated an already difficult situation: under new House rules, all money bills had to go through the Appropriations Committee. Instead of facing the Post Office Committee, whose members tended to favor the air mail, Praeger would have to contend with a budget-minded committee that was led by the formidable Martin B. Madden.

Destined to play a major role in the story of the air mail in the years to come, Congressman Madden liked to be known as one of the watchdogs of the Treasury; many observers considered him the "grimmest of them all." He was a self-made man, and he took pride in his struggle to overcome adversity and rise to a position of wealth and influence. Madden came to the United States from England at the age of five. His family settled in Cook County, Illinois. Forced to leave school at age ten, he took a job as a water carrier in a limestone quarry in Lemont, where he worked hard all day, then went to night school and studied business. At age nineteen he was general manager of the quarry, and by the time he reached thirty-five (1890) he was president of Western Stone Company, one of the largest producers of building stone in the world. Madden became involved in Chicago city politics in the 1890s, serving on the city council. Elected to the U.S. House of Representatives in 1904, he concentrated on financial issues. "He evinced a good deal of ability," his biographer has noted, "rather unusual activity, and a high degree of party regularity, the last marked by occasional streaks of intelligent independence." In 1921 he would help frame the bill to create the Bureau of the Budget. Seven years later, Madden would die of a heart attack while working at his desk in the room of the Appropriations Committee.[24]

Stressing economy of operations, the Post Office asked the Appropriations Committee for $3,500,000 to carry air mail during the fiscal year beginning July 1, 1921. Praeger again tried to argue that it cost no more to move mail by air than by rail. Madden was not impressed. According to his calculations, the price by air was $5.35 a ton-mile, compared to 7¢ a ton-mile by rail—and current schedules did not reveal any great savings in time. The experience gained from flying the transcontinental route "may be of some value from a military standpoint at some future period in our history," Madden admitted, "but from a purely mail standpoint I do not think the expenditure is justified." The committee voted $1,250,000 to continue the coast-to-coast service as an aeronautical experiment; there would be no funds for expansion.[25]

Even this modest allocation ran into trouble on the floor of the House. The air mail did not lack supporters, but Congressman Tincher was determined to make the same point of order that he had made the previous year. "The proposition of carrying mail by aero-

plane," he told the House on January 8, "is a failure from the standpoint of efficiency . . . and from the standpoint of economy." Pointing
out that the Air Mail Service lacked statutory authority, the Republican farmer-lawyer from Kansas made his point of order. The chair
sustained it, and funding for air mail was stricken from the postal appropriation bill.[26]

In the past, Praeger had had to work hard to mobilize support
to save the air mail. But not this time. Newspapers and magazines
throughout the country sprang to the Post Office's aid, attacking the
House and vigorously defending the Air Mail Service. The Spring-
field *Republican* spoke about Madden's "absurd misstatements" about
the high cost of air mail, while the *New York Times* noted the recent
establishment of air mail service between Peking and Tientsin and
raised the dire prospect that the United States would "fall behind
China in the expedition of mail" if the House's position was sustained
by the full Congress. Editorial support came from the *Omaha Bee*,
Pittsburgh *Post*, Dayton *News*, Atlanta *Journal*, New York *Tribune*, San
Francisco *Bulletin*, and other newspapers.[27]

Perhaps the most spirited and cogent defense of the Post Office appeared in *The Outlook*. This widely circulated magazine took issue with
charges that the Air Mail Service was extravagant, impractical, and
dangerous. To say that it cost more to carry mail by air than by rail was
no argument; it cost more by train than by boat, yet mail did not move
along the Erie Canal. Also, people who claimed that the air mail was
impractical belonged "in the class of those who ridiculed the Clermont
as she puffed her way slowly but surely up the Hudson." *The Outlook*
conceded that flying the mail carried an element of risk, but this was
not a good reason for abandoning the service. "The challenge," it argued, "is not to eliminate the dangers by leaving the air, but by fully
conquering it." Pointing to the broad national interest at stake in promoting the development of aeronautics, the magazine emphasized
that the Air Mail Service constituted the only encouragement by government to civil and commercial flying. "The country not only can afford its Air Mail," *The Outlook* concluded, "it must afford it."[28]

The influential National Advisory Committee for Aeronautics also
took a strong position in support of the Post Office. "The Air Mail
Service," it observed, "has given the best demonstration of the practicality of the use of aircraft for civil purposes and, in the face of many
obstacles, has accomplished remarkable results of real and permanent
value to the Nation at relatively slight cost." NACA urged Congress to
continue this "experimental laboratory" for the development of civil
aviation. Forwarding the resolution to Capitol Hill on January 24,

President Woodrow Wilson wrote: "I concur in the opinions expressed by the National Advisory Committee for Aeronautics and endorse its recommendation for continuance of the Air Mail Service."[29]

Congress went along. On January 25 the Senate Post Office Committee approved $1,500,000 for the air mail. The full Senate adopted the recommendation without debate. Later, the Senate-House conference committee accepted the Senate version of the Post Office appropriation bill, but it reduced funds for the air mail to $1,250,000.[30]

Although the air mail would continue for at least another year, congressional criticism of the Post Office did not slacken. In early February James B. Corridon of the Division of Railway Adjustments appeared before the House Post Office Committee in connection with a request for a $35,000,000 supplemental appropriation to cover an expected deficiency during the current fiscal year. Chairman Steenerson (termed by Lent "a man with a bitter hatred for the Postmaster General") used the occasion to question the department's juggling techniques for funding the air mail. Corridon acknowledged that up to January 31 the Post Office had transferred $448,000 from railroad appropriations to air mail, and he cited the legislative authority under which it had been done. Steenerson was not impressed, terming the statutory provisions "a kind of joker." Under the Post Office's interpretation of the law, the department's entire appropriation could be used for air mail if Burleson wanted to do so. This was *not* the intent of Congress, he grumbled, little realizing that the transfer of funds had just begun. By the end of the fiscal year—on June 30—$1,275,000 would be switched from rail to air.[31]

The Post Office came under heavier attack later in February when Congress heard from its Joint Commission on Postal Service. This body had been created by the Post Office appropriations law of 1920 and was one of many investigatory efforts sponsored by a Republican majority in Congress that was intent on embarrassing the Democratic administration. The commission took a special interest in the air mail. Senator Charles E. Townsend, chairman of the group, believed that the stated costs for the service had been "juggled," and he was determined to get to the bottom of the matter. "This Commission must look into the Air [Mail] Service," he told his colleagues, "and we must find out what it costs."[32]

Between February 21 and 23, the commission heard the report and testimony of Charles A. Howard, vice-president of the consulting firm (W. B. Richards & Company) that it had hired to investigate the Air Mail Service. Howard reviewed the abortive attempt by the Post Office to collect a surcharge for air mail. In May 1918 a bill had been rushed through Congress that levied a charge of 24¢ per ounce for air mail on the Washington–New York route. With declining demand for the service, the rate was reduced on July 15 to 16¢ an ounce for the first ounce, plus 6¢ for each additional ounce. The public remained unconvinced that the service was worth the price, and the Post Office lowered the fee on December 15 to a flate rate of 6¢ per ounce. But even this reduced rate failed to attract business. On July 18, 1919, the Post Office gave up and eliminated the surcharge. Air mail would cost 2¢ per ounce, the same as regular first-class mail; there would be no special stamp or marketing, and no guarantee that a letter would go by air.

At present, Howard stated, aircraft usually carried one pouch of first-class mail (1,600 to 2,500 letters), with the balance of the load in "ballast" mail, mostly circulars. It cost $29.65 to fly one pouch of mail from New York to Washington and $56.84 from New York to Cleveland. Comparable rail costs for a closed (unsorted) pouch were 15¢ and 41¢. Between April 1 and November 31, 1920, air mail from New York to Washington arrived on average fifty minutes late at the Main Post Office, saving only forty minutes over train mail. "We recommend an immediate discontinuance of the Washington–New York route," Howard testified. "It saves no time."

Howard also had done a detailed analysis of performance on the New York—Cleveland line. According to his calculations, performance on this route from April 1 to December 31, 1920, was 55 percent, much lower than the Post Office's figures. He had divided the number of trips made over the entire route by the number of trips scheduled; the Post Office based their performance figures on the number of trips started. With this "bookkeeping" device, an airplane could return in five minutes or be forced down along the way and have the mail go by train, and it still would be counted. In addition, the average delay on published schedules for the trips actually completed was three hours and thirty-three minutes, resulting in little savings in time over train mail. Howard was not prepared to make a recommendation about the transcontinental line without further investigation. Also, he refused to draw any broad conclusions about the viability of the Air Mail Service, emphasizing that the report dealt with the Service "purely from a post-office standpoint." Despite Howard's caution, the thrust of his investigation inevitably led to the conclusion that flying the mail had little value as a postal proposition.[33]

CONGRESSIONAL CRITICISM was the least of the Post Office's problems with the air mail. February 1921 also marked a tragic end to efforts to keep the twin-DH and JL-6 in service.

The Post Office had opened a 344-mile feeder line between Chicago and Minneapolis (with a refueling stop at LaCrosse, Wisconsin) on November 29, 1920. Praeger had assigned eight modified twin-DHs to the route and asked Superintendent Egge to give them a fair try. Led by E. Hamilton Lee and Lawrence H. Garrison, Egge's pilots made a valiant effort, but poor performance and mechanical problems continued to plague the aircraft.[34]

Egge was watching as Kenneth M. Stewart and mechanic George J. Sampson took off from Minneapolis for Chicago on February 3 in twin-DH Number 130. About six miles from the field, just after crossing the Minnesota River, the left engine failed. Unable to fly on one engine, the aircraft began losing attitude. Stewart corrected for the torque with right rudder while looking for a suitable landing field. Distracted, he failed to notice that the nose of the aircraft was rising. Sampson frantically pounded on the fuselage in an effort to attract his attention, but it was too late. The aircraft stalled and crashed, killing Stewart; Sampson survived with a broken arm and leg. Shortly thereafter, the twin-DHs were withdrawn permanently from service.[35]

The JL-6s, with modified fuel systems, also came back into operation during the winter of 1920–21. Restricted to the flat Chicago-Omaha portion of the transcontinental route, the novel all-metal airplanes continued to have problems. Dean Smith made sixteen trips in the Junkers, all ending in forced landings. Most happened when the benzol—with a freezing point of 41° F—crystallized and choked the fuel strainer, starving the engine of fuel. "I was mortally afraid of the things," Smith recalled.[36]

Following Stewart's fatal accident, JL-6s were assigned to the Chicago–Minneapolis route. William M. Carroll, Hiram H. Rowe, and Robert B. Hill flew the maiden trip on February 8, leaving Chicago for Minneapolis in Number 301. Bad weather forced a landing at Clinton, Wisconsin. The mail was sent by train, and the airmen ferried the craft back to Chicago later in the day.

The same three men tried again the following morning. Pilot Rowe and mechanic Hill occupied the cockpit, while pilot Carroll sat in the cabin with the mail sacks. An hour and a half from Chicago, the wind-driven fuel pump failed, causing severe backfiring. The crew landed at Lone Rock, made repairs, and took off. But the problem persisted, forcing a return to Lone Rock. Carroll was content to remain on the ground until a mechanic could be sent to repair the pump, but Rowe and Hill wanted to continue to the air mail field at LaCrosse, seventy miles distant, using a hand pump to get fuel to the engine if the wind-driven pump failed again. Carroll reluctantly agreed.

The Junkers climbed off the field at Lone Rock at 4:50 P.M. and arrived over LaCrosse at 5:45. The weather was clear, with the sun be-

ginning to set. People on the ground watched the silvery airplane
make a complete circle of the field at 2,000 feet, then turn around and
come in to land from the northeast. At 500 feet and three-quarters of
a mile from the field, the aircraft suddenly plunged into the ground
and exploded. Spectators rushed to the scene. Carroll lay on the
ground, about five feet from the right wing, holding an empty fire
extinguisher in his right hand. He was dead. Rowe and Hill were
found pinned in the cockpit, their bodies burned beyond recognition.[37]

The accident generated a storm of criticism. There were rumors of
deliberate sabotage, of German plots for revenge. Gov. J. A. O. Preus
of Minnesota called for an investigation. In an angry telegram to
Burleson, he announced that he would prefer to have the Chicago–
Minneapolis air mail service discontinued rather than see the "sacrifice of further lives by its operation with obsolete equipment." In
Washington, the House passed a resolution requesting Burleson to
provide the Post Office Committee with full information on the accident, while Congressman Steenerson sharpened his axe by schedul-
ing hearings to look into the situation.[38]

Superintendent Egge's preliminary report failed to explain the
tragedy. "It seems," he wrote, "Pilot Rowe lost control of the ship in a
glide, side-slipped and nose-dived." He was certain that there had *not*
been a fire in the air. Mechanics said that the engine had sounded
good when the Junkers circled the field. Carroll probably grabbed the
fire extinguisher when he realized that the aircraft was in trouble; it
was possible that a leak or the heat had emptied it. "The cause of the
accident," Egge concluded, "is a mystery."[39]

Praeger established a committee to make a more detailed inquiry.
Unfortunately, its work only testified to the embryonic character of accident investigation. The report of Jordan, pilot Randolph Page, and
Maj. William C. McChord of the Army Air Service, agreed in factual
detail with Egge's preliminary findings, but reached a dramatically
different conclusion. The most likely cause of the accident, it stated,
was an engine backfire that caused the fuel accumulated under the
engine to catch fire. As the fire was driven back toward the cockpit,
the reasoning went, Rowe tried to land but lost control of the aircraft
and crashed. Jordan later admitted that the conclusion was pure speculation. No one had observed a fire while the aircraft was in the air;
witnesses differed on whether or not a backfire had occurred; no au-
topsies had been done on the bodies of the crew. How could his committee reach the finding that a mid-air fire had caused the crash?
"From our general knowledge of the ship and what was likely to oc-
cur," Jordan explained.[40]

History has demonstrated that the Junkers all-metal monoplane

(JL-6/F.13) was not inherently dangerous. Between 1919 and 1932, 322 F.13s were built, saw service with airlines around the world, and had great success. As one authority has pointed out, the F.13 was "one of the real pioneers of early commercial air transport." But the early model used by the Post Office had proved a failure. Four JL-6s had crashed, killing seven crew members. The Post Office quietly disposed of the remaining four aircraft for $6,044.[41]

THE AIR MAIL SERVICE had been battered severely by critics who attacked it as uneconomical and unsafe. These assaults angered Praeger. With his term of office nearing an end, he looked for a way to show everyone how far aviation had come since May 1918, to demonstrate the potential of the air mail. Praeger finally decided to make a dramatic gesture: he ordered the mail carried from coast to coast by day *and* by night.[42]

The Post Office's record-breaking effort got underway on February 22 when two airplanes started out at opposite ends of the country, each carrying 350 pounds of mail, on a schedule that called for the transcontinental run to be made in thirty-six hours or less. The westbound sections, however, soon came to grief. Heavy icing over Pennsylvania caused Elmer G. Leonhardt to make a forced landing that damaged the tailskid and axle of his DH; he could not continue. Ernest M. Allison pressed on through the bad weather to Cleveland, where he transferred the mail to Walter J. Smith. Smith reached Chicago by mid-morning, but a combination of rain, snow, and fog to the west made it impossible to continue. If Praeger was going to make his point, the eastbound mail would have to get through.[43]

Farr Nutter and Raymond J. Little departed from San Francisco at 4:30 A.M.* Flying mostly in darkness, they crossed the Sierra Nevadas at altitudes reaching 18,000 feet, and landed at Reno shortly before 7 A.M. Samuel C. Eaton and William E. Lewis flew the mail to Elko in good weather, then changed to waiting airplanes for the flight to Salt Lake City. Eaton took off without incident at 9:31 A.M. Seven minutes later, Lewis followed. However, the recently hired pilot stalled his DH when 500 feet off the ground, crashed, and was killed. His mail pouches were gathered up, the broken ones turned over to the local post office, and the unbroken ones put aboard a standby aircraft. William F. Blanchfield got underway two minutes before noon.[44]

Eaton reached Salt Lake City at 11:30 A.M. and gave the mail to James P. Murray. En route to Cheyenne, Murray's DH developed an oil

*All times are local here and throughout this book.

leak, and he had to land at Rawlings. The leak was fixed, but Murray did not reach his destination until 4:57 P.M. Meanwhile, Blanchfield had arrived at Salt Lake City and passed his mail to Topliffe Paine, who landed at Cheyenne an hour after Murray.[45]

Frank R. Yager took Murray's mail to North Platte, arriving at 7:48 P.M. Jack Knight—sporting a nose that had been broken the previous week when he had made a forced landing on the side of a mountain east of Laramie—was waiting to take the mail to Omaha, but an ignition problem delayed his departure until 10:44 P.M. Flying by compass through broken clouds and catching only an occasional glimpse of the ground, Knight found Omaha at 1:10 A.M., February 23. By this time, Harry G. Smith already had arrived from Cheyenne with Blanchfield's mail.[46]

The mail had reached Omaha, but it seemed fated to go no further. The weather to the east was bad, and the only pilot available who knew the Omaha–Chicago route refused to fly. At this point, Knight stepped forward and volunteered. He had never been over the route

James H. ("Jack") Knight tests the radiotelephone.

by day, much less by night, but he did know Chicago. He studied a map while his DH (Number 172) was being serviced, then took off at 1:59 A.M.

Knight set a compass course to overhead Des Moines, 140 miles away, en route to a fueling stop at Iowa City. "It was dark as hob up there," he said later. Heavy clouds obscured the moon, producing a "sense of isolation that's hard to describe." An hour and five minutes after take-off he sighted the lighted dome of the state capitol as he passed over the southern edge of Des Moines. A layer of white clouds began to drift under him and Knight descended from 5,000 feet to 100 feet in an effort to keep sight of the ground. "Flying was pretty bad at this altitude," he noted. "The air was rough and valleys were packed with fog. Next I began to get snow flurries. . . ." He picked up railroad tracks that seemed headed in the right direction, followed them as closely as possible, and hit Iowa City "right on the nose." Now he had to find the airport. "I flew all around, in and out the town, dodging steeples and looking for that field." Ten anxious minutes later, he spotted several red flares on the ground. "I judged as well as I could the general characteristics of the field," he recalled, "and then by more luck than skill made a perfect landing at 4:45."[47]

While the DH was being refueled, Knight telephoned Chicago for a weather report. It was still bad. He had a sandwich and smoked several cigarettes while waiting for an improvement. He finally departed at 6:30 A.M. At first all went well, and Knight's main problem was to stay awake. He reached the Mississippi River at Clinton, Iowa, and met fog in the river valley. Unable to get underneath, he climbed to 5,000 feet, trusting that there would be clearer weather over Illinois. His faith was rewarded. After crossing the Fox River, he began to pick up familiar landmarks in the suburbs of Chicago. Then he spotted the airport. At this point, his trusty Liberty engine missed. "But as I was within gliding distance of the field," Knight remembered, "I said, 'Just spit, old boy, we're here!'" He landed at 8:40 A.M., completing what one newspaper hailed as a "feat without parallel in civil aviation."[48]

John O. Webster flew the mail to Cleveland, hugging the ground beneath low clouds. Battling snow and sleet, Ernest Allison finished the trip to New York, landing at 4:50 P.M., February twenty-third. Word was flashed to Washington, and there were reports of "great jubilation" in the Post Office.[49]

CONTINENT SPANNED BY AIRPLANE
MAIL IN 33 HRS 20 MIN

The front-page headline in the *New York Times* fulfilled Praeger's highest hopes. Mail had been carried the 2,666 miles between San Francisco and New York in 25 hours 53 minutes flying time at an average speed of 103 mph. The total elapsed time of 33 hours 20 minutes compared to a previous best transcontinental mail record of seventy-two hours by airplane and four and a half days by train. "There are critics who think that the Post Office Department's air mail service is dangerous and costly," a *Times* editorial stated, "but nothing ventured, nothing gained. The modern world demands efficiency and speed; aviation is international and competitive. The United States has distanced all countries in transportation of mails through the air."[50]

An obviously elated Praeger agreed, hailing the achievement as the "most momentous step in civil aviation." He termed Jack Knight's flight—over an unfamiliar route in darkness, through snow and fog—a "demonstration of the entire feasibility of commercial night flying." Orders had been given, he announced, for signal beacons and field lighting to be installed from Chicago to Cheyenne. The Post Office would begin regular night flying on May 1.[51]

IF NIGHT FLYING WOULD BEGIN IN MAY, Otto Praeger would not be there to supervise it. On March 3 Praeger and nine other senior postal officials hosted a farewell dinner for Postmaster General Burleson at the University Club in Washington. The men dined on filet of Potomac bass, braised Smithfield ham, and roast Maryland squab.[52] There is no record of what remarks were made at the dinner, but it seems likely that Burleson and Praeger at least touched on the air mail. Perhaps they recalled that winter morning only three years earlier when Burleson, looking out his office window, had asked if a regular air mail service could be maintained. Not really knowing what he was getting into, Praeger had said yes. He had made good on his promise.

The statistics for air mail under Praeger were impressive. Between May 15, 1918, and March 15, 1921, the Air Mail Service flew 1,683,589 miles and carried 1,559,269 pounds of mail. There had been 1,494 forced landings—up to February 28, 1921—half due to weather and half due to mechanical problems. (See Appendix B for statistical information.)

Considerable progress had been made in establishing the airplane as a legitimate vehicle of commerce. The Post Office had proved that airplanes could fly over long distances on a regular schedule, airways had been built, essential operational procedures developed, and cost information compiled. The Air Mail Service had functioned as a laboratory for practical experimentation, leading to improved fire protection and ignition systems, and better flight instruments; important tests had been made on radio aids to navigation. The wartime DH-4 had been turned into a trustworthy airplane, and various other designs had been tested (with poor results).

Progress had not come cheaply, as least in human terms. Although the Post Office produced statistics to show that Air Mail Service fatalities per miles flown were fewer than those in Great Britain or Canada, the toll in lives was no less appalling. Twenty-two crew members (eighteen pilots and four mechanics) had died during the past thirty-four months; two employees had perished while riding as passengers, and two mechanics had been killed when hit by propellers during attempts to start engines (a constant danger). The *New York Times* put it best:

> *Aviation owes a great deal to Otto Praeger . . . who has been indefatigable in establishing mail routes . . . but American aviation owes even more to the brave youngsters . . . who have attempted what has often seemed to be the impossible in flying according to schedule in all weather.*[53]

9 Time of Troubles

WARREN G. HARDING HAD LED the Republican party to a massive victory in the election of 1920. The former newspaper editor and lackluster politician from Ohio captured an unprecedented 60 percent of the popular vote; the GOP gained control of 303 of the 435 House seats and dominated the Senate by a margin of 59 to 37. Harding had struck a responsive chord when he told the people:

> *America's present need is not heroics, but healing; not nostrums, but normalcy; not revolution, but restoration; not agitation, but adjustment; not surgery, but serenity; not the dramatic, but the dispassionate; not experiment, but equipose; not submergence in internationality, but sustainment in triumphant nationality.*

Americans were tired of great crusades and good causes, both foreign and domestic. Suffering from severe inflation, troubled by strikes, Red scares, and race riots, they yearned for the seeming stability and tranquility of the past. More than anything else, one historian has pointed out, the vote revealed a "craving for what was described as a 'return to normalcy.'"[1]

Aware of his own limitations, Harding announced that he would seek the "best minds" to help govern the nation. Some of his senior appointments met this standard. For example, Charles Evans Hughes served with distinction as secretary of state, while Herbert C. Hoover used his considerable administrative skills to revitalize the Department of Commerce. On the other hand, Secretary of Interior Albert B. Fall and Attorney General Harry M. Daugherty fell far short of the mark. The new postmaster general, Will H. Hays, ranked somewhere in between.

A teetotaler and Presbyterian elder, Hays had pursued a legal career following his graduation from Wabash College in 1900. As so often happens, law led to politics. Hays began with local volunteer work, rising to the chairmanship of Indiana's GOP in 1914. Energetic and hardworking, the diminutive lawyer (5'6", 115 pounds) became head of the national party organization in 1918. Although the postmaster general traditionally had charge of dispensing party patronage, Hays had no intention of playing the role of political hack. "The postal establishment is not an institution for profit or politics," he said when he took office; "it is an institution for service." Hays pledged to reduce waste, promote efficiency, increase employee morale, and expand the merit system.[2]

Of all the postal problems facing the new administration, the state of the Air Mail Service bothered Hays the most. President Harding had made clear that his first priority would be to slash government expenditures, and he had cautioned department heads against creating deficiencies in the current budget. Hays was not at all happy to learn that the air mail had nearly exhausted its appropriation and would need additional funds. He opposed the "tremendous cost" of the service and believed that the Post Office should be relieved of supporting an enterprise of dubious postal value.[3]

On March 19, 1921, Hays expressed to Secretary of War John W. Weeks his disappointment about the lack of a "close relation" between the air services of the two departments. While the air mail had value "per se," the controlling element should be its contribution to the national defense. Hays wanted the "closest possible contact" with the Air Service. Indeed, he went on, "the activities of the Post Office Department might with propriety be more or less controlled by the War Department." He suggested that an officer from the Air Service be detailed to discuss the matter with the Post Office.[4]

Military airmen reacted with enthusiasm. Ever since the Armistice, they had wanted to take control of the Air Mail Service but had been opposed by a determined Otto Praeger. Now, the prize seemed about to drop into their laps. Lt. Col. J. E. Fechet, head of the Training and Operations Group, already had formulated ambitious plans to introduce night flying, obtain more efficient aircraft, develop radio, and expand service. Maj. Gen. Charles T. Menoher, chief of the Air Service, liked the idea. A closer relationship with the Air Mail Service would promote efficiency by eliminating needless duplication of facilities and programs; also, the postal operation could be developed into a potential Air Reserve. Menoher ordered Maj. Maxwell Kirby to investigate the situation and make a recommendation.[5]

Secretary of War Weeks wrote to Hays on April 14 and expressed his support of a closer relationship with the Post Office. There was no doubt, Weeks said, that cooperation would promote the "efficiency of the Air Service as a whole and best provide for having available in time of emergency adequate personnel and material for the Air Service's part in National Defense." Major Kirby would be calling at the Post Office to gather information for a report to General Menoher on how to implement the desired relationship.[6]

Kirby had no sooner begun his survey when Hays was given additional cause to be rid of the troublesome Air Mail Service. On April 21 Elmer R. Vanatta—in violation of standing orders against stunting in mail planes—decided to put on a show for spectators at Mitchel Field. Taking off in a DH, he attempted a 180° vertical turn when fifty feet off the ground. The plane sideslipped, hooked a wing, and crashed. Severely burned, Vanatta died nine days later.[7]

A second fatality occurred on April 29. J. Titus Christensen left Chicago at 7:05 A.M. with the eastbound mail. The weather worsened as he approached Cleveland, and Christensen landed twelve miles southwest of Sandusky to call ahead for a weather report. Cleveland reported a ceiling of 400 feet and visibility of three-quarters of a mile. Deeming this acceptable, Christensen took off and tried to stay underneath the overcast as he wound his way towards Cleveland. Following the Cuyahoga River, he flew into a trap. Christensen found himself in a pocket of clear air over the river, with tall buildings on each bank and high bridges ahead and behind. He threw the DH into a tight circle, trying to clear the obstacles, but he did not make it. He crashed into railroad tracks, about twenty feet from the river, and was killed instantly.[8]

The cycle of three was completed on May 7. Walter M. Bunting was coming in for a landing at Rock Springs, Wyoming, when he dove into the ground and was killed. There was no apparent cause for this accident, although Dean Smith offered one possible answer. Smith pointed out that Bunting had been badly injured in a crash the previous winter. Despite the fact that his coordination seemed poor when he got out of the hospital, he insisted that he was fit and ready to fly. As the Air Mail Service lacked the kind of close medical supervision that might have prevented a premature return to flying status, Bunting was taken at his word. He had been on his first trip when he was killed.[9]

The accidents were bad enough, but Hays had even more to worry about as he tried to unload the Air Mail Service on the military. In late April a recently discharged pilot, Carroll C. Eversole, delivered a statement to the Post Office in which he charged that thirteen pilots had been killed during the past year because of "gross mismanagement, inefficiency, and criminal negligence." Eversole also offered supporting statements from rigger Paul G. Rickel and from Christensen (written shortly before his death). Hays quietly ordered an investigation "to determine whether there had been any misconduct." [10]

Postal inspector Charles H. Clarahan began taking testimony in Chicago on May 7, with Eversole appearing as the star witness. The Junkers that had crashed in February 1921, Eversole claimed, had left Chicago with multiple fuel leaks because mechanics had been drunk during an overhaul of the tank. In fact, "midnight frolics" were common at Chicago, creating dangerous conditions. Management at all levels was to blame for the sad state of the Air Mail Service, forcing pilots to fly in bad weather with inadequate aircraft and wasting the taxpayer's money by purchasing such expensive fiascos as the Junkers and the twin-DHs. [11]

Clarahan tried to maintain secrecy, but the newspapers soon got wind of the story. On May 13 the *Chicago Daily Tribune* ran an eight-column banner headline on page one:

BLAME AIR CHIEFS FOR DEATHS

Hays immediately telegraphed Clarahan to extend his investigation to every air mail field in the country. With great fanfare, he promised to prosecute all members of the Service against whom charges of misconduct were substantiated. [12]

Charges and countercharges soon filled the press. Earl C. Zoll, who had taken over as general superintendent following Lent's resignation, labeled the accusations "absolutely false"; the air mail was being efficiently operated. "The charges are preposterous," Divisional Superintendent Majors announced, "and are simply the malice of former employees who have been waiting for a chance to attack the service because they are no longer in it. . . . We welcome investigation." Pilot William Hopson said that he had never seen a drunken pilot or mechanic on Checkerboard Field. Furthermore, the story about the fuel leaks in the Junkers was not true; he had examined the airplane before it took off and it was in perfect condition. "Eversole has been a bolshevik for months," Hopson said, "going around attempting to stir up trouble in the shops and among the pilots." [13]

The newspapers learned that Eversole had been fired following a parachute jump that officials said was unnecessary. On February 18 Eversole had bailed out of a twin-DH shortly after leaving Minneapolis. The incident had received wide publicity. "For the first time in the history of aviation in this country," one periodical stated, "an emergency escape has been made from a disabled aircraft through the means of a life pack or parachute." Eversole gave reporters a dramatic account of the incident: The right engine had begun to vibrate, causing the ship to go into a nosedive. Struggling in vain as the twin-

DH started to porpoise wildly, he finally had no choice but to use his Floyd Smith Company parachute. "The recent deaths in this division caused me to mention the value of parachutes to field officials," he told reporters. "I was informed a parachute was available for any pilot that wanted one. . . . I do not hesitate to say to you that it is my firm belief I would not be here today if I had not seen fit to use it." [14]

Air mail officials—and fellow pilots—had their doubts about Eversole's story. Eversole had come out to the field several hours early on the 18th, checked how the parachute was packed and how it fitted, then donned one for the first time. He took off, circled the field a couple of times, then jumped. The aircraft, engine idling, glided down and nearly landed itself before going through a fence and into a ditch. Most people believed that Eversole had been paid by the parachute manufacturer. He might have gotten away with it, Dean Smith has observed, "if he had waited til he was well out on his run, for the twin-DH was such a horrible plane one would tend to believe anything bad about it." Under the circumstances, however, Eversole was dismissed. [15]

Clarahan completed his investigation of the Air Mail Service at the end of May. He found no criminal behavior, and there were no prosecutions. Nonetheless, the Post Office dismissed six employees in Chicago, including Divisional Superintendent Majors. Outside of Chicago, only Divisional Superintendent Jordan got the axe. [16]

There is good reason to believe that Majors—and others—had been fired because Postmaster General Hays was looking for scapegoats. In March 1922, following Hays's departure from office, Majors asked to be reinstated. Postal officials examined the record, noting that Clarahan had recommended that Majors be removed for incompetence, gross carelessness, inefficiency, drunkenness, and disgraceful conduct on and off the field. However, all accusations had been made by Eversole and had not been corroborated by disinterested witnesses. Majors was not rehired, but the Post Office cleared his record by changing "removed" to "resignation" in the official files. [17]

In the midst of the public furor created by Eversole's accusations, Major Kirby delivered his report on the Air Mail Service to General Menoher. Air mail personnel, he told Menoher on June 7, were making every effort to insure the success of the operations, but efficiency was "extremely low" because of the absence of aeronautical experience on the part of management. The general superintendent, five divisional superintendents, and eight of nine field managers lacked pilot training. Also, most mechanics had not been trained for airplane work, aircraft were not properly inspected, and many ships in daily use should be condemned.

Kirby believed that the Air Service could cure these ills. He recommended that the military take charge of the equipment, maintenance, and operation of the air mail. All executives in operational positions should be replaced by individuals with flying backgrounds, airplanes should be rebuilt and repaired in Air Service repair depots, and pilots should be hired from those on the Air Service Reserve list.[18]

Although Brig. Gen. William Mitchell, now assistant chief of the Air Service, remained as enthusiastic as ever about military control of the air mail, other officers on Menoher's staff were beginning to have their doubts. Maj. William F. Pearson summarized their growing reservations in a lengthy memorandum of June 20. Congress, he pointed out, would likely appropriate the same amount of money for the Air Service for fiscal 1922 as it had the past year. Yet the military would be expected to operate the Air Mail Service in addition to its other duties. The Air Service already was short of personnel, and it would be impossible to divert people to the new task. Furthermore, it was no more logical for the military to take over the air mail than to assume control of the railroads or telegraph lines. "About all we could get out of it in taking over the Mail Service," he argued, "would be to have unloaded on us criticism relative to the efficiency of the service which has been heaped upon the Post Office and obtain no resulting benefit to the Air Service."[19]

In light of the economic realities of the Harding administration, Pearson's arguments made perfect sense to Menoher. He buried Kirby's report and informed the War Department that the Air Service had no wish to assume responsibility for the air mail.[20]

Hays was not prepared to give up without a fight. On June 27 he sent President Harding a file of correspondence relative to plans for closer coordination between the postal and military air service. "I think something must be worked out on this," he advised Harding. As usual, the President failed to act. With the military unwilling to take over the air mail, the Post Office was stuck with the task.[21]

HAYS SELECTED EDWARD H. SHAUGHNESSY to succeed Praeger as second assistant postmaster general. Although he knew little about aviation, Shaughnessy had an extensive background in rail transportation. Born in 1882, he found his first job at age sixteen as a telegrapher with the Chicago & Northwestern Railroad. He remained with the company until May 1917, slowly rising through the ranks from train dispatcher to trainmaster to assistant division superintendent. Volunteering for military service in 1917, Shaughnessy went to France where he took over operation of the military railroad network in the Verdun section of the western front. More responsible commands followed, and he finished the war as acting deputy director general of transportation for the AEF. He returned to the United States in September 1919, a lieutenant colonel with the Distinguished Service Medal. After a brief stay with the Chicago & Northwestern, he resigned to become assistant director for transportation of the American Petroleum Institute. His motives for accepting the government position are not recorded, but one suspects that he was attracted by the challenge of the job.[22]

Shaughnessy believed that the government should get out of the air mail business and allow private enterprise to do the job. However, he soon learned that existing legislation did not encourage commercial operations. Congress in 1920 had authorized the Post Office to contract for air mail with private individuals or companies "at a cost not greater than the same service by rail," with funds to come out of appropriations for railroad mail. In September 1920 the Post Office had awarded contracts for three routes to Alfred W. Lawson, the sole bidder. Lawson had proposed to operate, for one year, service between Pittsburgh and St. Louis ($147,000), New York and Atlanta ($300,000), and New York and Chicago via Pittsburgh ($236,000).[23]

Publisher of the first popular aviation magazine in America (*Fly*, 1908–1910), Lawson had established an aircraft company in Green Bay, Wisconsin, during World War I and built a few single-engine trainers. Primarily a promoter and organizer, he attracted several talented designers, including Vincent J. Burnelli and John Carisi. After the war, the Lawson Airplane Company produced the first multi-engine passenger aircraft to be designed in the United States. Acclaimed by one historian as a "historic milestone on the road to the commercial airliner," the C-2 was a twin-engine biplane with an enclosed cabin that could carry twenty-six passengers over a distance of 400 miles. Lawson demonstrated the airplane during the summer of 1919. Aware that it would be impossible to make money under the terms of the Post Office contract for air mail, he hoped to profit by combining mail and passenger service.[24]

In November 1920 Lawson had asked the Post Office for an extension from January to May 1921 in beginning operations on contract routes "for the reason that a much better service can be established in the spring of the year than in the middle of the winter." Also, Lawson said that it was taking more time than first estimated to secure proper landing fields and equipment. Asked for additional information on his plane, Lawson replied in December that he had made arrangements for the construction of ten C-2s, each designed to carry 1,500 pounds of mail and 4,500 pounds of passengers or express. Two airliners were "practically completed," and the other eight would be ready on May 1. Also, he had designed and was ready to start production on twenty smaller aircraft, capable of carrying 1,000 to 2,000 pounds of mail. Plans for securing landing fields were "nearly complete," while applications from 300 qualified personnel were on file. The airline would be organized shortly, with Lawson as director general and a consulting board of "five of the very best aircraft men in this country." It would be in the best interests of all concerned, Lawson concluded, for the extension to be granted.[25]

Painfully aware of the problems associated with starting an air route, a suspicious Praeger had ordered Carl Egge (superintendent of the St. Louis–Minneapolis line) to investigate Lawson's claims. The Lawson Airplane Company, Egge reported in late December 1920, occupied an office in the First National Bank Building in Milwaukee. Factories consisted of two large buildings in south Milwaukee. Lawson had two airplanes: the original C-2 (which was being rebuilt and was nearly finished) and a partially completed experimental aircraft (L-4) that featured three Liberty engines. Egge found some spruce and steel on hand, but nothing was being done on the construction of additional C-2s. Lawson, however, claimed that he planned to hire several hundred men in January and complete eight aircraft by April. The Lawson Air Line Company had been incorporated in Delaware with $2,000,000 in stock, but none had been sold. Lawson said that salesmen would be sent out in January, and he was confident that all the stock would be quickly sold. Egge concluded that prospects for the opening of service in May did not appear bright.[26]

Obviously alarmed by Egge's visit, Lawson wrote to Praeger on December 30 and assured him that "there isn't one doubt in my mind" that service would begin on May 13. "As far as I am concerned," he continued, "everything is in splendid condition and my plans are maturing in accordance with my expectations." Lawson followed up the letter by visiting Washington. Whether he fell victim to Lawson's salesmanship or whether he decided that the Post Office had nothing to lose, Praeger had granted the requested extension.[27]

On April 8, 1921, James B. Corridon, superintendent of the Division of Railway Adjustments, conferred with Lawson about the prospects of a May inauguration of contract service. Lawson said that two large aircraft were ready, but all construction work at his factory had been suspended because of lack of funds. No fields had been leased and no personnel hired. Under the circumstances, Corridon asked, would it be possible to begin operations in May? Lawson remained optimistic. He planned to borrow money in Pittsburgh, he had "verbal agreements" for fields, he would purchase small aircraft to carry the mail. If he could not operate all three routes, he would operate one. If he could not operate one, he would ask for an extension. "It is my judgment," Corridon informed Shaughnessy, "that Mr. Lawson will not be able to fulfill the terms of the contracts."[28]

Lawson finally accepted a measure of reality on April 20 and agreed to the cancellation, without penalty, of the contacts for two of the three routes. But he had not given up. He still hoped to inaugurate the New York–Pittsburgh–Chicago line on May 13. It was not to be. On May 8 Lawson and pilot Charles Wilcox tried to take off from a poor field in the trimotored L-4. Slowed by mud, the aircraft struggled to 100 feet before hitting the top of an elm tree. There were no injuries, but the aircraft was badly damaged. Lawson had run out of money and time.[29]

Following Lawson's misadventure, Shaughnessy recommended to Hays that the law be changed to permit private contractors to collect a surcharge for air mail. The first attempt by the Post Office to collect extra postage in 1918–19 had failed "because there was no well handled advertising or personal solicitation such as would be the case with a private company." The Air Mail Service had been started to demonstrate the practicality of commercial aviation. "This work has been done," Shaughnessy concluded, "and the time has arrived for the necessary constructive legislation to make it possible for private interests to get started."[30]

WHILE WAITING FOR CONGRESS TO ACT, Shaughnessy attempted to clean up what he saw as the mess left by his Democratic predecessor. Unhappy with Praeger's use of railroad funds for the Air Mail Service, Shaughnessy sought a ruling from the comptroller on the legality of this transaction. Railroad funds could be spent on air mail routes, he learned, except for the New York–San Francisco line for which Congress had made a specific appropriation. This posed a dilemma. Money to operate the transcontinental route would be exhausted by the end of May. Either Congress would have to approve an additional $125,000, or the line would have to be abandoned until the beginning of the new fiscal year on July 1.[31]

Shaughnessy recommended to Hays that the Post Office seek the necessary deficiency appropriation rather than disrupt service. At the same time, it should be made clear to Congress that "we are not responsible for the condition which is brought about by our desire to get four square in every particular."[32]

Shaughnessy also recommended that the New York–Washington and St. Louis–Minneapolis routes be discontinued. Although the comptroller had ruled that these lines could be operated without specific congressional authorization, the Post Office should not use a "technical interpretation of existing legislation" to evade the will of the legislature. Furthermore, it would make sense in light of the President's recent request to all departments to curtail expenses; it cost $11,286 per month to operate the New York–Washington route, and $22,508 for the St. Louis–Minneapolis service. Finally, with fast and frequent train service along both lines, air mail was "not of vital importance." [33]

Hays approved all requests. He sought and obtained the $125,000 from Congress; the Post Office abandoned the New York–Washington route on May 31 and closed the St. Louis–Minneapolis line on June 30. Only the transcontinental route remained in operation. [34]

Shaughnessy, meanwhile, undertook a thorough reorganization of the Air Mail Service. He closed Newark's Heller Field and the repair depot at Bustleton. Each division became responsible for modifying the de Havillands obtained from Army stores; this eliminated outside contracts (which cost $276,109 in fiscal 1921). Stressing efficiency and economy, Shaughnessy ordered personnel reduced from 521 to less than 400, with cuts beginning at the top. Headquarters lost the positions of superintendent of operations and maintenance, chief of flying, radio engineer, mechanical inspector, and consulting engineer. This left the general superintendent (with salary reduced from $4,800 to $3,800), his assistant, a superintendent of radio, and a chief clerk. Finally, beginning in July, the transcontinental service would carry mail point to point only, giving local communities the advantage of air mail and perhaps encouraging their political representatives to support air mail appropriations. [35]

Shaughnessy selected Carl Egge as the new general superintendent. A career postal employee, Egge began his government service at age 19 as a clerk in the post office at Grand Island, Nebraska. He transferred to the Railway Mail Service the following year, and rose slowly through the bureaucratic ranks. In 1904 he joined the inspection division, where he remained for fourteen years. Egge returned to the Railway Mail Service in August 1918 and was attached to Praeger's office. Prager came to admire Egge's work, especially his handling of the pilots' strike of July 1919. At Praeger's urging, Egge transferred to the Air Mail Service in May 1920 as superintendent of the St. Louis–Minneapolis line. Despite poor equipment and bad weather, Egge maintained an excellent performance record. Shaughnessy would have preferred as general superintendent someone with a technical background; however, when he was unable to identify a suitably qualified individual, he settled for Egge. [36]

Egge took office on June 15 and immediately launched a "safety first" campaign. "It is the policy of the present administration of the Air Mail Service," he wrote to all divisional superintendents, "to go to any extreme in order to prevent accidents." He asked that all personnel be encouraged to submit suggestions about ways and means to enhance safety so that these could be adopted throughout the Service.[37]

Egge cultivated relations with the Air Mail Pilots of America (AMPA), an organization formed in November 1920 "for the benefit of the Air Mail and the advancement of aviation." Previously, management's attitude had been antagonistic toward the group, viewing it as an embryonic union. Superintendent John E. Whitbeck had considered J. T. Christensen, first president of AMPA (killed flying the mail in April 1921), "a sea lawyer of some considerable ability" and had wanted to fire him. Egge, however, listened carefully to the complaints of Howard Brown, Christensen's successor. When Brown spoke out about the poor condition of aircraft on the Central Division, Egge immediately ordered the situation corrected. "We have become extremely careful in checking planes at all fields in this division," Superintendent Dunphy informed Egge, "and have condemned several because of split longerons. . . . I do not believe that Mr. Brown will need to complain on the condition of planes flown on the Central Division in the future."[38]

Pilots were polled about the use of parachutes. Most replied that they were not worth carrying although a few men on the Reno–San Francisco route decided to wear them. Egge made clear that Praeger's "fly or resign" was out; schedules were to be subordinated to safety. This radical change in attitude led to some confusion. On September 29, for example, William Hopson reached Chicago from Omaha after flying the last forty-five minutes of the trip in darkness and bad weather. Noting that Hopson had completed all his trips during the previous six weeks, Superintendent Dunphy wrote to Egge and asked that his performance on September 19 be commended by the department. An official at headquarters wrote on top of the letter: "I believe Hopson ought to be reprimanded for taking foolhardy chances." The record fails to show whether Hopson was commended or reprimanded.[39]

The first three months (July–September 1921) of the new fiscal year showed promising results in the areas of both safety and economy. The Air Mail Service, Egge reported to Shaughnessy, had flown over 390,000 miles and carried more than 10,000,000 letters. There had been only one fatality: Howard F. Smith crashed and was killed on July 16, shortly after taking off from San Francisco on a ferry flight.

Performance (trips completed) had averaged 98 percent at a cost per mile of 71¢ (compared to 87¢ for the same quarter in 1920). A delighted Shaughnessy told Egge: "This is a remarkably good showing."[40]

The second quarter was even better. Although performance dipped below 90 percent in November and December because of bad weather, air mail pilots flew 413,000 miles carried 11,600,000 letters, and did not suffer a single fatality.[41]

On January 6, 1922, Shaughnessy reviewed the progress of the Air Mail Service in a speech to the Washington section of the Society of Automotive Engineers. When the present administration took office, he said, it found that the air mail had made considerable progress; however, the situation "was not altogether satisfactory." There was criticism over the high loss of lives. Also, many in Congress objected to the manner in which the air mail had been extended and financed. The new administration had decided that it was necessary to start "a new deal all around." The Air Mail Service would be conducted in accordance with the intent of Congress and the desire of the President for economy. The Post Office would promote the development of aviation "in a much more beneficial way if we stopped the too rapid expansion, which through lack of sufficient facilities seemed to be making the air mail service an extra-hazardous occupation and instead concentrated our efforts on standardizing and perfecting the operation on a more restricted route."

Accordingly, Shaughnessy continued, the New York–Washington and St. Louis–Minneapolis routes had been abandoned at an annual savings of $675,000; staff had been reduced from 521 to 479, lowering the annual payroll from $864,321 to $787,620; equipment had been standardized through the exclusive use of DH-4s; and there had been only one fatality during 800,000 miles of flying over the past six months, compared to one fatality per 100,000 miles in 1920.

Shaughnessy concluded by reiterating the Post Office's support for air mail, but emphasizing that the government had no more wish to operate an air service than it did to operate steamboat or railway companies. It would continue to fly the mail "only until such times as the commercial interests of this country are ready to step in and take over the burden."[42]

Shaughnessy's success in getting "four square with the committees of Congress" seemed debatable as the legislature considered appropriations for the Air Mail Service. Director of the budget Charles G. Dawes had recommended $2,200,000 for the air mail in a budget for fiscal 1923 that emphasized economy and provided for a surplus. However, a subcommittee of the House Committee on Appropria-

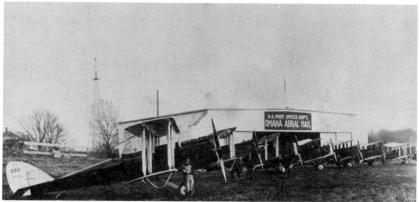

DHs lined up at Omaha, Nebraska, 1921.

tions reduced the figure to $1,935,000. Then, on January 11, 1922, the full committee voted to eliminate the entire appropriation. Opposition to the air mail, Chairman Madden explained, was based on grounds that the service had proven expensive and not particularly efficient.[43]

Shaughnessy, like Praeger before him, had to fight to save the air mail. At a meeting of NACA on January 26, he repeated his hope of operating the transcontinental route only until private enterprise could take over. He expected the Senate to reinstate the appropriation, as it had in the past, but he urged members of NACA to appear before the Senate committee and voice their support. Dr. Joseph S. Ames, chairman of the executive committee, assured him that NACA would render all possible assistance.[44]

On Saturday evening, January 28, Shaughnessy decided to take a respite from the burdens of office and accompany his wife and ten-year-old daughter to the Knickerbocker Theater to see the new silent comedy hit, *Get Rich Quick Wallingford*. They reached the theater, located at Columbia Road and 18th Street in the uptown apartment district in northwest Washington, shortly before 9 P.M. The Knickerbocker could seat 1,700 but was less than a third full; most people had been kept away by the heavy snow that had been falling since 5 P.M. the previous day. Shaughnessy and his family settled down in their seats to enjoy the film. The house lights dimmed and the orchestra began to play. Suddenly, a sharp crack resounded through the building. A fissure opened in the ceiling. Then, with a tremendous roar, the roof collapsed. Rescuers found the Shaughnessys buried in the rubble. His wife and child recovered from their serious injuries, but Shaughnessy died at Walter Reed Hospital on February 2, 1922, one of ninety-six people killed in the disaster.[45]

Shaughnessy's tragic death left to Postmaster General Hays the task of winning congressional support for the Air Mail Service that he had tried so hard to unload on the military just a few short months before. Hays, who would be leaving office on March 4 to become director general of the National Motion Picture Producers' Association, appeared before the Senate Appropriations Committee on February 23 and appealed for restoration of air mail funds. It would be a step in the wrong direction, he said, to abandon the service: "The future of the country is in the air." Eventually, commercial airlines would fly the mail, but the Post Office had to do the job until that happened. The committee agreed with Hays and voted to appropriate $1,900,000 for operation of the transcontinental line. The full Senate approved on March 19, and the House went along in conference.[46]

THE AIR MAIL SERVICE WAS FORTUNATE to survive during the first year of the Harding administration. As Hays later remarked, the pioneering venture had come "very close to singing its Swan Song."[47] Both Hays and Shaughnessy were convinced that their Democratic predecessors had badly mismanaged the enterprise. Flying the mail cost far too much, and the loss of life had generated adverse publicity.

While Hays believed in the future of aviation, he considered the Air Mail Service more valuable as a ready reserve for national defense than for postal operations. Military control of air mail, he had argued, would reduce costs and promote efficiency. Although initially interested in the proposal, the Army had decided that it could not bear the additional expense during a time of stringent economy in government.

Shaughnessy also wanted to end postal operation of the air mail. "I am of the opinion," he had informed Hays on May 12, 1921, "that our position in attempting to conduct such a highly technical means of transportation as airplane service is fundamentally unsound and should be relinquished to private industry without any delay whatsoever." He believed that the time had arrived for Congress to pass legislation that would enable commercial interests to take over the air mail.[48]

However, while waiting for Congress to act, Shaughnessy insisted that the Air Mail Service be operated economically and safely. He had reorganized the Service, abandoned collateral routes, standardized equipment, and generally brought stability to the operation. As a result of his efforts, costs went down, efficiency increased, and the accident rate improved dramatically.

Future prospects for the government-operated aerial enterprise nonetheless seemed bleak. The Post Office appeared content to continue daytime operations of the transcontinental route, flying the mail point to point in trusty DHs, until commercial airlines emerged to take over the business. For all practical purposes, the Air Mail Service had come to a dead end.

10 Aeromarine Airways

I F THE HARDING ADMINISTRATION really expected commercial airlines to spring up and relieve the government of responsibility for carrying the mail, it was doomed to disappointment. The fate of Inglis M. Uppercu and Aeromarine Airways was a case in point. There were a number of attempts to promote commercial aviation after the First World War, but Uppercu tried harder than anyone else—and came closer to success. Aeromarine Airways was amply financed and well managed. Its demise revealed with painful clarity the inability of private aeronautical ventures to succeed without the assistance and support of the federal government.[1]

Uppercu was born in 1875 in North Evanston, a pleasant suburb of Chicago, where his father practiced law. After the family moved to New York in 1888, he attended public school in Bay Ridge, Long Island, then graduated from Brooklyn Polytechnic Institute. Uppercu entered Columbia University Law School, intent on joining his father in a legal career, but he became so fascinated by automobiles that before taking a degree he left law school to do experimental work with the Neostyle Company and, later, the Duryea Automobile Company. In 1902 he organized his own firm, the Motor Car Company of New Jersey, and six years later secured the exclusive franchise for Cadillacs in the New York metropolitan area.[2]

While the Cadillac business meant high profits, it evidently did not provide the necessary challenge for a man who raced cars for the Vanderbilt Cup and managed bicycle races. Uppercu turned to aviation in 1908 and financed, for several hundred dollars, the Boland Aeroplane Company. This firm's main asset was Frank Boland, an imaginative designer with plans for a rear-engine, rudderless biplane, controlled by jibs and elevators. Despite the curious operating mechanism, Boland's airplane flew well enough to encourage production of a more advanced model. As so often happened in those early days, the venture ended in tragedy when Boland was killed while demonstrating the aircraft on a tour of Latin America in 1913.[3]

Uppercu maintained his interest in aviation, forming the Aeromarine Plane & Motor Company in 1914 to concentrate on the design and construction of seaplanes. In the summer of 1917, a few months after the United States entered World War I, Uppercu moved his company from Nutley, New Jersey, to sixty-six acres of choice land on Raritan Bay at Keyport, New Jersey. His hope for a Navy contract was realized when he received orders for 200 seaplanes valued at $2,000,000. In all, Aeromarine built some 300 aircraft during the war, and was one of the Navy's leading suppliers of training planes.[4]

The Armistice of November 1918 found Uppercu with perhaps the finest aircraft factory in the nation, encompassing sixteen fireproof buildings with a total floor space of 130,000 square feet. Facilities included a material testing laboratory, wood shop, hull shop, plating department, machine shop, propeller department, final assembly room, welding department, and motor department and testing laboratory. Every division had the latest equipment: automatic screw machines, lathes, grinders, drill presses, enamelling ovens, milling machines, a Sprague electric dynamometer, and so forth.[5]

Hoping to keep his superb facilities in operation, Uppercu searched far and wide for business. During the winter of 1918–19 he converted to civilian use several of the military trainers built by the company. Summer brought a contract from the Army Air Service to modify seventy-five observation planes. But the company was foundering. "We have tried in every way to turn our airplane plant into other purposes to help keep the airplane division in the plant," Uppercu testified before a congressional committee in December 1919, "but I must confess that we are losing a large sum of money every week, and that will run into several hundred thousand dollars this year." He was optimistic about the "ultimate destiny" of aviation, but "very dubious" about immediate financial return. He urged the government to assume regulatory authority over commercial aviation as a way to foster development, emphasizing that it was in the national interest for Washington to support the aircraft industry until the commercial market matured.[6]

Federal economic assistance was not forthcoming. Uppercu, in common with aircraft manufacturers in the United States and Great Britain, had to make his own way. Convinced—wrongly, as it turned out— that a civilian market could be developed and exploited, Uppercu embarked upon an ambitious scheme that began with the acquisition and modification of surplus military aircraft.

The Navy had huge stocks of surplus airplanes that, crated in warehouses, seemed fated to deteriorate to the point of uselessness. Uppercu saw commercial possibilities in two types of flying boats: the twin-engine F-5L biplane, which set an endurance record of twenty hours and nineteen minutes in 1919, and the HS-2L, a single-engine biplane with a wartime reputation for reliability. In February 1920 Aeromarine purchased the first of several F-5Ls and began converting it to an eleven-passenger airliner. Uppercu also sought an option to buy 135 HS-2Ls at $100 each, with an additional $2,000 payable to the Navy for each modified aircraft when resold. In effect, Aeromarine would become the Navy's exclusive sales agent for the disposal of this type of surplus equipment.[7]

Although Uppercu's proposal ran contrary to the military's policy of selling to the highest bidder on the open market, it won the key support of Rear Adm. William A. Moffett, chief of the Navy's newly created Bureau of Aeronautics. If sold on the open market in their present deteriorated condition, Moffett argued, the airplanes likely would fall into the hands of irresponsible individuals, intent on turning a quick profit. The Navy Department, he said, "should take responsibility for the safety of the general public and not offer for sale any Naval flying equipment which . . . will not reflect credit on the Department. The only conservative way to place these flying boats in the hands of the public is through a reputable concern which will overhaul them in an honest manner and place them in first-class condition. . . ." His recommendation to approve Uppercu's proposal was accepted by the secretary of the Navy.[8]

The first modified F-5L was completed in early summer 1920. Hailed as America's premier commercial airliner, it featured a spacious forward cabin that held six large wicker armchairs, upholstered in brown leather, three on each side of a central aisle; the rear cabin contained five seats and a divan. Mahogany veneer lined the soundproof interior, while carpet and drapes had accents of silver. There were dome lights for night flying, cigar lighters and vanity cases on the bulkhead, and windows that could be opened in flight should passengers desire a breeze. The three-man crew sat in an open cockpit between and above the passenger compartments. Two 400-hp Liberty engines provided a cruising speed of 75 mph and an endurance of six hours.[9]

Uppercu had a fine airplane. The next step, a giant one, was to find customers in the midst of an economic recession. Deciding to demonstrate the comfort and safety of air travel, Uppercu formed the Aeromarine Sightseeing and Navigation Company. The F-5L spent the rest of summer flying between New York City and the resorts of Atlantic City, Southampton, and Newport, carrying more than 1,000 passengers. Encouraged, Uppercu moved into the air transportation business in a major way by acquiring a controlling interest in Florida—West Indies Airways.[10]

News of commercial air transportation schemes had filled the pages of aeronautical journals in the postwar period, but few ever went beyond the planning stage. Aeromarine earlier had become involved in an attempt to operate one of the more discussed routes, Key West to Havana. In October 1919 Hannibal J. de Mesa, wealthy Cuban businessman and president of the Aerial League of Cuba, announced formation of the Compania Cubana Americana de Aviaçion. He ordered four modified single-engine seaplanes from Aeromarine, one of which flew from Keyport to Florida to initiate service to Havana in mid-November. Probably because of financial problems, the company operated only sporadically, mainly in Cuba, before disappearing from the scene.[11]

The venture that now attracted Uppercu to the airline business involved the same route. In 1919 a group of former servicemen, including Albert Tilt, Geoffrey H. Bonnell, and Alvin W. McKaig, sought to capitalize on Prohibition by establishing an air service between Key West and Havana. But after acquiring surplus airplanes, spare parts, and ground facilities, they ran out of cash. Unable to borrow operating funds from private sources, they went public in November, incorporating Florida—West Indies Airways under Cuban law. The founders planned to exchange their property and equipment for $650,000 in stock, and looked for public subscription to provide $200,000 in operating expenses.[12]

Investors stayed away in droves. Florida—West Indies then turned to the Post Office, hoping that the stability implied by a mail contract would attract capital. Supported by Praeger, the airline had secured the first airmail contract (F.M.-1) in American history on August 25, 1920. The one-year agreement, which had been hailed by Postmaster General Burleson as an "important forward step in improving postal communication with our Latin American neighbor," called for one trip daily, except Sunday, from Key West to Havana, beginning October 15, 1920. Florida—West Indies would receive $20,000 during the life of the contract for daily carriage of up to 500 pounds of regular mail, plus $1.68 per pound for letters bearing special airmail postage.[13]

The air mail contract may have been historic, but potential investors were not impressed, and the airline's stock remained unsold. While investors no doubt were disappointed by the airline's failure to obtain a reciprocal mail contract from the Cuban government, the major factor working against Florida—West Indies was a postwar recession that had dried up speculative capital. Only Inglis Uppercu, determined to create a market for commercial aircraft, showed interest. In October 1920 a merger took place that gave rise to Aeromarine–West Indies Airways. Although details of the arrangement were not announced, it is clear from subsequent events that Uppercu was the senior partner.[14]

The new company quickly moved to begin service across the Straits of Florida. Two of the converted F-5Ls, the *Santa Maria* and the *Pinta*, were given a gala send-off from New York's Columbia Yacht Club on October 23, with representatives of the Navy, Army Air Service, and Post Office attending. This occasion, noted Charles F. Redden of Aeromarine's engineering and sales division, "marks the first constructive step in the history of American rapid transportation toward the creation of regular passenger air lines." The slogan of the company would be "Safety first, last, and all the time." The advantages of travel by air, Redden promised, would be amply demonstrated.[15]

Twice-daily flights over the ninety-mile route from Key West to Havana started on November 1, 1920. Savings in time were considerable (one hour and fifteen minutes by air *versus* eight hours by steamship). Although it cost $75 to fly, as opposed to $16–20 by water, the airline managed to attract customers, no doubt lured by a sense of adventure. Over the next six months, as four additional F-5Ls came into service, traffic—including charters to Miami, West Palm Beach, and Bimini—amounted to some 1,100 passengers and 34,395 pounds of mail.[16]

Operational problems abounded. The *Nina* tore loose from its moorings in Havana's harbor during a storm and was destroyed, while pontoons were smashed against piers, jetties, and floating platforms with disconcerting regularity. Mildew in the wooden hulls became a major irritant. Radios were heavy (170 pounds) and unreliable. The airline learned from these difficulties: aircraft hulls were strengthened, new means of bracing for anchoring were devised, a redesigned wing section increased aerodynamic efficiency, and ventilators controlled (but did not conquer) mildew. One interesting innovation involved the use of carrier pigeons to improve communications; they turned out to be as unreliable as the radios.[17]

Management also underwent fundamental changes as Uppercu replaced the executives of the original company with his own men. Redden left engineering and sales to become president of the newly renamed Aeromarine Airways, pioneering U.S. Marine Corps aviator Bernard L. Smith took over operations, and Harry A. Bruno headed traffic and sales.[18]

By May 1921 the seasonal nature of the Key West–Havana route had become all too obvious. Aeromarine Airways surrendered its mail

The *Ponce de Leon* at anchor in Havana.

contract, placed four aircraft in storage, and sent one F-5L on a summer-long promotional tour. Commanded by Edwin C. Musick (who would become Pan American Airway's premier pilot during the 1930s), the *Santa Maria* undertook a 7,000-mile journey to New York, Toronto, Buffalo, Detroit, Chicago, New Orleans, and return to Key West. The aircraft stopped at every city and town of importance along the way, and Musick extolled the advantages of air travel to local businessmen and civic leaders.[19]

An equally ambitious promotional tour, using a newly remodeled HS-2L single-engine flying boat, departed from New York on July 7. The six-passenger aircraft, flown by Durston G. Richardson, called at cities bordering lakes George, Champlain, Ontario, Erie, Huron, and Michigan. Richardson made some 100 landings and carried more than 500 passengers during his 7,490-mile circumnavigation of the Great Lakes. "The most outstanding feature of the trip," recalled Sales Manager Bruno, "was its complete lack of air incidents. . . . This very pedestrian angle was just the thing we were after—to show that an airplane trip could be as mundane as an automobile jaunt but twice as fast, to say the least."[20]

Aeromarine Airways, which also operated an active summer charter schedule from New York City to Atlantic City and New England ports with the commercial version of the HS-2L, had an outstanding first year. During the twelve months ending October 20, 1921, the company flew 95,020 miles and carried 6,814 passengers without injury. As leading trade journal *Aviation* observed, this was a "truly remarkable showing" for America's pioneer airline.[21]

The 1921–22 season promised to be even better. Aeromarine Airways inaugurated regular bimonthly New York–Havana service (which proved to be irregular), and flew schedule flights to the popular rumfleet headquarters of Bimini and Nassau. The airline reduced the fare between Key West and Havana from $75 to $50. Passenger traffic tripled, and the increased revenue more than offset the lack of a mail contract.[22] The season's only sour note came in late March, when a commercial flying boat operated by a competing charter company crashed while en route to Bimini from Miami, killing five passengers.[23]

The wide publicity given this accident tended to undercut Aeromarine's efforts to convince the public that air travel was safe. As Redden stated in a telegram to a congressional committee that was considering federal regulation of flying: "When a mishap occurs, all aviation gets the blame." Air transportation was not dangerous, he stressed, "when rigorous inspection of equipment is provided." Unfortunately, strict safety procedures were exceptional. Redden urged the federal government to assume responsibility for inspecting aircraft and licensing pilots, otherwise "aviation [could not] progress as it should."[24]

The federal government was not unaware of the problem. On April 1, 1921, President Harding had asked NACA to form a special subcommittee to "take up vigorously and fully the question of Federal regulation of air navigation . . . ." The subcommittee recommended that the government establish a bureau of aeronautics in the Department of Commerce with authority to license and regulate aviators, aircraft, and airports. Senator James W. Wadsworth and others sponsored the necessary legislation, but Congress failed to enact it.[25]

While Congress debated, Aeromarine Airways continued to set traffic records. The winter season of 1921–22 turned out to be the best ever, with 755 flights conducted and 2,399 passengers safely carried. Summer saw the airline operating two divisions, Eastern and Great Lakes. Headquarters for the Eastern Division in New York was a new facility on the Hudson River at 82d Street, from which Aeromarine Airways not only flew the usual sightseeing and charter trips but also initiated daily scheduled service to Atlantic City. In all, the Eastern Division made 807 flights and carried 2,380 passengers. The new Great Lakes Division also was a huge success. In order to test the traffic potential indicated by the previous summer's promotional flights, on July 17 the airline inaugurated daily service between Cleveland and Detroit. The public responded with such enthusiasm that a second flight was soon added. During the two months it operated, this line carried 4,388 passengers.[26]

The airline headed south in the fall of 1922 with high hopes for the coming year. Redden secured a mail contract for the Key West–Havana route, and made ambitious plans to expand operations throughout the West Indies. Regular service began between Miami and Nassau, while survey flights were made and terminal facilities acquired for a route from Havana to Kingston via San Juan. Redden predicted a "very brilliant future" for overwater air service. "We now feel confident," he said, "that the time is not far distant when air travel will be accepted by the general public as a desirable and necessary means of transportation."[27]

While Redden's optimism was not unwarranted (as Pan American Airways would so forcefully demonstrate during the next decade), it did prove premature. On January 13, 1923, F-5L *Columbus* developed engine trouble while en route from Key West to Havana with seven passengers and 400 pounds of mail. Capt. C. W. Miller landed the aircraft in fifteen- to twenty-foot swells some twenty miles from Havana,

Aeromarine F-5L *Columbus*.

damaging the fuselage. Passengers and crew sought safety on top of the cabin as the hull began filling with water, but Edwin Atkins, a prominent Cuban sugar planter, his two sons (ages five and three), and their governess were swept overboard and drowned. A passing steamship rescued the remaining passengers and crew just before the *Columbus* heeled over and sank.[28]

This first fatal accident, coupled with the loss of F-5L *Ponce de Leon* in Havana's harbor during a storm, exposed the airline's shaky economic foundations, as neither aircraft was replaced. The absence of profit and loss statements makes it impossible to be precise about Aeromarine's financial status, but the company obviously was in deep trouble. Redden later testified that some routes made money, while others operated at a loss. Clearly, the seasonal need to relocate equipment was expensive, as were the construction and operation of fixed base facilities, especially Key West. Insurance, in the absence of federal regulation, amounted to 17.25 percent of total operating costs, or more than Aeromarine spent for fuel and labor. The available evidence suggests that the airline slowly had been losing money until the twin disasters in early 1923. Thereafter, rising maintenance costs reached prohibitive levels because aircraft hulls and engines were wearing out after more than two years of service. As Wing Commander M. G. Christie, British air attaché, noted in March 1923, "only the enthusiasm of a wealthy shareholder keeps the concern from closing down."[29]

Uppercu's enthusiasm, like his funds, had limits. While he derived a good deal of prestige from his efforts, culminating with his election as president of the Aeronautical Chamber of Commerce in 1922, the idea behind Aeromarine Airways was to create a market for airplanes by making the public "air minded," and by demonstrating the profitability of commercial aviation. But Uppercu was only proving that airlines could *not* be operated at a profit at this stage of technological development. It is hardly surprising that in nearly three years he had not found a single customer for the commercial F-5Ls or HS-2Ls, which had been modified at great expense. Furthermore, the Navy was now pressing for payment in full ($2,100 each) for ten HS-2Ls that had been acquired by Aeromarine Plane & Motor Company for a small down payment.[30]

Too late, perhaps, Uppercu turned to military sales in an effort to rescue his rapidly declining aircraft division. Three years of operational experience had led to development of a flying boat of advanced design, featuring a duraluminum hull. Initially intending to sell the airplane on the illusory civilian market, Uppercu now sought to interest the Navy. Prospects seemed good. Following extensive tests, Inspector W. G. Child reported to Washington that the aircraft "could easily be adapted for service of which the HS-2 is capable, but with greatly increased performance." At a minimum, he "strongly recommended" the purchase of several duraluminum hulls, modified for use with F-5Ls. Commander Holden C. Richardson, acting manager of the Naval Aircraft Factory and an expert on flying boats, agreed with Child. "The Aeromarine Company," Richardson wrote to Admiral Moffett, "deserves to be complimented upon its initiative and engineering skill in the production of the all-metal hull."[31]

While awaiting the Navy's decision, Uppercu continued to support Aeromarine Airways. The Eastern and Great Lakes divisions opened on schedule in the spring of 1923, but operations from New York were suspended in July. Service between Cleveland and Detroit continued throughout the summer, and the airline carried over 5,000 passengers without incident.[32]

In December, just as Redden announced plans for the winter season, Uppercu heard from the Navy. Although there was no question about the aircraft's technical excellence, the Bureau of Aeronautics wrote, "this development is not along the lines required by the service at the present time, and the Bureau's interest does not extend to the point of purchasing." Uppercu completed the assembly of twenty-five Martin bombers under a contract with the Army Air Service, then laid off his skilled mechanics and converted the plant's facilities to building buses and custom bodies for Cadillacs.[33]

Aeromarine Airways was finished. Uppercu had invested more than $500,000 in the enterprise, and he was not prepared to accept further losses. The airline suspended business at the beginning of the new year; a short time later Uppercu sold it to the Florida Railroad and Steamship Company for an undisclosed amount. In an attempt to continue service, the new owners approached the Department of Commerce for economic assistance on proposed Latin American routes, but the government was not interested. After a few charter flights, the airline passed from the scene.[34]

The demise of Aeromarine left only two small air carriers—the Seattle–Victoria Air Mail Line and the Gulf Coast Air Line—that flew on a regular basis. Edward Hubbard had been operating a contract mail service on the eighty-four-mile route between Seattle and Victoria, British Columbia, since October 1920. The Post Office paid Hubbard $200 per roundtrip (with a maximum of twelve trips per month) to expedite letters bound to and from the Orient by steamship. Merrill K. Riddick secured a similar contract in April 1923 to carry mail the eighty miles from New Orleans to Pilottown, a quarantine station at the tip of the Mississippi Delta that handled steamers on

Latin American routes. Beyond these tiny pioneering ventures, however, American commercial aviation did not exist.[35]

NOTED AERONAUTICAL AUTHORITY Edward P. Warner has emphasized that Aeromarine Airways stands as a "landmark in the record of commercial progress." The airline carried 30,000 passengers and flew more than 1,000,000 passenger-miles with only one serious accident in three and a half years. It had intelligent and imaginative management, generous financing, excellent equipment, and superb pilots. Its inability to survive emphasized, in a most dramatic manner, the limitations of private enterprise and the need for federal supervision and subsidy at this formative stage of aeronautics.[36]

The Harding administration had only to look abroad for further confirmation of these aeronautical facts of life. The British government also had wanted to avoid subsidy. As Air Minister Winston Churchill said in 1920, "Civil aviation must fly by itself." A private company tried to operate a London–Paris air service, but it could not compete against a generously subsidized French line. After British air transport came to a halt in February 1921, the government stepped in and began a program of economic assistance.[37]

Perhaps the American government might have acted if faced with Mexican competition. President Harding did support—unsuccessfully—"government aid" for the operation of merchant ships to enable Americans to compete with foreigners on the high seas. But this was an exception. Direct subsidy of private enterprise was something that Harding preferred not to contemplate. Also, while he favored federal regulation of aeronautics, Harding did not exert legislative leadership on the matter. And without presidential direction, Congress tended to agree on generalities but not specifics. This legislative vacuum, one perceptive student of government-business relations has observed, produced an anomaly: "The federal government, in the era of supposed high laissez-faire capitalism, remained the operator of the only significant commercial aerial entity—the United States Air Mail."[38]

11 The Lighted Airway

THE HEROIC AGE of the Air Mail Service seemed over when Paul Henderson became second assistant postmaster general in April 1922. As it turned out, this dynamic leader was destined to have an impact on the Service second only to Otto Praeger. Under Henderson's energetic and imaginative direction, postal airmen would continue to pioneer developments on the frontiers of aeronautics— especially in the untried area of night flying—while waiting for Congress to provide the necessary legislative foundation for commercial airlines.

Born in Kansas in 1884, Henderson grew up in Chicago and attended South Division High School, where he took an active part in track and debating. He wanted to go to college, but his father's death meant that there was no money for higher education. High school diploma in hand, Henderson went to work as a salesman for the Turner Brass Works. In 1907 he joined the Western Stone Company of Lemont, Illinois. Three years later, he married his high school sweetheart, Mabel B. Madden, daughter of Congressman Martin Madden. By 1916 Henderson was president of Western Stone, his rapid rise to the top no doubt facilitated by the fact that his father-in-law was part-owner and former head of the company. Volunteering for military service during the war, Henderson served in France as ordinance officer at Base No. 1, Saint-Nazaire. He returned home in 1919 and took a position as treasurer with the Andrews Engineering Company, a manufacturer of bridge operating equipment. Congressman Madden likely recommended his son-in-law for the appointment as second assistant postmaster general. If so, he picked a man perfectly suited for the job.[1]

Henderson got along well with Hubert Work, the new postmaster general. A physician with a reputation as a skilled clinician and psychiatrist, Work became interested in politics while practicing medicine in his adopted state of Colorado. He took an active part in the presidential campaign of 1920, organizing farmers for Harding. Offered the position of first assistant postmaster general, Work decided to enter public service. An enthusiastic and capable administrator who stressed businesslike efficiency in government operations, he won high marks from Hays—and a recommendation for promotion. Not sharing his predecessor's strong views about the air mail, Work was content to give Henderson a relatively free hand in developing the Service.[2]

Henderson favored private operation of the air mail, but he did not want the government-run Air Mail Service to stagnate while waiting for responsible commercial companies to appear. The obvious value of airplanes over trains lay in speed. However, flying at 90 to 100 mph during daylight, airplanes lost their advantage to trains with the setting sun. As Praeger had demonstrated with the day-and-night transcontinental flight of February 1921, the Air Mail Service would have to operate around the clock in order for the Post Office to take full advantage of the airplane's speed. Shortly after taking office, Henderson ordered an "intensive study of the question of night operation in all its phases."[3]

Night flying, Henderson learned, was not new. A number of prewar exhibition pilots had thrilled audiences with nighttime demonstrations. Also, bombing missions had been conducted during the war with primitive lighting equipment to assist the pilots. British bombers, for example, fearing collision in the dark, had operated singly, following courses worked out in advance and checked by visual reference to terrain features. Aircraft carried magnesium flares for illumination. A few airfields had electric beacons that would flash an identification letter in Morse code to guide pilots to the field. Landings normally were made with the aid of a few flares stuck in the ground. "It was found," Henderson noted, "that . . . there had been no regular or scheduled operation of aircraft at night excepting that which took place during the war and which was extremely hazardous."[4]

Henderson found that he could build on the preliminary work that had been done by Praeger. Following the successful coast-to-coast flight of February 22–23, 1921, Praeger had assigned Stanton to develop plans for permanent nighttime service. Like Henderson later, Stanton discovered that "we have learned nothing from war time night flying." Although operations between New York and Cleveland would not be possible owing to the mountainous nature of the terrain, he concluded that the route between Cleveland and Omaha could be flown in good weather. Stanton had drawn up a set of requirements: night landing fields had to be at least 2,000 feet by 1,500 feet, with excellent approaches; there should be a 500-watt revolving search-

Second Assistant Postmaster General Paul Henderson, July 1924.

light, projecting a beam parallel to the ground, to guide pilots to the field; a searchlight should project a beam along the ground and into the wind to illuminate the landing area and proper direction for approach; searchlights would be located along the route at fifty-mile intervals to provide directional guidance and to mark emergency landing fields; aircraft would carry wingtip flares for forced landings.[5]

A good deal of preparation took place during March and April 1921. After Praeger approved the establishment of a night airway between Chicago and Cheyenne, Stanton located fourteen emergency landing sites, contacted the Army Air Service about lighting equipment, conducted experiments at College Park, and surveyed pilots about their requirements for night operations. Christopher V. Pickup, who had over 250 hours of night flying experience with the Army and in exhibitions, suggested that each aircraft be equipped with a powerful searchlight, located underneath the wing and operated from the cockpit. "In a meeting of pilots," he wrote from Cheyenne, "it was the universal opinion that the most danger lies, not in getting lost or in forced landings, but mostly in case of rain or fog, the inability of one getting low enough to a railroad to fly with safety, and we came to the conclusion that a good light so arranged would be of the greatest help both from the standpoint of safety for the pilot and keeping a hundred percent schedule."[6]

It all came to naught. In May 1921 Shaughnessy had canceled the program. The Post Office had no plans for night flying, Egge reported after taking office as general superintendent. The decision had been made to develop the Service along lines of "safety and reliability" rather than to extend operations into new areas.[7]

After reviewing the past and consulting with technical experts (who agreed that night flying could be done but disagreed about *how* it could be accomplished), Henderson decided to press forward. On May 13, 1922, he hired Joseph V. Magee, an engineer from Cleveland, instructing him to find out if scheduled nighttime operations could be conducted with safety, and, if so, to do it.[8]

Over the next four weeks, Magee visited the Army Air Service's Engineering Division, General Electric's National Lamp Works, and the American Gas Accumulator Company. Although Henderson had told Magee to take all the time he needed, the assistant postmaster general soon grew impatient. On June 10 he asked Magee about the status of the preliminary report. "We are now assured of our appropriation for the next fiscal year," Henderson explained, "and I am anxious to advance this subject as rapidly as consistent with thorough research and careful study."[9]

Magee made his report on June 22. Night flying, he concluded, "can be made practical." However, "before any night flying program is carried out . . . it is necessary to continue research work which has been recently started along these lines. . . ." The problem was so new, and the special requirements so numerous, that it would be necessary to proceed "step by step," never losing sight of the fact "that the safety of the pilot is our first consideration."

Magee then outlined what he considered the "safest and most economical program to follow in developing night flying." There were four aspects of the problem: *(1)* suitable landing fields, *(2)* practical and efficient aerial lighthouses, *(3)* proper equipment for airplanes, and *(4)* proper airport lighting equipment.

Suitable landing fields: Fields must be clear of any obstruction to allow pilots to land upwind from any direction. New York's Hazelhurst and the new field at Chicago were suitable, but Cleveland, Bryan, and

Bellefonte were "positively out of the question for safe night flying." Emergency landing fields with clear approaches should be located approximately every twenty-five miles along the route.

Practical and efficient aerial lighthouses: Night operations required a light that could be seen by pilots for at least twenty-five miles when flying at a reasonable altitude. There were two possibilities. The American Gas Accumulator Company had an automatic acetylene-gas-operated beacon (of the type used for wartime operations in Europe) that had a range of thirty miles and could be left unattended for twelve months. The other possibility was a powerful incandescent searchlight that was being developed by the National Lamp Works. Tests would reveal the superior light for aerial operations.

Proper equipment for airplanes: The Air Service's Engineering Division recommended that all aircraft be equipped with electric landing lights, a good parachute flare, nonglow exhaust manifolds, a propeller with a dull finish to prevent reflected light from shining in the pilot's eyes, and green and red navigational lights. Lt. Donald L. Bruner had been experimenting with landing lights and expected to test a new design in the near future.

Proper airport lighting equipment: Terminal fields would require a beacon visible for at least twenty-five miles, low-powered boundary lights, an illuminated weathervane, obstacle lights, building floodlights to give a daytime perspective, and powerful incandescent floodlights to illuminate the point of touchdown. The Air Service had done considerable work on these problems, Magee noted, and had agreed to share their data with the Post Office. The National Lamp Works and American Gas Accumulator Company were preparing plans and cost estimates for field lighting systems.[10]

Henderson approved Magee's recommendation that Chicago's new Speedway Field be used as a laboratory to test various lighting designs, and that an airplane be equipped for night flying. This would be followed by the construction of a night airway from Chicago to Cheyenne. The Post Office would begin night flying, Henderson announced to the press, as soon as the engineering staff had completed the necessary preparations to insure that night operations could be conducted with safety.[11]

Magee worked through the summer and into the fall, installing and evaluating night flying equipment. He identified and surveyed thirty-two emergency fields between Chicago and Omaha. The Army Air Service fitted a postal DH with landing lights, navigation lights, cockpit lights, parachute flares, generator, battery, and starter. The equipment worked well, but the high landing speed of the brakeless DH posed problems for night operations. "I think," Magee noted, "it is practically agreed among the superintendents, managers and pilot personnel that the present type of DH is not suitable for safe night flying." [12]

Pleased with the technical progress, Henderson obtained Work's approval for an appropriation request of $2,500,000 for the fiscal year beginning July 1, 1923, with $1,000,000 to be used for night flying ($500,000 to light the airway from Chicago to Cheyenne and $500,000 to purchase suitable aircraft). However, Herbert M. Lord, who had replaced Dawes as director of the budget, refused to go along. The Post Office had asked for a total of $592,815,151. Lord cut only $2,560,960 from the request, but the biggest slice—$1,000,000 for night flying— came from the air mail. [13]

Work raised the matter at a cabinet meeting in late November, prompting President Harding to contact NACA. "The only possible object in maintaining an aerial postal service," Harding noted, "is the development of aviation." The Post Office, he continued, would like NACA's recommendation as to the "most promising program" to achieve this objective. [14]

NACA's executive committee met on December 12 and heard from Henderson on the problems and prospects of the air mail. With an appropriation of $1,500,000, Henderson explained, the Post Office would be able to continue only the transcontinental service. But there was so little time saved by air over rail on that route that Postmaster General Work would prefer to shut down the entire operation rather than keep going as usual. Night flying was essential to realize the potential of air mail. If private companies were ever to take over the air mail, the government would have to demonstrate the practicality of night flying to potential commercial operators. [15]

NACA agreed. "The fundamental purpose of the Air Mail Service," chairman Charles D. Wolcott wrote to Harding on December 20, "is to demonstrate the safety, reliability, and practicality of air transportation of the mails, and incidentally of air transportation in general." Important progress had been made in achieving these objectives; however, two important tasks remained. First, the Post Office had to show "that night flying is practical over a regular route and schedule" by developing a "chain of emergency landing fields, adequate lighting for night flying, improved methods of navigation through fog, storm, and darkness, and a specially trained personnel." Second, the Air Mail Service had to foster the development of an "efficient type of airplane for this special purpose." NACA recommended that the government continue to fly the mail until the Post Office had established a day-and-night transcontinental service of thirty-six hours or less and had made the route self-supporting through appropriate postage rates.

When this was accomplished, Wolcott concluded, "the further application of aircraft to the carrying of mail [should] be effected by contracts with private enterprise." [16]

"I am so lacking in expert information," Harding informed Wolcott on December 21, "that I do not venture to comment on the report. I have had a feeling that very practical results could be acquired through the development of night flying. Frankly, I do not think the present method of aerial and rail transportation to be worth the money expended upon it. I do hope that we may adopt a plan which will be productive of real development in aerial navigation." The President went on to say that he was forwarding NACA's report to Postmaster General Work "and authorizing his presentation to the Appropriations Committee of Congress if it meets with the approval of the Department." [17]

Unfortunately, when Harding sent NACA's recommendations to Work, his covering note raised the alarming prospect of discontinuing the transcontinental route. "My own thought has been," the President wrote, "that we might very largely diminish the expenditure on daytime flying in the postal service and appropriate the major portion of available funds to the development of night flying. Once that is proven to be feasible, we could embark very consistently on a more ambitious program. . . ." [18]

When the possibility of concentrating on the night airway from Chicago to Cheyenne had been raised at the meeting of NACA's executive committee on December 12, Henderson had stated that this could be done, but abandonment of the transcontinental service "would be a step backward, would waste the present investment in organization and equipment east of Chicago and west of Cheyenne, would alienate popular support of the Air Mail Service, and would have a serious reaction in Congress." Work now supported Henderson on this matter. The best way to proceed, he decided after receiving the NACA's report and the President's covering note, was to take advantage of Harding's authorization to seek additional funds from Congress and ignore his suggestion to cut back on daytime flying. [19]

Work found some support on Capitol Hill, but he failed to persuade Congress that night flying was more important than prudent fiscal policy. Harding and Lord were anticipating the first balanced budget since 1916 in fiscal 1923, with a surplus in fiscal 1924. With the economy reviving from its postwar slump, Congress was reluctant to tamper with the recommendations of the Bureau of the Budget. Under the circumstances, only a direct appeal from Harding would have produced action. And the President did not consider the matter sufficiently important to take such a step.

Henderson may have been disappointed, but he was not ready to give up. The Air Mail Service had a current appropriation of $1,900,000. Thanks to Shaughnessy's emphasis on economy, there would be a balance of approximately $200,000 that could be used to light the airway from Chicago to Cheyenne. Even if funds were not available to operate at night during the fiscal year that would begin in July 1923, Henderson decided to accomplish as much as possible with the money on hand. Like Praeger in 1921, he wanted to demonstrate the crucial difference that night flying could make in the delivery of mail.

Experimental night flying began in February 1923. Magee set up a course from North Platte to an emergency field twenty-five miles away to test rotating beacons, routing markers, terminal and emergency field lighting systems, and aircraft equipment. A number of pilots volunteered for the experiments, including Jack Knight, Frank Yager, Dean Smith, James F. Moore, Earl F. White, Ernest M. Allison, and Harry A. Chandler. Dean Smith later recalled the sense of adventure experienced during the early trials:

> I wish everyone could have the pleasure and excitement of those first hesitant probes across the dark plains. We were like children venturing from home, each time daring a bit farther, then running back filled with awe at what we had done. It felt empty and lonesome out there, even with the beacons flashing, four or five visible ahead; we felt the fear of the unknown, the excitement of pioneering, and the satisfaction of accomplishment.[20]

Initial results were promising. Magee reported in March that pilots had made helpful suggestions for improving aircraft equipment and that several types of large beacons were expected by the end of the month and would be tested to determine their maximum range under different weather conditions. Most important, Magee emphasized, "the first big step, namely, that of getting our men in the air at night with safe equipment, has been accomplished."[21]

Following completion of preliminary trials in mid-April, Henderson ordered Magee to build the world's first night airway. It took four months to complete the task. The 885-mile route included airfields at Chicago, Iowa City, Omaha, North Platte, and Cheyenne, each featuring a giant thirty-six-inch electric arc beacon that produced the most powerful artificial light ever created by man. A result of wartime developments by the Sperry Gyroscope Company, the beacon stood atop a thirty-five-foot tower and projected a beam of light equivalent to 450,000,000 candlepower at an angle of 2° above the horizon. Rotating three times a minute, the huge beacon was an impressive sight.

The night operations landing light that was developed mainly by the Army Air Service, 1923.

Visible from over 100 miles under ideal conditions, it first appeared to pilots as a yellow-green flash on the horizon, changing to greenish-white at a distance of fifteen to twenty miles, then becoming a vivid blue-white at ten miles. A Sperry searchlight of equal candlepower illuminated the landing area, while floodlights were aimed at hangars and other buildings, and red lights marked obstructions.

Thirty-four emergency fields were spaced approximately every twenty-five miles along the route, identified by eighteen-inch incandescent beacons that had been developed by General Electric's National Lamp Works. These 5,000,000-candlepower lights, flashing six times a minute and with a range of over thirty miles, were placed on fifty-foot towers that housed a gasoline generator at the base. Acetylene boundary lights of 5,000 candlepower blinked 250 times a minute from each corner of the field.

Two hundred and fifty acetylene beacons on six-foot pylons were strung out at three-mile intervals to mark the route across the prairies. Activated at night or during cloudy weather by a sun valve (invented by Dr. Gustaf Dalen of Sweden), the gas-fed lights blinked 150 times a minute and had a range of eight to twelve miles.[22]

Henderson wanted an aircraft for night flying that had a landing speed fifteen to twenty miles per hour lower than the DH's sixty mph, was more maneuverable at lower speeds, and had a greater carrying capacity. In March he had ordered experimental models from the Aeromarine, Curtiss, and Glenn L. Martin companies. Also, he had authorized Divisional Superintendent Whitbeck to proceed with plans for a specially modified DH. By August none of these airplanes was ready, and the Post Office had to equip regular DHs for night operations.[23]

With all preparations completed, Henderson ordered a four-day demonstration of the transcontinental day-and-night service. He met Egge in Chicago on August nineteenth. The two men drove to Omaha, where Henderson inspected the lighting facilities at the Fort Crook airfield, spoke with pilots, and reviewed plans for the trial. Everything seemed ready. "I do not think I ever saw more whole-hearted, enthusiastic devotion to duty," he told Egge, "than is evident at every hand. . . ."[24]

Thousands of spectators showed up on the evening of August 21 to be part of what one aeronautical periodical hailed as the "beginning of a new era in aviation." Henderson welcomed the honored guests, including Dr. George W. Lewis of NACA, Glenn Martin, W. J. Boots of the American Gas Accumulator Company, and M. L. Patterson of Sperry. As everyone waited for the westbound mail plane, one observer remembered:

> *The scene was impressively beautiful—the orderly stillness of the military post, the emptiness of the vast field and the vaster sky, the busy workers on parachutes, planes and lighting apparatus about the hangars, the powerful sweep of the huge beacon, the twinkle of the boundary and obstacle lights, the soft flapping of the wind cone, and more than all, the confident expectancy of the officials and men, from Henderson down to the mechanics solicitously inspecting the relay planes due to leave the instant the mail had been transferred.*[25]

The westbound mail was on the way. Eugene Johnson had left New York at 11:01 A.M., stopped at Bellefonte, and reached Cleveland at 4:14 P.M. Arthur R. Smith took the mail to Chicago, arriving at 6:50 P.M. Dean Smith had the first night portion of the schedule. The weather was perfect. The light of sunset lasted almost until Iowa City, then a huge harvest moon lit the landscape between Iowa City and Omaha. The flight was "duck soup," Smith recalled.[26]

Shortly before 11 P.M., a lookout on the tower of the huge Sperry beacon spotted Smith. The rotating beacon was turned off and the landing floodlights came on. Smith touched down at 11:02 P.M., the mail was swiftly unloaded and transferred to a waiting DH, and Jack Knight was on his way in three minutes.[27]

Knight reached Cheyenne at 2:50 A.M., following a stop at North Platte. Bad weather to the west caused Henry G. Boonstra to delay his departure until 5 A.M. After one unsuccessful attempt to get through, Boonstra took off again at 8:24 A.M., taking three hours to cover the 240 miles to Rock Springs. Robert H. Ellis then carried the mail to Salt Lake City, John W. Sharpnack continued to Elko, and Claire K. Vance completed the schedule to San Francisco at 6:24 P.M.[28]

Despite the delay of six hours, more than 30,000 people were at Crissey Field to greet Vance. He smiled "very broadly and happily" when Lillian Gatlin ("a real big Sister to all Fliers") approached the aircraft, shook his hand, and presented him with a small box. Inside, Vance found a four-leaf clover and a message: "For Claire K. Vance: With pride in your participation on the achievement of 28-hour San Francisco to New York U.S. Air Mail Service. And with four leaf clover non-stop wishes for continued four leaf clover success and happiness." Actually, the transcontinental flight had taken over thirty-four hours because of the weather delay at Cheyenne, but this did not diminish the importance of the accomplishment.[29]

Meanwhile, the eastbound schedule had run into trouble. Everything went according to plan until Rock Springs. H. A. Collison left for Cheyenne in mid-afternoon, flew into heavy fog, and had to land at Laramie, forty miles short of his destination. He made four attempts to penetrate the fog, but failed each time and had to return to Laramie. "I'll make Cheyenne if it's the last thing I ever do," Collison growled before leaving again at 10:15 P.M. It took him nearly two

The delayed eastbound mail arrives in New York, August 22, 1923.

hours to cover the forty miles, but he got through. By this time, however, Egge had ordered Frank Yager to leave Cheyenne for Omaha with local mail. The mail from San Francisco eventually went through to New York, but the schedule had been broken.[30]

All flights operated without delay over the next three days, attesting to the Post Office's careful preparation and the presence of good weather. Westbound schedules were completed in under thirty hours (29:44, 29:38, and 29:40), while eastbound trips, aided by favorable winds, did even better. The fastest time was recorded on August 23–24, when the San Francisco mail reached New York in 26 hours 14 minutes, establishing a new transcontinental speed record.[31]

The Post Office had taken a momentous step in the advancement of communications. In 1850 the fastest mail crossed the continent in twenty-four days, three by train and twenty-one by stagecoach. Ten years later, mail from the east coast reached St. Joseph, Missouri, by train in two and a half days; Pony Express completed the trip to the west coast in eight days. The opening of the transcontinental railroad after the Civil War sharply reduced travel time, enabling a special train in 1876 to go coast to coast in 100 hours. By 1923 regular trains took ninety-one hours for the trip. Now, the Air Mail Service had reduced transcontinental transit time by two-thirds.[32]

Congratulations poured in to the Post Office. "I have been watching the transcontinental Air Mail tests with intense interest," Congressman Madden stated, "and am delighted with the success attained." Praeger congratulated Henderson on the "splendid night flying performance" and predicted that regular service would be a "great contribution to commercial aviation in this country." NACA passed a special resolution, praising the Air Mail Service for an "epoch-making performance . . . that will have far-reaching results, not only in assuring the more rapid transportation of the mails, but also in stimulating the development of aviation for civil and commercial purposes, in lessening the handicap of natural barriers of distance between sections of the United States, and in promoting the unity of the American people."[33]

The Post Office basked in the warm light of public approval: *Aircraft Year Book* counted 644 favorable editorials from newspapers and periodicals in 250 cities across the country. "I think that the outstanding conclusion arrived at as a result of this experiment," Henderson reported to the postmaster general, "is that it is feasible and practical to operate aircraft at night over properly lighted and prepared airways." He recommended that the Air Mail Service be authorized to begin regular day-and-night transcontinental operations as soon as possible "consistent with sound preparation."[34]

Henderson looked forward to continued progress. He wanted to extend the lighted airway 150 miles west of Cheyenne and 150 miles east of Chicago. Aircraft with slower landing speeds than the DH had to be found, and experiments to develop a workable radiotelephone should go forward. The next step in air transportation, Henderson told the press, would be to carry passengers as well as mail. "I do not believe," he said, "that even Jules Verne . . . would be qualified to predict the developments of the next decade in the matter of aerial commercial navigation."[35]

Postmaster General Harry S. New, who had taken the position when Work was appointed secretary of the interior in March 1923, shared his predecessor's enthusiasm for the air mail. The former newspaper publisher and senator from Indiana authorized Henderson to include $1,500,000 for night flying in the Post Office's budget request for the coming fiscal year. But Director of the Budget Lord remained unpersuaded. In trimming $10,000,000 from New's requested $623,000,000, Lord again singled out the air mail for special treatment. Apparently knowing little and caring less about the value of the service, he slashed the air mail appropriation by 50 percent, from $3,000,000 to $1,500,000, thus eliminating funds for night operations.[36]

Henderson found himself in the same difficult position that he had been in the previous year. The President—this time Calvin Coolidge, who had become the nation's chief executive following Harding's death in August 1923—did not oppose additional funds for the air mail, but he was reluctant to interfere with the new budgetary process. Like Harding, he supported Lord's authority; he did not wish to go back to the prewar system that saw each department head negotiating separately with Congress for appropriations. The House Appropriations Committee, wielding enormous power under the new procedures, also had a vested interest in supporting the status quo. Members of the committee as individuals might favor more money for the air mail; however, in their collective capacity, they backed Lord.

Henderson appeared before a subcommittee of the House Appropriations Committee on December 31, 1923. Using his report to Postmaster General New on night flying as opening testimony, he followed by saying that it would be impossible to conduct regular night operations with only $1,500,000 for fiscal 1924. "Inasmuch as administrative officers of this Government are prohibited by law from urging appropriations in excess of those passed by the Director of the Budget," he observed, "there is no other comment that I may make on this subject."

Questioned by Chairman Madden, Henderson proceeded to comment a great deal on the subject. If the air mail was going to amount to anything, he responded, it must fly at night and with proper aircraft. The Post Office needed $150,000 to $200,000 to complete the lighting of airways, plus $1,300,000 for the development of suitable aircraft. "Do you think," Madden asked, "that expenditure for pioneer work in the development of commercial aeronautics would be money well expended?" His son-in-law replied:

> The air mail service is the only commercial aviation effort in the United States. Now, whether there ever will be commercial aviation or not, I do not know. Sometimes I think there will be and sometimes I think there will not. But there certainly never will be unless somebody tries it; and no private capital can afford to do the experimenting that would be necessary to develop it.[37]

Although sympathizing with Henderson's position, the legislators could not bring themselves to overturn Lord's decision. On January 29, 1924, the committee reported the Post Office appropriations bill without additonal funds for night flying. Even worse lay ahead. When Congressman La Guardia and others tried to amend the bill on the floor of the House, the entire air mail appropriation was eliminated on a point of order. Ironically, this action came on the same day that the National Aeronautic Association awarded the prestigious Collier Trophy to the Air Mail Service "for successfully demonstrating to the world the practicality of night flying in commercial aviation."[38]

The fate of the air mail again lay with the Senate. In an atmosphere made cordial by the appearance of a former colleague, Postmaster General New came before a subcommittee of the Senate Committee on Appropriations on February 18 and asked that funds be restored. Sen. Kenneth McKellar (Democrat, Tennessee), longtime champion of the air mail, gave New the opportunity to review the sad story of the Post Office's search for money. McKellar was the soul of understanding. "It was a matter of great disappointment to me that the Budget did not allow the $1,500,000 for night flying," McKellar commiserated. "I believe that the very greatest forward step of the year in aviation was the step taken by the Post Office Department in the establishment of those night flights." The full $3,000,000 should be restored, McKellar said. New replied—no doubt with a smile on his face— that he did not want to be placed in the position of appealing a decision of the bureau of the budget. McKellar was not concerned with this problem, nor were the other members of the subcommittee. They defied Lord and recommended $3,000,000 for the air mail. The Senate accepted the subcommittee's decision. The House went along after the conference committee reduced the appropriation to $2,750,000. Day-and-night transcontinental service, Postmaster General New announced, would begin at the start of the new fiscal year on July 1, 1924.[39]

PAUL HENDERSON HAD APPEARED at a crucial juncture in the history of the Air Mail Service. No longer animated by the pioneering spirit of Otto Praeger, the Service had become a routine, point to point, daytime operation that did not significantly advance either the mail or aeronautical technology. Henderson was not content with this situation. He knew little about aviation, but he saw clearly that progress would be limited until airmen had conquered the night. Bringing to the task a pragmatic managerial temperament associated with progressives such as Herbert Hoover, the widely admired secretary of commerce, Henderson systematically examined the problems associated with night flying, then took steps to overcome them.

Less inclined than Otto Praeger to become involved with operational details, Henderson left to subordinates the execution of his grand design. Carl Egge performed admirably, as did the pilots who volunteered for the experimental night flights. More than anyone else, however, engineer Joseph Magee was responsible for assembling the pieces that resulted in the world's first lighted airway.

Following careful preparations, the Post Office staged a spectacular demonstration of what day-and-night flying could accomplish. With time as a measure of distance, a thirty-hour transcontinental service reduced the United States to one-third of its former size. Everyone was impressed, except Budget Director Lord and the fiscal conservatives on the House Appropriations Committee. The Post Office had to struggle for funds to exploit this major technological triumph, demonstrating once again that politics held as many perils as the night sky for the Air Mail Service.

12 Safety First

PREOCCUPIED WITH PREPARATIONS for night flying and relations with Congress after he took office in April 1922, Henderson had left to Carl Egge, the general superintendent, details of day to day operations. Egge, in turn, relied on the divisional superintendents to a greater extent than had any of his predecessors. Washington became the administrative rather than operational center of the Air Mail Service under the new regime. Pilots and field managers no longer communicated directly with headquarters, as they had during the Praeger years; instead, they now faced a structured chain of command that kept all but the most important messages from reaching Egge's desk. "I consider my office [as] executive," Egge explained, "and it is believed advisable to have an executive employee in charge rather than an operations and maintenance official." This meant that chief clerk John W. Sutherin, rather than Charles Stanton, acted as general superintendent during Egge's absences. Stanton fumed, but not for long. Later in 1922 a team of postal inspectors recommended that the offices of Stanton and Edgerton (then superintendent of radio) be eliminated in the interest of administrative efficiency, and Egge complied. The departure of the two men who had done so much for the air mail left no one at headquarters with flying experience.[1]

By the end of 1922, the Air Mail Service had assumed the basic organizational structure that it would retain until its demise in 1927. The transcontinental route was divided into three administrative sectors. Superintendent John E. Whitbeck in New York (later, Cleveland) headed the Eastern Division and was responsible for fields at New York, Bellefonte, Cleveland, Bryan, and Chicago. From his headquarters in Omaha, Superintendent D. B. Colyer of the Central Division looked after Iowa City, Omaha, North Platte, Cheyenne, Rawlins, and Rock Springs. Field managers at Salt Lake City, Elko, Reno, and San Francisco reported to Arlen C. Nelson, superintendent of the Western Division, at his headquarters in Salt Lake City. (In 1924 a new Mountain Division took charge of the route from Cheyenne to Rock Springs, causing adjustment of responsibilities in the Central and Eastern divisions.) With ninety-two aircraft, forty pilots, and twenty-eight radio operators, the Air Mail Service had an accounting value of $2,800,000 in aircraft, engines, motor vehicles, spare parts, hangars, and other buildings.[2]

The move toward centralized retrenchment that had begun under Shaughnessy and continued under Henderson led to the closure of the warehouse at Newark and establishment of a permanent repair facility at Chicago. This came at a time when the Air Mail Service decided to terminate its lease at Checkerboard Field and move flight operations to nearby government-owned land on the spacious grounds adjacent to the Edward Hines Hospital. The Post Office erected a two-story brick repair depot, with 58,100 square feet of floor space for warehouse, garage, test stand, factory, and assembly room. With completion of two hangars, 100 feet by 100 feet, and a hard-surfaced L-shaped runway, air mail operations shifted to the new Speedway Field in the Chicago suburb of Maywood.[3]

The decision to establish a permanent repair base may have been taken largely for economic reasons, but it had important—and positive—operational consequences. Previously, each division had been responsible for assembling and reconditioning the DHs that arrived in crates from surplus Army stores. Although the Eastern Division had a reputation for turning out fine airplanes, the other divisions often produced inferior machines that caused pilots to complain about shoddy workmanship. Now, with improved quality control, the Chicago repair depot turned out rebuilt DHs that compared favorably to those produced by the Army Air Service's excellent maintenance shops.

Lt. Corliss C. Moseley had occasion to inspect the Chicago DHs; he came away impressed. The postal de Havillands, he reported to his superiors, had important modifications that might well be incorporated into military aircraft. For example, Air Service mechanics did not inspect DHs as carefully as they should because so much of the aircraft was inaccessible; mechanics often failed to take off seven or eight screws and open an inspection port to look at a cotter key. The Post Office simplified the inspection process by installing easily opened inspection doors at key locations. Other improvements included heavy axles, an easily reached emergency fuel cut-off valve, a Pyrene extinguisher system for engine fires that a pilot could activate by pulling a release ring, a reinforced cockpit, and double hinges on all elevators, ailerons, and rudder controls. Moseley identified a total of twenty-two changes that "embody not only simplicity but safety to the last degree . . . ."[4]

Harry W. Huking had cause to be grateful for the sturdy character of the postal de Havillands. Leaving Reno in DH Number 167 at 4:26 P.M., May 19, 1922, with the westbound mail, he had trouble climbing and holding altitude. Even with full throttle, the engine would turn over at only 1500 rpm instead of the usual 1600. Reluctant to go back to Reno and default the trip, he decided to press on over the cloud-covered Sierra Nevadas. The engine held at 1500 rpm for an hour, then suddenly dropped below 1400. "This brought me down into the storm which was a corker," Huking recalled. As he passed through 14,000 feet, his engine quit. Huking cut the switches and glided down through the clouds. If he had cleared the mountains and was over the Sacramento Valley, and if there was enough ceiling, there would be nothing to worry about. His last memory of the day's events was that of trees whizzing by "awfully close."

Huking had crashed into Blue Camp Rock, six miles north of Grass Valley, near the California-Nevada border. The DH was a complete washout. A farmer found Huking unconscious in the cockpit and took him to the hospital. The pilot did not regain consciousness for five days. The following week, with no apparent ill effects other than black eyes and a broken nose, Huking returned to flying status.[5]

Even more impressive testimony to the durability of the aircraft— and the pilots—of the Air Mail Service came on December 15, 1922. Henry G. Boonstra took off from Salt Lake City for Rock Springs at 7:30 A.M. He flew low, under a solid layer of clouds, trying to stay at least 200 feet from the rugged terrain. Without warning, a strong gust of wind pushed Boonstra's DH into Porcupine Ridge, southeast of Coalville, Utah. He had no time to turn, reduce power, or cut the switches. The airplane smashed into the ground at flying speed, the landing gear collapsed, and the DH slid on its belly over the ridge before coming to a stop.

Bruised but alive, Boonstra now found himself on an almost inaccessible mountain ridge over 9,400 feet high, and far from civilization. He reported what happened next:

> I took the [airplane] compass and my traveling bag and started on my journey toward civilization. The ridge was bare of snow, but before I had gone a hundred yards down the north slope, I was floundering in snow to my waist. I used the bag in one hand and a stuffed pair of trousers in the other to help support my weight on the snow and started crawling down the slope through the woods. Progress was slow and tiresome, necessitating frequent stops for rest, but I kept at it all day and night and at daybreak came to the edge of the woods. The temperature was below zero and during rest periods I could feel my feet getting numb. The only sign of habitation I could see was a barn about three miles

straight ahead. I struggled toward the barn throughout the day with the blizzard raging and at times obscuring all vision. Progress was fearfully slow and my leg muscles were almost refusing to function. About three P.M. *I came close enough to the barn to see that there was no house there, but could see one about three-quarters of a mile further. I made up my mind to reach the barn—it was debatable whether or not I could reach the house. However, I reached it about six* P.M. *and was taken in and taken care of. I had food and water, my flying clothes taken off, my feet soaked and rubbed in snow, and went to bed.*

Boonstra rested for two days, while divisional superintendent Arlen C. Nelson led a massive ground and air search for the missing pilot. Finally able to ride a horse, Boonstra traveled ten miles to the nearest telephone and called Salt Lake City. He was back flying the Salt Lake City–Rock Springs route a few days later.[6]

Maybe he should have stayed on the ground. Less than three weeks after plowing into the side of Porcupine Ridge, Boonstra again found himself in trouble. He departed from Rock Springs in DH Number

Pilots Henry G. Boonstra (*left*) and James F. Moore, September 1920.

247 at 7:05 A.M., January 4, 1923, for Salt Lake City. Running into heavy snowstorms over the Wasatch Range and unable to stay underneath, Boonstra decided to fly over the storm. He climbed in and out of clouds at 18,000 feet when his engine stopped. Boonstra plunged into the heart of the storm and lost his bearings as the aircraft went into a spin. He recovered, but the disoriented pilot could see nothing outside the aircraft and fell into another spin. Boonstra regained control, only to have the terrifying cycle repeat itself three more times. Just as he was recovering from the fifth spin, the DH hit the ground, bounced, and came down again minus wings and landing gear. The force of the second collision with the earth tore the motor and gas tank from their mounting. Boonstra lay unconscious in what remained of the twisted and broken fuselage. He awoke three hours later, covered in blood from cuts about the face, and with a broken nose. He climbed out of the debris, put on the snowshoes that Superintendent Nelson had placed on all aircraft following Boonstra's previous adventure, and started toward Upton, Utah. About an hour from the crash site, he met one of the search parties that had been sent out to look for him. The intrepid Boonstra would continue to fly the mail over the mountains for the Air Mail Service and Boeing Air Transport for the next decade—and die of natural causes in 1984 at age ninety-four.[7]

The "safety first" program initiated by Shaughnessy and continued by Henderson produced dramatic results (although a number of close calls testified to the role of Chance). During a twelve-month period that ended in July 1922, pilots flew over 1,750,000 miles and carried nearly 1,225,000 pounds of mail without a fatal accident. NACA passed and sent to Postmaster General Work a special resolution of congratulations on the year's performance; it expressed the hope that the air mail's achievement "would serve to inspire public confidence in the safety and utility of airplane transportation under competent management and control."[8]

This happy record came to an end on September 7, 1922. Walter J. Smith was on special assignment to carry mail from the Indiana State Fair at Indianapolis to Cleveland. Apparently wanting to impress the thousands of spectators at the fair grounds, he banked sharply at 200 feet after take-off. The unforgiving DH stalled and spun into the ground. Taken to the hospital in critical condition, Smith died the next morning.[9]

Although the Post Office prohibited stunt flying in mail planes, it proved impossible to restrain the high spirits of some pilots. Paul S. Oakes was another airman who paid a high price for violating departmental regulations. Assigned to test fly DH Number 223 at Cheyenne on January 18, 1923, Oakes took mechanic's helper W. R. Acer along for the ride. To give his passenger a thrill and to entertain spectators on the ground, Oakes put the DH through a series of acrobatic maneuvers, including low-level steep wingovers. While making an abrupt turn downwind at 500 feet, the plane stalled, plunged into the ground nose first, and burst into flames. Oakes and Acer died in the crash.[10]

The Air Mail Service suffered a weather-related fatality the following month. Elmer G. Leonhardt was en route from Bellefonte to Cleveland with the westbound mail on February 26 when he became trapped in dense fog near Meadville, Pennsylvania. In trying to set down in a field, he hooked the landing gear of the DH on a double-wire fence, flipping the plane on its back. Leonhardt was thrown out and killed.[11]

Following Leonhardt's death, the Air Mail Service went another six months and flew nearly 1,000,000 miles without a fatality. Henderson could point with pride to the fact that only three pilots had been killed during his first eighteen months in office, and two of these accidents (Walter Smith and Oakes) could be attributed to pilot error. Night flying experiments had been conducted without a major accident or serious injury, the new repair depot at Chicago was producing DHs that even the Army Air Service admired, and relations with the pilots could not have been better.

The wheel of Fate took another turn on September 7, 1923. Harwell C. Thompson left Cleveland in good weather at 8:07 A.M. with mail for Chicago. About 9:30 a farmer living one mile east of Colton, Ohio, saw Thompson heading west at a low altitude and heard the engine "making very loud reports." The aircraft began a wide turn around the farmhouse, gliding down with the engine throttle back, and was about to land when some cattle shifted into its path. The engine exploded to life, only to fall silent a moment later. The airplane dropped like a rock, nose first and left wing low, hitting the ground at an angle of 120°. Thompson's seat belt broke loose at the fitting, and he was thrown into the inner-bay stagger wires of the left wing. Pinned in the wreckage by the main gas tank, he died after being taken to the hospital.

The engine from the DH was brought to Chicago for inspection. Mechanics discovered a tooth missing from each of the cam shaft drive gears, causing the engine to fire out-of-time and accounting for the loud noise heard by the farmer. Thompson's attempt to apply power and clear the cattle had stripped six teeth from the generator gear, stopping the engine cold.[12]

Three months later, on December 6, Howard C. Brown was flying between Cleveland and Chicago in clear weather. At 10:30 A.M. the sound of an engine attracted the attention of W. H. Sedgwick, a postal employee at Castalia, Ohio. He looked up and saw a DH falling toward the ground, obviously out of control. Running about one-quarter of a mile to the site, he found that the severely injured pilot had managed to crawl ten feet from the burning airplane. Sedgwick pulled him further away and cut off his smoldering clothing. Brown was rushed to a hospital at Sandusky with a broken nose, badly shattered left leg, internal injuries, and third-degree burns on the back, leg, hands, and arms.

William P. Hoare, chief mechanic at Cleveland, visited the hospital at 2 P.M. and was able to have a brief conversation with Brown.

"How are you feeling, Brownie?"

"My leg is broken and my nose is broken but down below is giving me most trouble."

"How did it happen, Brownie?"

"The universal broke. I thought I'd be able to make Bryan with it."

Brown said to tell his wife that he was "banged up a little" but would be all right in a few days. He died at 5:30 P.M. from internal bleeding.

Hoare examined the burned wreck and found that the control stick, which operated the ailerons and elevators, had separated from the "U" fitting that secured the stick to the main assembly. The cause was a defective weld. The stick bore the marks of the Army Inspection Service and had been passed "OK." Sloppy workmanship by the manufacturer had conspired with an Army inspector's negligence to kill a pilot.[13]

A third fatality occurred on the day before Christmas 1923. James F. ("Dinty") Moore encountered a stiff headwind at 1,000 feet while en route from North Platte to Cheyenne. He dropped down to 100 feet, where he found calmer air. A Union Pacific section crew watched as Moore skimmed across a valley two miles west of Egbert, Wyoming. Everything appeared normal until the airplane neared low bluffs at the end of the valley; then instead of gaining altitude it sank and plowed into the slope, a few feet from the top. The propeller cut a ridge in the earth as the DH careened across the ground before collapsing in a heap about 100 feet from the point of first impact. The section crew found Moore inside the cockpit, pinned by the wings. Freeing him from the wreckage, they carried him to the hospital at Burns. The badly injured pilot, suffering from a broken back and crushed chest, died without regaining consciousness.

Assistant divisional superintendent Frank M. Towers led an inspection party to the wreckage that same day. He noted that both switches were one, throttle advanced, and stick control assembly intact. On Christmas Day he wired Egge: "Our investigation resulted that pilot flying low [and] struck a down trend of air sinking plane into side of bluff." Egge passed the information to Henderson, who was spending the holidays with his family in Chicago. "It seems," Egge noted, "the accident [was] due to the hazard of flying and not to defective equipment." Henderson nevertheless suspended operations until January 2 and ordered all airplanes thoroughly inspected.[14]

Henderson called all supervisors to Chicago for a "safety first" conference on December 30. Pilots R. C. ("Tex") Marshall, Randolph G. Page, and George I. Myers represented the Air Mail Pilots of America (AMPA). Presenting an analysis of the fatal accidents over the past four years, Marshall pointed out that eighteen of twenty-five fatalities had occurred in de Havillands. Of the eighteen, eight were due to weather, six to stalls, two to stunt flying, one to mechanical failure, and one to inexperience. The delicate stalling characteristics of the DH had caused six accidents and was a factor in several of the weather-related crashes. Clearly, Marshall concluded, a more stable aircraft would contribute significantly to improved safety.[15]

Henderson could only agree, but there was no easy solution to this problem. Everyone at the conference knew that in April the Post Office had purchased three new planes from Curtiss for $30,000. Featuring a 160-hp C-6 engine, Reed duraluminum propeller, and streamlined wing-type radiator, the aircraft had proved too small and too slow. In July two other planes had been acquired from Aeromarine for $39,000. Although lovely to look at, with a semimonocoque fuselage of duraluminum and fabric-covered wooden wings that

Superintendent John E. Whitbeck's modified DH became known as "Miss Maternity."

had been coated with aluminum paint, the performance of the Liberty-powered biplane had not lived up to expectations. Equally unsatisfactory had been three Glenn L. Martin planes, each powered by a 200-hp Wright E-4 engine, that had cost $58,800 in precious appropriations. Superintendent Whitbeck had obtained better results by modifying a standard DH with Aeromarine wings and a streamlined radiator and engine cowling, but Henderson did not believe that the slightly improved performance justified large-scale procurement.[16]

Henderson told Marshall that he had not given up the search for a better airplane. In fact the department's budget for the next fiscal year had contained a request for $1,500,000 to purchase such a plane (if it could be found). Although the Bureau of the Budget had turned down the appropriation, Henderson hoped to have the funds restored. He then exhorted the assembled pilots:

> *Now boys let's forget the Air Mail percentage. I mean this, forget the percentage we are now making, and put forward first and foremost,* Let's stop killing men. *Let's make the game safer with DHs until we can do better. If it's necessary to run at twenty-five percent in order to make the game safe, why, let's do that. I had rather run at twenty-five percent and not kill a man than run at ninety-six percent and kill someone.*

Henderson emphasized that one out of every eight pilots employed by the Post Office had been killed since he had taken office. If the deaths did not stop, he promised to put an end to the Air Mail Service.[17]

The conference was followed by a letter from Henderson to each pilot, stressing safety. In addition, Egge invited Frank P. Yager, president of AMPA, to write to him on all matters of concern to pilots. "We are real sincere in our ambition to make a safety record," Egge said, "even at the cost of the performance record."[18]

Yager sent to the thirty-four members of AMPA (seven pilots did not belong to the organization) a report of the Chicago conference and a copy of Marshall's accident analysis. "Without wishing to reflect upon anyone who has given his All for the service," Yager wrote in a covering letter, "I believe we can learn from his misfortune, and while the element of chance cannot be entirely eliminated from our occupation, it can be materially lessened. Flying the mail is a serious occupation, and if you will only remember when you are tempting the Goddess of Chance that you alone do not bear the consequences of your actions or misjudgment but that it is reflected upon the service as a whole as well as jeopardizing the positions of your brother pilots. Let us keep this in mind for a better and more substantial Air Mail."[19]

Two airmen tempted the Goddess of Chance only two months later, on March 7, 1924. Leonard B. Hyde-Pearson, a much-decorated veteran of the Royal Air Force, left Bellefonte for Cleveland in DH Number 327 at 2:30 P.M. He flew into a snowstorm near Grampian, Pennsylvania, crashed into a tree at the top of a mountain, and was killed. A note for his brother pilots, to be opened in the event of his death, read: "I go west, but with a cheerful heart. I hope what small sacrifice I have made may be useful to the cause [of advancing aviation]."[20]

Earlier that same day E. Hamilton Lee took off from Iowa City for Chicago. Running into snowstorms, Lee had to land three times to wait for conditions to improve. Shortly after taking off from a field near Rock Falls, he flew into a "blind black blizzard." Trying to land, Lee went through a fence and hit a tree stump that flipped the DH on its back and wiped out the wings, propeller, rudder, and radiator. Pitched out of the cockpit, Lee walked away with a few bumps and bruises.[21]

Superintendent Colyer was not at all pleased when he read Lee's report. Lee was not adhering to the "safety first" policy. "He took unnecessary chances in bad weather," Colyer informed Egge, "and only by good luck was he able to escape without serious injury." Colyer recommended that disciplinary action be taken against Lee "to act as a warning to all other pilots who might be inclined to go too far."[22]

Egge agreed that Lee "certainly did not carry out the instructions recently issued by the office relative to flying in bad weather." On the other hand, Lee was one of the oldest flyers in the Service (and a favorite of Egge's). He had made only a few forced landings and was "rated as a conservative pilot." Egge ordered a mild rebuke: Lee lost mileage pay by being deprived of one mail trip.[23]

The accident rate did go down in 1924, and it improved further during 1925, 1926, and 1927. Yet the higher fatalities of 1921–23 had not been abnormal. A comparison with the experiences of the Army Air Service makes the point:

ARMY AIR SERVICE

	Fatal accidents	Deaths	Accident per miles flown
1921	36 (12 in training)	69	1: 141,127
1922	27 (5)	48	1: 178,311
1923	26 (4)	41	1: 217,392

AIR MAIL SERVICE

	Fatal accidents	Deaths	Accident per miles flown
1921	7	9	1: 273,247
1922	1	1	1:1,756,803
1923	5	6	1: 374,084

The records of the Army Air Service and Navy, together with incomplete statistics from Great Britain and France, indicate that fatal accidents occurred at the rate of approximately 1 per 200,000 miles. By this measure, the Air Mail Service had better than average years in 1921 and 1923, and an exceptionally good one in 1922 (giving rise to Henderson's expectations about safety). But by any measure, the primitive state of aeronautics—aircraft, engines, airports, instruments, and radio—made flying a hazardous occupation during the early 1920s.[24]

HENDERSON CONTINUED TO STRESS safety as he prepared for the beginning of regular day-and-night transcontinental service on July 1, 1924. "I am very optimistic as to the success of the new venture," he wrote to Egge on June 10. "I am very anxious that, in our enthusiasm to succeed, we take no unnecessary hazards. The 'safety first' program which was adopted several months ago has, I feel confident, been successful, and in this new undertaking we must not for a moment abandon our well founded theory of 'safety first.'"[25]

Henderson also decided that the time had come to test the economic potential of air mail. For the first time since 1919, mail would require special postage. Henderson established three zones (New York–Chicago, Chicago–Cheyenne, Cheyenne–San Francisco) and levied an 8¢ surcharge per zone. In 1918 it had cost 24¢ to carry a letter from New York to Washington; now, 24¢ could take the letter from New York to San Francisco. "Beginning with July 1," Henderson pointed out, "the entire character of the Air Mail Service will change. From that date the Air Mail will be performing a tangible rather than an intangible service."[26]

While Magee supervised extension of the night airway from Chicago to Cleveland and from Cheyenne to Rock Springs, Henderson continued to search for a replacement for the DH. In April 1924 the Post Office invited proposals for a plane with a landing speed of 50 mph or less, cruising speed of at least 95 mph, service ceiling of 15,000 feet, and payload of not less than 1,000 pounds. However, as new aircraft could not possibly be ready during 1924, Henderson could only continue to look for ways to improve the performance of the standard DH.[27]

The most promising schemes to modify the postal DH came from Grover Loening and Giuseppe M. Bellanca. These talented aeronautical engineers, both destined to stand in the forefront of American aircraft designers, were trying to survive the lean postwar years by capitalizing on their experiments with more efficient airfoils. The Post Office purchased ten sets of wings from Loening and four from

**Carl F. Egge (*left*)
and Dean Smith,
Omaha, Nebraska,
July 1, 1924.**

Bellanca. Installed on standard DHs, both modifications resulted in reduced landing speeds, better maneuverability at low speeds, and higher cruising speeds. "These remodeled airplanes give us a prompt and timely equipment for night flying." Henderson noted, "during the year or so that the airplane industry will require to develop the new types of planes. . . ."[28]

Transcontinental day-and-night service began on schedule when Wesley L. Smith left New York shortly after 10 A.M., July 1, 1924, circled the field, and "headed west into invisibility and aviation history." Carrying 455 pounds of mail (including a letter from President Coolidge to Gov. F. W. Richardson of California), Smith reached Cleveland seventeen minutes ahead of schedule and passed his cargo to Warren Williams. Transfers at Chicago, Omaha, Cheyenne, Rock Springs, Elko, Salt Lake City, and Reno went smoothly, and the mail arrived in San Francisco at 5:45 P.M. local time, July 2, exactly on schedule (34 hours 45 minutes elapsed time).[29]

Claire K. Vance inaugurated eastbound service on July 1, departing foggy San Francisco at 6 A.M. Schedule was maintained until a tardy mail truck caused a half hour's delay at Cleveland. Wesley Smith tried to make up the time, but was frustrated by unusual easterly winds.

The eastbound transcontinental mail is unloaded at Omaha, Nebraska, during the early morning of July 2, 1924.

He reached New York at 5:11 P.M., July 2, forty-six minutes behind schedule (32 hours 21 minutes elapsed time).[30]

During the first week of operations, all westbound trips arrived in San Francisco close to schedule. Eastbound service suffered only one major interruption. On July 7 Charles Yager left Cheyenne at 7:51 P.M., ahead of a storm that was approaching from the northwest. At Lodgepole, Nebraska, he could see the lights of the emergency field at Chappell, ten miles ahead, but a dark storm obscured the beacon at Big Springs, twenty miles further east. He decided to land at Chappell and wait for the thunderstorm to pass. Everything was normal as Yager approached the field, but then a severe gust of wind struck the airplane. "Found myself sitting on the prairie clear of the ship," Yager reported, "with a terrific wind blowing from west and slightly south." His seat belt had snapped and he had been thrown clear of the demolished DH, suffering only a painful but not serious back injury. Assistant superintendent Oscar C. Wilke testified to Yager's luck. Except for aircraft destroyed in fire, he observed, this was the "most complete washout I know of on the Central Division." He salvaged only two ailerons, the instrument board and instruments, and a few wires and fittings.[31]

Occasional delays during the last three weeks of July failed to dilute Henderson's pleasure with the month's performance. The air mail flew 173,910 miles in July, Henderson reported to Postmaster General New, averaging 39 hours 49 minutes on the westbound schedule and 36 hours 21 minutes on the eastbound, compared to a best train mail time of 86 hours westbound and 90 hours eastbound. Results were especially impressive in view of the poor weather that had plagued the nighttime portion of the route between Chicago and Cheyenne.

"There were frequent storms," Henderson explained, "amounting in certain instances to cloudbursts and tornadoes. There were many electrical storms. Weather conditions such as these are even a greater menace to aviation than more severe rain and snowstorms experienced in other seasons of the year. The very fact that these storms come up quickly and that they are severe while they last creates an unusual hazard." Yet, despite these conditions, there had been only one serious accident (Yager). Pilots were being properly cautious and "have learned to land at night on the emergency field . . . and wait for safe flying weather." Also, the lighting system had worked well, with no major failures. Finally, the morale of the pilots and ground personnel was "all it should be."[32]

In several instances, Henderson continued, aircraft had approached New York and San Francisco in the early evening, but because of darkness had been forced to land and spend the night short of their destinations. Orders have been given to light courses from Mather Field in the Sacramento Valley to San Francisco, and from New York into New Jersey. "This should make our future performance better," Henderson predicted.

Turning to revenue, Henderson said that the Air Mail Service had mounted an "intensive campaign of traffic solicitation," primarily through postmasters and business organizations along the route. Revenue for July had been $51,500, averaging $1,660 a day. Although income remained substantially below operating costs, Henderson expected the situation to improve with time.

On the whole, the first month's day-and-night service had lived up to expectations. Henderson concluded:

> *As far as the physical operation of this continuous New York to San Francisco route is concerned, I now have no hesitancy in predicting its success. Whether or not the service will be supported by the public to the degree which will warrant its continuation, is still open to question. It would seem to me that, at the end of say five or six months, we should take stock of the whole operation, its cost, its income, its performance, and then perhaps arrive at some conclusions as to its future.*[33]

Henderson's prediction of operational success proved accurate. Over the next five months, performance continued to improve as pilots learned to cope with bad weather at night. "At first," Dean Smith recalled, "we canceled whenever the weather was doubtful." However, after running into unexpected weather en route, pilots realized that they could handle most situations. With reasonable horizontal visibility, the flat route between Chicago and Cheyenne could be flown under clouds at 200 feet, nearly as low as in daytime. Except for the heaviest downpours, rain was not a problem; the flashing beacons could be kept in sight as they glistened through the moisture. Thunderstorms, Smith observed, "were far more impressive at night, and their electrical displays were terrifying to me. Alone in the black, with the exposed and defenseless feeling of an open cockpit, the crashing thick streaks of fire were awful in their might, and, perhaps the greatest danger, blinding." Experience showed, however, that most storms "were more sound and fury than actually violent," and it was possible to pick one's way through. "We had to be careful, though," Smith noted, "for some of these storms were treacherous, and occasionally we would blunder into a solid wall of rain, or find ourselves in black cloud, and we had to be alert to instantly turn and fly back out, sometimes in turbulence that taxed our strength."

Yet the darkness held marvels as well as danger for the tiny band of airmen who penetrated the night sky over the Midwest during the summer and autumn of 1924. Few could articulate this sense of wonder better than Dean Smith:

> *Clear black nights with no haze, were, I thought, the most beautiful, and even more so, best to fly rather than the full moon ones that filled all space with milky radiance. On these dark nights, after the eye pupils had dilated to the full, the sky was ablaze with stars, the lights of the towns and villages were lovely sprawls, and the revolving beacons flashed sparks in a row stretching far ahead, a hundred miles or more. Occasional meteors would strike a match across the sky, and sometimes flare so bright I'd blink and duck my head against the sudden light, and then laugh at my needless fright.*[34]

The approach of winter increased the hazards of night flying, bringing sudden snowstorms that could obscure beacons and blot out the horizon. Snow began to fall at sunset on December 21 and grew heavier as the hours passed. Dean Smith was eastbound from Omaha to Chicago. The weather forced him to fly over the now familiar route at altitudes lower than on any previous night trip, at times skimming over railroads and highways at altitudes of no more than 100 feet. "For such a trip," he cautioned, "experience was paramount."[35]

On that same night Clarence A. Gilbart (hired the previous August) went out to face the weather that had challenged the veteran Smith. Shortly after 7 P.M. Chicago operations telephoned the caretaker of the emergency field at McGirr, Illinois (fifty miles west of Chicago) and reported that two westbound sections had taken off, flown by Gilbart and Reuben L. Wagner. Caretaker Paul V. Eakle turned off the noisy gasoline electric generator and put the field's revolving beacon on battery power, the better to hear the aircraft. The night was black and the snow was increasing. At 7:40 P.M. he saw pinpoints of red and green lights over the field at about 300 feet. He responded to the pilot's landing-light signal by waving his flashlight, then followed routine procedure and telephoned ahead to the next emergency field at Franklin Grove and reported the passage. At 8 P.M., with no sight or sound of the second section, Eakle called Franklin Grove and Chicago and learned that two sections had passed Aurora, the emergency field between Chicago and McGirr. As only one flight had reached McGirr, Chicago ordered a search.

Eakle called farmers who lived on the dirt road that ran along the route of flight between Aurora and McGirr. Ascertaining that the airplane had been last heard at Kanesville, a hamlet thirteen miles east of McGirr, he could narrow the search area. Volunteers began looking for the lost airplane as the snowstorm turned into a blizzard. They tramped through the night in vain. It was not until dawn that a farmer discovered the DH in a plowed field only 800 feet from his farmhouse; noise of the crash had been masked by the storm. The pilot was not with the plane. Searching in a circular direction, they located Gilbart's body a half mile away. It was a grisly sight. Gilbart apparently had been caught in the snowstorm at a low altitude, became disoriented when he lost ouside visual reference, and decided to use his parachute (still an optional piece of equipment for pilots). Realizing that he was close to the ground, he pulled the ring to deploy the parachute as soon as he jumped over the side. The canopy went over the horizontal stabilizer, and Gilbart went under. When the shroud lines severed, he free-fell to earth, hitting the stump of a tree, head first, before going into a crack between the ground and wood. "His body rammed in after," Dean Smith recalled, "until it was just a lump with only his shoes showing at the top."[36]

PUBLIC SUPPORT of the air mail failed to match the improvement in service that came with night flying. In late August 1924 Egge informed traffic manager Luther K. Bell that Postmaster General New was disappointed with results to date. New believed that air mail volume should be twice the current level; also, he had received numerous complaints about delays. Egge counseled Bell to avoid mail that involved close rail connections because "postmasters and railway mail service people fail to dispatch mail to our line and we are the goat." He suggested that better results could be obtained by promoting the service with companies directly along the route, pointing out that Sears Roebuck had become interested in the air mail and was spending $150 a day for postage.[37]

Henderson took the lead in a campaign to whip up enthusiasm for the air mail. In articles and speeches, he emphasized that air mail was fast, reliable, and safe—with only 120 pounds of mail destroyed out of 360,000 pounds carried. "The service is yours to patronize," he told audiences. "It is presented as a business proposition, though naturally it has an intense patriotic appeal. But the Air Mail, being put to work for you, can develop and expand only to the degree in which you visualize its remarkable contribution to business efficiency and patronize it accordingly."[38]

Nothing helped. Traffic failed to increase, and expenses continued to run twice as much as income on the transcontinental route. Henderson had only to look at the numbers to measure the lack of progress:[39]

MONTH	DAY	NIGHT	TOTAL	Letters carried	Excess postage
		Miles flown			
July	177,216	35,626	212,842	770,120	$ 51,622
August	163,809	42,535	206,344	776,200	51,118
September	156,519	49,334	205,853	782,240	48,494
October	153,092	63,338	216,430	855,080	59,750
November	152,462	72,574	225,036	768,040	50,586
December	151,048	66,118	214,166	790,536	56,783
	954,146	329,525	1,283,671	4,742,216	$320,529*

*including adjustments

People were slow to change their habits. It would take a dramatic event—Charles Lindbergh's transatlantic flight in 1927—to make the nation "air minded."

Henderson nonetheless remained optimistic. Although it cost $2.60 a ton-mile to move mail by air (compared to 25¢ a ton-mile to carry freight and express over the highways by truck), he was confident that the cost could be brought down as soon as a more suitable aircraft was available. "I predict air transportation at a cost of less than 30 cents a ton-mile," he told an audience at New York University, "with speeds approximately 100 mi/hr. I predict a nation-wide connecting up of all important commercial and industrial centers, with air mail operating at night between such of these centers as are approximately 1,000 to 1,400 miles apart." The Post Office did not intend to stand still. Next year would see overnight mail service between New York and Chicago, followed by lateral extensions of the transcontinental route. The future of the air mail remained bright.[40]

The Bureau of the Budget and Congress apparently agreed. The Post Office asked for $2,600,000, including funds to operate the New York–Chicago overnight service, for the fiscal year beginning July 1, 1925. Never before had things gone so smoothly. The Bureau of the Budget approved the request without cutting a penny, the House Committee on Appropriations went along without a single objection, and no one raised a point of order when the appropriations bill came up for a vote on the House floor. Henderson must have had the feeling that he was doing something right.[41]

As editor of *Jane's All the World's Aircraft* and *The Aeroplane*, English journalist and expert aeronautical commentator Charles G. Grey was especially well qualified to place the accomplishments of the Air Mail Service in a broad context. Americans, he wrote following a visit to the United States, apparently had been shown optimistic maps of airline networks from London to Moscow and been told wonderful stories of the success of civil aviation in Europe. They tended to believe that Europe was ahead of the United States simply because passengers were being carried. This view was false. The only airlines in regular operation were flown by Imperial Airways from London to Paris (250 miles) and from London to Cologne (300 miles). Imperial received a subsidy of £100,000 per year, guaranteed for ten years. Airplanes on the subsidized French line from Paris to London started regularly but arrived intermittently. Imperial and KLM operated a London–Rotterdam–Amsterdam route with regularity; however, they seldom carried a full load. The same was true with Deruluft's Konigsburg–Moscow service. Other lines flew only from time to time. "So," the outspoken Englishman concluded, "barring Imperial Airways and the Royal Dutch line, one may say that Civil Aviation is a joke and rather a poor one at that."

In comparison, the "U.S. Post Office runs what is far and away the most efficiently organised and efficiently managed Civil Aviation undertaking in the world. That 3,000 mile trip, with its 1,400 miles in the dark, day in and out all the year round, is a wonderful affair." The secret to the success of the Air Mail Service, Grey explained, was that the "real work was done on the ground, not in the air." Henderson put it best when he said, "An airway exists on the ground, not in the air." Concentrating its efforts on lighting and preparing the transcontinental route, the Post Office had developed a system that was a "model for the world." Europeans had not understood this. "Our idea," he noted, "is to build and organise elaborate terminal aerodromes, equip them with radio gear and all the comforts of home and then push the aircraft into the air relying on what we hope to be infallible engines."

Grey much preferred the American system. "In spite of funny old-fashioned wooden hangars and dirt floors," he wrote, "the mechanics maintain their old war-time ships in beautiful order. And in spite of high landing speeds the pilots do not crash them. The mails are run astonishingly close to schedule time. The casualties are amazingly few. In fact the complete outfit is a wholly admirable institution which reflects credit on everybody concerned."[42]

13 Nor Gloom of Night

DEVELOPMENT OF THE overnight mail route between New York and Chicago ranks high among the Air Mail Service's most significant contributions to the advancement of commercial aviation in the United States. The Allegheny Mountains might lack the majestic peaks of the Rockies, but the densely wooded hills of Pennsylvania early gained the respect of air mail pilots. Storms were frequent and violent. Clouds often lay on top of the hills, and fog obscured the rolling valleys. A pilot forced to make an emergency landing usually looked in vain for a field large enough to safely accommodate a DH. Although "Hell Stretch" was a term used more by reporters than postal airmen, the air route over the Alleghenies posed a constant challenge to the experienced pilots who attempted to maintain regular daytime schedules between New York and Chicago. Nighttime operations would test their professional skills to the limit.

On July 10, 1924, Henderson was in Chicago to promote the newly opened transcontinental service at a meeting of the Illinois Bankers Association. While the bankers expressed interest in the air mail, they pointed out that most of their business lay with New York. The Post Office's schedule called for mail to leave Chicago at 7:35 A.M. and arrive in New York at 5:05 P.M. As the mail would not be delivered until the following morning, along with the train mail, there was little advantage in paying a premium rate for the air service. However, if the mail could leave Chicago at the end of the business day and reach New York for the start of the next business day, the "float" or transit time for checks and other negotiable paper would be reduced by one day. This would mean millions of dollars to the banks.[1]

Henderson appreciated the compelling logic of the bankers' suggestion. Even before the transcontinental route opened, he had realized that the commercial future of the air mail lay in providing overnight service between large business centers. However, Henderson wanted to proceed with caution. "Night flying on schedule had never been attempted anywhere in the world," he later pointed out. "We were literally blazing a new trail in aviation. . . . After the Service demonstrated its ability to fly at night over this level region [between Chicago and Cheyenne], I felt would be time enough to undertake the more difficult mountain sections."[2]

But increased pressure from the financial community on Postmaster General New, together with the initial success of night operations on the transcontinental route, caused Henderson to act more speedily that he had planned. In September he ordered Traffic Manager Bell to make an intensive survey of business interest in New York–Chicago overnight service. At the same time, he asked Egge to conduct an engineering study of the route between New York and Cleveland (the level ground between Cleveland and Chicago was already lighted).[3]

Both men came back with optimistic reports. Bell predicted 1,000 pounds of mail nightly from New York and 350 pounds from Chicago, far exceeding current daytime loads. Egge was equally sanguine. Building a night airway over the Alleghenies would not be easy, he concluded, but it could be done. On November 14 Henderson announced that a New York–Chicago overnight service would begin in April 1925.[4]

Egge placed John E. Whitbeck in charge of the challenging task of building the new night airway. Known as "Pinkwhiskers" because of his pinkish-colored Van Dyke beard (originally grown to cover a scar and kept as a trademark), Whitbeck had been superintendent of the Eastern Division since 1920. The former Navy machinist's mate and wartime captain in the Engineering Division of the Army Air Service was exceedingly proud of his technical expertise. As men who fly airplanes do not always see eye to eye with those who maintain them, relations between Whitbeck and the pilots tended to be tense at times. "Jack was a great showman with lots of ego," one colleague explained, "and we needed it in the mechanical end—we had plenty of it in the pilot group—but he pushed the mechanical and technical side." Eventually, many pilots would come to value Whitbeck's efforts to improve the DH. His work in this area, R. C. ("Tex") Marshall emphasized, "was the reason many pilots lived."[5]

The first requirement of the new airway was improved terminal facilities on the east coast. On November 1 Whitbeck signed a lease with John R. Hadley, Sr., for seventy-seven acres of level ground, located five miles from New Brunswick, New Jersey. One hour by fast mail train from the New York General Post Office, free from the fog and smoke that plagued operations at Hazelhurst, and affording clear approaches from all directions, Hadley Field seemed ideal for night re-quirements. Preparations began at once. Crews covered and graded an open ditch, laid 2,000 feet of eight-inch tile to improve drainage, erected radio masts, installed fifty boundary lights, and made provisions for floodlights and revolving beacons. The Post Office spent $20,000 for an 85 x 100 foot hangar that could accommodate five aircraft. Favored by good weather, the workmen completed their tasks in short order. On December 15 daytime transcontinental operations shifted from Hazelhurst to Hadley.[6]

Whitbeck, meanwhile, had been surveying the route to Cleveland. Driving over the back roads of Pennsylvania, he searched for emergency landing sites that were level, relatively free of timber, easily accessible and well drained. This proved no easy task. "Suitable plots of forty acres or more, which do not require extensive preparation," Whitbeck noted, "simply do not exist through Pennsylvania." Even when fields were located, he still had to find the owners to negotiate leases. This often caused problems because most of the mountain property was held for coal and timber rights, and the owners were scattered throughout the country.[7]

The need for clear approaches from all directions meant that the daytime fields at Bellefonte and Cleveland could not be used for night operations. While field manager Fred G. Gelhaus prepared a new field at Bellefonte, Whitbeck put pressure on Cleveland city manager W. R. Hopkins to make good on his earlier promise of a new municipal airport. "Some real progress has been made in determining the best night flying course between Cleveland and New York," Whitbeck reported to Egge in late December, "and most of the emergency fields have been tentatively located, so that it now begins to look as though Cleveland (the most important) would be the last field to be ready for night flying on the Eastern Division, and there will be a considerable amount of work at Cleveland, even after the field is available."[8]

January and February 1925 brought heavy snowfall to Pennsylvania (some locations recorded fifty-one inches in January alone), slowing work on the airway. The pace quickened in mid-March with the return of good weather. Whitbeck signed leases (usually for ten to twelve dollars per acre per year) for emergency fields at Tamaqua, Ringtown, Numidia, Elysburg, Sunbury, Woodward, Snowshoe, Du-Bois, Brookville, and Clarion. All required extensive work. At Clarion, fourteen acres of timber had to be removed; workmen had to tile and grade three open ditches at DuBois, cut down 300 trees at Sunbury and 100 at Numidia. After blasting out tree stumps (it took two tons of dynamite to clear one field), the ground was leveled and boun-

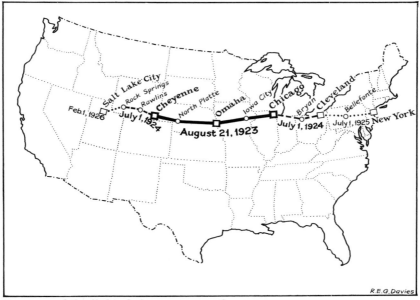

Progress of the lighted airway, 1923–26.

dary lights were strung out at 100-yard intervals to mark the emergency landing area. General Electric twenty-four-inch beacons that rotated six times a minute at an angle of 2.5° above the horizon were mounted on fifty-foot towers to identify the location. After caretakers were hired and given rudimentary training in weather observation, the emergency fields were ready for business.[9]

On May 30, 1925, Charles H. Ames, Dean Smith, and Wesley Smith made the first practice night flights from Hadley to Sunbury and return. The trials continued into June, with all pilots assigned to Cleveland and New York making at least one night flight over the route and a daytime landing at all emergency fields. On June 13 the new field at Bellefonte—two miles southeast of the old location—became operational. And, after numerous delays, the impressive Cleveland Municipal Airport (later named after City Manager Hopkins) opened on June 28.[10]

The night airway between New York and Cleveland was one of the wonders of early aviation. Hadley Field, Bellefonte, and Cleveland featured new 500,000,000-candlepower arc floodlights with Fresnel lenses one meter in diameter that turned the landscape for nearly a mile around (in a half-circle) as light as day. Yet, unlike previous designs, at no point did the floodlights' rays extend more than fifteen feet above the ground; pilots could land directly into the lights without experiencing a blinding glare. Another powerful searchlight stood atop a hangar, fifty feet from the ground. Revolving six times a minute, the 5,000,000-candlepower beacon shot an intense beam of light into the darkness at an angle of 1° above the horizon.

Departing from Hadley Field, a pilot picked up the first of forty-six specially designed routing beacons at Somerville, New Jersey, twenty miles to the northwest. Four headlights of the type used on Ford automobiles had been set to cast a beam ½°, 1°, 1½°, and 2° above the horizon; a pilot could see one of the headlights, revolving counterclockwise at ten times per minute, from any altitude. A red light on top warned him that this was a routing beacon and not an emergency field.

The first 2,500,000-candlepower beacon marking an emergency field appeared at Whitehouse. A pilot flew over flat terrain for the next eighty miles, noting three more emergency landing areas as he neared the Blue Mountains. Five emergency fields could be found along the thirty miles of heavily wooded hilly terrain between New Tripoli and Ringtown, then another five fields to Bellefonte. Fifteen more emergency fields lay between Bellefonte and Cleveland.[11]

The Post Office spent $127,715 to light the 399-mile airway between New Brunswick and Cleveland ($23,307 for three regular fields, $57,665 for twenty-nine emergency fields, and $46,742 for forty-six electric and ten gas routing beacons). By comparison, it cost $63,910 to light the 327 miles between Cleveland and Chicago.[12]

Over 15,000 spectators packed Hadley Field on July 1, 1925, for the start of the night mail. The first airplane was scheduled to leave at 10:30 P.M., but Dean Smith was sent ahead with three sacks of mail (eighty-seven pounds) because of anticipated heavy volume for the inaugural flight. Postmaster General New appeared on the scene after Smith's departure and spoke to the crowd, recalling the days of the Pony Express and citing the words of Herodotus that were carved over the entrance to the New York Post Office: "Neither snow nor rain . . . nor gloom of night stays these couriers from the swift completion of their appointed rounds." The government would continue to fly the night mail for the time being, he said, but looked forward to the day when private companies would take over the task. New then walked over to James D. Hill and handed him a sack of mail: "Here, take it; good luck to you." After this sack joined the thirty-five others that had been loaded onboard, Hill climbed into the cockpit of his DH and started the engine. Over 1,000 cars trained their headlights on the field in a symbolic gesture as Hill made a short run across the ground, then disappeared into the night.[13]

Chicago saw a similar scene. Henderson and Egge joined a group of dignitaries and thousands of spectators to bid farewell to the two pilots who would carry the eastbound mail. Moments before the departure of Shirley J. Short, two large boxes of flowers arrived from the downtown post office. One was from Vice-President Charles G. Dawes to President Coolidge's father, who was recovering from an operation in Plymouth, Vermont; the other was being sent by radio station WHT to actress Grace George in New York. Following appropriate remarks by Dawes and Henderson, Short lifted off into the twilight at 7:40 P.M. Most of the crowd remained on the field to witness George I. Myers's nighttime departure at 9:40 P.M.[14]

The eastbound schedule went smoothly. Short reached Cleveland at 10:30 P.M., where over 200,000 people were on hand to celebrate the opening of the new airport. Paul F. Collins then carried the mail to Hadley, arriving at 2:00 A.M. The second eastbound section, flown by Charles Ames, reached New Brunswick without incident at 4:37 A.M.[15]

Dean Smith, meanwhile, had run into trouble with the westbound mail. It was a clear night, with excellent visibility, when Smith left Hadley Field. "My spirits were high," he recalled, "elated by the prospect of easily accomplishing an important flight." He followed the beacons to Bellefonte, landed at the new field, refueled, and took off for Cleveland. Clearing the high ridges of Rattlesnake Mountain, he was approaching Clearfield at 8,000 feet when a great spout of steam and boiling water gushed from the front of his engine. The motor quit "without even a residual cough." Smith put his DH into a glide, headed toward the revolving beacon of the emergency field at Clearfield, and dropped one of the two magnesium parachute flares that he carried.

"It was a weird, wild scene," Smith remembered, "the ball of fire in the air, a snake of smoke rising from it; the dark pushed back, but its wall not far; the plane, illuminated by the flare, gliding down, the twin beams of its landing lights probing ahead; and the lights of the small field a rectangle below with the arm of its beacon sweeping around in beckoning gesture." Smith's first emergency night landing was perfect. Without turns or slips, he brought the DH over the boundary lights, set down, and rolled to a stop.

Smith telephoned Cleveland and reported the trouble. He was told that Lloyd W. Bertaud would fly in with a replacement aircraft. When Bertaud arrived, he informed Smith that a tremendous crowd was waiting for him in Cleveland. Smith asked if the airplane had enough fuel to cover the 180 miles to Cleveland; otherwise, he would have to go back to Bellefonte, thirty minutes away. "There ought to be enough," Bertaud answered. Smith decided to press on.

The westerly wind grew stronger as Smith headed toward Cleveland. He flew as low as possible to keep out of the wind, but his ground speed continued to slow, while the needle on his fuel gauge crept toward the peg. The DH had an eight-gallon gravity-feed emergency tank in the center section of the upper wing, usually permitting twenty minutes of cruising. Smith decided that if he could reach the emergency field at Solon (fifteen minutes from Cleveland) on the main tank, he would have enough fuel to complete the trip. He switched to the emergency tank just to make sure that it would work. It did, so he switched back to his main tank.

About five miles east of Solon, the engine coughed, sputtered, and died. "I nearly broke my fingers twisting on the emergency valve," Smith recalled; but nothing happened. He continued to twist the valve, trying to clear what was probably an air lock in the line. At the same time, he popped an emergency flare. The harsh light of the flare revealed only rolling hills that were covered with clumps of trees. Flying at 1,000 feet with no chance of reaching a suitable field, Smith headed for a tiny clearing near a farmhouse. Approaching the site, he threw the DH into a skid, held the nose up, and dropped the trailing wing until it hooked the ground. The airplane cartwheeled, the wings crumpled, and it slapped on its back with a thud. Somehow, the landing lights survived to shine through the dirt and give the impression of fire. A miraculously uninjured Smith was out of the DH and fifty feet away "in a matter of seconds." He walked the short distance to the farmhouse and knocked on the door. A voice inside answered: "Who are you? What do you want?" Smith told the suspicious farmer that he had just landed an airplane in his yard and would like to use the telephone. The farmer wanted to see some money to pay for the call. Finally, he opened the door and allowed Smith to contact anxious officials at Cleveland. Ordered to take the mail to the emergency field at Solon, he then had to dicker with the farmer for the use of his car. Negotiations completed, the two men walked to the demolished airplane to retrieve the mail. The DH was a sorry sight, lying on its back with the landing gear sticking up into the air, wings crumpled. The farmer carefully surveyed the scene, then commented, "Hmmptf, do you always land this way?" The chagrined pilot took the mail to Solon, where Art Smith picked it up. It finally reached Chicago at 8:20 A.M., two hours after the second section had arrived.[16]

The New York–Chicago overnight service proved an immediate success, carrying 1,199,480 letters (approximately 30,000 pounds) during the first three months of operation and generating revenues of $45,703 (at 10¢ per ounce). The mail moved with a speed that later generations of postal patrons might envy. Lester D. Gardner, editor of *Aviation*, conducted a test of the service in July that produced impressive results. At 5:30 P.M., July 8, he dropped a letter into one of the special red, white, and blue air mail boxes near the Flatiron Building in New York City. It was addressed to the Postmaster at Chicago, with instructions to return upon receipt. The letter reached the Main Post Office at 6:30 p.m., went to New Brunswick by fast mail train, and was carried by truck to Hadley Field in time for the 10:30 P.M. departure of the night mail. It arrived at the Chicago Post Office at 8 A.M., July 9, then was returned to Maywood Field for the night flight. The New York Post Office received the letter at 10 A.M., July 10, and delivered it to the offices of *Aviation* at 225 Fourth Avenue at 11 A.M. Gardner immediately telegraphed Postmaster General New: "Congratulations on the fastest mail service in the world." [17]

MAINTAINING SCHEDULES AT NIGHT over the Alleghenies made unprecedented demands on the pilots, and called forth an unprecedented response. A number of air mail pilots had experimented with instrument flying before 1925. Usually, this involved climbing through clouds en route to a destination that was reported clear. "Prior to our obtaining the turn Gyro," Dean Smith recalls, "I, and others, were able to fly for ten or fifteen minutes while attempting to climb on top of cloud layers. We made no attempt to hold a compass course, but locked the rudder as best we could, watched the air speed, and, if we felt too much wind on one cheek, gingerly lifted the wing a bit. Still, often as not, the plane would get away from us and we would spin down, to pull out at the bottom of the cloud layer." [18]

The gyroscopic turn indicator, key instrument for early "blind" flying, was developed at the end of World War I largely through the efforts of Charles H. Colvin of the Sperry Gyroscope Company. Colvin left Sperry in 1919 and formed the Pioneer Instrument Company. Both Sperry and Pioneer continued work on the turn indicator during the 1920s, and early models were tested by the Air Mail Service, Navy, and Army Air Service. In January 1923 Pioneer put out an improved design, produced under a Sperry license. Known as a turn-and-bank indicator, it featured a gyro-erected needle showing direction and rate of turn, and a bubble inside a liquid-filled tube that served as a lateral inclinometer. [19]

Most air mail pilots showed little interest in the new instrument, preferring to hug the ground and trust their senses in bad weather. But a few intrepid airmen, like Dean Smith, Wesley Smith, Arthur R. Smith, and R. C. Marshall experimented with the device. Marshall, for example, would pull up into an overcast on his regular run and try to control the airplane by reference to his instruments. At first, he

Veteran pilot R. C. ("Tex") Marshall logged 3,675 hours between 1920 and 1927.

quickly lost control and came spinning out of the clouds. But with trial and error, he grew more confident. He learned to turn 180° in clouds, then 360°, using the position of the turn indicator needle and a clock to time his turns when the spinning compass proved useless. No doubt, Marshall recalled, his flying was sloppy and erratic by later standards, but nonetheless "I could control the plane and keep it generally headed the way I wanted to go somewhere about the altitude I wanted to use." [20]

Problems developed and solutions emerged as the first instrument pilots honed their skills. Turn indicators were too sensitive for flying in rough air, and the venturis that provided air to spin the gyros clogged at the first sign of ice. The situation improved when turn indicators were damped so that they would respond only to turns large enough to affect the compass; venturi tubes were mounted near the exhaust pipes of the engine, where the heat prevented ice from forming. As the bubble-bank indicators—used to keep the plane level in straight flight and to bank it properly in turns—were difficult to use and hard to see, Wesley Smith enlisted the services of Howard F. Salisbury, an air mail instrument technician at Cleveland, to design a more effective device. With the help of a glassblower at Cleveland Hospital,

Salisbury came up with a curved tube, six inches around, filled with alcohol (or kerosene), and containing a steel ball one inch in diameter, that proved far superior to the Pioneer indicator.[21]

Sporadic individual experiments with instrument flying evolved in 1925 into an informal, cooperative group effort among the men who flew the night mail over the Alleghenies. Pilots based at Hadley Field (Wesley Smith, Dean Smith, James Hill, Harry Chandler) and at Cleveland (Paul Collins, Charles Ames, Lloyd Bertaud, Earl F. Ward) exchanged ideas as they pushed back the frontiers of flight. Sometimes the price of new knowledge came high.[22]

Charles Ames was one of those tough and determined men who seemed attracted to the ranks of the Air Mail Service. Early in his flying career, Ames nearly died in a serious accident that left his right knee completely rigid. An infection drained pus through several openings into the joint, and the surgical dressing had to be changed each day, but Ames kept on flying. A progressive pilot, he worked hard on developing instrument skills. One technique he used to cross over a ridge that was covered by clouds was to pull up into the overcast and rely on his instruments for several minutes before dropping down into clear skies in the valley on the other side.[23]

On October 1, 1925, Ames reported to Hadley Field for the night schedule to Cleveland. The weather had been miserable for three days, but the situation was improving. At 9 P.M. Bellefonte reported an overcast ceiling of 1,500 feet, visibility "two lights west, one east," haze, winds from the southwest at 6 mph, temperature 50° F, and barometer 30.2 inches of mercury. Reports of en route weather indicated that Woodward Pass had the lowest ceiling, as usual, of 800 feet. With a reasonable possibility of getting through, Ames hobbled out to DH Number 385 and took off at 9:58 P.M.

Ames was due at Bellefonte at 11:30 P.M. When he did not arrive by midnight, officials at the field telephoned caretakers along the route for information. The last definite report put Ames over Millheim light, between Woodward and Bellefonte, at 11:35 P.M.

Fog prevented an air search on October 2, but a ground party covered the course between Millheim and Bellefonte and found nothing. The weather cleared on October 3, permitting Air Mail and Army pilots to search the area east and west of Bellefonte. Again, the air and ground effort failed to reveal any sign of Ames. The next day, with the story of the pilot's disappearance being given wide publicity, reports began to come in that placed Ames far north and south of course. The search expanded, with troops from the Pennsylvania National Guard joining in.

On October 6 pilots scattered handbills over the widening search area, offering a $500 reward for information. Newspapers began to speculate that Ames may have absconded with a large amount of cash that was onboard the airplane. Postmaster General New denied that Ames had been carrying money. "There is not doubt in my mind," New said, "that Ames met with the saddest kind of a sad fate."

It was not until October 11 that a ground party searching Nittany Mountain, four miles west of Bellefonte, found Ames. He was in the cockpit of his DH, safety belt broken, feet wrapped around the control stick. He had died when his head hit the instrument board. The airplane had crashed 200 feet from the summit of the mountain, and had been masked by the foliage of oak trees.

Field manager Gelhaus headed an investigating team that inspected the wreck on October 12. The airplane had been directly on course, switches on, and throttle advanced. Ames obviously had flown into the side of the mountain. Their report noted that there had been a sharp drop in barometric pressure in the area following Ames's departure from Hadley Field. Ames may have been trying to clear the mountain on instruments, relying on his altimeter, when he crashed.[24]

The altimeter used by the Air Mail Service had been developed during World War I and was not adequate for the demands of instrument flying. Recording up to 20,000 feet with one revolution of the indicator hand on the dial, the altimeter's scale was so fine that it could not be read with accuracy in hundreds of feet. Also, adjustments for en route changes of pressure could not be made; the pilot could only set the pointer on zero before departure.

Howard Salisbury, the Cleveland instrument technician, had been a good friend of Ames's. Following Ames's death, Salisbury talked with instrument manufacturers and military experimenters about ways to improve the altimeter. "No one," Salisbury recalled, "had a direct answer how to correct the trouble." He finally discovered a report about a German mountain climbing altimeter with two dials that allowed the user to make barometric corrections. After much trial and error, Salisbury modified an altimeter by putting a barometric scale on the fixed inner plate of the instrument and cutting a window in the outer, movable dial. "This proved quite satisfactory," Salisbury noted, "so about ten of the altimeters were revised and calibrated in the small shop at the Cleveland Air Mail Field. The shop facilities were meager . . . hand tools, a barometer and a homemade bell jar (made from a cheese jar and a surface plate). The tests were successful and the pilots were pleased." The Air Mail Service took the adjustable altimeter to the Taylor and Pioneer instrument companies. Soon, pilots had "real 'store bought' altimeters with a barometric correction built in." The Kollsman Instrument Company later refined and perfected the instrument. "Thus," Salisbury concludes, "the death of an Air Mail pioneer, Charlie Ames, was the reason for development of the barometric correction on our altimeters. The honor should be his and he and many others in the Air Mail Service did not die entirely in vain. The very foundation of modern Air Transportation was laid . . . by these men."[25]

As instruments improved and experience accumulated, pilots would gain confidence in their ability to fly without outside visual reference. But first a formidable mental block had to be overcome. "It is difficult now for one to understand the mental hazard involved," Dean Smith has emphasized, "for before it had been ingrained in us that we would invariably lose control if we flew blind any length of time." Slowly, they learned to trust their instruments, even when their senses denied the readings on the gauges. When they found that they could hold the airplane level in flight, they tried turns. Finally, they deliberately put the plane into a spin and attempted to recover by a one-two-three method: one, use the rudder to center the turn indicator; two, use the ailerons to place the metal ball of the bank indicator in the center of the tube; and three, use the elevator to stabilize the airspeed.[26]

After experimenting with the most effective arrangement of instruments for "blind" flying, the pilots reached general agreement on a design that placed the magnetic compass at the top center of the instrument board, with the turn indicator, bank indicator, and airspeed indicator directly in line underneath. The altimeter was placed to the left of the bank indicator and the tachometer to the right. Engine instruments were on the extreme right of the panel, with lighting instruments, switches, and clock on the extreme left.[27]

"IF THE TERMINAL FIELDS have fair weather," Wesley Smith noted, "we can fly through anything between them, except ice-forming clouds." However, much remained to be done to improve the reliability of the air mail. "We need a beacon ray that will penetrate the storms and guide us to the fields in bad weather," he pointed out, "and we need communication between the field and the plane en route to warn us to changes in the weather."[28]

During 1925 the Air Mail Service explored the use of radio, both for communications and as an aid to navigation. This was part of an attempt to place aeronautical experimentation on a more systematic basis, the first such effort since budgetary restraints in 1922 had brought an end to the work done at College Park under Stanton and

Edgerton. In January 1925 Egge asked Henderson for permission to establish an "experimental laboratory" to test radio direction finding instruments, a radio compass, altimeter, and other flight instruments, and to evaluate new types of aircraft for night operations. He wanted $20,000 to build the necessary buildings at a new facility, and permission to hire Edward P. Warner of the Massachusetts Institute of Technology, a prominent aeronautical engineer, as a part-time consultant to supervise the work.[29]

"I have given a great deal of thought to this proposed operation," Henderson wrote to Egge in February. "I feel confident that if we get it properly organized it will be productive of much good." The experimental station was to emphasize the practical application of existing equipment. "We must not permit ourselves to engage in tests which are super-technical," he stressed. "We don't care to know why a thing fails if it fails." Professor Warner agreed to become responsible for the technical direction of the work. He planned to consult with the National Bureau of Standards, the Army Air Service Engineering Division, and other agencies and individuals in an effort to discover "just what has been done up to the moment in the matter of aids to air navigation." He would recommend the purchase of radio equipment and supervise tests to determine "if there are any of these devices sufficiently worthy of adoption by the Air Mail Service." Again, Henderson emphasized, "we must avoid . . . experiments which do not lead anywhere."[30]

On March 15, 1925, Egge created the Development Division. Selecting Monmouth, Illinois, as the site for the new section, he contracted for a two-plane hangar that also would house a workshop, radio laboratory, and offices. Harry G. Smith, a pilot who had an engineering background and managerial experience, became superintendent and took charge of a small staff that included engine expert Oscar C. Wilke, radio specialist Carl B. Hempel, and test pilot Frank H. Burnside.[31]

By summer Smith had a variety of projects underway. After developing devices to measure landing speed, the division conducted extensive performance tests on two aircraft that had been submitted by manufacturers as replacements for the DH. Storage batteries were compared, and a shortwave tube transmitter examined. The most promising line of investigation, Smith believed, lay in Hempel's work on the four-course, low frequency, radio directional beacon. At a time when the lighted airway between New York and Chicago was being hailed as a great achievement, Smith looked forward to the day when it would be replaced by a "radio airway." And that day, he was convinced, was near.[32]

Hempel went to McCook Field in July and discussed with Army Air Service technicians their progress in perfecting the directional radio beacon that had been developed by the National Bureau of Standards after World War I. Results, he learned, had been encouraging, although many problems remained to be solved. With components acquired at McCook, Hempel built a radio beacon adjacent to the flying field at Monmouth. Improving the original equipment, he developed a simplified airborne receiver, and he made the first successful voice transmission over the antenna and transmitter that carried the navigational signal. But experiments revealed that the beacon did not have sufficient power to overcome bad static conditions during electrical storms. Also, the cost of the transmitter was prohibitive, while the eighty-five-foot antenna towers posed a hazard to pilots using the airfield.[33]

Hempel made considerable progress in resolving these problems. "We are at present on the threshold of securing an improved radio beacon," Smith reported in November, "in which the original objections have been overcome. The beacon on which we are now working will be comparatively inexpensive, will have an effective range, and will be of small physical dimensions. The results obtained in the last few days have proved that this can be made practical in a very short time." But Smith would not have the opportunity to see this important work through to completion: a new regime had ordered the abandonment of the Development Division.[34]

On August 1, 1925, W. Irving Glover replaced Henderson, who left the Post Office to become general manager of National Air Transport, a well-financed company that had been organized following passage of the Air Mail Act of 1925 (see Chapter 14). Born in Brooklyn in 1879 and educated in the public schools of New York City, the new second assistant postmaster general was a self-made man who took his first job in the woolen industry at age eighteen. Eager to succeed, he went to night school for technical courses in spinning and weaving; he ended up as New York sales representative for the Phoenix Woolen Company of Stafford, Connecticut. Active in Republican politics, Glover moved to New Jersey, where he was elected to the state assembly in 1917. Hays offered him the position of third assistant postmaster general in 1921 and he accepted. During the next four years, Glover proved an effective administrator, establishing a new philatelic division and developing a method to sell foreign money orders to patrons of the Post Office's money order system.[35]

The Air Mail Service seemed to be making important technical and commercial progress when Glover took office. Traffic on the night schedule between New York and Chicago was increasing daily, the transcontinental route carried 1,415,640 letters in July and generated an all time high of $75,764 in excess postage, orders had been given to light the airway between Rock Springs and Salt Lake City, and work at the Development Division gave promise of important results. Glover, however, saw only waste, inefficiency, and possible corruption. On August 5 he ordered the chief inspector to make a "complete and thorough investigation of the Air Mail Service."[36]

Charles H. Clarahan, inspector-in-charge at New York City and an old hand at air mail investigations, headed a team of four inspectors who launched a comprehensive inquiry on August 13. Two months later, they submitted a report that seemed to confirm Glover's worst fears. The Air Mail Service, their report claimed, was poorly organized and overstaffed. Henderson had erred in moving the headquarters to Omaha in October 1924; it should be returned to Washington. Employment had grown from 425 in March 1921 to 626 (excluding 118 caretakers) in September 1925. "From our observation at the different fields," the inspectors wrote, "it was evident to us that there are more employees than are necessary at this time and that the force could be reduced materially without affecting the efficiency of the service."[37]

Nor were the inspectors impressed with the dependability of the transcontinental route. Their report featured a table documenting an unreliable performance during the winter, and improvement with the weather:[38]

Month	Trips Scheduled	Incompleted*	Completed on time	Completed less than 4 hrs. late	Completed 4 to 14 hrs. late	Completed 14 to 20 hrs. late	Completed more than 20 hrs. late
1924							
Nov. 14–30	34	15	10	1	0	3	5
December	62	49	8	0	0	2	3
1925							
January	62	46	7	1	0	2	6
February	54	35	9	3	0	2	5
March	60	31	17	6	1	3	2
April	60	28	20	8	0	4	0
May	62	16	28	11	0	6	1
June	60	10	24	16	4	6	0
July	62	3	22	28	6	3	0
Aug. 1–18	36	4	8	14	7	2	1
	552	237	153	88	18	33	23

*Incomplete trips are those where mail was transported by railroad train over part of the route. The reports for February 28 and March 1 are missing.

THE INSPECTORS' most scathing criticism came in the area of "unnecessary expenses." Since its inception, the Air Mail Service had spent $900,000 on airplanes from private manufacturers and "none of the planes has been found to be adapted to the service." Over $12,000 had gone to the Westinghouse Electric Company for aircraft radio equipment that had been tested and discarded; $10,000 had been wasted on an experimental radio altimeter, and another $2,500 for a useless wind indicator. A Sunday visit to the Development Division indicated "that little of importance was being done" at the facility. The inspectors recommended that Monmouth be abandoned and that aeronautical equipment prove its utility *before* being purchased.[39]

Carl Egge was singled out for special treatment. According to the inspectors, an examination of his railroad meal checks revealed consistently inflated claims for travel expenses. On fifteen occasions during the past year he had claimed $23.50 (total) for meals when receipts showed that he had paid only $14.85. He had used a government car for questionable trips that involved visits to relatives in Nebraska, and he had claimed business expenses while staying with relatives. Also, he had hired his daughter as a clerk and chauffeur to accompany him on these trips. Finally, they reported, Egge had put his brother-in-law on the payroll as caretaker at Grand Island, Nebraska, at a salary of $300 a year more than other caretakers.[40]

At the end of thirty-five pages of criticism, the inspectors wrote:

> *In conclusion this investigation has convinced us that the Air Mail Service as conducted by General Superintendent Egge is not well organized or supervised. There are too many employees on the pay roll when the needs of the service are considered; poor judgment has been exercised in the purchase of equipment before its adaptability was known; little regard for conservation of Government funds has been shown by gross extravagances and waste in purchases and by the considerable amounts expended in unnecessary travel by General Superintendent Egge. . . .*[41]

The report contained forty-three recommendations to improve conditions, including Egge's dismissal. Glover approved most of them, but Egge's situation created a dilemma. Glover wanted to get rid of him; however, how does one fire the head of the widely esteemed Air Mail Service at a time when the government's air policy was coming under attack at the court martial of Billy Mitchell? In the end, postal officials opted for discretion and compromise. On October 25 the *New York Times* reported that Egge had resigned because of "ill health." Actually, he had been demoted to divisional superintendent.[42]

THE AIR MAIL SERVICE had compiled a remarkable record of achievement under Henderson and Egge. The two men had been the driving force behind the construction of the transcontinental airway and the development of night flying. Their impressive accomplishments had been widely—and justly—acknowledged. As the *New York Times* pointed out in July 1925: "One of the most wonderful things in the world is the United States air mail service. It has its equal nowhere for distance flown and service rendered."[43]

In sharp contrast stands the internal indictment of the Air Mail Service's management. Certainly, there were in the organization flaws that merited correction. Henderson had erred in transferring the headquarters to Omaha. Egge tended to delegate too much authority to divisional superintendents without exerting the necessary oversight. But most complaints were unfounded or overstated. Postal inspectors lacked the background to understand the peculiar requirements of a pioneering aeronautical enterprise. Also, one suspects that Glover wanted a negative report, perhaps to support the argument that government was incapable of conducting an efficient business enterprise.

Lt. J. Parker VanZandt, a more informed (and sympathetic) critic, during the summer of 1925 also looked into the operation of the Air Mail Service. His most serious complaint centered on its failure "to make *systematic use of recorded experience.*" Overconcerned with day to day operations, air mail officials lacked the scientific spirit that was necessary for continued progress in solving the problems of air transportation. Establishment of the Development Division represented a belated attempt to correct this situation. Ironically, one of the central complaints of the postal inspectors was the "waste" of government funds on experimental work, leading Glover to close the division.[44]

Perhaps it no longer mattered. The Air Mail Act of 1925 and the appearance of contract carriers meant that the days of the government-owned Service were numbered. Postal officials no longer spoke about the future of the Air Mail Service; it was time for private enterprise to step in and take over the Post Office's unwanted burden.

14 Passing into History

GOVERNMENT OWNERSHIP of the Air Mail Service had never sat well with Republican advocates of private enterprise. Postmaster General Hays and his successors would have welcomed the appearance of private companies to perform the task, but Congress was reluctant to provide the necessary financial incentives and regulatory structure. With an emphasis on economy, a lack of public pressure for action, and little in the way of executive leadership, Congress seemed far more interested in investigating than legislating when it came to aeronautics. Although, as one historian has pointed out, the failure of Aeromarine Airways and other private ventures demonstrated "that government was the indispensable partner of American aeronautics," it was not until 1925 and 1926 that the federal government laid the foundations for the American airline industry.[1]

While "subsidy" generated as much support as "bolshevism" in the America of Harding and Coolidge, the idea of "compensation" came from a long and honorable tradition. The road to "compensation"— with governmental payments to private companies exceeding air mail revenue by $53,000,000 from 1926 to 1933—had begun in December 1921, when Halver Steenerson, Republican from Minnesota and chairman of the House Post Office Committee, introduced a bill to pay private contractors for carrying air mail. This modest proposal called for the Post Office to charge 6¢ an ounce, three times the first class rate for mail (2¢ an ounce), with the contractor receiving the surcharge (4¢). His bill, Steenerson emphasized, was intended to stimulate discussion; "I have no pride in authorship of it. . . ."[2]

Second Assistant Postmaster General Shaughnessy testified that he approved "in principle" the proposed legislation; it was a "step in the right direction, along the lines that the Post Office Department would like to see developed because we feel that sooner or later the department should give up the operation of the Air Mail Service. . . ." However, Shaughnessy pointed out that it would be difficult to arrive at a fair rate of compensation under the formula and suggested a pound-per-mile structure.[3]

Egge brought up another point when he appeared before Steenerson's committee. Potential contractors, he said, wanted a guaranteed minimum. "The people who are interested in investing their money believe that the contract should be drawn with a minimum-load clause, so much per mile per pound or per ton-mile and be guaranteed a certain load."[4]

C. G. Peterson of the Wright Aeronautical Corporation told the committee that his company would bid for a mail contract only if there was a reasonable chance of breaking even. Would Wright bid on a contract if the bill passed in its present form, asked Congressman C. William Ramseyer? "No, Sir," Peterson replied, "we would not." Would any other responsible company?" "No, sir." What would attract private companies, Ramseyer inquired? The best policy, Peterson said, would be to guarantee a minimum load. "I do not think Congress will stand at this time for a bill which authorizes a subsidy to the air mail service," Ramseyer pointed out. "There has been no intention on our part of ever desiring a subsidy for carrying mail," Peterson assured the New York Republican. "A subsidy . . . is something in addition to cost. We are not asking anything in addition to our cost."[5]

Although the House failed to act on Steenerson's bill, or on similar proposals submitted in 1922 by Congressmen Ramseyer and M. Clyde Kelly, Republicans on the Post Office Committee continued their efforts to design legislation that would satisfy businessmen and their colleagues on the touchy matter of subsidy. In February 1924 Congressman Kelly introduced a bill which he believed would do the trick. It authorized the postmaster general to contract for the transportation of mail by air at a rate not to exceed four-fifths of the revenue derived from a postage charge of 10¢ per ounce (or fraction thereof). Also, contractors could carry first class mail, receiving up to four-fifths of the revenue from such mail. "This permits the expansion of the air mail service without burden upon the taxpayers," Kelly explained, "and also permits the firm contracting to carry such mail to secure full loads of common mail until such time as the use of the air mail has increased sufficiently to furnish capacity loads for the mail aircraft at the rates contracted for."[6]

Kelly's bill sailed through Congress with little debate and no changes, and President Coolidge signed it into law on February 2, 1925. The Air Mail Act, historian Thomas Walterman has emphasized, represented a "giant stride toward comprehensive aid and regulation to aviation . . . ." It drew highly influential businessmen and financiers into aeronautics and led to the rapid growth of new companies. This increased commercial activity, in turn, "made eventual regulation by the federal government inevitable."[7]

The first sign of a quickening of interest in commercial aviation came in April when Henry Ford opened a private air freight service between Detroit and Chicago. For the time being, Ford announced, the line would carry only company cargo. However, this was just the beginning. Ford said that he was prepared to take a more active role in aviation. "There is no doubt in the world," he proclaimed, "that commercial aviation—passenger and freight transportation—can be successful."[8]

The aeronautical community hailed Ford's entry into the struggling air transportation industry with an enthusiasm that had not been seen since the heady post-Armistice days. Ford, after all, was the symbol of the prosperity of the 1920s. A hard-headed, pragmatic businessman who had risen to the highest rank in the nation's industrial hierarchy, he gave commercial aviation a credibility that it had not formerly had. "People said that if Ford had faith in aircraft," one reporter noted, "then flying must be practical."[9]

Excitement over Ford's announcement had hardly begun to die down when even bigger news came out of Chicago. On May 21 Howard E. Coffin announced the formation of National Air Transport (NAT). Capitalized at $10,000,000, with $2,000,000 already paid in by the company's organizers, NAT represented the "most ambitious attempt to promote air transportation in this country." Its board of directors—a veritable Who's Who of the nation's financial and industrial establishment—included Philip K. Wrigley, Lester Armour, William A. Rockefeller, C. F. Kettering, and John Hays Hammond. Coffin would be president of the new enterprise, while Clement M. Keys, head of the Curtiss Aeroplane & Motor Company, would be chairman of the important executive committee. Coffin persuaded Paul Henderson to leave the Post Office and become general manager, effective August 1.[10]

The summer of 1925 saw businessmen in every section of the country scrambling to get on the commercial aviation bandwagon. The *New York Times* counted at least fifty projects that were underway by late August. While some evidenced more enthusiasm than funding, many were well financed and managed. Certainly there was no lack of applicants when the Post Office called for bids on the first contract routes to be awarded under the Air Mail Act. "This is not a question of bargain counter competition," Postmaster General New warned. He intended "to exercise the most extreme care in scrutinizing bids and making these awards."[11]

On October 7, 1925, New announced the names of the first successful applicants for contract air mail:

Boston–New York (C.A.M. 1)	Colonial Air Transport
Chicago–St. Louis (C.A.M.2)	Robertson Aircraft Corporation
Chicago–Dallas (C.A.M. 3)	National Air Transport
Salt Lake City–Los Angeles (C.A.M. 4)	Western Air Express
Elko–Pasco (C.A.M. 5)	Walter T. Varney

All contractors bid for maximum compensation under the law (80
percent), except Robertson (67.5 percent). These awards, New observed, marked an "epoch in the history of the American post office.
Upon the result of this enterprise . . . depends the future of aerial
transport in the United States." [12]

As plans for commercial aviation developed during 1925, demands
for federal regulation increased. NAT took the lead in bringing pressure on President Coolidge for action. Coffin wanted Washington "to
safeguard aerial navigation by the establishment of airports, emergency landing fields, beacon lights, weather reports and radio service." There should be rules for the safe operation of aircraft and the
certification of pilots. "This is a public duty," he said, "which cannot
longer be ignored." [13]

For the previous six years, however, the government had managed
to avoid the question of regulation. The National Advisory Committee
for Aeronautics (NACA) had concluded in 1919 that federal control
of aerial navigation was essential for the development of civil aviation. President Wilson endorsed a bill, drafted by NACA, to create an
agency within the Commerce Department that would exert the necessary authority, but Congress had failed to act. Although bills modeled
on the NACA proposal were introduced in 1920, they became swept
up in the unification controversy. Both Harding and Coolidge voiced
their support for federal regulation, then stood aside and watched as
Congress became mired in debates over states' rights. As historian
Nick Komons has observed, until 1925 the question of civil air regulation remained in the hands of special interest groups. The issue
"never caught fire; it never became a party issue. It was just another
topic on the edge of legislative authority. Legislators could not become
excited over an issue that lacked public sentiment. . . . And such public sentiment was lacking because commercial aviation did not exist on
a scale that could attract public attention." [14]

Passage of the Air Mail Act and the appearance of large commercial
companies meant that the federal government could no longer defer
action. Also, events during the fall of 1925 focused additional public
attention on aeronautics. On September 3 the U.S. Navy airship *She-*

nandoah crashed during a thunderstorm, killing fourteen crew members. Two days later Billy Mitchell issued a public statement that blamed the accident on "incompetency, criminal negligence and almost treasonable administration" by the War and Navy Departments. In the wake of Mitchell's outburst—one that would soon lead to his court martial—President Coolidge appointed a special board, headed by Dwight W. Morrow, "to make a study of the best means of developing and applying aircraft in national defense." [15]

The Morrow Board, which included Howard Coffin of NAT among its members, sat for eight weeks and took testimony from ninety-nine witnesses. Henderson appeared on September 23. Commercial aviation, he said, did not need a subsidy; it did require "Federal sympathy and understanding, and active Government cooperation." Specifically, the government had three responsibilities to commercial aviation. First, it had to take over and maintain existing interstate airways; second, it should inspect aircraft and license pilots; and third, it should contract for carrying mail by air. One can only imagine that Coffin nodded in sympathy as Henderson testified. [16]

President Coolidge released the report of the Morrow Board on December 2. On the question of civil aviation, the board endorsed the creation of a bureau of air navigation in the Department of Commerce, extension of air mail routes, and federal support for airways, weather forecasting, and air navigation facilities. Twelve days later, Congressman Florian Lampert (Republican, Wisconsin) made public the results of an exhaustive House investigation that also contained recommendations for federal regulation of civil aviation through a bureau in the Commerce Department. "With both Morrow and Lampert in such close agreement," Komons has noted, "the civil aviation issue appeared all but settled." [17]

Secretary of Commerce Herbert Hoover took the lead in shaping the necessary legislation. Although generally opposed to federal regulation, preferring the notion of an "associative state" in which government fostered voluntary cooperative efforts by private industry, he earlier had concluded that aviation was an exception. Convinced that there would be no progress without the government's assistance, he drew on historical precedent (especially federal support for shipping) in drafting the administration's bill. Introduced in the Senate by Hiram Bingham (Republican, Connecticut), the bill charged the government with responsibility for establishing and maintaining airways and aids to navigation, licensing pilots and aircraft, investigating accidents, and in general taking steps to foster air commerce. It did not create a new bureau in the Commerce Department, as Hoover preferred to handle the additional responsibilities through existing agencies.[18]

With Coolidge exercising unusual legislative leadership, the bill sailed through the Senate, passing by voice vote on December 16. The House debated at more length before sanctioning its own version the following April. A conference committee quickly resolved the differences, and Coolidge signed the Air Commerce Act on May 20, 1926.[19]

Hailed by NACA as the "legislative corner stone for the development of civil and commercial aviation in America," the new law had been demanded by an industry that saw federal regulation as essential to progress. An administration sympthetic to the needs of business had responded, at least after aviation had begun to attract the interest of Ford, Wrigley, Rockefeller, and other prominent supporters of the GOP. Private enterprise now had the legal foundations necessary to build an airline industry.[20]

Although Postmaster General New wanted to withdraw from the Air Mail Service "as soon as possible," he intended to move cautiously. Contract carriers would be restricted at first to collateral routes, and the Post Office would continue to operate the New York–San Francisco main line. Only after private companies had demonstrated that they were capable of maintaining the transcontinental route would New turn over to them the "backbone of the system."[21]

SECOND ASSISTANT GLOVER selected Stephen A. Cisler to replace Egge as general superintendent. A career postal employee, Cisler started at the bottom, taking his first job at age nineteen as a mailing clerk in the Denver Post Office. Three years later (1891), he joined the Railway Mail Service. Cisler acquired a wide range of experience over the next twenty-two years, working in the Sea Post Service, Rural Free Delivery Service, and as a postal inspector. "He is the one man under my personal observation," a superior wrote, "whose love of work outruns every other interest in existence." Promoted in 1913 to superintendent in the Railway Mail Service, Cisler gained a reputation as an effective administrator and troubleshooter. In April 1922 Postmaster General Work sent him in the Seventh Division of the Railway Mail Service at St. Louis to "clean up an unfortunate situation." Cisler reduced the division by 225 men, cut annual appropriations by $1,000,000, and incurred the wrath of the powerful Railway Clerks Association. A delighted Work, however, praised him as "one of the best, if not the most efficient Division Superintendent . . . in the service."[22]

In September 1925 Glover spoke to Postmaster General New about

Stephen A. Cisler.

the need to replace Egge. When New asked whom he had in mind for the position, Glover suggested Cisler. "Fine," New replied, "go ahead. He is just the man for the job." Cisler took over on October 26 with instructions to place the Air Mail Service "on a high plane of efficiency upon which it does not rest at the present time."[23]

Cisler found that discipline had tended to relax under Egge, although the situation was nowhere close to the anarchic conditions described by Dean Smith in his autobiography, *By the Seat of My Pants* (1961). A talented writer, Smith was the only air mail pilot to publish his memoirs, and later accounts of the Air Mail Service took his recollections at face value. While portions of his book are faithful to the realities of the Service, numerous exaggerations severely distort the way it really was.

Smith, for example, described how easy it was to find a job with the Air Mail Service when he signed up in April 1920. Flying for the Post Office, he wrote, was considered the "next thing to suicide." The pilots were a hard-drinking lot, and many would drink and fly. He told how H. T. Lewis had shown up for a trip "stumbling and weaving," climbed into the airplane, took off, then flew superbly. "The daily operation of the Air Mail," he stressed, "was conducted with immense informality. We landed along the route in fields or pastures as the whim struck us—to relieve ourselves, to visit with acquaintances we'd met on some forced landing, or perhaps because we liked the looks of some place we'd never been. It was also common practice to give rides to our friends." [24]

To begin with, a position with the Post Office was a plum. The Air Mail Service, Praeger testified in January 1920, had a waiting list of 200 to 300 pilots, mostly military trained; thus, only the most experienced airmen, with a minimum of 500 hours, were considered. By 1924 the waiting list had grown to 600 to 800. As Wesley Smith observed, "the Service had the pick of the best flyers in the country who intended to keep on flying [after the war]." [25]

Certainly the job was dangerous, but postal pilots made more money than airmen anywhere in the world. In 1920 pilots were paid a base yearly salary of $2,000, plus 5¢ a mile. By 1924 the base pay was $2,000 to $2,800, depending on the route, with experience increases to a maximum of $3,600; mileage pay ranged from 5¢ for Cleveland–Cheyenne daytime flying to 14¢ for Rock Springs–Salt Lake City and Reno–San Francisco night flying. Four pilots collected over $4,000 in mileage pay alone in 1924, and one (H. T. Lewis) made $5,582. This came at a time when the average annual wage in the United States was $1,300; postal employees averaged $1,900 and Egge made $5,200. In short, pilots were extremely well paid for their fifty to sixty flying hours a month—and they earned their money. [26]

The Air Mail Service had strict rules against drinking and flying. As veteran pilot R. C. Marshall emphasized, "If you showed up for a flight with liquor on your breath, you were fired." But Egge did make two exceptions to this rule. In November 1924 Jack Knight reported for duty at Cheyenne under the influence of alcohol. Ground personnel allowed him to make his trip, and he was sober by the time he reached Omaha. Egge ordered an investigation. Knight admitted that he had consumed several drinks before coming out to the airfield but denied that he was intoxicated. "He did admit," Egge told Henderson, "that he had made a fool of himself." Despite an earlier letter to all employees that drinking would result in immediate dismissal, Egge decided to make an exception in Knight's case. He simply could not bring himself to fire the most celebrated pilot in the Air Mail Service, the hero of the first transcontinental flight, the leader in night flying. Instead, Egge grounded Knight for fifteen days, costing him about $250 in mileage pay. [27]

The following week Dean Smith showed up at the Omaha airfield at 2:30 A.M. for his trip to Chicago. Night manager H. S. Long observed the obviously drunk pilot staggering toward his airplane; he told him to go home to bed. Smith refused. Long and mechanic Henry A. Mossman tried to restrain Smith as H. T. Lewis got ready to take his trip. Smith became violent. "During this final encounter," Long reported, "I received a blow on the head and a bloody nose, also tore the skin on my knuckle [dragging] Smith off the plane. Mechanic Mossman was also hit a few times to the tune of the rarest profanity in the modern dictionary." [28]

Despite abundant evidence to the contrary, Smith denied that he had been intoxicated, although he did allow that he had consumed two or three drinks. This posed a problem for Egge. "Unfortunately," he explained to Henderson, "because of the precedent established in Knight's case it did not seem just to separate Smith. . . ." Egge assigned Smith to reserve status for sixty days, costing him $800 to $1,000 in flying pay. He informed Smith and Knight that any repetition would mean dismissal, then wrote to all divisional superintendents "advising them that my action in the Knight and Smith cases should not be accepted as a precedent; that dismissal would immediately follow in case an employee violated our rules relative to the use of intoxicants." [29]

There were a few hard-drinking, high-living pilots with the air mail, but most were sober, sensible individuals. Wesley Smith, for example, hardly fits the role of daredevil of the skies. A graduate of the University of California (with a degree in mechanical engineering) who learned to fly during the war, Smith had two passions: flying and grand opera. He joined the Air Mail Service in November 1919 and quickly gained a reputation as a determined bad-weather pilot. When not battling the elements, Smith studied French and German, and took voice and piano lessons. He married his music teacher and began to raise a family. His dreams of a career in grand opera were not to be realized. As his wife explained, Smith had a good baritone voice, "but he had trouble keeping on key." Abandoning his musical ambitions (but not his love of music), Smith concentrated on developing his piloting skills. He went on to pioneer instrument flying, deliver professional papers on the subject, and write the best early textbook on air operations. [30]

The archival record, as well as the testimony of pilots, makes clear that the Air Mail Service *never* was operated in casual fashion. Born during the war, with a majority of its personnel trained by the military, the Service emphasized discipline from the beginning. Free spirits, like Dean Smith and Randolph Page, bent the rules from time to time, but infractions, when detected, did not go unpunished. The mail flew on schedule. Delays and forced landings required detailed

Wesley L. Smith.

explanations. Professionalism characterized the Air Mail Service, and this trait passed on to the commercial airlines that followed.

Cisler, however, believed that standards should be tightened. In a long overdue reform, he required pilots to take annual physical examinations, with eye tests every six months. He dismissed one pilot whose personal problems—drinking and marital—had gotten into the newspapers and "brought discredit" on the Service, and he accepted the resignation of another pilot following an accident in which drinking was suspected.[31]

Otherwise, Cisler soon realized that conditions throughout the Service were nowhere near as bad as he had been led to believe, and few major changes were required. He did abolish the Development Division, arrange for headquarters to return to Washington at the beginning of the new fiscal year on July 1, 1926, institute tighter administrative procedures for expenditure of funds, and reduce employees from 712 in October 1925 to 553 in May 1926.[32]

Operations changed little. Revenue on both the transcontinental route and the New York–Chicago overnight service fell by 20 percent during the winter of 1925–26, as delays and cancellations increased. Pilots continued to challenge the bad weather, fighting lonely battles in the sky with a skill and tenacity that few could appreciate, but they often found it impossible to get through. Despite the inherent hazards of attempting to maintain a daily schedule across the continent, the Air Mail Service's safety record remained impressive. Yet every loss was painful, and the single fatality that occurred during 1926 was especially so.

Arthur R. Smith belonged to that pre–World War I group of exhibition pilots who introduced the airplane to people around the world. After gaining fame for his daring feats of airmanship at the 1915 San Francisco World's Fair, he toured the Orient, made the first night flight over Tokyo, and was decorated by the Japanese government. Smith served as a test pilot with the Army during and after the war, specializing in night flying. Joining the Post Office in 1923, he was considered to be an excellent bad-weather pilot. "Slight of stature, plumpfaced and rosy cheeked," one friend described him, "his sparkling eyes and cheery smile gave one the impression of a school boy about to experience the thrill of his first flight as he donned his flying suit and climbed into his plane." A quiet man, Smith lived with his parents and was active in church affairs.[33]

Smith left Chicago for Bryan with the eastbound night mail at 7:35 P.M., February 12, 1926. He was flying a Curtiss Carrier Pigeon, a Liberty-powered biplane that the Post Office had purchased and was testing under operational conditions. Shortly after 10 P.M., Smith crashed into woods near Montpelier, Ohio, six miles from Bryan. The Curtiss burst into flames and was consumed; Smith's body was found in the cockpit, burned beyond recognition.

An investigation failed to determine the cause of the accident. The weather in the area had been good, with a ceiling of 1,000 feet and visibility of two miles. Smith had been traveling in a southwesterly direction, away from Bryan, at low altitude and high speed, when he hit the top of a tall tree. The most frequently advanced theory was that Smith climbed above the overcast after leaving Chicago, then encountered a patch of low clouds when he tried to descend.[34]

The Curtiss Carrier Pigeon that Smith had been flying was one of several aircraft being considered by the Post Office as a replacement for the venerable de Havilland. For a time, the Curtiss seemed the front-runner, especially after a performance survey by National Air Transport resulted in the purchase of ten airplanes (hailed as the single largest commercial order for aircraft ever placed in the United

States). The Post Office, however, announced in May 1926 that Douglas had won the competition. A single-engine biplane, powered by a 400-hp Liberty engine (as required by postal specifications), the Douglas M4 was the clear choice of air mail pilots. Featuring such welcome innovations as brakes and a tail wheel instead of a skid, it could carry 1,000 pounds of mail at 145 mph and land at 52 mph. In a move designed to stimulate the aircraft industry, Postmaster General New ordered forty planes at $11,900 each. The Air Mail Service later would acquire eleven additional Douglas biplanes, allowing it to fly out in style.[35]

The task of phasing the new airplanes into service fell largely to D. B. Colyer. This worked out well. Cisler may have had managerial skills, but he lacked aeronautical experience. As Wesley Smith wrote in his diary following his first encounter with Cisler: "He is awfully ignorant of things Aerial . . ." Colyer, on the other hand, had an extensive background in all phases of aviation. A wartime pilot, he joined the Air Mail Service in 1919. Serving in turn as field manager, chief of flying, and divisional superintendent, he was promoted to assistant

The Douglas M4.

general superintendent in April 1926. He became head of the Air Mail Service in October when Cisler left the Post Office for a financially attractive position with Sears, Roebuck and Company.[36]

As usually happens with new aircraft, the Douglas had its share of problems. Wesley Smith, assigned to ferry an M4 from the factory in Santa Monica to New York, encountered one problem that caught his attention. En route to Las Vegas, Smith was dismayed to find that the engine exhaust pipe had set fire to the fuselage. Fortunately, he managed to land before the flames spread. The manufacturer had to remove all the original pipes and replace them with seamless Shelby tubing.[37]

Pilots discovered that the Douglas did not carry ice well. "The ice would form on the wings and struts," Wesley Smith recalled, "and the latter would almost tear themselves out of the plane with their powerful vibration." The vibration lessened when stainless steel was used in place of duraluminum for the struts connecting the wings. Nonetheless, ice remained a deadly menace for the intsrument flying pioneers of the Air Mail Service.[38]

Warren Williams could bear witness to Wesley Smith's judgment that the "greatest of all our problems is ice." When he left Cleveland at 1:30 A.M., December 23, 1926, with 321 pounds of mail for Chicago, the sky was overcast and Bryan was reporting a 1,500-foot ceiling and three miles' visibility. Williams flew underneath the overcast until low clouds at Woodville blocked his way. Rather than return to Cleveland, he decided to fly on top. The clouds seemed only 1,000 feet thick, and he expected them to extend for no more than twenty to thirty miles. After ten minutes, however, the cloud layer began to thicken. Williams went on instruments and started to climb. The Douglas rapidly collected ice, and the controls grew "mushy." His turn indicator went out after the venturi opening froze over; the compass began to spin; the altimeter unwound. Williams fought unsuccessfully to control the aircraft. With the ground approaching, he cut the throttle and jumped. He pulled his rip cord, and floated down safely from 300 feet, making the air mail's second (and last) successful parachute jump.[39]

After numerous close calls, icing claimed a victim on April 22, 1927. John F. Milatzo, an enthusiastic instrument pilot, departed from Chicago in Douglas Number 626 at 9:45 P.M., April 21, carrying 327 pounds of mail for New York. Milatzo flew into a sleet storm, collected ice, and landed at the Goshen emergency field shortly after 11 P.M. He stayed on the ground for an hour, waiting for the storm to pass. After receiving a report of good weather at Bryan, Milatzo started out again. He did not get far. Twenty miles from Goshen, the Douglas

Randolph Page crashes the Douglas M4 Number 629 when attempting to take off from a field near Clarence, Iowa, September 16, 1926.

crashed into a field during a severe snow and sleet storm. Milatzo died, the last pilot to lose his life while flying for the Post Office.[40]

By April 1927 Douglas M4s had replaced DHs on mail routes from New York to Salt Lake City. Their greater range and speed enabled the Post Office to eliminate intermediate stops (except in bad weather) at Bellefonte, Bryan, and Rawlins, and on eastbound trips at Iowa City, North Platte, and Rock Springs. The pilots grew increasingly enthusiastic about the Douglas. After the "bugs" were worked out, Wesley Smith boasted, "we had the finest airplane in the world." The public began to use the air mail as never before. Excess postage rose to over $100,000 a month in August 1926, and remained at that level throughout the winter. Mail loads increased after February 1, 1927, when the Post Office eliminated the zonal system of charges in favor of a flat rate of 10¢ per half ounce for air mail carried between any two points in the country.[41]

The contract carriers also were doing well. Henry Ford obtained a postal contract and on February 15, 1926, began to carry mail from Detroit to Cleveland and Chicago on his private freight line. Walter T. Varney opened a route from Elko, Nevada, to Pasco, Washington, on April 6; however, he had to suspend service and seek an extension when his Curtiss C-6s, with a 150-hp engine, could not complete the northbound portion of the trip because of headwinds. Robertson Aircraft Corporation started service between St. Louis and Chicago with DH-4s on April 15. Two days later, Douglas M2s of Western Air Express connected Salt Lake City and Los Angeles. The giant National Air Transport got underway on May 12, using Curtiss Carrier Pigeons between Chicago and Dallas. Between February 1926 and April 1927, route mileage increased from 328 to 4,713, and monthly compensation rose from $466 to $121,987.[42]

The time was approaching for the government to turn over the transcontinental route to private companies. In January 1927 Postmaster General New awarded the Chicago–San Francisco segment to Boeing Air Transport, but he delayed a decision on the eastern section after North American Airways (in which several pilots had a financial interest) underbid National Air Transport. North American never had a chance against the politically well-connected NAT. In April New gave the choice New York–Chicago route to NAT as the "lowest and best responsible bidder."[43]

On April 15 Colyer resigned to take a position with Boeing Air Transport, leaving to A. E. Peterson the task of winding up the affairs of the Air Mail Service. The Post Office relinquished the Chicago–San Francisco route to Boeing at midnight, June 30, with little fanfare. Cleveland, however, staged a civic celebration on August 31 to mark the transfer of the New York–Chicago section to NAT. More than 10,000 people showed up at the municipal airport to watch air mail pilots drop magnesium flares, a former Miss America christen NAT airplanes, and other festivities. The high point of the evening came at 12:58 A.M., September 1, when Stephen T. Kaufman arrived with the mail from Hadley. When his wheels touched the ground, the Air Mail Service came to an end. Appropriately, NAT operations manager Wesley Smith directed NAT pilot Warren Williams to carry the mail through to Chicago in a Douglas M4 that had been purchased from the Post Office.[44]

The government promptly disposed of the assets of the Air Mail Service. The Commerce Department took over the radio service, including seventeen stations and forty-four operators, and the equipment and personnel of the lighted airway. Fifteen Douglas M4s were transferred to the War Department, five went to Commerce, and one to NACA. The balance were sold at approximately 50 percent of cost to air mail contractors. Disposal of the recently purchased aircraft raised some complaints, and Postmaster General New had to defend the sale. As it turned out, the government probably did well to unload them. With the bulky, water-cooled Liberty engine rapidly giving way to a new generation of high power, lightweight, reliable air-cooled engines (built by Wright and Pratt & Whitney), the Douglas biplane was obsolete. Postal garages acquired useable shop material and equipment, with the balance sold as surplus. Most of the precious human assets of the Service, the highly skilled pilots and trained technicians, joined Boeing Air Transport and NAT, the predecessor companies of what later became United Air Lines.[45]

Memories of the Air Mail Service soon faded, lost amid the overwhelming public reaction to Charles Lindbergh's dramatic New York–Paris flight in May 1927. "Ask people about the Air Mail," Dean Smith wrote in 1976, "and they are apt to recall that Lindbergh was a mail pilot, which he was not . . . ." Commercial aviation in the United States did not begin when the former chief pilot for Robertson Aircraft Corporation, a contract mail carrier, crossed the Atlantic. Certainly, Lindbergh's heroic journey provided a significant stimulus for aviation: investors poured millions of dollars into the developing industry, thousands of young men learned to fly, municipalities across the country built airports, and an "air-minded" public patronized the air mail with unprecedented enthusiasm. But the rapid progress of air transportation after 1927 would not have been possible if sound foundations had not already existed. Lindbergh realized this. "To me," he reflected about the effect of his flight, "it was like a match lighting a bonfire. I thought thereafter that people confused the light of the bonfire with the flame of the match, and that one individual was credited with doing what, in reality, many groups of individuals had done." Among these groups, the U.S. Air Mail Service was in the forefront.[46]

Conclusion

THE AIR MAIL SERVICE formed part of a continuing effort by the United States Post Office to employ innovative means to advance the mail. In 1813 Congress authorized the Post Office to transport mail by steamboat, this only five years after Robert Fulton's first experiments on the Hudson River. In 1838 Congress declared railroads to be post roads. The early years of the twentieth century, the progressive era, saw the Post Office eagerly adopt "modern" methods, such as pneumatic tube lines, mechanical mail sorters, postage meter machines, post office conveyer belts, streetcars, and automobiles to improve service.

Aviation promised a quantum leap in the rapid delivery of mail, presenting an irresistible opportunity for Albert S. Burleson and Otto Praeger. No doubt politics played a part in the decision to establish the air mail. Certainly, the two men were aware of the broad advantages to society of advancing important government and business letters. But the desire for speed carried its own imperative. "The search for faster and faster ways of carrying the mail," one postal historian has poined out, "has gone on continuously regardless of the urgency of its contents and seems to have been inspired by demands that were perhaps partly emotional." John Wanamaker, the great postmaster general of the 1890s, put it best when he said: "The swiftest mail is not fast enough." [1]

In their search for speed, Burleson and Praeger demanded of aeronautics a punctuality that challenged existing standards of mechanical reliability and operational techniques. Praeger constantly searched for ways to improve performance, experimenting with airplanes, instruments, and radio aids to navigation. Meanwhile, he insisted that the mail be carried in all weather conditions. Responding to the challenge, postal airmen developed their piloting skills to an unprecedented degree, becoming the finest contact, bad weather pilots in the world.

Postmaster General Burleson favored permanent governmental control of the air mail, believing that the Post Office could operate the service more efficiently and economically than private enterprise. His Republican successors disagreed. Advocates of free enterprise, they wanted private companies to perform the task. However, as demonstrated by Aeromarine Airways and the experience in European nations, commercial airlines were not viable without liberal government contracts and regulation. While Congress debated proposals for appropriate compensation and the character of a federal regulatory structure, a sometimes reluctant Post Office continued to sponsor the most significant civil use of airplanes in the United States.

Fortunately for the Air Mail Service, Paul Henderson provided a leadership that was second only to Praeger's. Henderson's style—and role—was different from his predecessor's. Praeger restlessly pushed expansion of air mail routes, displaying the spirit of a true pioneer as he probed the limits of the new technology. Cautious and patient, Henderson brought stability and order to the Air Mail Service when it was most needed. Whereas Praeger concerned himself with every detail of the operation, Henderson preferred to set broad objectives, then delegate responsibility for their execution to his subordinates. Henderson built on the foundations that had been laid by Praeger: he perfected the transcontinental air route, one of the truly epic achievements of early aviation, and he developed night flying and the lighted airway, placing the United States far ahead of the world in these important areas.

"There has been no more valuable experiment in aeronautics," NACA concluded about the Air Mail Service, "and certainly none that contributed more directly to the demonstration of the practical value of air transportation and the advancement of aeronautics generally." The *New York Times* agreed: "The significance of the United States air mail service will be missed if it is not understood to be the pioneer of commercial aviation extending to every part of the country." Operating the transcontinental route, day and night, with remarkable regularity and safety, the Air Mail Service revealed the potential of air transportation and attracted the interest of commercial developers. Beyond question, the modern airline industry stems directly from the pioneering efforts of the Post Office.[2]

Commercial air carriers owe another debt to the Air Mail Service. The experience gained between 1918 and 1927 proved invaluable in establishing airline operating techniques. Postal airmen set the standard of excellence in bad weather and night flying for airline pilots; they fostered public expectations of regularity and punctuality that compelled the rapid development of radio aids to navigation and instrument flying. And this operational heritage, one astute European writer has emphasized, "helped create the ascendency in air transport which the Americans were to win in the 1930s and which they retain to this day."[3]

Despite constant congressional complaints of extravagant expenditures on an enterprise of dubious value, the Air Mail Service did not cost much. Congress appropriated a total of $17,400,000 for the Service. Deducting receipts from postage and estimating the real value of inventory and capital items on hand in August 1927, the net cost came to $10–12,000,000. When considering what European nations received for a comparable sum spent on developing and subsidizing air transport, Edward P. Warner stresses, "the American people had a very great bargain."[4]

The human cost is another matter. Thirty-four pilots died while on duty with the Air Mail Service. Placed in the context of fatalities per miles flown in military aviation in the United States or in commercial aviation abroad, the number of dead is not unusual. In fact, the Air Mail Service had an excellent safety record for its time, except during the years 1920 and 1921, when seventeen pilots were killed. But this was small comfort to the widow of Max Miller, the father of Lyman Doty, the mother of Art Smith, or the family and friends of all the young men who gave their lives in the pursuit of progress. The historian can only record their deeds and honor their memory.

Appendix A

Chronology of the U.S. Air Mail Service

1910

June 13	Charles K. Hamilton flies round trip between New York and Philadelphia
June 14	Congressman Morris Sheppard introduces bill that directs postmaster general to study feasibility of air mail service

1911

September 23	Earle H. Ovington makes first official U.S. air mail flight at Garden City, New York, international aviation meet

1915

September 1	Otto Praeger appointed second assistant postmaster general

1916

December 4	National Advisory Committee for Aeronautics in its annual report recommends establishment of an air mail service

1918

February 12	Post Office calls for bids to construct five aircraft for Washington–New York air mail service
May 10	Congress passes bill for air mail postage charge of 24¢ per ounce
May 15	Army Air Service pilots inaugurate air mail service from New York (Belmont Park) to Washington (Polo Field) via Philadelphia (Bustleton)
July 15	Air mail postage reduced to 16¢ per ounce
August 10	Last day of mail flying by Army Air Service
August 12	Civilian pilots begin operation of air mail service by Post Office; College Park, Maryland, replaces Polo Field as Washington terminal
September 5–11	Post Office surveys New York–Chicago route
November 11	Armistice signed
December 6	Benjamin B. Lipsner resigns as general superintendent of Air Mail Service
December 15	Air mail postage reduced to 6¢ per ounce

December 16	Air Mail Service suffers first fatality when Carl B. Smith crashes at Elizabeth, New Jersey
December 18	Post Office opens New York (Belmont Park)–Cleveland (Woodland Hills)–Chicago (Grant Park) route
December 22	New York–Chicago service suspended

1919

May 15	Post Office reopens Chicago–Cleveland route (via Bryan, Ohio)
July 1	Chicago–Cleveland route extended to New York (via Bellefonte, Pennsylvania)
July 18	Post Office eliminates surcharge for air mail; postal airplanes henceforth carry random selection of mail
July 22–26	Air mail pilots strike
October 8–31	Army Air Service conducts Transcontinental Reliability and Endurance Test
December	Heller Field, Newark, New Jersey, replaces Belmont Park as New York terminal of Air Mail Service

1920

January	Post Office moves from Chicago's Grant Park to Checkerboard Field in suburban Maywood
March	Cleveland's Woodland Hills Park abandoned in favor of Glenn Martin Field
July 1	Post Office leases Hazelhurst Field, Hempstead, Long Island, from Curtiss Aeroplane & Motor Company to serve as eastern terminal for transcontinental route; Newark's Heller Field remains terminal for New York–Washington route
August 16	Post Office opens Chicago–St. Louis route
August 25	Florida-West Indies Airways awarded first foreign air mail contract for Key West–Havana route
September 1	Max Miller and Gustav Reierson killed in crash of JL-6 Number 305
September 8	Post Office opens transcontinental service
October	Aeromarine Plane & Motor Company acquires controlling interest in Florida–West Indies Airways (later renamed Aeromarine Airways)
November	Air Mail Pilots of America organized
November 29	Post Office opens Chicago–Minneapolis route

1921

February 22–23	Post Office demonstrates day-and-night transcontinental service
March 4	Warren G. Harding inaugurated as President; Will H. Hays replaces Albert S. Burleson as postmaster general
April	Post Office closes Newark's Heller Field
April 11	Edward H. Shaughnessy appointed second assistant postmaster general, replacing Otto Praeger
May 31	New York–Washington route abandoned
June 15	Carl F. Egge takes office as general superintendent of Air Mail Service

| June 30 | Post Office closes St. Louis–Chicago–Minneapolis route |
| September | Post Office moves from Marino Field, San Francisco, to Army's Crissey Field |

1922

January 28	Edward H. Shaughnessy fatally injured in Knickerbocker Theater disaster
March 4	Hubert Work replaces Will H. Hays as postmaster general
April	Paul Henderson appointed second assistant postmaster general
July 16	Air Mail Service completes one year without a fatal accident

1923

February	Experimental night flying begins at North Platte, Nebraska
February 1	Collier trophy awarded to Air Mail Service for year's greatest achievement in aviation (operation of transcontinental route for one year without a fatal accident)
February 22	Harry S. New replaces Hubert Work as postmaster general
August 2	Warren Harding dies; Calvin Coolidge becomes President
August 21–24	Post Office operates experimental day-and-night transcontinental service, using Chicago–Cheyenne lighted airway

1924

February 9	Air Mail Service wins Collier trophy for second time for pioneering work in night flying
July 1	Post Office inaugurates regular day-and-night transcontinental service; air mail requires special postage for first time since 1918 (8¢ to 24¢, depending on distance)
December 15	Post Office moves from Hazelhurst Field, Long Island, to Hadley Field, New Brunswick, New Jersey

1925

February 2	President Coolidge signs Air Mail Act
March 15	Air Mail Service establishes Development Division at Monmouth, Illinois
May 21	National Air Transport formed
July 1	Post Office inaugurates New York–Chicago overnight air mail; postal rate fixed at 10¢ per ounce
August 1	W. Irving Glover replaces Paul Henderson as second assistant postmaster general
September 3	U.S. Navy dirigible *Shenandoah* crashes near Cambridge, Ohio
October 7	Post Office awards first contracts under Air Mail Act

October 26	Stephen A. Cisler replaces Carl F. Egge as general superintendent of Air Mail Service
October 28	Court martial of Col. William ("Billy") Mitchell begins
December 2	President Coolidge releases report of Morrow Board
December 7	Col. William Mitchell found guilty of conduct prejudicial to good order and military discipline

1926

February 15	Henry Ford carries first domestic contract mail from Detroit to Cleveland
May	Post Office selects Douglas M4 to replace DH-4
May 20	President Coolidge signs Air Commerce Act
July 1	Post Office discontinues rebuilding DH-4s at Chicago Repair Depot as Douglas M4s come into service
October	D. B. Colyer replaces Stephen A. Cisler as general superintendent of Air Mail Service

1927

January 13	Air mail pilot Shirley Short awarded Harmon Trophy
February 1	Post Office eliminates zonal charges for transcontinental air mail in favor of flat rate of 10¢ per half ounce
April 15	A. E. Peterson replaces D. B. Colyer as general superintendent of Air Mail Service
April 22	Air Mail Service suffers last fatality when John F. Milatzo crashes near Goshen, Indiana
May 20–21	Charles A. Lindbergh flies from New York to Paris
July 1	Boeing Air Transport begins operation of Chicago–San Francisco portion of transcontinental route
September 1	National Air Transport takes over New York–Chicago route, marking end of government-operated Air Mail Service

Appendix B

Operating Statistics

Statement of Performance, May 15, 1918–June 30, 1924

Month	Trips scheduled	Trips de-faulted	Trips uncom-pleted	Miles flown with mail	Total miles (including test & ferry)	Mail carried (number of letters)	Cost of service	Forced landings Me-chanical	Others
1918									
May 1–15	60	11	—	5,324	7,234	190,000	$ 3,682.11	2	2
June	100	4	—	10,685	14,155	523,240	9,922.71	4	4
July	108	2	—	11,855	14,601	678,680	10,001.46	4	4
August	109	0	—	11,984	15,120	663,520	9,555.67	1	1
September	100	0	—	10,900	15,263	608,000	9,638.74	2	1
October	108	0	—	11,617	12,671	671,520	9,841.76	2	0
November	104	2	—	11,118	13,689	674,160	10,673.68	0	1
December	104	32	—	8,415	9,815	711,120	13,300.46	7	11
	793	32	—	81,898	102,548	4,720,240	76,616.59	22	24
1919									
January	108	16	—	9,653	11,138	724,200	$ 13,741.58	1	5
February	97	5	—	9,307	10,982	619,560	13,645.16	6	8
March	106	4	—	10,699	10,835	701,240	13,880.29	5	5
April	107	2	—	11,105	11,497	667,080	13,516.44	2	7
May	146	3	—	22,578	23,397	1,065,060	17,715.66	3	9
June	160	0	—	30,835	45,978	1,425,880	30,891.62	4	4
July	178	5	6	56,577	62,175	1,948,160	41,134.36	7	5
August	176	2	6	58,022	69,095	2,274,800	40,614.59	3	6
September	172	1	2	56,308	64,736	2,226,720	34,861.53	5	6
October	178	13	29	50,437	59,530	2,203,800	35,609.03	11	19
November	177	5	18	41,757	50,605	2,163,360	31,127.58	6	14
December	156	31	19	35,788	41,327	1,649,840	33,909.86	16	9
	1,761	87	(80)	393,066	461,295	17,669,700	320,647.70	69	97

Month	Trips scheduled	Trips defaulted	Trips uncompleted	Miles flown with mail	Total miles (including test & ferry)	Mail carried (number of letters)	Cost of service	Forced landings Mechanical	Others
1920									
January	169	46	22	33,952	40,458	1,725,000	$ 52,551.66	16	10
February	146	33	15	32,647	38,158	1,489,680	46,004.12	4	1
March	210	41	17	37,861	46,990	1,694,440	44,785.71	12	8
April	208	28	9	41,890	47,881	1,682,640	55,343.40	28	7
May	232	21	7	54,318	64,982	2,044,480	57,004.83	17	11
June	260	56	17	49,867	62,463	2,360,200	80,209.43	29	9
July	260	7	7	69,140	74,002	2,736,040	85,993.59	25	14
August	368	21	19	73,456	116,023	2,925,600	73,026.93	39	29
September	696	194	30	105,847	132,202	3,646,000	108,751.76	47	30
October	750	157	57	123,274	154,486	3,581,660	123,618.68	54	59
November	758	183	77	114,750	139,757	3,492,080	121,501.18	85	69
December	884	222	105	127,306	131,040	3,597,680	131,205.96	89	138
	4,941	1,009	382	864,128	1,048,444	30,975,500	979,997.25	445	385
1921									
January	850	153	87	132,679	139,609	3,377,400	$ 136,488.61	117	131
February	782	122	71	130,431	143,655	3,525,400	131,855.43	82	122
March	918	47	59	171,593	186,625	4,404,680	152,442.27	64	123
April	884	47	36	171,156	186,950	4,711,120	147,890.64	79	107
May	850	17	20	168,397	181,216	4,602,920	125,754.74	72	81
June	832	3	10	166,956	185,091	4,233,520	127,479.83	57	51
July	624	1	6	130,555	148,684	3,091,040	109,799.11	34	29
August	693	4	13	134,549	149,432	3,387,200	106,986.98	32	30
September	657	6	8	125,914	148,099	3,536,040	102,998.45	13	26
October	714	7	7	138,759	158,971	3,962,280	122,205.51	23	21
November	672	39	46	117,529	143,145	3,740,760	117,417.83	17	74
December	726	66	37	125,416	141,256	4,047,920	118,264.70	42	46
	9,202	512	400	1,713,934	1,912,733	46,620,280	1,499,584.10	632	841

Month	Trips scheduled	Trips de-faulted	Trips uncom-pleted	Miles flown with mail	Total miles (including test & ferry)	Mail carried (number of letters)	Cost of service	Forced landings Me-chanical	Others
1922									
January	699	66	32	119,966	137,687	3,731,320	$ 116,553.07	31	44
February	635	77	15	107,944	118,084	3,716,080	86,898.29	24	28
March	729	39	22	134,503	150,664	4,932,480	95,884.94	13	57
April	675	23	16	127,634	134,003	4,652,120	80,066.05	17	69
May	702	8	8	136,973	149,285	4,875,520	79,611.22	17	46
June	702	5	1	138,185	147,955	5,316,160	78,480.86	18	9
July	675	0	2	133,809	142,429	4,793,840	88,427.66	11	6
August	729	0	0	145,896	160,381	5,401,440	121,270.00	8	6
September	688	2	1	135,997	146,331	6,160,160	126,075.56	15	13
October	706	3	9	138,307	176,913	6,125,800	341,770.51	22	15
November	677	24	18	127,805	144,834	5,593,120	98,686.71	20	37
December	674	45	21	123,070	148,237	5,189,840	103,649.95	10	37
	8,291	292	145	1,570,089	1,756,803	60,487,880	1,417,374.82	206	367
1923									
January	702	40	20	129,289	141,954	5,695,960	$ 146,067.44	14	36
February	621	38	13	114,424	129,173	4,921,920	100,319.45	22	34
March	729	24	22	137,200	153,968	6,637,720	177,965.95	12	38
April	675	23	9	128,483	139,773	6,118,129	235,219.01	12	24
May	702	4	3	138,085	154,844	5,599,200	173,723.59	13	19
June	702	2	4	138,272	170,191	5,738,720	213,975.76	17	14
July	675	1	1	133,550	155,248	5,151,400	236,160.54	24	14
August	674	0	0	134,470	215,518	5,751,480	153,820.74	16	9
September	648	12	8	125,265	158,449	5,145,920	130,415.38	11	15
October	729	13	9	141,058	187,494	5,618,240	128,964.50	11	40
November	675	18	9	128,938	150,359	5,092,920	100,218.52	14	26
December	540	50	13	96,246	113,451	3,924,320	113,571.66	9	32
	8,072	225	111	1,545,280	1,870,422	65,295,920	1,910,422.54	175	327

Month	Trips scheduled	Trips defaulted	Trips uncompleted	Miles flown with mail	Total miles (*including test & ferry*)	Mail carried (*number of letters*)	Cost of service	Forced landings Mechanical	Forced landings Others
1924									
January	702	53	16	127,422	143,386	4,733,800	110,824.72	21	31
February	648	46	14	117,793	133,149	4,373,520	103,747.62	10	37
March	702	49	17	127,402	142,624	4,730,880	104,735.87	7	57
April	702	17	6	134,926	147,405	5,312,200	102,362.35	8	24
May	702	14	2	136,078	157,049	5,409,360	103,758.18	11	18
June	615	5	4	119,615	149,119	4,757,320	107,416.25	12	24
	4,071	184	59	763,236	872,732	29,317,080	632,488.99	69	191
GRAND TOTAL	37,131	2,341	1,123	6,931,631	8,024,977	255,086,600	$6,837,487.99	1,618	2,232

Source: U.S. Post Office, "Statement of Performance from May 15, 1918, to December 31, 1923," Records of the Superintendent, Air Mail Service; Aeronautical Chamber of Commerce, *Aircraft Year Book, 1925* (New York, 1925), p. 271.

STATEMENT OF PERFORMANCE, JULY 1, 1924–AUGUST 31, 1927

Fiscal year	Miles flown with mail	Total miles including test & ferry	Mail carried *number of letters**	Forced landings Mechanical	Forced landings Others
July 1, 1924–June 30, 1925	2,076,764	2,501,555	9,300,520	174	586
July 1, 1925–June 30, 1926	2,256,137	2,547,992	14,145,640	155	707
July 1, 1926–June 30, 1927	2,329,553	2,583,006	22,385,000	140	881
July 1, 1927–August 31, 1927	173,987	195,712	3,338,080	7	31
	6,836,441	7,828,265	49,169,240	476	2,205

*All mail bore special air surcharge.

Source: Post Office, "Air Mail, 1918–1927," U.S. Postal Service Library.

Appendix C

Rules for Government Pilots

(c. October 1918)

All pilots will see to it that these rules are strictly enforced. All infractions will be followed by immediate censure.

1. Pilots will not perform any stunts with mail aeroplanes or put them through any unnecessary strains.

2. Before starting a flight inspect your ship thoroughly and report any defect or negligence on the part of the crew to the chief mechanic and see to it that this defect is remedied before beginning the flight.

3. Before starting on a flight the motors will be run for ten minutes at about 800 R.P.M. to warm them up. This gives an even and equal expansion, lengthening the life of the motor.

4. Pilots will observe a 50 foot dead-line from all buildings and will not take off directly in front of the hangars. Taxi out into the field at least 50 or 75 yards before taking off.

5. Never taxi away from dead-line without the assistance of a mechanic at the wing tip. Be sure that your fire extinguishers are easily accessible.

6. Carry an emergency tool kit, spark plugs, etc.

7. In case of forced landing, first, to save time and to rush assistance when the plane comes down, you are instructed to put in two calls, one for each field you are between, and when one has answered cancel your other call. The relief ship should carry mechanic and the necessary repair parts. The mail should proceed to its destination in the relief plane with the regular mail pilot. THE MAIL MUST PROCEED BY AEROPLANE TO ITS DESTINATION AT ALL HAZARDS AND WITH THE LEAST DELAY. Upon the field receiving such a call, they will notify by wire or telephone the Division Superintendent and will rush a relief plane to the scene of forced landing at once. Not a minute must be wasted in going to the relief of the plane that is down or in starting the mail from the disabled plane on to its destination. If the relief plane finds that field in which the plane has had the forced landing is not suitable for landing, the pilot should land in the nearest available field and with the aid of the nearest help, team or automobile, transfer the mail and pilot to the relief ship so that the mail can go on to its destination.

Upon making forced landing in freezing weather, the pilot is first instructed to drain all water from his radiators, also to turn over the motor to insure complete drainage so as to prevent any part of the motor from freezing.

8. If it is necessary to make a forced landing, get necessary assistance SO AS NOT TO DELAY MAIL IN ANY RESPECT.

9. In case of forced landing in a strange field, make sure that there are no obstacles in the path of your getaway.

10. Carry maps unless you are absolutely sure of the country to be covered.

11. If possible fly over 5000 feet, preferably 8000 feet.

12. Never fly over cities unless you have a safe altitude.

13. Pilots landing with mail should have the right of way over all others.

14. No pilot should carry passengers in Aerial Mail ships unless by written authority of the Second Assistant Postmaster General, or the Superintendent of the Aerial Mail Division.

15. Under no circumstances will the weight of the mail be reduced in order to take a passenger unless authority is given by the Superintendent.

16. Test flights will not last longer than 45 minutes.

17. Hangars must be cleared by at least 50 feet.

18. Compasses must be consulted at all times while in flight. There is absolutely no excuse for pilots deviating from their course if this instruction is followed to the letter. Check up your flights as to compass courses, wind strengths and directions, and keep a relative time table over prominent landmarks. These observations will get you to your destination with least delay to the mail during periods of poor visibility.

19. Always note in pilot's report whenever a ship is delayed more than 10 minutes in getting away, stating whether it be due to the failure of the mail arriving at the field on time or otherwise.

20. When proper authority has been granted for passengers to be carried, the representative at the starting point should place his O.K. on the letter authorizing flight, and when the destination is reached by the aviator and passenger, the passenger will then affix his signature on the letter of authorization and the representative will then forward it to the Division of Aerial Mail Service for the files.

21. Mail will be locked in compartment by the manager of the field and each pilot must carry a key on a chain fastened to his belt or clothing. Each manager and aviator must receipt for the key issued to him and be responsible for its safe keeping, and must keep it on his person at all times. Pilots and managers should take every precaution for the safety of the mail in their custody as some of the mail going by aeroplane is very valuable.

22. Pilots drinking intoxicating liquors within twenty-four hours previous to flying will be punished by their dismissal from the service.

23. Winter clothing. The winter clothing will be in the custody of the field managers who will issue it to the pilot for use while flying, and upon completing his flight the suit must be returned to the field manager and not worn or carried off the field. No exceptions to this rule will be permitted.

24. Inspections must be made beforehand, with a sufficient margin before flying time to allow for minor repairs or a shift to a better ship.

25. Detailed instructions to be issued on this subject from time to time.

26. Ships should never be placed so that a strong propeller blast is thrown into hangars or against ships.

Source: Air Mail Service, General Records of the Superintendent, College Park, 1918–28.

Appendix D

Statement of Fatalities in the U.S. Air Mail Service

Name	Position	Date	Plane	Remarks
Carl B. Smith	Pilot	Dec. 16, 1918	DH #97	Lost control of aircraft and crashed at Elizabeth, N.J.
August Thiele	Mechanic	Jan. 8, 1919	Standard #4	Struck on head by propeller while starting plane at Dunellen, N.J.
Frank McCusker	Pilot	May 25, 1919	DH #61	Jumped from plane at 200 feet at first indication of fire; en route Cleveland–Chicago
Charles W. Lamborn	Pilot	July 19, 1919	DH #82	Lost control of aircraft in fog en route Bellefonte–Cleveland
Lyman W. Doty	Pilot	Oct. 14, 1919	Curtiss R #32	Encountered poor visibility en route Washington–New York; struck tree while attempting to land near Catonsville, Md.
John P. Charlton, Jr.	Pilot	Oct. 30, 1919	DH #77	Became lost while flying from Bellefonte to New York; nosed over when landing at Long Valley, N.J., to seek directions

Name	Position	Date	Aircraft	Circumstances
Clayton W. Stoner	Pilot	March 10, 1920	DH #65	Hit tree in fog while flying from Chicago to Cleveland
Harry C. Sherlock	Pilot	March 30, 1920	DH #72	Hit smokestack of factory while landing at Heller Field, Newark, N.J.
Richard W. Wright	Pilot	April 10, 1920	Curtiss R #49	Passenger with pilot Hogue ferrying plane Bustleton–Newark; plane caught fire and Wright jumped or fell from altitude of 200 feet
Clarence Stapleton	Clerk	April 11, 1920	JN-4H #44303	Passenger in unauthorized flight with pilot F. A. Robinson; plane spun into ground at Heller Field
W. J. McCandless	Div. Supt.	May 12, 1920	DH #79	Passenger with pilot H. W. Johnston; ferrying plane Omaha–Iowa City; crashed while attempting to land near Oskaloosa, Iowa, to get directions
N. C. Montis	Mechanic	June 6, 1920	Martin #204	Flying with pilot J. P. Harris; crashed after engine failed on take-off from Cleveland
Charles Nanista	Helper	Aug. 8, 1920	Twin-DH #117	Struck on head by propeller at Chicago Field
Robert Gautier	Pilot	Aug. 16, 1920	DH #31704	Struck radio mast in rain while practicing landings at College Park, Md.
Max Miller	Pilot	Sept. 1, 1920	JL #305	Aircraft caught fire en route New York–Cleveland; crashed near Morristown, N.J.
Gustav Rierson	Mechanic	Sept. 1, 1920	JL #305	
Walter H. Stevens	Pilot	Sept. 14, 1920	JL #308	Aircraft caught fire en route Cleveland–Chicago; landed safely but exploded on ground
Russell L. Thomas	Mechanic	Sept. 14, 1920	JL #308	
Frederick A. Robinson	Pilot	Sept. 27, 1920	DH #31697	Ran into cables across Susquehanna River near Millersburg, Pa., en route New York–Cleveland

Name	Title	Date	Aircraft	Description
Bryan McMullen	Pilot	Oct. 15, 1920	DH #76	Crashed while landing in fog near Batavia, Ill., en route Chicago–Omaha
John P. Woodward	Pilot	Nov. 7, 1920	DH #178	Hit side of hill in bad weather near Tie Siding, Wyo., en route Salt Lake City–Cheyenne
Kenneth M. Stewart	Pilot	Feb. 3, 1921	Twin-DH #130	Crashed near Mendota, Minn., following engine failure
Hiram H. Rowe	Pilot	Feb. 9, 1921	JL #301	Crashed at LaCrosse, Wis., while on ferry flight Chicago–Minneapolis; Rowe was pilot, Carroll was learning route, and Hill was flight mechanic
William M. Carroll	Pilot	Feb. 9, 1921	JL #301	
Robert B. Hill	Mechanic	Feb. 9, 1921	JL #301	
William E. Lewis	Pilot	Feb. 22, 1921	DH #67	Plane stalled and crashed on take-off from Elko, Nev.
Elmer R. Vanatta	Pilot	April 21, 1921	DH #160	Plane stalled and crashed on take-off from Mitchel Field, N.Y.; pilot died of burns on April 30, 1921
James Titus Christensen	Pilot	April 29, 1921	DH #196	Hit concrete abutment on approach to Cleveland in bad weather
Walter M. Bunting	Pilot	May 7, 1921	DH #176	Crashed while attempting to land at Rock Springs, Wyo., in good weather
Howard F. Smith	Pilot	July 16, 1921	DH #222	Plane stalled and crashed on take-off from Marina Field, San Francisco
Walter J. Smith	Pilot	Sept. 7, 1922	DH #227	Plane stalled and crashed after take-off from Indianapolis Fair Grounds; pilot died of injuries on Sept. 8, 1922
Paul S. Oakes	Pilot	Jan. 18, 1923	DH #223	Crashed while testing plane at Cheyenne; Acer was passenger
W. R. Acer	Helper	Jan. 18, 1923	DH #223	
Elmer G. Leonhardt	Pilot	Feb. 26, 1923	DH #291	Crashed while attempting to land in bad weather at Meadville, Pa.

Harwell C. Thompson	Pilot	Sept. 7, 1923	DH #283	Crashed while attempting forced landing at Colton, Ohio, with engine problems
Howard C. Brown	Pilot	Dec. 6, 1923	DH #318	Crashed at Castalia, Ohio; cause, defective welding of control stick
James F. Moore	Pilot	Dec. 24, 1923	DH #315	Flew into hill near Egbert, Wyo., while flying low to avoid severe headwind
Leonard B. Hyde-Pearson	Pilot	March 7, 1924	DH #327	Crashed in bad weather near Grampian, Pa., en route Bellefonte–Cleveland
William F. Blanchfield	Pilot	Aug. 1, 1924	DH #297	Stalled and crashed while making unauthorized flight over cemetery during funeral for Air Mail helper
Clarence A. Gilbart	Pilot	Dec. 21, 1924	DH #311	Crashed near Goshen, Indiana, in snow and sleet storm
Charles H. Ames	Pilot	Oct. 1, 1925	DH #385	Flew into Nittany Mountain near Bellefonte in bad weather
Arthur R. Smith	Pilot	Feb. 12, 1926	Curtiss Carrier Pigeon #602	Hit trees near Montpelier, Ohio, en route Chicago–Bryan
John F. Milatzo	Pilot	April 22, 1927	Douglas #626	Crashed near Goshen, Indiana, in snow and sleet storm

Source: Records of the Post Office Department.

Notes and Abbreviations

Abbreviations Used in the Notes

The major source of archival material used for this study was found in the Records of the Post Office Department, Record Group 28, National Archives, Washington, D.C. At the time these records were consulted (1976), they were organized as follows:

Bureau of the Second Assistant Postmaster General
Immediate Office, Correspondence Relating
    to Air Mail Service, 1921–27   2PMG/IOC (AM)
Immediate Office, Memoranda, 1914–29   2PMG/IOM
Division of Air Mail Service   AMS
  General Classified Records, 1918–25   AMS/GCR
  General Records of the Superintendent,
    College Park, Maryland, 1918–25   AMS/GRS (CP)
  Records of the Superintendent,
    1924 [1918]–1926   AMS/RS
  Circular Letters, Memoranda, and
    Instructions, 1924–26   AMS/CLM1
  First Flights, 1919–57   AMS/FF
  Personnel Files   AMS/PF

In addition to the above, these sources are abbreviated in the Notes as follows:

Army Air Forces, Central Decimal Files   AAF/CDF
Air Mail Pilots of America   AMPA
Bureau of Aeronautics (Navy)   BuAer
National Archives   NA
National Advisory Committee for Aeronautics   NACA
National Air and Space Museum   NASM
Post Office Department   POD
Record Group   RG
United States Postal Service   USPS

Chapter 1

1. Harold E. Morehouse, "Charles K. Hamilton," n.d., and Norman E. Borden, Jr., "Charles Keeney Hamilton," n.d.; both in the historical files of the National Air and Space Museum, Smithsonian Institution, Washington, D.C.

2. Ibid.; *Aircraft* 1 (September 1910), 251.
3. Morehouse, "Hamilton," and Borden, "Hamilton."
4. *New York Times*, June 14, 1910; *Fly* 2 (July 1910), 5–6, 12.
5. Ibid.
6. *Fly* 2 (July 1910), 5–6, 12.
7. Ibid.
8. Morehouse, "Hamilton."
9. *Fly* 2 (July 1910), 1; *Literary Digest* 40 (June 25, 1910), 1246–48.
10. Henry Ladd Smith, *Airways: The History of Commercial Aviation in the United States* (New York, 1944), p. 54; Lewis L. Gould, *Progressives and Prohibitionists: Texas Democrats in the Wilson Era* (Austin, 1973), pp. 94–95.
11. Donald B. Holmes, *Air Mail: An Illustrated History, 1793–1981* (New York, 1981), pp. 5–21.
12. POD, "Aeroplane Service Data," December 23, 1914, AMS/FF; C. R. Rosenberry, *Glenn Curtiss* (Garden City, N.Y., 1972), pp. 294–95.
13. POD, memorandum, November 10, 1910, historical files, Library of the U.S. Postal Service, Washington, D.C. On Hitchcock's career, see Edward C. Smith, "Frank Harris Hitchcock," in Harris E. Starr (ed.), *Dictionary of American Biography*, Supplement 1 (New York, 1944), pp. 409–410.
14. The world's first officially sanctioned air mail service took place in India on February 20, 1911. See Holmes, *Air Mail*, pp. 41–43.
15. Previous accounts of the first authorized air mail flight in the United States contain a number of errors. For example, Holmes, *Air Mail*, pp. 53–57, and Donald Dale Jackson, *Flying the Mail* (Alexandria, Va., 1982), state that Hitchcock handed the first sack of mail to Ovington; Jackson (p. 20) even reproduces a picture of the event. But Hitchcock was not present; the picture was taken on September 25. Part of the problem is reliance on the faulty recollections of Hitchcock, who confuses his visit of September 25 with September 23 in a letter to Ovington, October 7, 1931, in NASM Historical Files. Also, Ovington's memory of events is flawed, as can be seen by comparing his memorandum, undated but written not long after the event (in AMS/FF) with his later account, "The First Aerial Mail-Man," *Western Flying* 1 (March 1926), 7, 23. For a more accurate picture of events on Long Island, interested readers are referred to the following contemporary accounts: New York Daily *Tribune*, September 22–27, 1911; *New York Times*, September 22–27, 1911; *Fly* 4 (November 1911), 11–16, which contains the photograph of Bartsch handing the mail to Ovington; and *Aero Club of America Bulletin* 1 (January 1912), 13–15, which featured the photograph of Hitchcock and Ovington, taken on September 25.
16. W. W. Dickson to Hitchcock, September 21 and 23, 1911, USPS Historical Files.
17. Exactly who flew the mail during the meet has never been resolved. Arnold, for example, later wrote in *Global Missions* (New York, 1949), p. 71, that he had been one of the pilots, while a memorandum, POD, "Aeroplane Mail Service Data," December 23, 1914, AMS/FF, indicates that mail was carried by Ovington, Beck, Arnold, Milling, Ely, T. G. Ellyson, Edward Lee Hammond, and George W. Beatty. Contemporary accounts of the air meet, which lost interest in the air mail after the first few days, state that Ovington made most trips, with Sopwith and Beck flying at

least one trip each. It can be argued that only Ovington took an oath of office as a temporary mail carrier and therefore could—and did—claim to be the only *official* air mail pilot.

18. POD, *Annual Report of the Postmaster General, 1911* (Washington, D.C., 1912), pp. 11, 145.
19. U.S. House of Representatives, Subcommittee No. 1 of the Committee on the Post Office and Post Roads, *Hearings: Post Office Appropriation Bill, 1913*, 62d Congress, 2d sess. (1912), p. 293.
20. *Congressional Record*, 62d Cong., 2d sess. (April 20, 1912), pp. 5063–66.
21. "Aeroplane Service Data," December 23, 1914, AMS/FF. See also Thomas J. O'Sullivan and Karl B. Weber, *History of the United States Pioneer and Government-Operated Air Mail Service, 1910–1928* (Philadelphia, 1973).
22. *Flying* 2 (March 1913), 18.
23. Ibid. 2 (April 1913), 14.
24. Arthur S. Link, *Wilson: The New Freedom* (Princeton, 1956), pp. 135–36.
25. Richard Winston Howard, "The Work of Albert Sidney Burleson as Postmaster General," M.A. thesis, University of Texas, 1938, is best for Burleson's background and career as postmaster general, but see also Gould, *Texas Democrats*. Gerald Cullinan, *The Post Office Department* (New York, 1968), and Ross A. McReynolds, "History of the United States Post Office, 1607–1931," Ph.D. dissertation, University of Chicago, 1935, are hostile. Cullinan writes (p. 126) that Burleson "was a coarse, vain, and excessively arrogant man, and his eight years as Postmaster General are generally considered to have been the most disastrous in the history of the postal establishment." A scholarly biography of Burleson—and a dispassionate assessment of his tenure at the Post Office—is badly needed.
26. POD, *Annual Report of the Postmaster General, 1913* (Washington, D.C., 1914); Burleson to Woodhouse, November 21, 1913, USPS Historical Files.
27. Burleson to Finley, December 8, 1913, USPS Historical Files.
28. U.S. House of Representatives, *Report No. 126* [December 10, 1913], 63d Cong., 2d sess. (Washington, D.C., 1913).
29. *Congressional Record*, 63d Cong., 2d sess. (December 15, 1913), pp. 929–36.
30. The best account of NACA is Alex Roland, *Model Research: The National Advisory Committee for Aeronautics, 1915–1958* (Washington, D.C., 1985).
31. Praeger, "Moss from a Rolling Stone," unpublished autobiography, Papers of Otto Praeger, in the possession of the Praeger family, Rye, N.Y. See also George Langley Conner, "A Brief Biography of Hon. Otto Praeger," NASM Historical Files.
32. Grey to Praeger, October 30, 1930, Praeger Papers; New York *Herald Tribune*, February 13, 1948.
33. Praeger, "Moss," and Conner, "Praeger."
34. Praeger, "Moss."
35. Koenigsberg, *King News: An Autobiography* (Philadelphia, 1941), pp. 35–37.
36. Praeger, "Moss."
37. Ibid.; Carl H. Scheele, *A Short History of the Mail Service* (Washington, D.C., 1970), pp. 138–39.

38. *Flying* 5 (March 1916), 53–59, 62–63.
39. Burlseon to Bankhead, March 8, 1916, USPS Historical Files; Paul T. David, *The Economics of Air Mail Transportation* (Washington, D.C., 1934), pp. 8–9.
40. Burleson to Bankhead, May 9, 1918, printed in *Congressional Record*, 65th Cong. 2d sess. (May 13, 1918), 643; POD, *Annual Report of the Postmaster General, 1916* (Washington, D.C., 1917), p. 46.
41. *Flying* 5 (December 1916), 452–54; *New York Times*, November 4, 1916.
42. *New York Times*, November 14, 1916; *Flying* 5 (January 1917), 504–506; Howard L. Scamehorn, *Balloons to Jets: A Century of Aeronautics in Illinois, 1855–1955* (Chicago, 1957), pp. 99–100.
43. Praeger to Richardson, November 23, 1916, and Richardson to Praeger, December 2, 1916, Subject-Classified Files, Box 23, National Advisory Committee for Aeronautics, RG 235, NA; NACA, *Second Annual Report, 1916* (Washington, D.C., 1917), pp. 10–11.
44. John Victory, "Twentieth Anniversary of the Air Mail," May 14, 1938, NACA Suitland Files, Box 40; NACA, "Minutes of a Special Meeting of the Executive Committee," March 29, 1917, NACA Subject-Classified Files, Box 3; James Clark Edgerton, "Horizons Unlimited," unpublished autobiography, in the possession of the Edgerton family, Miami Springs, Florida.
45. Praeger, "Moss."
46. Praeger to NACA, January 24, 1918, NACA Subject-Classified Files, Box 23.
47. Ibid.
48. DeKlyn to NACA, January 29, 1918, NACA Subject-Classified Files, Box 19; Edgerton, "Horizons Unlimited."
49. Wayne E. Fuller, *The American Mail* (Chicago, 1972), p. 9.
50. Howard, "Burleson," pp. 118–22; Burleson, "Telegraph and Telephone in Government Hands," *American Review of Reviews* 58 (December 1918), 619–24.

Chapter 2

1. POD, press release, February 12, 1918, AMS/GCR; *Aviation* 4 (February 15, 1918), 99–100.
2. Deeds to Maj. Gen. George O. Squier, April 9, 1918, and Praeger, "Memorandum for the Postmaster General on Army Cooperation in the Aerial Mail Service," June 20, 1918; both in AAF/CDF 311.125, Records of the Army Air Force, RG 18, NA.
3. Agreement between Praeger and Deeds, March 1, 1918, AAF/CDF 311.125.
4. Office of the Chief Signal Officer, "Memorandum to All Divisions," March 1, 1918, AAF/CDF 311.125.
5. Conner to Praeger, April 3, 1918, AMS/GCR.
6. "Report on Actions Taken by the Flying Branch in Regard to the Aerial Postal Route," April 11, 1918, AAF/CDF 311.125; *Aviation* 4 (April 15, 1918), 389; Edgerton, "Horizons Unlimited."
7. "Report on Actions," April 11, 1918, AAF/CDF 311.125; Edgerton, "Horizons Unlimited."
8. Praeger, "Army Cooperation," June 20, 1918, AAF/CDF 311.125.
9. Bane to Squier, April 24, 1918, AAF/CDF 311.125.

10. Baker to Burleson, April 23, 1918, AAF/CDF 311.125.
11. Praeger, "Army Cooperation," June 20, 1918, AAF/CDF 311.125;
    Praeger, "Moss." The exact date of this meeting is uncertain, but it took
    place between April 23 and 27.
12. Praeger, "Army Cooperation," June 20, 1918, AAF/CDF 311.125;
    Burleson to Senator Kenneth McKellar, January 6, 1920, published in
    Congressional Record, 66th Cong., 2d sess. (January 20, 1920), 1088. On
    Fleet's background and subsequent career, see William Wagner, *Reuben
    Fleet and the Story of Consolidated Aircraft* (Fallbrook, Cal., 1976).
13. Fleet to Chief of Training, April 27, 1918, and Fleet to Praeger April 30,
    1918, both in AAF/CDF 311.125; Fleet, "Fifty Years of Airmail," pri-
    vately printed, 1968, copy in author's collection.
14. Edgerton, "Horizons Unlimited." On Culver, see Edith Dodd Culver,
    The Day the Air-Mail Began (Kansas City, 1971).
15. Edgerton, "Horizons Unlimited."
16. Ibid.; Fleet to Chief of Air Service, May 18, 1918, AAF/CDF 311.125.
    Fleet gives a slightly different account of events in "Fifty Years of
    Airmail."
17. Edgerton, "Horizons Unlimited."
18. My account of the first flight from Washington is taken from *Air Service
    Journal* 2 (May 23, 1918), 737—43; Washington *Evening Star*, May 16,
    1918; *New York Times*, May 16, 1918; and Fleet to Chief of Air Service,
    May 18, 1918, AAF/CDF 311.125. Lipsner, *The Airmail—Jennies to Jets*
    (Chicago, 1951), p. 23, passes along a fanciful story of the day's events
    that has been repeated by authors who failed to consult contemporary
    sources.
19. Fleet to Chief of Air Service, May 18, 1918, AAF/CDF 311.125; Wash-
    ington *Evening Star*, May 16, 1918.
20. *Air Service Journal* 2 (May 23, 1918), 727—43; *New York Times*, May 16, 1918.
21. Edgerton, "Horizons Unlimited"; *Air Service Journal* 2 (May 23, 1918),
    727—43.
22. *New York Times*, May 17, 1918.
23. Edgerton, "Horizons Unlimited"; *Air Service Journal* 2 (May 23, 1918),
    727—43.
24. Fleet to Chief of Air Service, May 18, 1918, AAF/CDF 311.125;
    Edgerton, "Horizons Unlimited." Fleet, "Fifty Years of Airmail," says
    that he escorted Boyle, but it is clear from Fleet's report of May 18,
    1918, and Edgerton's memoirs, that it was Edgerton who provided the
    escort.
25. Fleet to Chief of Air Service, May 18, 1918, AAF/CDF 311.125.
26. Ibid.; POD, "Flight Data," n.d. [1918], AMS/FF.
27. *Air Service Journal* 2 (May 23, 1918), 743.
28. Fleet to Chief of Air Service, May 18, 1919, AAF/CDF 311.125; Brig.
    Gen. C. M. Saltzman, "Memorandum for the Air Division," April 18,
    1918, AAF/CDF 311.125; Fleet, "Fifty Years of Airmail."
29. *New York Times*, May 21, 1918.
30. Dean C. Smith, "Pilot's Progress," in the Dean Smith Collection, Trans-
    portation History Foundation, University of Wyoming. Smith published
    a shorter version of his autobiography as *By the Seat of My Pants* (Boston,
    1961). Smith and other pilots solved the R-4's control problems by using
    a rubber shock absorber to ease the strain, fastening one end to a ring

on the front wall of the cockpit and wrapping the other around the
control column.
31. Smith, "Pilot's Progress."
32. Edgerton, "Horizons Unlimited"; *New York Times*, May 22, 1918.
33. Praeger, "Moss."
34. Culver to Praeger, June 3, 1918, AAF/CDF 311.125.
35. Carlton Kemper, "Log Report," May 31, 1918, AMS/GCR. In "Horizons
    Unlimited," Edgerton confused the date of Praeger's familiarization
    flight—and the results.
36. Praeger to Weidenbach, with covering note, June 1, 1918, AAF/CDF
    311.125.
37. Weidenbach to Chief of Operations Section, June 1, 1918, with Goodier's
    annotation; Weidenbach, memorandum of conversation with Praeger on
    June 1 and 4, 1918; Weidenbach to Chief of Operations Section, June
    11, 1918; all in AAF/CDF 311.125.
38. Edgerton, "Horizons Unlimited"; POD, press release, June 18, 1918,
    AMS/GCR.
39. *New York Times*, June 4, 7, and 12, 1918.
40. Edward P. Warner, *The Early History of Air Transportation* (York, Pa.,
    1938), p. 6.
41. Ibid., pp. 10, 14−15; *Flying* 7 (July 1918), 522.
42. Praeger, "Army Cooperation," June 20, 1918, AAF/CDF 311.125.
43. Weidenbach to Goodier, June 11, 1918; Weidenbach to Col. H. H.
    Arnold, June 17, 1918; both in AAF/CDF 311.125.
44. Kenly to March, September 5, 1918; Baker to Burleson, June 26, 1918;
    March to Kenly, July 25, 1918; all in AAF/CDF 311.125.
45. Burleson to Edgerton, June 1918, quoted by George L. Conner in
    the fragments of his manuscript on the origins of the Air Mail Service,
    NASM Historical Files; Edgerton, "Horizons Unlimited." Edgerton's
    weather logs are at NASM.
46. Willoughby became chief of intelligence for Gen. Douglas MacArthur
    during World War II. He may have changed his name (to his mother's
    maiden name) because of anti-German feeling in the United States.
    See Frank Kluckhorn, "Heidelberg to Madrid—The Story of General
    Willoughby," *Reporter* 7 (August 18, 1952), 25−30.
47. Praeger to Willoughby, July 13, 1918, AAF/CDF 311.125.
48. POD, press release, August 5, 1918, AMS/GCR.
49. *Aerial Age Weekly* 7 (August 12, 1918), 1070−71.
50. Burleson to Baker, August 19, 1918, AAF/CDF 311.125.
51. Praeger, "Army Cooperation," June 20, 1918, AAF/CDF 311.125;
    Praeger, "Moss."
52. *Flying* 7 (July 1918), 525.

Chapter 3
1. POD, press release, July 18, 1918, AMS/GCR.
2. Lipsner, *Airmail*, passim.
3. Praeger, "Memorandum for the Postmaster General on Army Cooperation in the Aerial Mail Service," June 20, 1918, AAF/CDF 311.125;
   Praeger to the Adjutant General, War Department, July 8, 1918, the
   Papers of Benjamin B. Lipsner, Division of Postal History, National Museum of American History, Smithsonian Institution, Washington, D.C.

4. Praeger to W. C. Jenkins, June 12, 1918, AMS/GCR. Emphasis in original.

5. Miller to Praeger, June 27, 1918, AMS/Miller PF.

6. Lipsner, *Airmail*, p. 77.

7. Ibid., pp. 77–78; *Flying* 7 (September 1918), 711; *Aerial Age Weekly* 7 (September 9, 1918), 1268.

8. *Flying* 7 (September 1918), 705–711.

9. Ibid.

10. POD, flight logs, 1918, AMS/FF.

11. POD, press release, August 31, 1918, AMS/GCR.

12. Shank to Lipsner, August 28, 1918, AMS/Shank FF.

13. L. T. Bussler to Col. T. H. Bane, October 1, 1918. AMS/GCR. The Pentz and other compasses are discussed in John A. C. Warner, "Aircraft Compasses," Part III of NACA Report No. 128 ("Direction Instruments"), published in NACA, *Seventh Annual Report, 1921* (Washington, D.C., 1922), pp. 616–45.

14. Lipsner's "Instructions" can be found in AMS/GRS (CP). For the dispatch board, see *Aerial Age Weekly* 7 (September 9, 1918), 1268–69.

15. Martin to Lipsner, August 20, 1918, Lipsner Papers; Lipsner, *Airmail*, pp. 174–76.

16. Lipsner, *Airmail*, pp. 174–76.

17. *New York Times*, May 28, 1918; *Flying* 7 (September 1918), 711; Praeger, "Moss."

18. Edgerton, "Horizons Unlimited."

19. Burleson to Baker, August 27, 1918, AAF/CDF 311.125.

20. Kenly to March, August 28, 1918, AAF/CDF 311.125.

21. March to Kenly, September 3, 1918; Kenly to March, September 5, 1918; March to Kenly, September 9, 1918; all in AAF/CDF 311.125.

22. Memorandum for Jordan, unsigned but corrections in Lipsner's handwriting, AMS/GCR.

23. *Aerial Age Weekly* 7 (September 16, 1918), 1310; *New York Times*, September 3, 1918.

24. Reports of the flight by Miller and Gardner were published in *Flying* 7 (October 1918), 819–21. See also *New York Times*, September 6, 7, 10, and 11, 1918. Gardner's crash was noted in Praeger to Burleson, "Report on Aeroplane Mail Service," May 15, 1919, USPS Historical Files.

25. *Aerial Age Weekly* 7 (September 16, 1918), 1310, 1313–14.

26. U.S. House of Representatives, Subcommittee of the Committee on the Post Office and Post Roads, *Hearings: Claims for Construction of Hangars and Maintenance of Flying Fields—Air Mail Service*, 67th Cong., 4th sess. (Washington, D.C., 1923), pp. 73–74; *New York Times*, October 23, 1918.

27. *New York Times*, September 30, 1918; Elton W. Downs, "Contributions of U.S. Army Aviation to Uses and Operation of Aircraft," Ph.D. dissertation, University of Wisconsin, 1959, pp. 30–31.

28. *Aviation* 5 (November 1, 1918), 422; Praeger to Burleson, "Report on Aeroplane Mail Service," May 15, 1919, USPS Historical Files. Correspondence regarding Newton's accident and his wife's pension claim can be found in AMS/Newton PF. Although the claim listed September 25, 1918, as the date of the accident, contemporary documentation indicates that October 18, 1918, is correct.

29. Capt. C. B. Hammond and 1st Lt. Charles W. Lamborn, "Memorandum

for Colonel Woods," December 16, 1918, enclosing statement by Shank,
AAF/CDF 231.21.

30. *Aerial Age Weekly* 8 (October 28, 1918), 370.

Chapter 4

1. David Burner, "1919: Prelude to Normalcy," in John Braeman, *et al.*
   (eds.), *Change and Continuity in Twentieth-Century America: The 1920's* (Columbus, Ohio, 1967), pp.3–31.
2. Manufacturers Aircraft Association, *Aircraft Year Book, 1919* (New York,
   1919), p. 11.
3. *Aerial Age Weekly* 8 (December 9, 1918), 655.
4. Lt. Col. B. F. Castle to Kenly, November 12, 1918, reporting a conversation with Praeger, AAF/CDF 311.125; POD, *Annual Report, 1918* (Washington, D.C., 1919), pp. 16–19.
5. Praeger to W. C. Potter, assistant director of aircraft production, November 21, 1918, and Burleson to Potter, November 21, 1918, AAF/CDF
   311.125.
6. U.S. House of Representatives, Committee on the Post Office and
   Post Roads, *Hearings*, 65th Cong., 3d sess. (Washington, D.C., 1918),
   pp. 48–66.
7. *New York Times*, December 7, 1918.
8. Ibid., December 8, 1918.
9. Lipsner, *Airmail*, pp. 173–91.
10. *Aerial Age Weekly* 8 (November 18, 1918), 520; (December 9, 1918), 655,
    673; memorandum of meeting in Lipsner's office, December 3, 1918,
    Lipsner Papers. Lipsner's return to Washington on November 14, four
    days before Gardner was fired, is confirmed by C. N. Moore and C. H.
    Clarahan, "Investigation of Expense Account of B. B. Lipsner," De-
    cember 24, 1918, AMS/Lipsner PF.
11. Praeger's orders, usually handwritten notes, can be found in AMS/
    Lipsner PF.
12. POD, press release, March 17, 1920, AMS/GCR.
13. Edgerton, "Horizons Unlimited."
14. Praeger, "Order," December 15, 1918, AMS/Edgerton PF.
15. Jordan to Praeger, December 9, 1918, and Praeger to Jordan, December
    11, 1918, AMS/GCR.
16. Edgerton to Praeger, December 17, 1918, AMS/GCR.
17. New York *Tribune*, December 19, 1918, and *New York Times*, December
    19, 1918.
18. New York *Tribune*, December 19, 1918.
19. *Chicago Daily Tribune*, December 20, 1918; *New York Times*, December 21,
    1918; New York *Tribune*, December 21, 1918.
20. Kemper to Superintendent, AMS, December 21, 1918, AMS/GCR.
21. Newton to Bussler, December 21, 1918, AMS/Newton PF; *New York
    Times*, December 22, 1918.
22. POD, press release, December 21, 1918, and Praeger to Manager, Bel-
    mont Field, December 21, 1918, AMS/GCR.
23. DeHart to Bussler, December 28, 1918, and L. D. Smith to Bussler, De-
    cember 28, 1918, AMS/Doty PF.
24. Newton to Bussler, December 28, 1918, AMS/Doty PF; POD, press re-
    lease, December 30, 1918, AMS/GCR.

25. Castle, "Memorandum for the Executive Officer," November 7, 1918, AAF/CDF 311.125.
26. Castle to Kenly, November 12, 1918, AAF/CDF 311.125.
27. Kenly to Ryan, November 13, 1918, AAF/CDF 311.125.
28. Praeger memorandum, November 13, 1918, AAF/CDF 311.125.
29. Woods to Praeger, confirming an earlier conversation, November 23, 1918, and Potter to Burleson, November 21, 1918, AAF/CDF 311.125. See also Downs, "Contributions," pp. 32−36.
30. *Congressional Record*, 65th Cong., 3d sess. (December 17, 1918), pp. 573−77. For La Guardia's wartime service, see James J. Hudson, *Hostile Skies: A Combat History of the American Air Service in World War I* (Syracuse, N.Y., 1968), pp. 242−48.
31. *Congressional Record*, 65th Cong., 3d sess. (December 18, 1918), pp. 626−29; *New York Times*, December 19, 1918.
32. New York *Herald*, December 21, 1918.
33. Moore and Clarahan, "Investigation," December 24, 1918, AMS/Lipsner PF.
34. Praeger testified on January 9 and 10. U.S. Senate, Committee on Post Office and Post Roads, *Hearings*, 65th Cong., 3d sess. (Washington, D.C., 1919), pp. 70−111.
35. *Congressional Record*, 65th Cong., 3d sess. (January 31, 1919), pp. 2435−36.
36. Ibid. (February 1, 1919), p. 2518; (February 19, 1919), p. 3790.
37. Edgerton, "Horizons Unlimited."

Chapter 5
 1. *Aerial Age Weekly* 8 (January 13, 1919), 896.
 2. Edgerton, "Horizons Unlimited"; Praeger testimony, January 29, 1920, U.S. Senate, Subcommittee of the Committee on Post Offices and Post Roads, *Hearings*, 66th Cong., 2d sess. (Washington, D.C., 1920), pp. 43−72.
 3. Interview with Stanton, April 18, 1976; Maj. Nathan Levinson to Edgerton, December 19, 1918, AMS/Stanton PF; John R. M. Wilson, *Turbulence Aloft: The Civil Aeronautics Administration Amid Wars and Rumors of War, 1938−1953* (Washington, 1979), pp. 70−71.
 4. Lee to Lipsner, October 16, 1918, AMS/Lee PF; Miller to Lipsner, December 27, 1918, Lipsner Papers. Lee gives a somewhat different account of the circumstances of his hiring in his unpublished autobiography, copy in NASM Historical Files.
 5. Edgerton to L. D. Smith, January 25, 1919, AMS/L. D. Smith PF.
 6. Edgerton to Divisional Superintendents, January 28, 1919, AMS/GRS (CP); Air Mail Service, *General Directions to Entire Personnel*, n.d. [1919], AMS/GRS (CP).
 7. McCusker to Edgerton, February 5, 1919, and Edgerton to McCusker, February 8, 1919, AMS/McCusker PF; Edgerton to Praeger, February 26, 1919, AMS/GCR.
 8. Anglin, "Report," July 1, 1919, AMS/Anglin PF; Stanton to Powers, July 7, 1919, AMS/GRS.
 9. Edgerton, "Horizons Unlimited"; Praeger, "Memorandum on Changing De Haviland Planes for Postal Service," December 19, 1919, printed in U.S. House of Representatives, Select Committee on Expenditures in the

War Department, *Hearings Before Subcommittee No. 1 (Aviation)*, 66th Cong., 1st sess. (Washington, D.C., 1920), pp. 4009–11.
10. Praeger to Jordan, April 8, 1919, AMS/GCR.
11. Praeger to Jordan, April 8, 1919, and Jordan to Praeger, April 14, 1919, AMS/GCR.
12. Praeger to Burleson, "Report on Aeroplane Mail Service," May 15, 1919, USPS Historical Files.
13. Ibid.; *New York Times*, May 15, 1919.
14. *Aerial Age Weekly* 9 (May 26, 1919), 545.
15. Edgerton to Praeger, May 20, 1919, AMS/Edgerton PF.
16. *Aerial Age Weekly* 9 (June 9, 1919), 643.
17. McCusker to Praeger, December 12, 1919, AMS/McCusker PF.
18. Jordan to Praeger, December 12, 1919, AMS/McCusker PF.
19. *New York Times*, June 26, 1919.
20. Burleson to Steenerson, July 2, 1919, AMS/McCusker PF.
21. POD, press release, June 21, 1919, AMS/GCR.
22. *New York Times*, July 2, 1919.
23. Jordan to Praeger, July 5, 1919, AMS/Biffle PF.
24. Praeger to Jordan, July 7, 1919, AMS/Biffle PF.
25. Biffle to Edgerton, July 9, 1919, and Jordan to Edgerton, July 10, 1919, AMS/Biffle PF.
26. Anglin, "Report," July 11, 1919, AMS/Anglin PF.
27. Ellis, "Report," July 15, 1919, AMS/Ellis PF.
28. Stanton to Praeger, August 4, 1919, and Praeger to Stanton, August 5, 1919, AMS/Lamborn PF.
29. Powers to Praeger, July 22, 1919, and Praeger to Powers, July 22, 1919, AMS/GRS (CP); Egge to Praeger, July 22, 1919, AMS/RS.
30. Egge to Praeger, enclosing statements, July 22, 1919, AMS/RS.
31. Ibid.
32. Ibid.; *New York Times*, July 25, 1919; Lee to the author, April 4, 1976; interview with Stanton, April 18, 1976.
33. Egge to Praeger, July 27, 1919, AMS/RS; *New York Times*, July 25, 1919.
34. Egge to Praeger, July 27, 1919, AMS/RS.
35. *New York Times*, July 25, 1919.
36. Egge to Praeger, July 27, 1919, AMS/RS.
37. Ibid.
38. Ibid.; interview with Stanton, August 5, 1976.
39. *New York Times*, July 25, 1919.
40. Ibid.; POD, press release, July 25, 1919, AMS/GCR.
41. *Congressional Record*, 66th Cong., 1st sess., appendix, pp. 9046–47; interview with Stanton, August 5, 1976; *New York Times*, July 26, 1919.
42. *Aerial Age Weekly* 9 (August 4, 1919), 968, reported that attorney James H. Conklin and E. Hamilton Lee also were present. Conklin may have advised Anglin, but he did not attend the meetings. Lee took part only during the last hour on July 27 in order to clarify his petition for reinstatement.
43. Buente, "Report on Conference," July 27, 1919, AMS/GCR.
44. Lee to Praeger, July 26, 1919, and Praeger to Lee, July 27, 1919, AMS/Lee PF; Lee to Jerome Lederer, October 30, 1975, copy supplied to the author by Lee.

45. *New York Times,* July 28, 1919.
46. The *Times* also stated that the pilots had secured a raise in pay as a result of the strike. There was an adjustment in the area of per diem: pilots could claim $1.50 without receipts for each one-way trip flown over the route to which assigned; in the event of forced landing and failure to complete the trip, pilots would be entitled to actual expenses (vouchers required), with a maximum of $3 a day for subsistence. It is not clear, however, that these adjustments were a result of the strike. Acting Postmaster General J. D. Koone, "Order No. 3387," July 31, 1919, AMS/GRS (CP).
47. See George E. Hopkins, *The Airline Pilots: A Study in Elite Unionization* (Cambridge, Mass., 1971), pp. 20–27.
48. "Application for Employment as Pilot, Aerial Mail Service," September 1919, AMS/GCR.
49. Anglin to Praeger, October 16, 1919, with Praeger annotation, AMS/Anglin PF; Leon D. Smith to Second Assistant Postmaster General, August 17, 1922, AMS/L. D. Smith PF.
50. NACA, *Fifth Annual Report, 1919* (Washington, D.C., 1920), pp. 26, 40.
51. Interview with Stanton, August 5, 1976; Edgerton, "Horizons Unlimited."
52. Praeger to Burleson, "Report on Aeroplane Mail Service," May 15, 1919, USPS Historical Files.

Chapter 6
1. Text of Praeger's speech at the Sixth Annual convention of Dixie Overland Highway Association, Demopolis, Alabama, August 15, 1919, released in advance by POD, Office of Information, August 12, 1919, AMS/GCR.
2. Praeger testimony, January 9, 1919, U.S. Senate, Committee on Post Offices and Post Roads, *Hearings,* 65th Cong., 3d sess. (Washington, D.C., 1919), pp. 70–111; Praeger to Burleson, "Report on Aeroplane Mail Service," May 15, 1919, USPS Historical Files.
3. Praeger, "Memorandum on Aerial Mail Service, January 30, 1919, reprinted in *Congressional Record,* 65th Cong., 3d sess. (January 31, 1919), 2436–37; Praeger testimony, December 19, 1919, U.S. House of Representatives, Select Committee on Expenditures in the War Department, *Hearings Before Subcommittee No. 1 (Aviation),* 66th Cong., 1st sess. (Washington, D.C., 1920), pp. 4009–35; Jordan to Praeger, March 14, 1919, AMS/Jordan PF; *Aerial Age Weekly* 8 (March 10, 1919), 1347.
4. POD, Office of Information, April 7, 1919, AMS/GCR.
5. Aviation 6 (July 1, 1919), 576.
6. Ibid.; "Planes Used in the Air Mail Service," September 17, 1924, Records of the Select Committee of Inquiry into the Operations of the U.S. Air Services, 1924–1925, U.S. House of Representatives, RG 233, NA; Praeger testimony, January 29, 1920, U.S. Senate, Subcommittee of the Committee on Post Offices and Post Roads, *Hearings,* 66th Cong., 2d sess. (Washington, D.C., 1920), pp. 43–72.
7. *Aerial Age Weekly* 10 (September 29, 1919), 84.
8. Praeger testimony, January 29, 1919, U.S. Senate, Subcommittee of the Committee on Post Offices and Post Roads, *Hearings,* 66th Cong., 2d sess. (Washington, D.C., 1920), pp. 43–72.

9. *Aviation* 7 (January 1, 1920), 475–76.
10. *Aerial Age Weekly* 10 (November 24, 1919), 286; POD, Office of Information, November 15, 1919, AMS/GCR.
11. Belmont to Praeger, September 11, 1919, AMS/GCR; *Aerial Age Weekly* 10 (January 26, 1920), 565, and (February 9, 1920), 626.
12. *Aerial Age Weekly* 10 (December 22, 1919), 364; Dean Smith, "Pilot's Progress."
13. Stevens to Praeger, December 3, 1919, AMS/Stevens PF.
14. Stevens to Praeger, January 13, 1920, AMS/Stevens PF.
15. Knight, "Report," January 19, 1920, AMS/Knight PF.
16. Praeger to McGrath, February 6, 1920, AMS/McGrath PF.
17. "Planes Used in the Air Mail Service," September 17, 1924.
18. Rexmond C. Cochrane, *Measures for Progress: A History of the National Bureau of Standards* (Washington, D.C., 1966), pp. 142, 196; Radio Laboratory, Bureau of Standards, "Localized Signalling System for Airplane Landing," June 2, 1920, National Bureau of Standards, General Records of J. Howard Dellinger, Box 4, RG 167, NA.
19. Ibid.; Edgerton to Stanton, January 2, 1919, AMS/Stanton PF.
20. Edgerton, "Radio as Applied to Air Navigation in the Air Mail Service," *U.S. Air Service* 5 (February 1921), 12–14.
21. Ibid.; Edgerton, "Horizons Unlimited."
22. McGregor, "Beam Dream," in Dale Nielson (ed.), *Saga of the U.S. Air Mail Service, 1918–1927* (privately printed, 1962), pp. 16–17.
23. Edgerton, "Radio"; J. L. Bernard and L. E. Whittemore, "Radio Communication with Postal Aeroplanes," *Aerial Age Weekly* 13 (April 11, 1921), 105–06; (April 18, 1921), 127–29; (April 25, 1921), 155–57, 163.
24. Edgerton, "Horizons Unlimited."
25. *New York Times*, October 8, 1919.
26. Details of preparation can be found in AAF/CDF 373, and Office of Director of Air Service, "Report on First Transcontinental Reliability and Endurance Test," February 5, 1920, *Air Service Information Circular* I. See also Ray L. Bowers, "The Transcontinental Reliability Test," *Airpower Historian* 8 (January 1961), 45–54, and (April 1961), 88–100.
27. *New York Times*, October 9, 1919.
28. Ibid.
29. Ibid.
30. *San Francisco Chronicle*, October 9, 1919.
31. Except where noted, details of the race are taken from *New York Times*, October 9–31, 1919.
32. *Chicago Daily Tribune*, October 18, 1919.
33. *New York Times*, September 8 and 12, 1922.
34. Bowers, "Transcontinental Reliability Test," 97–98.
35. Quoted in Warner, *Early History of Air Transportation*, p. 17.
36. *New York Times*, October 21, 1919.
37. Lt. Col. Jack W. Heard, "To Whom It May Concern," September 20, 1918; Doty to Praeger, December 2, 1918; medical report of May 8, 1919; Edgerton to Doty, May 12, 1919; Col. Albert E. Truby to Edgerton, June 25, 1919; all in AMS/Doty PF.
38. S. Swann to Praeger, October 15, 1919; Praeger to W. M. Doty, October 16, 1919; W. M. Doty to Praeger, December 7, 1919; all in AMS/Doty PF.
39. Stanton to Praeger, November 10, 1919, AMS/GRS (CP).

40. POD, *Annual Report of the Postmaster General* (Washington, D.C., 1921), p. 60.
41. P. Smith to Stanton, January 15, 1920, AMS/P. Smith PF.
42. Edgerton to P. Smith, February 3, 1920, AMS/P. Smith PF.
43. Nielson (ed.), *Saga*, p. 99; Stephen G. Janas to the author, February 26, 1976; diary of Wesley L. Smith, April 10, and 12, 1920, in the possession of the Smith family, Mountain Lakes, N.J.
44. *New York Times*, April 11, 1920; New York *Tribune*, April 12, 1920.
45. P. Smith to Edgerton, April 17, 1920, AMS/P. Smith PF.
46. W. L. Smith to Praeger, April 27, 1920, AMS/W. L. Smith PF; W. L. Smith diary, April 27 and May 1, 1920.
47. Knight to Riddell, May 4, 1920, AMS/Knight PF.
48. POD, press release, May 15, 1920, AMS/GCR.
49. Noville to Praeger, July 11, 1920, AMS/Noville PF.

Chapter 7
1. Frederic L. Paxson, *American Democracy and the World War*, 3 vols. (Berkeley, Cal., 1936–48), III (*Postwar Years: Normalcy, 1918–1923)*, pp. 5–6.
2. Praeger testimony, December 10, 1919, U.S. House of Representatives, Committee on the Post Office and Post Roads, *Hearings*, 66th Cong., 2d sess. (Washington, D.C., 1920), 142–59.
3. Praeger to W. A. Ellis, January 3, 1920, AMS/GCR.
4. *Aerial Age Weekly* 10 (January 26, 1920), 565.
5. David, *Economics of Air Mail*, p. 8.
6. Praeger testimony, January 29 and February 9, 1920, U.S. Senate, Subcommittee of the Committee on Post Offices and Post Roads, *Hearings*, 66th Cong., 2d sess. (Washington, D.C., 1920), pp. 43–72, 259–72. See also Burleson, "The Story of Our Air Mail," *The Independent* 102 (April 3, 1920), 8, 35–36.
7. *New York Times*, February 17, March 30, and May 30, 1920.
8. POD, "Amount Expended for Air Mail Service by Fiscal Years," September 17, 1924, Records of the House of Representatives, Select Committee of Inquiry into Operations of the U.S. Air Services.
9. Praeger to Bussler, March 17, 1920, AMS/Bussler PF; interview with Stanton, April 18, 1976.
10. Winfield Scott Downs (ed.), *Who's Who in Engineering, 1948* (New York, 1948), p. 1185; *Aviation* 9 (November 22, 1920), 319; John J. Smith to the author, April 24, 1976.
11. Interview with Stanton, April 18, 1976; Lent, "Memoirs," in the possession of Jesse M. Davidson, Bronx, N.Y.
12. U.S. House of Representatives, Subcommittee of the Committee on the Post Office and Post Roads, *Hearings: Claims for Construction of Hangars and Maintenance of Flying Fields—Air Mail Service*, 67th Cong., 4th sess. (Washington, D.C., 1923), pp. 9–13.
13. Ibid., pp. 13–27.
14. Praeger testimony, January 29, 1920, U.S. Senate, Subcommittee of the Committee on Post Offices and Post Roads, *Hearings*, 66th Cong., 2d sess. (Washington, D.C., 1920), pp. 43–72; Manufacturers Aircraft Association, *Aircraft Year Book, 1920* (New York, 1920), pp. 217–20; Dean Smith to the author, March 9, 1976.
15. POD, Office of Information, December 2, 1919, AMS/GCR.

16. Praeger to Senator Charles B. Henderson, February 28, 1920, AMS/ GCR.
17. Lent, "Memoirs."
18. Kenneth Munson, *Airliners between the Wars, 1919–1939* (New York, 1972), pp. 150–51; Peter W. Brooks, *The Modern Airliner: Its Origins and Development* (London, 1961), pp. 18–19, 52–55.
19. Lent, "Memoirs"; Maj. Gen. Mason M. Patrick to I. B. Dunlap, January 21, 1922, AAF/CDF 452.1.
20. Larsen to Menoher, June 3, 1920, AAF/CDF 452.1.
21. Ocker to Menoher, May 27, 1920, and Hartney to chief, training and operations group, June 11, 1920, AAF/CDF 452.1; *U.S. Air Service* 3 (July 1920), 17–19, 33.
22. Monher to Larsen, June 4, 1920, AAF/CDF 452.1; Menoher to the technical committee, Aeronautical Board, July 12, 1920, Records of the Aeronautical Board, Box 3, RG 334, NA.
23. Lent, "Memoirs"; interview with Stanton, April 18, 1976.
24. "Report on Accident Resulting in McCandless' Death," May 19, 1920, AMS/McCandless PF. The Chicago–Omaha route had been opened, briefly, in January 1920. Walter J. Smith flew a survey flight on January 7, followed by regular mail service on January 9. However, bad weather and equipment shortages forced abandonment of the route after a few days. See *New York Times*, January 9, 1920, and Edgerton, "Horizons Unlimited."
25. Praeger to C. A. Parker, June 23, 1920, AMS/Howard M. Gurney PF.
26. Lent, "Memoirs."
27. Edgerton, "Horizons Unlimited."
28. Ibid.
29. Ibid.
30. Ibid.
31. Ibid.
32. Stevens to Parker, August 12, 1920, AMS/Stevens PF.
33. Robinson, "Report on Twin D.H. 118," August 12, 1920, AMS/Robinson PF.
34. Stanton to Praeger, August 23, 1919, AMS/GCR.
35. Ibid.
36. Miller to Colyer, August 16, 1920, AMS/Miller PF; W. L. Smith, "The Ill-Fated Junker Mailplanes," n.d., W. L. Smith Papers.
37. W. L. Smith, "Junker Mailplanes."
38. Whitbeck to Praeger, September 1, 1920, AMS/GCR; telegram, Whitbeck to Praeger, September 1, 1920, and Paul Smith to Praeger, September 2, 1920, AMS/Miller PF; *Washington Times*, September 1, 1920; *New York Times*, September 2, 1920; Capt. A. R. Christie to Chief of Air Service, September 3, 1920, AAF/CDF 452.1.
39. *Washington Herald*, September 2, 1920; material in AMS/Miller PF; interview with Daisy Marie Miller Ricker, July 15, 1976.
40. New York *Sun*, September 3, 1920; *New York Times*, September 3, 1920.
41. *New York Times*, September 9–12, 1920; *Aerial Age Weekly* 12 (September 13, 1920), 5.

Chapter 8

1. *U.S. Air Service* 4 (October 1920), 28.
2. *New York Times*, September 15, 1920; Gurney to Praeger, September 16, 1920, and Majors to Praeger, October 15, 1920, AMS/Stevens PF.
3. *New York Times*, September 16, 1920.
4. *Aviation* 9 (November 22, 1920), 319; Praeger to Lent, Stanton, and Egge, September 15, 1920, AMS/GCR.
5. Lent, "Memoirs"; POD, Office of Information, October 1, 1920, AMS/GCR.
6. Ibid.
7. *U.S. Air Service* 4 (October 1920), 29; Stanton to Praeger, October 18, 1920, AMS/GCR.
8. Stanton to Praeger, October 18, 1920, AMS/GCR.
9. Ibid.; Egge to J. E. Lamiell and J. V. Holtby, May 17, 1921, AMS/RS; Stanton to Praeger, October 12, 1920, AMS/GCR.
10. Stanton to Praeger, October 18, 1921, AMS/GCR.
11. U.S. Air Mail Service, *Pilots' Directions: New York–San Francisco Route* (Washington, D.C., 1921), pp. 17–20; A. K. Lobeck, *Airways of America* (Port Washington, N.Y., 1970; first published in 1933), pp. 89–11; Moore to Colyer, November 30, 1920, AMS/Moore PF.
12. Murray to Dunphy, October 20, 1920, AMS/Murray PF.
13. *New York Times*, November 8, 1920.
14. U.S. Air Mail Service, *Pilots' Directions*, pp. 21–27; Lobeck, *Airways*, pp. 113–37; F. E. Caldwell to Egge, February 24, 1923, AMS/GCR.
15. Kelly to Maj. H. H. Arnold, September 22, 1920, AMS/Jordan PF.
16. Conner to Praeger, November 6, 1920, AMS/Jordan PF.
17. Jordan to All Employees, December 1, 1920, AMS/Jordan PF; Jordan testimony, February 25, 1921, U.S. House of Representatives, Committee on the Post Office and Post Roads, *Hearings: Air Mail Service*, 66th Cong., 3d sess. (Washington, D.C., 1921), pp. 40–41.
18. "Proceedings of Board of Inquiry," January 5, 1921, AMS/Boggs PF.
19. Ibid.
20. Edward M. Boggs to Burleson, January 8, 1921, and clipping from *Los Angeles Times*, January 8, 1921, AMS/Jordan PF.
21. Jordan to Praeger, January 10, 1921, AMS/Jordan PF.
22. Barber to Praeger, January 15, 1921, and Nelson to Praeger, January 14, 1921, AMS/Jordan PF.
23. Assistant Attorney General R. P. Stewart to Burleson, January 10, 1921, AMS/Jordan PF; Praeger to Stanton, February 19, 1921, AMS/Boggs PF.
24. L. Ethan Ellis, "Martin Barnaby Madden," *Dictionary of American Biography*, 12 (New York, 1933), pp. 180–81; *Biographical Dictionary of the American Congress, 1774–1961* (Washington, D.C., 1961), p. 1251.
25. *Congressional Record*, 66th Cong., 3d sess. (January 7, 1921), p. 1121.
26. Ibid. (January 8, 1921), pp. 1174–76.
27. *Literary Digest* 68 (January 29, 1921), 16–18.
28. *The Outlook* 127 (January 19, 1921), 84.
29. U.S. Senate, *Document No. 358*, 66th Cong., 3d sess. (Washington, D.C., 1921).
30. *New York Times*, January 26, February 18, 25, and 26, 1921. The Air Mail Service later secured an additional $175,000 in a supplemental appropriation.

31. U.S. House of Representatives, Committee on the Post Office and Post Roads, *Hearings: First Deficiency Bill, 1921—Air Mail Service*, 66th Cong., 3d sess. (Washington, D.C., 1921).

32. "Minutes of the Second Meeting of the Advisory Council, Joint Commission on Postal Service," August 21, 1920, U.S. Congress, Records of the Joint Commission on the Postal Service, 1920–1924, RG 148, NA.

33. U.S. Congress, Joint Commission on the Postal Service, *Hearings: The Postal Service* (Washington, D.C., 1923), pp. 77–89, 91–95, 123, 179–80. See also David, *Economics of Air Mail*, pp. 24–27.

34. Egge to J. E. Lamiell and J. V. Holt, May 17, 1921 (two letters), AMS/RS.

35. Egge to Praeger, February 7, 1921, and E. R. White to Walter Sweeney, March 3, 1921, AMS/Stewart PF.

36. D. Smith, "Pilot's Progress."

37. Egge to Praeger, February 10, 1921, AMS/ Carroll PF. U.S. House of Representatives, Committee on the Post Office and Post Roads, *Hearings: Air Mail Service*, 66th Cong., 3d sess. (Washington, D.C., 1921).

38. *New York Times*, February 11, 1921.

39. Egge to Praeger, February 10, 1921, AMS/Carroll PF.

40. U.S. House, *Hearings: Air Mail Service*, 66/3.

41. Munson, *Airliners*, pp. 150–51; Post Office, "Planes Used in the Air Mail Service," September 17, 1924, Records of the U.S. House of Representatives, Select Committee of Inquiry into Operations of the U.S. Air Services.

42. *New York Times*, February 23, 1921.

43. Ibid.; Praeger to Burleson, February 24, 1921, AMS/GCR.

44. Ibid.

45. Ibid.

46. Ibid.

47. Knight to Praeger, February 23, 1921, AMS/Knight PF. Knight is quoted extensively in Donald Wilhelm, "Flying the Mail," *World's Work* 42 (May 1921), 49–59.

48. Ibid.; *New York Times*, February 25, 1921.

49. *New York Times*, February 24, 1921.

50. *New York Times*, February 24 and 25, 1921.

51. *New York Times*, February 24, 1921.

52. "Menu for Farewell Dinner for Albert Sidney Burleson," March 3, 1921, Burleson Papers.

53. *Aviation* 10 (May 2, 1921), 559; *New York Times*, February 25, 1921.

Chapter 9

1. Paxson, *American Democracy*, III, 162. See also Wesley M. Bagby, *The Road to Normalcy: The Presidential Campaign and Election of 1920* (Baltimore, 1962), and Robert K. Murray, *The Harding Era* (Minneapolis, 1969).

2. Stanley Coben, "Will H. Hays," in John A. Garraty (ed.), *Dictionary of American Biography*, Supplement 5 (New York, 1977), pp. 280–82; Murray, *Harding Era*, pp. 304–306; Samuel McCune Lindsay, "The New Cabinet and Its Problems," *American Review of Reviews* 63 (April 1921), 381–93.

3. White to All Superintendents and Field Managers, February 28, 1921, AMS/GRS (CP): Hays, *The Memoirs of Will H. Hays* (Garden City, N.Y., 1955), pp. 302–304.

4. Hays to Weeks, March 19, 1921, AAF/CDF 311.125.
5. Fechet to Menoher, March 17, 1921, and Menoher to the Adjutant General, April 2, 1921, AAF/CDF 311.125.
6. Weeks to Hays, April 14, 1921, Papers of Warren G. Harding (microfilm edition), reel 142.
7. Yager to All Members, Air Mail Pilots of America, January 23, 1924, AMS/Yager PF; Dean Smith, "Pilot's Progress."
8. H. B. Shaver to Zoll, June 15, 1921, AMS/Christensen PF; Yager to All Members, AMPA, January 23, 1924, AMS/Yager PF.
9. Dean Smith, "Pilot's Progress."
10. *Chicago Daily Tribune*, May 13 and 14, 1921; *Chicago Daily News*, May 13, 1921; *New York Times*, May 14 and 15, 1921.
11. Ibid.
12. Ibid.
13. Ibid.
14. *New York Times*, June 1, 1921; *Aviation* 10 (March 28, 1921), 408.
15. Dean Smith, "Pilot's Progress"; Dean Smith to the author, March 9, 1976; Egge to John Holtby, May 17, 1921, AMS/RS.
16. Also fired were S. M. Moore, Jr. (Majors's assistant), field manager Paul L. Dumas, purchasing agent Carl Nickell, and mechanics Paul B. King and D. A. Martin. See Conner to C. A. Parker, May 31, 1921, AMS/Majors PF, and Shaughnessy to Jordan, June 18, 1921, AMS/Jordan PF. Clarahan's report could not be located in the records of the Air Mail Service or Postal Inspection Service.
17. Correspondence in AMS/Majors PF.
18. Kirby to Menoher, June 7, 1921, AAF/CDF 311.125.
19. Mitchell to Shaughnessy, June 7, 1921, Mitchell Papers; Pearson memorandum, June 20, 1921, AAF/CDF 311.125.
20. Pearson to Frank, June 20, 1921, and Pearson to Menoher, September 2, 1921, AAF/CDF 311.125.
21. Hays to Harding, June 27, 1921, enclosing correspondence, Harding Papers, reel 142. See also Alfred F. Hurley, *Billy Mitchell: Crusader for Air Power* (New York, 1964), pp. 63–64.
22. *Aviation* 10 (April 25, 1921), 530; "Edward Henry Shaughnessy," *National Cyclopaedia of American Biography* 19 (New York, 1926), pp. 358–59.
23. POD, *Annual Report of the Postmaster General, 1920* (Washington D.C., 1921), p. 63; *New York Times*, July 2 and September 11, 1920.
24. Cy Q. Faunce, *The Airliner and Its Inventor, Alfred W. Lawson* (Columbus, Ohio, 1921); Alfred W. Lawson, *Lawson: Aircraft Industry Builder* (Detroit, 1943); Richard P. Hallion, *Legacy of Flight: The Guggenheim Contribution to American Aviation* (Seattle, 1977), pp. 8–10.
25. Lawson to Praeger, November 17 and December 4, 1920, AMS/GRS (CP).
26. Egge to Praeger, December 22, 1920, AMS/GRS (CP).
27. Lawson to Praeger, December 30, 1920, and Corridon to Shaughnessy, April 11, 1921, AMS/GRS (CP).
28. Corridon to Shaughnessy, April 11, 1921, AMS/GRS (CP).
29. Corridon to Shaughnessy, April 20, 1921, AMS/GRS (CP); *Chicago Daily Tribune*, May 9, 1921; Hallion, *Legacy*, pp. 9–10.
30. Shaughnessy to Hays, May 12, 1921, 2PMG/IOC (AM).
31. Shaughnessy to Hays, May 9, 1921, Harding Papers, reel 142.
32. Ibid.

33. Ibid.
34. *New York Times*, May 27, 1921; *Aerial Age Weekly* 13 (June 13, 1921), 316.
35. Shaughnessy to Hays, May 12, 1921, 2PMG/IOC (AM); Shaughnessy memorandum, June 15, 1921, AMS/GCR; Shaughnessy speech to the Washington section, Society of Automotive Engineers, January 6, 1922, *Aviation* 12 (January 23, 1922), 96–99.
36. Egge to J. E. Lamiell and J. V. Holtby, May 17, 1921, AMS/RS; material in AMS/Egge PF; C. H. Clarahan, et al., "Investigation of Air Mail Service," October 8, 1925, 2PMG/IOM.
37. Quoted in Whitbeck to All Personnel, June 20, 1921, AMS/GCR.
38. Whitbeck to Praeger, March 9, 1921, AMS/Christensen PF; Dunphy to Egge, August 5, 1921, AMS/Brown PF.
39. Whitbeck to Stanton, October 3, 1921, and Egge to Whitbeck, November 2, 1921, AMS/GCR; Dunphy to Egge, September 20, 1921, AMS/Hopson PF.
40. Egge to Shaughnessy, October 12 and 19, 1921, and Shaughnessy to Egge, October 12, 1921, AMS/GCR.
41. POD "Statement of Performance," n.d. [1924], AMS/RS.
42. *Aviation* 12 (January 23, 1922), 96–99.
43. *New York Times*, January 12, 1922; *Aerial Age Weekly* 14 (January 23, 1922), 461.
44. *Congressional Record*, 67th Cong., 2d sess. (January 13, 1922), 1163; NACA, "Minutes of Regular Meeting of Executive Committee," January 26, 1922, NACA Suitland.
45. Washington *Evening Star*, January 29, 1922; *New York Times*, January 29 and 30, 1922; *Aviation* 12 (February 13, 1922), 199.
46. *Aerial Age Weekly* 14 (March 6, 1922), 609; *New York Times*, February 24, March 5, 19, and May 14, 1922.
47. Hays, *Memoirs*, pp. 302–04.
48. Shaughnessy to Hays, May 12, 1921, 2PMG/IOC (AM).

Chapter 10

1. My earlier version of this account of Aeromarine Airways appeared as "At the Dawn of Commercial Aviation: Inglis M. Uppercu and Aeormarine Airways," *Business History Review* 53 (1979), 180–93; reprinted with permission.
2. "Inglis Moore Uppercu," *The National Cyclopedia of American Biography* 36 (New York, 1950), 284–85; "Inglis M. Uppercu: A Biographical Sketch," *U.S. Air Service* 7 (November 1922), 21–22; obituary, *New York Times*, April 8, 1944. Uppercu held the Cadillac franchise until 1931.
3. *Aerial Age Weekly* 8 (October 21, 1918), 303. Frank Boland's career is sketched in David R. Winans, *Wheels, Wings, and Waves: Highlights of 200 Years of Transportation in New Jersey* (privately printed, 1975), pp. 3–4.
4. Manufacturers Aircraft Association, *Aircraft Year Book, 1919* (New York, 1919), pp. 59–75; Aeromarine Plane & Motor Company to Bureau of Supplies and Accounts, Navy Department, April 16, 1919, Bureau of Aeronautics, General Correspondence (1925–42), QM 18, Box 4361, RG 72, NA
5. Alexander Klemin, "Plant of the Aeromarine Plane & Motor Company," *Aviation* 10 (February 7, 1921), 171, 174–76.

6. Manufacturers Aircraft Association, *Aircraft Year Book, 1920* (New York, 1920), pp. 147–156; Uppercu testimony, December 11, 1919, U.S. House of Representatives, Subcommittee of the Committee on Military Affairs, *Hearings: United Air Service*, 66th Cong., 2d sess. (1921), p. 335.

7. Aeromarine Plane & Motor Company to the Secretary of the Navy, January 30, 1920; memorandum, Secretary of the Navy to the Chief of Bureau of Supplies and Accounts, "Sale of 1 F-5-L Flying Boat to Aeromarine Plane & Motor Company," February 28, 1920; both in BuAer GC (1917–25), 3146-aa-15, Box 175.

8. Memorandum, Moffett to the Secretary of the Navy, "Proposal for Purchase of HS-2-L Flying Boats," November 15, 1920, BuAer GC (1925–42), QM 18, Box 4361; memorandum agreement between Bureau of Supplies and Accounts and Aeromarine Plane & Motor Company, December 14, 1920, BuAer GC (1917–25), 3146-pp-99, Box 173; *U.S. Air Service* 4 (January 1921), 20.

9. Paul G. Zimmermann, "Adapting an F-5L Flying Boat to Air Transport," *Aviation* 9 (September 1, 1920), 87–99; *New York Times*, November 7, 1920.

10. *U.S. Air Service* 4 (November 1920), 22–23; *Aerial Age Weekly* 12 (November 8, 1920), 249–50.

11. *New York Times*, October 20 and 27, 1919; *Aerial Age Weekly* 10 (October 13–20, 1919), 155–56; *Aircraft Year Book, 1920*, pp. 151–55; Aeromarine Plane & Motor Company, *The Log of an Aeromarine* (Keyport, 1920); an undated newspaper clipping supplied to the author by Mrs. Durston G. Richardson, whose husband was employed by the Cuban Company.

12. Alvin W. McKaig to the Secretary of the Navy, November 17, 1919, enclosing "Prospectus of the Florida-West Indies Airways," BuAer GC (1917–25), 3066-17, Box 156; McKaig testimony, February 3, 1920, U.S. Senate, Subcommittee of the Committee on Post Offices and Post Roads, *Hearings*, 66th Cong., 2d sess. (1920), pp. 143–55. McKaig stated that $250,000 initially had been raised by the group, but this figure may have been intended to impress outsiders rather than reflect the company's true state of affairs.

13. U.S. House of Representatives, Committee on the Post Office and Post Roads, *Hearings: First Deficiency Bill, 1921—Air Mail Service*, 66th Cong., 3d sess. (1921); U.S. Senate, Document No. 70, *Air Mail Contracts*, 72d Congress, 1st sess. (1931), p. 8; Burleson to the Secretary of State, September 4, 1920, State Department Decimal File 811.71237, RG 59, NA.

14. *Aviation* 9 (November 1, 1920), 226–27, 230; *U.S. Air Service* 4 (November 1920), 22–23; *Aerial Age Weekly* 12 (November 8, 1920), 249–50. On the airline's failure to make an agreement with Cuba, see testimony by Egge, December 16, 1920, U.S. House of Representatives, Subcommittee of the Committee on Appropriations, *Hearings: Post Office Appropriation Bill, 1922*, 66th Cong., 3d session (Washington, D.C., 1920), pp. 66–68. Later attempts to secure a Cuban contract also came to naught. See Charles F. Redden to the editor, Air Service News Letter, April 23, 1925, AAF/CDF 311.125. *Aircraft Year Book, 1921* (Boston, 1921), p. 13, incorrectly states that Florida–West Indies secured a mail contract from the Cuban government.

15. *Aerial Age Weekly* 12 (November 8, 1920), 249–50. Five additional F-5Ls,

Nina, Columbus, Balboa, Ponce de Leon, and *Mendoza,* would follow over the next four months.

16. *Aviation* 11 (November 28, 1921), 622–23; Aeronautical Chamber of Commerce, *Aircraft Year Book, 1923* (New York, 1923), pp. 17–23. The figure for mail carried, higher than the 24,002 pounds claimed by Aeromarine Airways in their first annual report, is taken from Post Office Department records. See U.S. Senate, Document No. 70, *Air Mail Contracts,* p. 8.

17. *Aircraft Year Book, 1923,* pp. 17–22; *Aviation* 12 (June 26, 1922), 752; Earl D. Osborn, "A Seaplane Base for Commercial Air Transport," *Aviation* 16 (February 4, 1924), 123–24. Osborn reports on the carrier pigeons: "Of the birds released from planes only a small percentage returned, probably due to lack of training, though some were killed by hawks."

18. Bruno discusses his role with Aeromarine Airways in *Wings Over America: The Story of American Aviation* (Garden City, N.Y., 1944), pp. 108–122. Smith's interesting career is outlined in Reginald Wright Arthur, *Contact! Careers of U.S. Naval Aviators Assigned Numbers 1 to 2000* (Washington, D.C., privately printed, 1967).

19. Redden, "Commercial Aviation," *Aviation* 12 (January 2, 1922), 11–12. Musick's career is sketched in William S. Grooch, *From Crate to Clipper with Captain Musick* (New York, 1939).

20. Bruno, *Wings Over America,* pp. 15–17; *Aviation* 11 (October 3, 1921), 392–94.

21. *Aviation,* 11 (October 10, 1921), 427; 12 (April 24, 1922), 485; D. G. Richardson to John C. Leslie, September 13, 1971. The author is indebted to Mr. Leslie, retired executive vice-president of Pan American Airways, for a copy of this letter. Richardson, who went on to a distinguished career with Pan American, American Overseas Airlines, Guest Airlines, and the Agency for International Development, died in 1974.

22. *Aviation* 12 (April 3, 1922), 401.

23. The charter company, Aero Limited, had been founded in 1919 and operated a route structure parallel to Aeromarine Airways': Miami to Bimini and Nassau in the winter, and New York to Atlantic City and New England resorts during the summer. See *Aviation* 10 (May 9, 1921), 590, for information on this little-known pioneer company.

24. *Aviation* 12 (April 3, 1922), 401. Wing Commander M. G. Christie, British air attaché, agreed with Redden. "No financial backing," he reported to London, "and consequently no real development can be hoped for in this country until Civil Aviation receives legalised status and protective regulation through Federal Legislation." See "Annual Report of the British Air Attaché Washington for 1922," March 31, 1923, Records of the Air Ministry, AIR 2/246, Public Record Office, London.

25. NACA, *Seventh Annual Report, 1921* (Washington, D.C., 1922), pp. 13–15; Nick A. Komons, *Bonfires to Beacons: Federal Civil Aviation Policy under the Air Commerce Act, 1926–1938* (Washington, D.C., 1978); Thomas Worth Walterman, "Airpower and Private Enterprise: Federal-Industrial Relations in the Aeronautics Field, 1918–1926," Ph.D. dissertation, Washington University, 1970.

26. *Aviation* 12 (April 24, 1922), 578; 13 (July 24, 1922), 94–95; *Aeronautical Digest* 1 (August 1922), 25; *New York Times,* December 19, 1922.

27. Redden, "The Outlook for Commercial Aviation in America," *Aeronautical Digest* 2 (February 1923), 100–102; *New York Times*, January 10, 1923; *Aircraft Year Book, 1923*, p. 22; *Aviation* 14 (January 8, 1923), 49. The mail contract provided for one trip daily, except Sunday, with 150 pounds of mail for $50 a flight (600 pounds and $200 on Wednesday). See U.S. Senate, Document No. 70, *Air Mail Contracts*, p. 8.

28. *Aviation* 14 (January 22, 1923), 124.

29. Redden, "Outlook for Commercial Aviation"; Redden testimony, January 16, 1925, U.S. House of Representatives, Select Committee of Inquiry into Operations of the United States Air Services, *Hearings*, 68th Cong., 2d sess. (1925), pp. 1024–33; *Aircraft Year Book, 1923*, pp. 17–22; "Annual Report of the British Air Attaché Washington for 1922." Loss of the *Ponce de Leon* is detailed in Bernard Smith's photographic collection, made available to the author by Mr. Smith's stepdaughter, Mrs. Millard Brundage.

30. Redden to Secretary of the Navy Edwin Denby, December 22, 1922; Denby to Redden, February 7, 1923; Secretary of the Navy, General Correspondence (1916–1922), 26983, Box 2124, RG 72, NA.

31. *Aviation* 15 (October 20, 1923), 550–52; Child to Chief of the Bureau of Aeronautics, March 31, 1923, and Richardson to Chief of the Bureau of Aeronautics, August 22, 1923, BuAer GC (1925–42), QM 18, Box 4362.

32. *New York Times*, July 22 and October 16, 1923. The airline charged $40 for a one-way trip between Cleveland and Detroit. This compared to a rail fare of $4.25.

33. Bureau of Aeronautics to Aeromarine Plane & Motor Company, December 7, 1923, BuAer GC (1925–42), QM 18, Box 4362; *Aviation* 15 (December 10, 1923), 714. Uppercu retained a small engineering staff until October 1924. See *Aviation* 17 (October 13, 1924), 1133.

34. Redden to Moffett, January 14, 1924, BuAer GC (1925–42), QM 18, Box 4362; *Aeronautical Digest* 4 (February 1924), 100; *U.S. Air Services* 9 (February 1924), 56; Wesley Phillips Newton, *The Perilous Sky: U.S. Aviation Diplomacy and Latin America, 1919–1931* (Coral Gables, 1978), p. 63.

35. R. E. G. Davies, *Airlines of the United States Since 1914* (rev. ed., Washington, D.C., 1982), pp. 11–12.

36. Warner, *Early History of Air Transportation*, p. 31. See also Smith, *Airways*, pp. 87–88.

37. H. Montgomery Hyde, *British Air Policy Between the Wars, 1918–1939* (London, 1976), pp. 127–34.

38. Walterman, "Airpower and Private Enterprise," p. vi.

Chapter 11

1. W. David Lewis and Wesley Phillips Newton, "Paul Henderson," in John A. Garraty (ed.), *Dictionary of American Biography*, Supplement 5 (New York, 1977), pp. 294–95; *Aviation* 12 (April 24, 1922), 468; Josephine Henderson Humphries to the author, February 10 and 14, 1976; Floranne Henderson Passino to the author, February 22, 1976.

2. Eugene P. Trani, "Hubert Work," in John A. Garraty (ed.), *Dictionary of American Biography*, Supplement 3 (New York, 1973), pp. 845–46.

3. Henderson, "Report to the Postmaster General on the Post Office's Night Flying Experiments, August 21–24, 1923," AMS/GCR.

4. Ibid.; Glenn L. Martin, "Night Flying Made Practical Through Artificial Light," *U.S. Air Service* 8 (August 1923), 25–28; Neville Jones, *The Origins of Strategic Bombing* (London, 1973), pp. 200–01.
5. *U.S. Air Service* 5 (March 1921), 13–16.
6. Dunphy to Zoll, March 23, 1921; Praeger to Majors, March 24, 1921; Shaughnessy to Bane, April 12, 1921; Pickup to Praeger, March 31, 1921; all in AMS/GCR.
7. Egge to Clayton E. Rice, June 21, 1921, AMS/GCR.
8. Henderson speech, September 12, 1922, *Aviation* 13 (October 16, 1922), 502.
9. Henderson to Magee, June 10, 1922, AMS/GCR.
10. Magee to Henderson, June 22, 1922, AMS/GRS (CP).
11. Ibid.; Henderson to Congressman Cassius C. Dowell, August 18, 1922, AMS/GRS (CP); *Aviation* 13 (October 16, 1922), 502.
12. Magee to Egge, October 5, 1922, AMS/GCR; C. Eugene Johnson, "Report on Night Flying Equipment on Ship 242," n.d. [November 1922], AMS/Johnson PF.
13. U.S. House of Representatives, Subcommittee of the Committee on Appropriations, *Hearings: Post Office Appropriation Bill, 1924* 67th Cong., 4th sess. (Washington, D.C., 1922).
14. Harding to Wolcott, December 4, 1922, NACA Suitland.
15. NACA, "Minutes of Special Meeting of Executive Committee," December 12, 1922, NACA Suitland.
16. Wolcott to Harding, December 20, 1922, NACA Suitland.
17. Harding to Wolcott, December 21, 1922, NACA Suitland.
18. Harding to Work, December 21, 1922, Harding Papers, reel 183.
19. NACA, "Minutes," December 12, 1922, NACA Suitland.
20. Dean Smith, "Pilot's Progress."
21. Magee to Egge, March 14, 1923, AMS/GCR.
22. P. R. Bassett, "Night Flying," *U.S. Air Service* 8 (March 1923), 23–27; M. L. Patterson, "Night Flying Progress," *U.S. Air Service* 8 (November 1923), 30–32; Manufacturers Aircraft Association, *Aircraft Year Book, 1924* (New York, 1924), pp. 41–43.
23. Henderson, "Report," September 13, 1923, AMS/GCR.
24. *U.S. Air Service* 8 (September 1923), 10.
25. *Aviation* 15 (August 20, 1923), 209; *Aircraft Year Book, 1924*, p. 46.
26. *Aeronautical Digest* 3 (October 1923), 223–31; Smith, "Pilot's Progress."
27. Ibid.
28. Henderson, "Report," September 13, 1923, AMS/GCR.
29. *Aeronautical Digest* 3 (October 1923), 223–31.
30. Ibid.; Henderson, "Report," September 13, 1923, AMS/GCR.
31. Ibid.
32. *Aeronautical Digest* 3 (October 1923), 224.
33. *Aviation* 15 (September 3, 1923), 226–69; Praeger to Henderson, August 27, 1923, AMS/GCR; NACA to Postmaster General New, September 13, 1923, AMS/GCR.
34. *Aircraft Year Book, 1924*, p. 52; Henderson, "Report," September 13, 1923, AMS/GCR.
35. *Aviation* 15 (October 22, 1923), 521–23; Henderson statement, August 28, 1928, AMS/GCR.
36. John D. Hicks, "Harry Stewart New," in John A. Garraty (ed.), *Dictionary*

of American Biography, Supplement 2 (New York, 1958), pp. 486–87; New testimony, February 18, 1924, U.S. Senate, Subcommittee of the Committee on Appropriations, *Hearings: Treasury and Post Office Departments, Appropriation Bills, 1925*, 68th Cong., 1st sess. (1924), pp. 108–109.

37. U.S. House of Representatives, Subcommittee of the Committee on Appropriations, *Hearings: Post Office Appropriation Bill, 1925*, 68th Cong., 1st sess. (1924), pp. 156–83.
38. *Aviation* 15 (February 25, 1924), 201; *New York Times*, February 10, 1924.
39. U.S. Senate, Subcommittee of the Committee on Appropriations, *Hearings: Treasury and Post Office Departments, Appropriations Bills, 1925*, 68th Cong., 1st sess. (1924), pp. 108–109; *New York Times*, February 27, March 30, and May 5, 1924.

Chapter 12
1. Egge, "Memorandum for Inspectors Fitch and Rapp," May 16, 1922, AMS/RS; Edgerton to Egge, November 20, 1922, AMS/Edgerton PF; Stanton to Henderson, December 11, 1922, AMS/Stanton PF.
2. Aeronautical Chamber of Commerce, *Aircraft Year Book, 1923* (New York, 1923), pp. 299–300.
3. *Aviation* 13 (September 25, 1922), 387; Egge testimony, December 19, 1922, U.S. House of Representatives, Subcommittee of the Committee on Appropriations, *Hearings: Post Office Appropriation Bill, 1924*, 67th Cong., 4th sess. (1922), pp. 229–46.
4. Moseley to Patrick, June 6, 1923, AAF/CDF 311.125.
5. Huking to Nelson, June 22, 1922, and Huking report, March 22, 1925, AMS/Huking PF.
6. Boonstra to F. A. O'Leary, field manager, Salt Lake City, December 26, 1922; Egge to Nelson, December 19, 1922; Nelson to Egge, December 21, 1922; all in AMS/Boonstra PF.
7. O'Leary to Egge, January 25, 1923, AMS/Boonstra PF. For a portrait of Boonstra with Boeing Air Transport, see Charles F. Blair, *Red Ball in the Sky* (New York, 1969), pp. 8–24.
8. *Aviation* 13 (July 31, 1922), 128; (September 25, 1922), 386.
9. W. L. Smith Diary, September 7 and 8, 1922, W. L. Smith Papers; *New York Times*, September 8, 1922; Yager to All Members, AMPA, January 23, 1924, AMS/Yager PF.
10. Tower to Egge, January 17, 1924, AMS/Moore PF; Yager to All Members, AMPA, January 23, 1924, AMS/Yager PF; Dean Smith, "Pilot's Progress."
11. W. L. Smith diary, February 26, 1923, W. L. Smith Papers; New York *Tribune*, February 27, 1923; Yager to All Members, AMPA, January 23, 1924, AMS/Yager PF.
12. R. L. Wagner to Egge, September 22, 1923, and Inspector L. J. Brennan, "Case No. 57182-D," March 2, 1924, AMS/Thompson PF.
13. Shaver to Egge, December 10, 1923; Whitbeck to Egge, December 10, 1923; Magee to Egge, December 11, 1923; all in AMS/Brown PF.
14. Colyer to Egge, December 24, 1923; Tower to Egge, December 24 and 25, 1923; Egge to Henderson, December 25, 1923; Egge note, n.d. [December 25, 1923]; Tower to Colyer, December 31, 1923; all in AMS/Moore PF.

15. Yager to All Members, AMPA, January 23, 1924, enclosing analysis of accidents, AMS/Yager PF.
16. On the Curtiss, Aeromarine, and Martin airplanes, see *Aviation* 15 (September 3, 1923), 270–75. The modified DH is described in Whitbeck, "Performance Test Report, U.S. Mail W.M.-1 No. 299 (remodeled)," August 13, 1923, copy courtesy of Mrs. Whitbeck. The fate of these aircraft is discussed in C. H. Clarahan, et al., "Investigation of the Air Mail Service, 2735-H," October 8, 1925, 2PMG/IOM.
17. Quotes in Yager to All Members, AMPA, January 23, 1924, AMS/Yager PF.
18. Ibid.; Egge to Yager, January 18, 1924, AMS/Yager PF.
19. Yager to All Members, AMPA, January 23, 1924, AMS/Yager PF.
20. W. L. Smith diary, March 8, 1924, W. L. Smith Papers; *Aviation* 16 (April 7, 1924), 368.
21. Lee, "Report," March 7, 1924, AMS/Lee PF.
22. Colyer to Egge, March 10, 1923, AMS/Lee PF.
23. Egge to Colyer, March 26, 1924, AMS/Lee PF.
24. U.S. House of Representatives, Select Committee of Inquiry into Operations of the United States Air Services [Lampert Committee], *Hearings*, 68th Cong. (Washington, D.C., 1925), pp. 774–80.
25. Quoted in Egge to All Personnel, June 11, 1924, AMS/RS.
26. Ibid.
27. *Aviation* 16 (April 21, 1924), 422.
28. *New York Times*, May 12, 1924; *U.S. Air Services* 9 (June 1924), 49; Jay P. Spenser, *Bellanca C.F.: The Emergence of the Cabin Monoplane in the United States* (Washington, D.C., 1982), p. 42. A later poll of pilots revealed that sixteen of nineteen preferred the Bellanca over the Loening modification. Marshall, "Monthly [AMPA] News Letters," March 15, 1926, AMS/Marshall PF.
29. W. L. Smith diary, July 1 and 2, 1924, W. L. Smith Papers; *New York Times*, July 2 and 3, 1924; Henderson to New, August 6, 1924, AMS/RS.
30. Ibid.
31. Yager, "Report," July 12, 1924; Wilke to Colyer, n.d. [July 1924]; AMS Yager PF.
32. Henderson to New, August 6, 1924, AMS/RS.
33. Ibid.
34. Dean Smith, "Pilot's Progress."
35. Ibid.
36. Ibid.; Paul V. Eakle, "A Tragedy Flying the Christmas Mail," in Nielson (ed.), *Saga*, pp. 41–43.
37. Egge to Bell, August 27, 1924, 2PMG/IOC (AM).
38. *Aviation* 17 (August 25, 1924), 910–11; *New York Times*, December 7, 1924; *U.S. Air Services* 9 (September 1924), 29–30.
39. Aeronautical Chamber of Commerce, *Aircraft Year Book, 1925* (New York, 1925), p. 269.
40. *Aviation* 17 (October 22, 1924), 1254.
41. U.S. House of Representatives, Subcommittee of the House Committee on Appropriations, *Hearings: Post Office Appropriation Bill, 1926*, 68th Cong., 2d sess. (Washington, D.C., 1924).
42. C. G. Grey, "Civil Aviation in the United States," *Aviation* 18 (January 5, 1925), 16–17.

Chapter 13

1. Aeronautical Chamber of Commerce, *Aircraft Year Book, 1925* (New York, 1925), pp. 38–39.
2. Henderson, "The Air Mail—Its Future," *Aero Digest* 6 (March 1925), 127–29, 168.
3. Ibid.
4. Ibid.; *Aircraft Year Book, 1925*, pp. 38–39; *New York Times*, November 15, 1924.
5. "Pinkwhiskers," *Air Mail Pioneers News*, May/July 1962.
6. *Aviation* 17 (December 1924), 1328–29; Whitbeck to Egge, December 27, 1924, AMS/GCR.
7. Whitbeck to Egge, December 27, 1924, AMS/GCR; *Aviation* 19 (July 13, 1925), 38–40.
8. Whitbeck to Egge, December 27, 1924, AMS/GCR.
9. Whitbeck to Egge, March 18, 1925, AMS/GCR; *Aviation* 19 (July 13, 1925), 38–40.
10. W. L. Smith diary, May 30 and June 27, 1925, W. L. Smith Papers; Whitbeck to Egge, June 18, 1925, AMS/GCR.
11. *Aviation* 19 (July 13, 1925), 38–40; Roger Dane, "Midnight Suns of the Air Mail," *Aero Digest* 7 (July 1925), 359–60.
12. "Air Mail Service," n.d. [c. June 30, 1926], AMS/GCR.
13. *Aviation* 19 (July 13, 1925), 38–40; *New York Times*, July 2, 1925.
14. *Aviation* 19 (July 13, 1925), 38–40.
15. Ibid.
16. Dean Smith, "Pilot's Progress;" *New York Times*, July 3, 1925. The *Times* attributed the delay to "severe head winds" and a problem with a generator.
17. *Aviation* 19 (July 20, 1925), 69.
18. Dean Smith to the author, August 5, 1976.
19. M. M. Titterington, Pioneer Instrument Company, to Lt. E. W. Rounds, August 9, 1921, NASM Historical Files; Praeger to C. W. Ramseyer, July 30, 1919, *Congressional Record*, Appendix, 66th Cong., 1st sess., p. 9047; *Aviation* 13 (June 6, 1921), 301, and 14 (January 29, 1923), 131.
20. R. C. Marshall, "Needle, Ball, and Airspeed," *Air Facts* 33 (August 1970), 23–30.
21. Wesley Smith, *Air Transport Operation* (New York, 1931), pp. 209–212.
22. Dean Smith, "Pilot's Progress."
23. Arthur LaRoc, "The Physical Standards of New Air Regulations," *Aero Digest* 10 (March 1927), 178; Howard F. Salisbury to Dale Nielson, March 19, 1965, Edwin C. Cooper Collection, San Diego Aero-Space Museum.
24. Whitbeck to Egge, October 5, 1925, AMS/GCR; *New York Times*, October 3, 12, and 18, 1925; POD press release, October 9, 1925, AMS/Ames PF; W. L. Smith diary, October 1–12, 1925, W. L. Smith Papers; Investigating Committee, "Report on Wreck of Air Mail Plane 385," October 12, 1925, AMS/Ames PF; Jesse Davidson, "Death of an Airman," in Nielson (ed.), *Saga*, pp. 18–25.
25. Salisbury to Nielson, March 18, 1965, Cooper Collection, San Diego Aero-Space Museum.
26. Dean Smith to the author, August 5, 1976; Dean Smith, "Pilot's Progress."
27. Wesley Smith, "How I Fly at Night," *Journal of the Society of Automotive Engineers* 19 (September 1926), 228–33.

28. Ibid.
29. Egge to Henderson, January 23, 1925, AMS/RS.
30. Henderson to Egge, February 28, 1925, AMS/RS.
31. *Aviation* 18 (May 27, 1925), 579.
32. Harry Smith to Cisler, November 28, 1925, 2PMG/IOC (AM).
33. Ibid.; *Aviation* 19 (November 16, 1925), 720.
34. Harry Smith to Cisler, November 28, 1925, 2PMG/IOC (AM).
35. *Aviation* 18 (June 15, 1925), 669.
36. C. H. Clarahan, et al., "Investigation of Air Mail Service," October 8, 1925, 2PMG/IOM.
37. Ibid.
38. Ibid.
39. Ibid.
40. Ibid.; Clarahan and W. J. Marles, "Case 2735-H. Special," October 1, 1925, 2PMG/IOC (AM).
41. Clarahan, et al., "Investigation."
42. Ibid. Glover to Cisler, September 17, 1925, copy supplied to the author by J. P. Cisler; "Service Record of Carl F. Egge," AMS/Egge PF.
43. *New York Times*, July 1, 1925.
44. VanZandt, "Brief Critical Estimate of Post Office Air Mail Operations," August 1, 1925, AAF/CDF 311.125.

Chapter 14
1. Walterman, "Airpower and Private Enterprise," p. 184.
2. David, *Economics of Air Mail*, p. vii; U.S. House of Representatives, Committee on the Post Office and Post Roads, *Hearings: Commercial Aviation—Air Mail Service*, 67th Cong., 2d sess. (Washington, D.C., 1922), p. 41.
3. House, *Hearings: Commercial Aviation*, p. 41.
4. Ibid., p. 34.
5. Ibid., pp. 44–46.
6. David, *Economics of Air Mail*, pp. 54–59; Kelly, "Outflying the Eagles," *Aero Digest* 5 (July 1924), 10–11, 38.
7. Walterman, "Airpower and Private Enterprise," pp. 415–16.
8. *U.S. Air Service* 10 (May 1925), 18–20.
9. *New York Times*, August 23, 1925.
10. *Aviation* 18 (June 1, 1925), 598–600.
11. *New York Times*, August 3, 1925; *U.S. Air Services* 10 (November 1925), 25.
12. *U.S. Air Services* 10 (November 1925), 25.
13. *Aviation* 18 (June 1, 1925), 598–600.
14. Komons, *Bonfires to Beacons*, pp. 35–64.
15. Ibid., pp. 74–75.
16. U.S. President's Aircraft Board, *Hearings* (Washington, D.C., 1925), pp. 306–307.
17. Komons, *Bonfires to Beacons*, pp. 78–79; Walterman, "Airpower and Private Enterprise," pp. 475–76.
18. For Hoover's role, see the excellent article by David D. Lee, "Herbert Hoover and the Development of Commercial Aviation, 1921–1926," *Business History Review* 58 (1984), 78–102.
19. Walterman, "Airpower and Private Enterprise," pp. 494–511.

20. NACA, *Annual Report for 1926* (Washington, D.C., 1927), pp. 64–66.
21. U.S. House of Representatives, Subcommittee of the Committee on Appropriations, *Hearings: Post Office Appropriation Bill, 1927*, 69th Cong., 1st sess. (1925), pp. 159–70; New, "Transcontinental Trails Blazed by the Air Mail Lines," *Aero Digest* 9 (August 1926), 87.
22. Memorandum, "Stephen Arnold Cisler," n.d., and Work, "Memorandum for Senator Phipps," n.d. [April 1923], AMS/Cisler PF.
23. Glover to Cisler, September 17, 1925, copy supplied to the author by J. R. Cisler.
24. Dean Smith, *Seat of My Pants*, pp. 103, 140–42.
25. Praeger testimony, January 29, 1920, U.S. Senate, Subcommittee of the Committee on Post Office and Post Roads, *Hearings*, 66th Cong., 2d sess. (Washington, D.C., 1920), pp. 43–72; Henderson testimony, December 17, 1924, U.S. House of Representatives, Select Committee of Inquiry into Operations of the United States Air Services, *Hearings*, 68th Cong. (Washington, D.C., 1925), p. 275; Harold G. McCoy, "The Story of Cleveland's Lindy," *Cleveland Press*, November 30, 1928.
26. Egge to Henderson, June 18, 1924, AMS/GCR; Egge to H. G. Smith, D. B. Colyer, and W. E. LaFollette, February 7, 1925, AMS/GCR; U.S. Department of Commerce, *Historical Statistics of the United States* (Washington, D.C., 1961), p. 91.
27. Interview with Marshall, April 8, 1976; Egge to Henderson, December 5, 1924, AMS/Knight PF.
28. Long to Colyer, December 2, 1924, AMS/Dean Smith PF.
29. Egge to Henderson, December 5, 1924, AMS/Knight PF.
30. McCoy, "Cleveland's Lindy," *Cleveland Press*, November 27–December 22, 1928; interview with Mrs. Wesley L. Smith, August 17, 1976; biographical material in AMS/W.L. Smith PF. The textbook is *Air Transport Operation* (New York, 1931).
31. Cisler to Glover, November 23, 1925, June 24, and September 30, 1926; Glover to Cisler, November 30, 1925; all in 2PMG/IOC (AM).
32. Annotation to Clarahan et al., "Investigation of the Air Mail Service," October 8, 1925, 2PMG/IOM: Cisler to Glover, May 11, 1926, 2PMG/IOC (AM): *Aviation* 20 (June 28, 1926), 983.
33. V. E. Bertrandias, "Barnstorming in Japan with Art Smith," *U.S. Air Services* 9 (July 1924), 29–30; H. B. Shaver to Cisler, February 16, 1926, AMS/GCR.
34. H. B. Shaver, S. J. Short, and L. Harris to Cisler, February 13, 1926, AMS/Arthur Smith PF; Shaver to Cisler, February 16, 1926, AMS/GCR.
35. *U.S. Air Service* 10 (August 1925), 17–18; *New York Times*, May 6, 1926; R. C. Marshall, president, AMPA, "Monthly Newsletter," March 15, 1926, AMS/Marshall PF: *Aviation* 19 (August 24, 1925), 210–11; Glover, "History of the Air Mail Service," in Wenneman, *Municipal Airports*, p. 291.
36. W. L. Smith diary, "November 6, 1925, W. L. Smith Papers; Colyer to L. D. Gardner, October 8, 1926, AMS/Colyer PF; Henderson to Cisler, September 29, 1926, copy supplied to the author by J. P. Cisler.
37. W. L. Smith diary, August 24, 1926, W. L. Smith Papers; McCoy, "Cleveland's Lindy," *Cleveland Press*, December 13, 1928.
38. E. P. Critchley to Egge, November 10, 1926, AMS/W. L. Smith PF: McCoy, "Cleveland's Lindy," *Cleveland Press*, December 14, 1928.

39. Wesley Smith, "How I Fly at Night," *Journal of the Society of Automotive Engineers* 19 (September 1926), 228–33; Egge to Colyer, December 27, 1926, quoting report by Williams, AMS/Williams PF.
40. Luther Harris to Colyer, April 23, 1927, AMS/Milatzo PF.
41. Glover, "History of the Air Mail Service," in Wenneman, *Municipal Airports*, pp. 291–92; McCoy, "Cleveland's Lindy," *Cleveland Press*, December 13, 1928.
42. Davies, *Airlines of the United States*, pp. 39–54; POD, *Annual Report of the Postmaster General, 1928* (Washington, D.C., 1928), p. 132.
43. *New York Times*, March 30, April 4 and 6, 1927.
44. Glover to Colyer, April 6, 1927, AMS/Colyer PF; *New York Times*, July 1, 1927; *Cleveland Press*, September 1, 1927.
45. Glover, "History of the Air Mail Service," in Wenneman, *Municipal Airports*, pp. 294–95; *New York Times*, June 13 and 15, 1927.
46. Dean Smith to the author, March 9, 1976; Lindbergh, *Autobiography of Values* (New York, 1977), p. 310.

Conclusion

1. Fuller, *America Mail*, pp. 9–10. Wanamaker is quoted by Scheele, *History of the Mail Service*, p. 113.
2. NACA, *Annual Report for 1927* (Washington, D.C. 1928), p. 20; *New York Times*, July 1, 1925; Jerome Lederer, *Safety in the Operation of Air Transportation* (Burlington, Vt., 1939).
3. Brooks, *Modern Airliner*, pp. 43–44.
4. David, *Economics of Air Mail*, pp. 48–53; Warner, *Early History of Air Transportation*, p. 29.

Bibliography

Manuscripts

Air Ministry of Great Britain. Records. Public Record Office, London, England.

Burleson, Albert S. Papers. Library of Congress, Washington, D.C.

Coolidge, Calvin. Papers. Microfilm edition.

Cooper, Edwin C. Collection. San Diego Aero-Space Museum, San Diego, California.

Harding, Warren G. Papers. Microfilm edition.

Hoover, Herbert C. Papers. Hoover Presidential Library, West Branch, Iowa.

Lipsner, Benjamin B. Papers. Division of Postal History, National Museum of American History, Smithsonian Institution, Washington, D.C.

Mitchell, William. Papers. Library of Congress, Washington, D.C.

Praeger, Otto. Papers. In the possession of the Praeger family, Rye, New York.

Smith, Wesley L. Papers. In the possession of the Smith family, Mountain Lakes, New Jersey.

United States Aeronautical Board. Records. Record Group 334, National Archives, Washington, D.C.

United States Army Air Forces. Records. Record Group 18, National Archives, Washington, D.C.

United States Department of Commerce. Records. Record Group 40, National Archives, Washington, D.C.

United States Department of the Navy. Records. Record Group 72, National Archives, Washington, D.C.

United States Department of State. Records. Record Group 59, National Archives, Washington, D.C.

United States (Congress) Joint Commission on the Postal Service. Records. Record Group 148, National Archives, Washington, D.C.

United States (House of Representatives) Select Committee of Inquiry into the Operations of the U.S. Air Services. Records. Record Group 233, National Archives, Washington, D.C.

United States National Advisory Committee for Aeronautics. Records. Record Group 255, National Archives, Washington, D.C.

United States National Air and Space Museum. Historical Files. Smithsonian Institution, Washington, D.C.

United States National Bureau of Standards. Records. Record Group 167, National Archives, Washington, D.C.

United States Post Office. Records. Record Group 28, National Archives, Washington, D.C.
United States Postal Service. Historical Files. U.S. Postal Service Library, Washington, D.C.
Warner, Edward P. Papers. New York Public Library, New York, New York.
Wilson, Woodrow. Papers. Library of Congress, Washington, D.C.

Unpublished Works
Conner, George L. "A Brief Biography of Hon. Otto Praeger," and fragments of a manuscript on the origins of the Air Mail Service. National Air and Space Museum, Smithsonian Institution, Washington, D.C.
Downs, Elton W. "Contributions of U.S. Army Aviation to Uses and Operation of Aircraft." Ph.D. dissertation, University of Wisconsin, 1959.
Duke, Escal F. "The Political Career of Morris Sheppard, 1875–1941." Ph.D. dissertation, University of Texas, 1958.
Edgerton, James Clark. "Horizons Unlimited." In the possession of the Edgerton family, Miami Springs, Florida.
Howard, Richard Winston. "The Work of Albert Sidney Burleson as Postmaster General." M.A. thesis, University of Texas, 1938.
Lee, E. Hamilton. Untitled memoirs. National Air and Space Museum, Smithsonian Institution, Washington, D.C.
Lent, Leon B. "Memoirs." In the possession of Jesse M. Davidson, Bronx, New York.
McReynolds, Ross A. "History of the United States Post Office, 1607–1931." Ph.D. dissertation, University of Chicago, 1935.
Miller, Max. Logbook. Division of Postal History, National Museum of American History, Smithsonian Institution, Washington, D.C.
Praeger, Otto. "Moss from a Rolling Stone." In the possession of the Praeger family, Rye, New York.
Smith, Dean C. "Pilot's Progress." Transportation History Foundation, University of Wyoming, Cheyenne, Wyoming.
Walterman, Thomas Worth. "Airpower and Private Enterprise: Federal-Industrial Relations in the Aeronautics Field, 1918–1926." Ph.D. dissertation, Washington University, 1970.

Published Documents
U.S. Air Mail Service. *Pilots' Directions: New York–San Francisco Route.* Washington, D.C., 1921.
U.S. Congress. *Congressional Record* (1910–27).
U.S. Congress. House of Representatives. Subcommittee of the Committee on Appropriations. *Hearings: Post Office Appropriation Bill, 1922.* 66th Cong., 3d sess., 1920.
U.S. Congress. House of Representatives. Subcommittee of the Committee on Appropriations. *Hearings: Post Office Appropriation Bill, 1924.* 67th Cong., 4th sess., 1922.
U.S. Congress. House of Representatives. Subcommittee of the Committee on Appropriations. *Hearings: Post Office Appropriation Bill, 1925.* 68th Cong., 1st sess., 1924.
U.S. Congress. House of Representatives. Subcommittee of the Committee

on Appropriations. *Hearings: Post Office Appropriation Bill, 1926.* 68th Cong., 2d sess., 1924.

U.S. Congress. House of Representatives. Subcommittee of the Committee on Appropriations. *Hearings: Post Office Appropriation Bill, 1927.* 69th Cong., 1st sess., 1925.

U.S. Congress. House of Representatives. Subcommittee of the Committee on Appropriations. *Hearings: Post Office Appropriations Bill, 1928.* 69th Cong., 2d sess., 1926.

U.S. Congress. House of Representatives. Subcommittee of the Committee on Military Affairs. *Hearings: United Air Service.* 66th Cong., 2d sess., 1921.

U.S. Congress. House of Representatives. *Hearings: Air Service Unification.* 68th Cong., 2d sess., 1925.

U.S. Congress. House of Representatives. Subcommittee No. 1 of the Committee on the Post Office and Post Roads. *Hearings: Post Office Appropriation Bill, 1913.* 62nd Cong., 2d sess., 1912.

U.S. Congress. House of Representatives. Committee on the Post Office and Post Roads. *Hearings.* 65th Cong., 3d sess., 1918.

U.S. Congress. House of Representatives. Committee on the Post Office and Post Roads. *Hearings.* 66th Cong., 2d sess., 1920.

U.S. Congress. House of Representatives. Committee on the Post Office and Post Roads. *Hearings: Air Mail Service.* 66th Cong., 3d sess., 1921.

U.S. Congress. House of Representatives. Committee on the Post Office and Post Roads. *Hearings: First Deficiency Bill, 1921—Air Mail Service.* 66th Cong., 3d sess., 1921.

U.S. Congress. House of Representatives. Committee on the Post Office and Post Roads. *Hearings: Commercial Aviation—Air Mail Service.* 67th Cong., 2d sess., 1922.

U.S. Congress. House of Representatives. Subcommittee of the Committee on the Post Office and Post Roads. *Hearings: Claims for Construction of Hangars and Maintenance of Flying Fields—Air Mail Service.* 67th Cong., 4th sess., 1923.

U.S. Congress. House of Representatives. Subcommittee of the Committee on the Post Office and Post Roads. *Hearings: Pay of Air Mail Contractors.* 69th Cong., 1st sess., 1926.

U.S. Congress. House of Representatives. Select Committee of Inquiry into Operations of the United States Air Services. *Hearings.* 68th Cong., 1925.

U.S. Congress. House of Representatives. Select Committee of Inquiry into Operations of the United States Air Services. *Report.* 68th Cong., 1925.

U.S. Congress. House of Representatives. Select Committee on Expenditures in the War Department. *Hearings Before Subcommittee No. 1 (Aviation),* 66th Cong., 1st sess., 1920.

U.S. Congress. Joint Commission on the Postal Service. *Hearings: The Postal Service.* Washington, D.C., 1925.

U.S. Congress. Senate. *Document No. 70: Air Mail Contracts.* 72d Cong., 1st sess., 1932.

U.S. Congress. Senate, Subcommittee of the Committee on Appropriations. *Hearings: Treasury and Post Office Departments, Appropriation Bills, 1925.* 68th Cong., 1st sess., 1924.

U.S. Congress. Senate. Committee on Post Offices and Post Roads. *Hearings.* 65th Cong., 3d sess., 1919.

U.S. Congress. Senate. Subcommittee of the Committee on Post Offices and Post Roads. *Hearings.* 66th Cong., 2d sess., 1920.
U.S. National Advisory Committee for Aeronautics. *Annual Report* (1915–1927). Washington, D.C., 1916–28.
U.S. Post Office. *Annual Report of the Postmaster General* (1911–1928). Washington, D.C., 1912–29.
U.S. President's Aircraft Board. *Hearings.* Washington, D.C., 1925.
U.S. President's Aircraft Board. *Report of the President's Aircraft Board.* Washington, D.C., 1925.

Correspondence and Interviews
Allison, Ernest M., correspondence, November 27, 1967.
Cisler, J. P., correspondence, April 27 and May 20, 1976.
Goettel, Elinor, correspondence, May 16 and July 1, 1976.
Humphries, Josephine Henderson, correspondence, February 10 and 14, 1976.
Janas, Stephen G., correspondence, February 26, 1976.
Lee, E. Hamilton, correspondence, April 27, 1976.
Marshall, R. C., correspondence, March 28, 1976; interview, April 8, 1976.
Passino, Floranne Henderson, correspondence, February 22, 1976.
Praeger, Otto, Jr., correspondence, September 2, 1976.
Ricker, Daisy Marie (Miller), interview, July 15, 1976.
Riddick, Merrill K., correspondence, April 22 and June 13, 1983.
Smith, Dean C., correspondence, March 9, July 2, and August 5, 1976.
Smith, Zelma, interview, August 17, 1976.
Stanton, Charles I., correspondence, August 11, 1976; interviews, April 18 and August 5, 1976.

Newspapers and Periodicals
Aerial Age (New York), 1915–23 [published as *Aerial Age Weekly*, 1915–22]
Aero Digest, 1921–27 [published as *Aeronautical Digest*, 1921–24]
Aeronautics (London), 1916–25
Aircraft Journal, 1919–20
Air Service Journal, 1918–19
Aviation, 1916–27 [published as *Aviation and Aeronautical Engineering*, 1916–October 1920, and as *Aviation and Aircraft Journal*, November 1920–21]
Chicago Daily Tribune, 1918–27
Chicago *Daily News*, 1918–27
Flight (London), 1916–25
Fly: The National Aeronautic Magazine, 1910–12
Flying, 1912–21 [published until October 1912 as *Aero Club of America Bulletin*; absorbed by *Aerial Age Weekly*, August 1, 1921]
Literary Digest, 1910–28
New York Times, 1910–27
U.S. Air Services (Washington, D.C.), 1919–27 [published as *U.S. Air Service*, 1919–24]
Washington *Evening Star*, 1918–27
Washington Post, 1918–27

Books

Aeromarine Plane & Motor Company. *The Log of an Aeromarine.* Keyport, N.J., 1920.

Aeronautical Chamber of Commerce. *Aircraft Year Book* (1922–1928). New York, 1922–28.

Air Mail Pioneers. *The Roll Call.* Privately printed, 1956.

Arnold, H. H. *Global Mission.* New York, 1949.

Arthur, Reginald Wright. *Contact! Careers of U.S. Naval Aviators Assigned Numbers 1 to 2000.* Privately printed, 1967.

Bagby, Wesley M. *The Road to Normalcy: The Presidential Campaign and Election of 1920.* Baltimore, 1962.

Bilstein, Roger E. *Flight in America, 1900–1983.* Baltimore, 1984.

———. *Flight Patterns: Trends of Aeronautical Development in the United States, 1918–1929.* Athens, Ga., 1983.

Blair, Charles F. *Red Ball in the Sky.* New York, 1969.

Brooks, Peter W. *The Modern Airliner: Its Origins and Development.* London, 1961.

Bruno, Harry A. *Wings Over America: The Story of American Aviation.* Garden City, N.Y., 1944.

Burner, David. *Herbert Hoover.* New York, 1979.

Cochrane, Rexmond C. *Measures for Progress: A History of the National Bureau of Standards.* Washington, D.C., 1966.

Collins, Paul F. *Tales of an Old Air-Faring Man.* Stevens Point, Wis., 1983.

Courtney, Frank T. *Flight Path.* London, 1972.

Cullinan, Gerald. *The Post Office Department.* New York, 1968.

Culver, Edith Dodd. *The Day the Air Mail Began.* Kansas City, Kan., 1971.

David, Paul T. *The Economics of Air Mail Transportation.* Washington, D.C., 1934.

Davies, R. E. G. *Airlines of the United States Since 1914.* Rev. ed., Washington, D.C., 1982.

———. *A History of the World's Airlines.* London, 1964.

Dichman, Ernest W. *This Aviation Business.* New York, 1929.

Dickey, Philip S., III. *The Liberty Engine, 1918–1942.* Washington, D.C., 1968.

Faunce, Cy Q. *The Airliner and Its Inventor, Alfred W. Lawson.* Columbus, Ohio, 1921.

Francillon, René J. *McDonnell Douglas Aircraft Since 1920.* London, 1979.

Freudenthal, Elsbeth E. *The Aviation Business: From Kitty Hawk to Wall Street.* New York, 1940.

Fuller, Wayne E. *The American Mail.* Chicago, 1972.

Gardner, Lester D. (ed.). *Who's Who in American Aeronautics.* New York, 1925.

Glines, Carroll V. *The Saga of the Airmail.* Princeton, 1960.

Gould, Lewis L. *Progressives and Prohibitionists: Texas Democrats in the Wilson Era.* Austin, Texas, 1973.

Grooch, William S. *From Crate to Clipper with Captain Musick.* New York, 1939.

Hallion, Richard P. *Legacy of Flight: The Guggenheim Contribution to American Aviation.* Seattle, 1977.

Hawley, Ellis W. (ed.). *Herbert Hoover as Secretary of Commerce: Studies in New Era Thought and Practice.* Iowa City, Iowa, 1981.

Hays, Will H. *The Memoirs of Will H. Hays.* Garden City, N.Y., 1955.

Hicks, John D. *Republican Ascendancy, 1921–1933.* New York, 1960.

Holland, Maurice. *Architects of Aviation.* Freeport, N.Y., 1971.
Holley, I. B., Jr. *Ideas and Weapons.* New Haven, Conn., 1953.
Holmes, Donald B. *Air Mail.* New York, 1981.
Hopkins, George E. *The Airline Pilots: A Study in Elite Unionization.* Cambridge, Mass., 1971.
———. *Flying the Line: The First Half Century of the Air Line Pilots Association.* Washington, D.C., 1982.
Hudson, James J. *Hostile Skies: A Combat History of the American Air Service in World War I.* Syracuse, N.Y., 1968.
Hughes, Arthur J. *History of Air Navigation.* London, 1946.
Hurley, Alfred F. *Billy Mitchell: Crusader for Air Power.* New York, 1964.
Hyde, H. Montgomery. *British Air Policy Between the Wars 1918–1939.* London, 1976.
Jackson, Donald Dale. *Flying the Mail.* Alexandria, Va., 1982.
Joint Committee on Civil Aviation of the U.S. Department of Commerce and the American Engineering Council. *Civil Aviation: A Report.* New York, 1926.
Jones, Neville. *The Origins of Strategic Bombing.* London, 1973.
Keen, Ronald. *Wireless Direction Finding.* 4th ed., London, 1947.
Kelly, Clyde. *United States Postal Policy.* New York, 1932.
Knappen, Theodore Macfarlane. *Wings of War: An Account of the Important Contributions of the United States to Aircraft Invention, Engineering, Development and Production during the World War.* New York, 1920.
Koenigsberg, M. *King News: An Autobiography.* Philadelphia, 1941.
Komons, Nick A. *Bonfires to Beacons: Federal Civil Aviation Policy under the Air Commerce Act, 1926–1938.* Washington, D.C., 1978.
Lawson, Alfred W. *Lawson: Aircraft Industry Builder.* Detroit, 1943.
Lederer, Jerome. *Safety in the Operation of Air Transportation.* Burlington, Vt., 1939.
Leuchtenburg, William E. *The Perils of Prosperity, 1914–1932.* Chicago, 1958.
Lindbergh, Charles A. *Autobiography of Values.* New York, 1977.
Link, Arthur S. *Wilson: The New Freedom.* Princeton, 1956.
Lipsner, Benjamin B. *The Airmail—Jennies to Jets.* Chicago, 1951.
Lobeck, A. K. *Airways of America.* Port Washington, N.Y., 1970 (first published in 1933).
Loening, Grover. *Takeoff Into Greatness.* New York, 1968.
Mann, Arthur. *LaGuardia: A Fighter Against His Times, 1882–1933.* Philadelphia, 1959.
Manufacturers Aircraft Association. *Aircraft Year Book* (1919–1921). New York, 1919–21.
McCoy, Donald R. *Calvin Coolidge: The Quiet President.* New York, 1967.
———. *Coming of Age: The United States during the 1920's and 1930's.* Baltimore, 1973.
Miller, Ronald, and David Sawers. *The Technical Development of Modern Aviation.* London, 1968.
Mingos, Howard. *The Birth of an Industry.* New York, 1930.
Morris, Lloyd, and Kendall Smith. *Ceiling Unlimited.* New York, 1953.
Munson, Kenneth. *Airliners between the Wars, 1919–1939.* New York, 1972.
Murray, Robert K. *The Harding Era.* Minneapolis, 1969.
———. *The Politics of Normalcy: Government Theory and Practice in the Harding-Coolidge Era.* New York, 1973.

Newton, Wesley Phillips. *The Perilous Sky: U.S. Aviation Diplomacy and Latin America, 1919–1931.* Coral Gables, Fla., 1978.
Nielson, Dale (ed.). *Saga of the U.S. Air Mail Service, 1918–1927.* Privately printed, 1962.
Noggle, Burl. *Into the Twenties: The United States From Armistice to Normalcy.* Urbana, Ill., 1974.
O'Sullivan, Thomas J., and Karl B. Weber. *History of the United States Pioneer and Government-Operated Air Mail Service, 1910–1928.* Philadelphia, 1973.
Paxson, Frederic L. *American Democracy and the World War.* 3 vols., Berkeley, Cal., 1936–48.
Perrett, Geoffrey. *America in the Twenties.* New York, 1982.
Rae, John B. *Climb to Greatness: The American Aircraft Industry, 1920–60.* Cambridge, Mass., 1968.
Rickenbacker, Edward V. *Rickenbacker.* Englewood Cliffs, N.J., 1967.
Rohlfing, Charles C. *National Regulation of Aeronautics.* Philadelphia, 1931.
Roland, Alex. *Model Research: The National Advisory Committee for Aeronautics, 1915–1958.* 2 vols., Washington, D.C., 1985.
Roper, Daniel C. *The United States Post Office.* New York, 1917.
Roseberry, C. R. *Glenn Curtiss.* Garden City, N.Y., 1972.
Rubenstein, Murray, and Richard M. Goldman. *To Join with the Eagles: Curtiss-Wright Aircraft, 1903–1965.* Garden City, N.Y., 1974.
Scamehorn, Howard L. *Balloons to Jets: A Century of Aeronautics in Ilinois, 1855–1955.* Chicago, 1957.
Scheele, Carl H. *A Short History of the Mail Service.* Washington, D.C., 1970.
Schlaifer, Robert. *Development of Aircraft Engines.* Boston, 1950 (includes S. D. Heron, *Development of Aviation Fuels*).
Schlesinger, Arthur M., Jr. *The Crisis of the Old Order, 1919–1933.* Boston, 1957.
Serling, Robert J. *The Only Way to Fly: The Story of Western Airlines, America's Senior Air Carrier.* Garden City, N.Y., 1976.
Setright, L. J. K. *The Power to Fly: The Development of the Piston Engine in Aviation.* London, 1971.
Shamburger, Page. *Tracks Across the Sky.* New York, 1964.
Smith, Dean. *By the Seat of My Pants.* Boston, 1961.
Smith, Henry Ladd. *Airways: The History of Commercial Aviation in the United States.* New York, 1942.
Smith, Wesley L. *Air Transport Operation.* New York, 1931.
Soule, George. *Prosperity Decade.* New York, 1947.
Spenser, Jay P. *Bellanca C.F.: The Emergence of the Cabin Monoplane in the United States.* Washington, D.C., 1982.
Spero, Sterling Denhard. *The Labor Movement in a Government Industry: A Study of Employee Organization in the Postal Service.* New York, 1927.
Sullivan, Mark. *Our Times: The United States, 1900–1925.* 6 vols., New York, 1926–35.
Thomas, G. Holt. *Aerial Transport.* London, 1920.
Travelers Insurance Company. *Airplanes and Safety.* Privately printed, 1921.
Turner, P. St. John, and Heinz J. Nowarra. *Junkers.* London, 1971.
Trani, Eugene P., and David L. Wilson. *The Presidency of Warren G. Harding.* Lawrence, Kan., 1977.
United States Congress. *Biographical Directory of the American Congress, 1774–1971.* Washington, D.C., 1971.

Villard, Henry Serrano. *Contact! The Story of the Early Birds.* New York, 1968.
Wagner, William. *Reuben Fleet and the Story of Consolidated Aircraft.* Fallbrook, Cal., 1976.
Warner, Edward P. *The Early History of Air Transportation.* York, Pa., 1938.
———. *Technical Development and Its Effect on Air Transportation.* York, Pa., 1938.
Wenneman, Joseph H. *Municipal Airports.* Cleveland, 1931.
Whitnah, Donald R. *A Histroy of the United States Weather Bureau.* Urbana, Ill., 1961.
———. *Safer Skyways: Federal Control of Aviation, 1926–1966.* Ames, Iowa, 1966.
Wilson, Joan Hoff. *Herbert Hoover: Forgotten Progressive.* Boston, 1975.
Wilson, John R. M. *Turbulence Aloft: The Civil Aeronautics Administration Amid Wars and Rumors of War, 1938–1953.* Washington, D.C., 1979.
Winans, David R. *Wheels, Wings, and Waves: Highlights of 200 Years of Transportation in New Jersey.* Privately printed, 1975.

Articles

Anon. "Inglis Moore Uppercu." *The National Cyclopedia of American Biography* 36 (1950), 284–85.
Anon. "Martin Barnaby Madden." *Biographical Dictionary of the American Congress* (Washington, D.C., 1961), p. 1251.
Anon. "Martin Barnaby Madden." *The National Cyclopedia of American Biography* 34 (1948), 420.
Ames, Joseph S. "Commercial Flight." *Aeronautical Digest* 11 (May 1923), 321–23, 380.
Bassett, P. R. "Night Flying." *U.S. Air Service* 8 (March 1923), 23–27.
Bell, Luther K. "The Future of the Air Mail." *Outlook* 139 (January 28, 1925), 141–44.
Bernard, J. L., and L. E. Whittemore. "Radio Communication with Postal Aeroplanes." *Aerial Age Weekly* 13 (April 11, 1921), 105–106; (April 18, 1921), 127–29; (April 25, 1921), 155–57, 163.
Bilstein, Roger. "Technology and Commerce: Aviation in the Conduct of American Business, 1918–1929." *Technology and Culture* 10 (1969), 392–411.
Black, Archibald. "European Air Transport." *Aero Digest* 8 (March 1926), 121–23, 170.
———. "Night Flying Equipment." *Aeronautical Digest* 11 (June 1923), 431–33, 457–58.
Bowers, Ray L. "The Transcontinental Reliability Test." *Airpower Historian* 8 (January 1961), 45–54; (April 1961), 88–100.
Brancker, Sefton. "The Lessons of Six Years' Experience in Air Transport." *The Journal of the Royal Aeronautical Society* 29 (November 1925), 552–85.
Burleson, Albert Sidney. "The Story of Our Air Mail." *The Independent* 102 (April 3, 1920), 8, 35–36.
———. "Telegraph and Telephone in Government Hands." *American Review of Reviews* 58 (December 1918), 619–24.
Burner, David. "1919: Prelude to Normalcy." John Braeman, et al. (eds.), *Change and Continuity in Twentieth-Century America: The 1920's* (Columbus, Ohio, 1967), pp. 3–31.

Claudy, C. H. "Why the Mail Plane?" *Scientific American* 126 (April 1922), 250–51.

Coben, Stanley. "Will H. Hays." John A. Garraty (ed.), *Dictionary of American Biography*, Supplement 5 (New York, 1977), pp. 280–82.

Courtney, Frank T. "The Practical Difficulties of Commercial Flying." *The Journal of the Royal Aeronautical Society* 28 (January 1924), 35–41.

Cross, Carolyn. "Possibilities of Aeroplane Mail Service." *The Postmasters' Advocate* 20 (May 1915), 241–42.

Dane, Roger. "Midnight Suns of the Air Mail." *Aero Digest* 7 (July 1925), 359–60.

Davis, W. Jefferson. "Clearing the Air for Commerce." *Annals of the American Academy of Political and Social Science* 131 (May 1927), 141–50.

Day, W. J. "The Aerial Night Mail." *U.S. Air Services* 9 (July 1924), 24–26.

Dellinger, J. H. "Applications of Radio in Air Navigation." *Engineers and Engineering* 43 (1926), 301.

———, and Haraden Pratt. "Development of Radio Aids to Air Navigation." *Institute of Radio Engineers Proceedings* 16 (1928), 890–920.

Eakle, Paul V. "A Tragedy Flying the Christmas Mail." Dale Nielsen (ed.), *Saga of the U.S. Air Mail Service, 1918–1927* (privately printed, 1962), pp. 41–43.

Edgerton, James C. "Radio as Applied to Air Navigation in the Air Mail Service." *U.S. Air Service* 5 (February 1921), 12–14.

Ellis, L. Ethan. "Martin Barnaby Madden." *Dictionary of American Biography* 12 (New York, 1933), 180–81.

Fairchild, Muir S. "Experimental Night Flying by Flight Test Section, McCook Field." *Aerial Age Weekly* 13 (August 8, 1921), 516–17.

Franklin, W. S., and M. H. Stillman. "NACA Report No. 128: Direction Instruments," part I ("Inclinometers and Banking Indicators"). NACA, *Seventh Annual Report, 1921* (Washington, D.C., 1922), pp. 597–611.

Glover, W. Irving. "The Air Mail." *Annals of the American Academy of Political and Social Science* 131 (May 1927), 43–48.

———. "History of the Air Mail Service." Joseph H. Wenneman, *Municipal Airports* (Cleveland, 1931), pp. 281–98.

Gregg, W. R. "Meteorological Service for Commercial Aeronautics," *U.S. Air Service* 12 (February 1927), 17–23.

Grey, C. G. "American Impressions." *Aviation* 17 (October 20, 1924), 1165–66.

———. "Civil Aviation in the United States." *Aviation* 18 (January 5, 1925), 16–17.

———. "Impressions of Aviation in America." *Aviation* 17 (October 6, 1924), 1082–83.

———. "Post Impressions of American Aviation." *Aviation* 17 (December 15, 1924), 1395–97.

Guggenheim, Harry F. "Aviation and Confidence." *Aviation* 20 (February 22, 1926), 250–51.

Hays, Will H. "The Human Side of the Postal Service." *American Review of Reviews* 64 (December 1921), 625–40.

Henderson, Paul. "The Air Mail—Its Future." *Aero Digest* 6 (March 1925), 127–29, 168.

Hersey, Mayo D. "Aeronautic Instruments." *Aviation* 8 (July 1, 1920), 437–40.

Hicks, John D. "Harry Steward New." *Dictionary of American Biography*, Supplement 2 (New York, 1958), pp. 486–87.

Hoff, N. J. "A Short History of the Development of Airplane Structures." *American Scientist* 34 (1946), 212–25, 270–88.

Hunsaker, J. C. "The Story of Transportation by Air." *Aviation* 14 (February 19, 1923), 215–18.

Hunt, Franklin L. "NACA Report No. 132: Aeronautic Instruments." National Advisory Committee for Aeronautics, *Seventh Annual Report, 1921* (Washington, D.C., 1922), pp. 805–814.

Jolliffe, C. M., and Elizabeth Zandonn. "Bibliography of Aircraft Radio." *Institute of Radio Engineers Proceedings* 16 (1928), 985–99.

Kelly, M. Clyde. "Outflying the Eagles." *Aero Digest* 5 (July 1924), 10–11, 38.

Kennedy, Thomas Hart. "Our Westbound Route to the East." *U.S. Air Services* 9 (August 1924), 7–14.

Leary, William M. "At the Dawn of Commercial Aviation: Inglis M. Uppercu and Aeromarine Airways." *Business History Review* 53 (1979), 180–93.

Lee, David D. "Herbert Hoover and the Development of Commercial Aviation, 1921–1926." *Business History Review* 58 (1984), 78–102.

Lewis, W. David, and Wesley Phillips Newton. "Paul Henderson." *Dictionary of American Biography*, Supplement 5 (New York, 1977), pp. 294–95.

Lindsay, Samuel McCune. "The New Cabinet and Its Problems." *American Review of Reviews* 63 (April 1921), 381–93.

Luckey, G. P. "Aerial Navigation Instruments." *U.S. Air Services* 9 (January 1924), 35–38.

Marshall, R. C. "Needle, Ball, and Airspeed." *Air Facts* 33 (August 1970), 23–30.

Martin, Glenn L. "Night Flying Made Practical Through Artificial Light." *U.S. Air Services* 8 (August 1923), 25–28.

Martin, E. Stockton. "Safety in Aviation." *Aviation* 10 (March 14, 1921), 336.

Marvin, Charles F. "The Weather Bureau and Aviation." *Aeronautical Digest* 11 (January 1923), 6.

McConnell, Burt M. "The Air Mail Pilot." *Review of Reviews* 76 (August 1927), 167–73.

———. "The Air Mail Service Makes Good." *Review of Reviews* 71 (March 1925), 301–306.

McCoy, Harold G. "The Story of Cleveland's Lindy." *Cleveland Press*, 23 parts, November 27–December 22, 1928.

Meisinger, C. LeRoy. "The Aviator and the Meteorologist." *U.S. Air Services* 8 (May 1923), 31–32.

———. "Interpretation of Meteorological Map." *Aviation* 13 (December 11, 1922), 774–76.

Mingos, Howard. "Flying the Mails." *New York Times*, December 26, 1920.

Mitchell, William. "The Air Mail Service." *American Review of Reviews* 62 (December 1920), 625–32.

Moran, C. "The Gay White Way of the Air Mail." *U.S. Air Services* 9 (February 1924), 34–38.

Morgan, T. A. "Instruments for Cross Country Flying." *Aerial Age Weekly* 8 (February 3, 1919), 1029.

Murphy, W. H., and L. M. Wolfe. "Stationary and Rotating Equi-Signal Beacons." *Journal of the Society of Automotive Engineers* 19 (1926), 209.

Noorduyn, R. B. C. "Air Lines and Some of Their Problems." *Aerial Age Weekly* 14 (January 30, 1922), 492–94, 503.

Osborn, Earl D. "Preparing the Night Airway." *Aviation* 18 (June 1, 1925), 604–605.

Ovington, Earle. "The First Aerial Mail-Man." *Western Flying* 1 (March 1926), 7, 23.

Patterson, M. L. "Night Flying Progress." *U.S. Air Service* 8 (November 1923), 30–32.

Post, George B. "Aspects of Commercial Aviation in the U.S.A." *Annals of the American Academy of Political and Social Science* 131 (May 1927), 71–78.

Praeger, Otto. "Air Mail Service Saves Public $100,000 a Year." *U.S. Air Services* 3 (April 1920), 29.

Rowe, A. P. "Aerial Navigation." *The Journal of the Royal Aeronautical Society* 27 (1923), 450–54.

Ruhl, Arthur. "'It's a Temperamental Job!'" *New Republic* 28 (September 28, 1921), 126–28.

Searle, Frank. "Requirements and Difficulties of Air Transport." *Aviation* 12 (February 20, 1922), 220–23.

Shaughnessy, E. H. "The United States Air Mail Service." *Aviation* 12 (January 23, 1922), 96–98.

Smith, Wesley L. "How I Fly at Night." *Journal of the Society of Automotive Engineers* 19 (September 1926), 228–33.

Stewart, Harry A. "Our Postmen of the Skies." *American Magazine* 97 (February 1924), 14–15, 155–60.

Sweeney, Stephen B. "Some Economic Aspects of Aircraft Transportation." *Annals of the American Academy of Political and Social Science* 131 (May 1927), 159–181.

Sylvander, R. C., and E. W. Rounds. "NACA Report No. 128: Direction Instruments." National Advisory Committee for Aeronautics, *Seventh Annual Report, 1921* (Washington, D.C., 1922), pp. 646–63.

Thomas, G. Holt. "Commercial Aeronautics." *The Aeronautical Journal* (October–December 1917), 369–89.

Trani, Eugene P. "Hubert Work." John A. Garraty (ed.), *Dictionary of American Biography*, Supplement 3 (New York, 1973), pp. 845–46.

Wardrop, G. Douglas. "The Liberty Motor." *Aerial Age Weekly* 8 (December 16, 1918), 706–17; (December 23, 1918), 762–65.

Warner, John A. C. "NACA Report No. 128: Direction Instruments." National Advisory Committee for Aeronautics, *Seventh Annual Report, 1921* (Washington, 1922), pp. 616–45.

Whitbeck, John E. "Operation of the Air Mail Lines." *Aero Digest* 8 (April 1926), 185–87, 240–41.

Wilhelm, Donald. "Flying the Mail." *World's Work* 42 (May 1921), 49–59; (June 1921), 199–204.

Wimperis, H. E. "Air Navigation." *The Journal of the Royal Aeronautical Society* 23 (1919), 445–61.

Young, Clarence M. "Civil Aeronautics in America." *Aero Digest* 11 (December 1927), 644–52.

Zimmermann, Paul G. "Adapting an F-5L Flying Boat to Air Transport." *Aviation* 9 (September 1, 1920), 87–99.

Index